CW00870844

Native Waters

Native Waters

✦

A Few Moments In A Small Wooden Boat

Roger Emile Stouff

iUniverse, Inc.
New York Lincoln Shanghai

Native Waters
A Few Moments In A Small Wooden Boat

Copyright © 2005 by Roger Emile Stouff

All rights reserved. No part of this book may be used or reproduced by any means, graphic, electronic, or mechanical, including photocopying, recording, taping or by any information storage retrieval system without the written permission of the publisher except in the case of brief quotations embodied in critical articles and reviews.

iUniverse books may be ordered through booksellers or by contacting:

iUniverse
2021 Pine Lake Road, Suite 100
Lincoln, NE 68512
www.iuniverse.com
1-800-Authors (1-800-288-4677)

ISBN: 0-595-34316-3

Printed in the United States of America

This is for all my relations.
Most especially Nicholas Leonard, Lydia Marie, Emile Anatole and Josephine Faye.
I am, because of you.

Contents

Introduction

These are musings along the road. They are the puzzled, often bemused and sometimes-inconsolable observations of someone in search of what Richard Bode called the quest for an authentic life. That life, not even perceived when these writings first began, is much closer today but still too far away to grasp.

They were written as a twice-weekly column called "From the Other Side" during the years from 1998-2004 for the *St. Mary and Franklin Banner-Tribune*. Though I actually began writing the column in about 1982, the years mentioned are those which directly preceded the death of my father, and an awakening of a sort I never predicted.

A member of the Chitimacha Tribe of Louisiana, born to a father who had been the last traditional chief of the tribe as well as its first elected chairman, and a mother who was French-Acadian, or Cajun, I rejected both worlds and searched, in vain, for some third existence, which ultimately was an illusion. The life I sought was one of career success, and fraught with disappointments and harsh lessons. A jaunt to the New Orleans area to pursue, and I believed to advance, my journalism career taught me that it was in the end far better to be a big fish in a little pond than the obverse, and returning to my little hometown, back to the reservation, felt like defeat and failure. Over the years that followed, I was to learn differently.

As a Native American, spirits surrounded me, calling out but ignored. They spoke of the things that should have really mattered, but I refused to listen. Instead, the lure of success and material possessions obsessed me. Yet, I was always aware of a world just on the edge of my perception, an otherness that perhaps subconsciously permeated the naming of the column even far back when it was begun, when I dreamed of occupying an editor's desk and awards and accolades from my peers. As an Acadian, I relished the simple ethics of hard work and hard play, but hid what slight accent I might have picked up from my maternal lineage, never learned the language they spoke so fluently when I was a child.

From both worlds a love for the water was inevitable. There, and only there, did I feel content, complete. I did not know why. When out of a boat, I walked on concrete to prevent my feet from ever touching the land of my ancestors, so I would not feel them, not hear them. I huddled behind computers and newsprint searching for truth, finding only confusion and chaos in the police reports, government meetings and obituaries chronicling four column inches of a life precious. Under each bold-type name, the list of survivors, those who died before, visitations, service times and burial places seemed far insufficient to describe a life, much too cold to convey the spirit which had passed into the Creator's hands.

In the years approaching my father's death, I began to realize that what I searched for was right under my feet all along. What I learned, as I feared, was the threat of oppression, the prejudice that he had endured, which my grandparents had endured, on the paternal and maternal lineages of my descent. In my quest to become faceless, I had succeeded all too well and become nameless as well. In those final years, I began to see through the eyes of those who came before me, and I wrote what I saw, and for the first time in 20 years of writing "From the Other Side," I stepped off the concrete, and readers responded with surprising heartfelt empathy.

I suspect that they were reacting to the personal familiarity of the search. The quest for an authentic life. Many didn't even know they were searching. But somehow, in my ramblings about my life and my ancestors, in my dreaming about wooden boats and forgotten songs, their own searches perhaps became more clear.

The search is not over. I still do not know where this stranger in this strange land truly belongs. Every step along the way augments the lines on the map, the winds on the charts. Off the edge of the map, where there be dragons, the search will end.

Of course, there are thanks in order, far too many to list here, but most particularly to Allan Von Werder, publisher of *The St. Mary and Franklin Banner-Tribune*, for allowing me the opportunity to tell the stories of my people and my waters; my editor, Vanessa Pritchett, for keeping my dashes and semi-colons consistent with the Associated Press Stylebook, no matter how stubbornly I resisted; Deanna and Jim Birkholm for allowing me to write for their outstanding website, Fly Anglers Online, as a columnist; all the good, kind folks who have responded to these words over the years; and last but in every way first above all others, Susan, always the rudder and keel staying my course.

The Chitimacha language, as used in this work, is mostly derived from the works of John R. Swanton, ethnologist for the former United States Bureau of American Ethnology. It does not have the benefit of modern research, as does the language as resurrected by the Chitimacha Tribal government and now taught to our people of all ages. But my use of the earlier version is intentional. Our language is a private thing, to me, something to be held close and treasured. Thus I have intentionally used Swanton's conventions when referring to place names, proper names and so forth. For instance, my use of *Sheti imasha* would under the revised structure be *Siti imaxa.* An official dictionary of the language is in planned publication, but until then, I will use the conventions mentioned. There is also a splattering of my grandmother's written interpretations of the words and names spoken to her by the elders.

The first set of these musings chronicles the painful side of discovery: Learning who I am and what place I hold in the world. The rest of the collection contains observations recited from the vantage of someone who had but one foot slipped from the raceway, limping sadly along but at once aware of all the other racers and their blinders as they plunge forever forward toward a mysterious, fabled finish line. They outline the life, set down on a calendar from January to December, though the years have mingled within the months, of a person born of water. Both chronicle a life thus far, and in their amusement and in their dismay, collectively they are a vision from the other side.

Amidships

o o o o o o o o o o o o o o o o o o o o o o o o o o o o o o o

"The water's murmur is the voice of my father's father."

—*Chief Seatl, Dwamish*

January

This is how my world begins.

The Creator of all things moved in thunder across a great sphere of water and knew that perfection was the sole proprietorship of gods, so he formed the land.

He did this by commanding Crawfish to swim down below the waters and, doing what Crawfish still does today, bring up mud into a mound like a volcano's throat—more and more, until the mud pierced the surface and dried under the sun. Crawfish continued to work, now snug and dry within the tunnel passage of his mound, bringing up mud, which spread and radiated, dried and hardened, and in this way, the Creator of all things sundered perfection by making the land, and isolated men by forcing them to live upon it.

Rivers moved across what had been created, for water is intolerant of imperfection. The edge of the sea laps at the margins of Crawfish's labor, sifting it away, but rivers move the earth from here to there, dumping it back into floodplains and basins. Lakes collect and persist, pools of grace to remind those who live too far from the sea of what lies beyond.

There are only three things constant from aft of my life to where I now sit, slightly more than amidships: Crawfish continues to build the land, water continues to confront it, and the infinite journey between the two.

January. Everything seems to slow, as if saturated with winter.

The October call of moving ignored, my English Springer spaniel, Mocha, stalks around the yard, padding over brown leaves and grass. Sometimes she sniffs at the air, nostrils flaring. She is breathing deeply of winter. The fence surrounding the back yard has imprisoned her, forbidden her instincts to move when October arrived, so she trudges through January and sniffs at winter. At times, she mysteriously curls into a ball, right there on the dead grass in the wide open, sleeping as a chill wind blows through the tufts of her hair. I can't comprehend why she does it, but I suspect she is making peace with the ghosts of winter. Springers are water dogs, but the fence forbids her the water, so she makes truce with the land.

January, and the skies are vivid blue and silent. There are few birds to sing. In the morning, squirrels dance across the pasture behind the house, bounding and nibbling at things I can't quite make out. Their red tails bristle at the sound of a passing car or a barking dog. They scurry up leafless trees to hide from winter.

So much to see, so much to learn. Things I have never seen before, because I never had the notion in January to look. Along Bayou Teche, the brown water scarcely moves, and it has fallen so much I can see the things that, in the summer and fall, lurked beneath. Shards of broken glass and ceramic; aluminum cans turned black with sludge and mud; chunks of foam and fragments of fishing tackle, muddy nylon braid from which dangle rusty hooks dulled by the water's rush. Winter reveals to humanity the refuse of its ignorance.

Across the bayou, a bank of white clamshell reminds me of something I had forgotten. When I was a lad, there was an old house on the opposite bank, its long ago paint peeled away, but it had a railed back porch and huge steps leading to the house which sat there, naked, abandoned and forlorn. I used to imagine I might take a boat across the bayou and go explore it, finding perhaps an Indian head penny in the crack of a floorboard, or the yellowed, fading letters of some heartbroken young girl pining over the loss of a suitor. I'd imagine carefully making my way through silent hallways, along faded walls save for squares and rectangles and the occasional oval of white where picture frames once hung, taken away by whoever lived here when they departed. Perhaps, I thought, I might find a cache of gold in the attic, or old books and maps to ponder. Maps fascinate some children, and I could imagine myself tracing lines with my finger, following winding rivers and roads and boundaries. Over the following years I passed that old house in my boat, reminding myself that I would explore it soon, but as time and the brush encroached, it faded from my memory.

Now, beyond the white shell, a thicket of trees grows dense, mostly chicken trees and chinaberry, immigrant invaders. I wonder if the old house is still within that briar patch, or if it has fallen and its timbers rotting away, the stately porch crumbled.

Beneath my feet, bristly cypress needles cover the wet ground near the bayou with a carpet of ocher, leaving just a few patches of black soil visible. In one patch, tracks of some animal that passed that way when the ground was softer head off south. Cypress knees stick knobby heads out of the rusty red carpet, faces wrinkled like an old man's, spiraling wood grain converging into tight circles like eyes. The elephant ears along the water's edge are dead, for the bayou has receded many feet from where they grew waist-deep in the summer. At the top of the ridge, a camphor tree is green and shiny. But at the edge of the bayou farther along, the thorn tree has died. I mourn for it quietly; every Chitimacha family had a thorn tree, and this was, as far as I know, the last on the reservation.

High in the branches of a tall, spindly pecan tree, the absence of leaves reveals a soup bowl shape of twigs and branches, a bird's nest gone unnoticed when the pecan was clothed in green, banana-shaped leaf. Like the house across the bayou, the nest is abandoned now, but perhaps in the spring its residents will return.

A cold breeze rushes by, and I shudder against it, climbing the ridge across the landscape back to the house. I pass where the fig tree that died last year was rooted, and mourn for it silently as well. I miss its skeletal form, the anticipation of watching it for buds to signal the advent of spring, for the little mottled-brown bird that always came to sing to me in years past, surviving disbelief.

Before going in, to the warmth of the house where I'll shed my coat and shoes, settle into my chair and sip hot coffee with Patches snuggled up beside me in a tortoise shell calico ball of warmth, I stare back over the fingernail of land between house and bayou. In a few acres of imperfect but beloved earth surrounding the house where I struggle to keep winter at bay, the world accepts and comforts itself under the spell of the season. It reminds me that I don't look and don't see often enough. Each season of the earth's turning has beauty and magic all its own.

So it's only fitting that I turn now in winter, look aft, and remember.

There is a fire out there, somewhere in the swamp. I have searched for it my entire life. It is an eternal fire. A sacred flame. In that primordial, ancient world of water it did not exist, but then, what use is fire to a world of water?

Long after Crawfish created the world by the Creator's bequest, a giant snake came upon my ancestors. From tail to fang, it measured in the miles. Many Chitimacha warriors confronted it, shooting it with arrows and piercing it with spears, and it took many years to kill. Where its gargantuan body lay and decomposed, a deep ravine formed and water flowed into it, sought it out, occupied and enveloped it. When it filled, my father's grandfathers called it *Teche*, their word for snake and when my mother's French-Acadian grandfathers saw it, they called it Bayou Teche and set about searching for divinity along it.

My father's people called themselves *Sheti imasha.* It was a name composed of words that sought to touch the face of the Creator.

Over thousands of years, that greatest of all rivers, the Mississippi, ran a reckless and wandering course across the southern margin of Louisiana. It would flow here for a time, somewhere else for a few millennia, abruptly move and begin anew somewhere else. For a time, the river ran through the great snake's deathbed, as well as west and east of it. Water found its way into the new land the river had relocated from much farther north, and formed a giant complex of large, joined lakes, the closest of which my father's people called *Sheti.*

They came from Natchez, my father's people. There was some sort of rift, some manner of division. They touched a brand to the eternal flame that burned for so long at Grand Village and moved south, carrying the flame with them, to be attended night and day, never allowed to expire, for that would mean the end of all things. Perhaps this ending would mean water would again engulf the world as it had twice before. When they came here, they found the only graceful, poetic balance of water and land in all of creation: These majestic swamps and marshes, the towering salt domes and great shell reefs, the rivers slicing courses through the earth, the abundance, the safety. They looked upon that great lake, named it, and themselves forever more became *Sheti imasha*, people of the lake.

Several thousand years later, I sit beside the window of a house built by poor people in a rich land, and look out at the final days of winter. The days are growing longer. Dawn comes earlier, the sunsets later. Last night, I noticed winged insects on the window screen. There are bright red cardinals perching on the fence, watching the dog closely, eager for an opportunity to steal from her food bowl. When I open the back door or come around the corner of the house, they flutter away, red embers whirling into the trees. Within the barren limbs, they look like signal flags—markers so that spring can find its way.

Milkweed and other late-winter plants spring up along the edges of the fence, the house, at the base of trees. Moist, fresh clover makes green mounds here and there around the otherwise dead-brown yard. At the foot of the back steps, a brown anthill pocked with tiny cavern openings marks the return of the red ants from beneath the ground where they fled to escape the cold.

Old Man Winter knows his days are short. Slipping in and out of consciousness, he is sometimes lucid, sometimes drifting off into oblivion. Winter storms in the north are the final gasps of dying breath, mighty exhalations of essence.

The frozen rivers that are his veins will thaw soon, the white snow that is his skin will begin to flail.

Winter was a time of misery all of my life. Winter was when dad couldn't go to divinity. The waters turned brown with sediment from cold rains, spring brought the melt of snows and ice far north down the Mississippi and into the Atchafalaya River, fanning it out across the basin. At times, where sediments laid by the Red River were drawn up, carried along and strewn over the basin, the water would turn red like the Nile transformed into blood.

Thankfully, the winters here are short and usually mild. Dad would grumble about the cold, make his way to the carbon black plant each weekday and retreat to the workshop on the weekends while the boat stayed dusty in the boat shed and the water in Bayou Teche went somewhere we couldn't follow. As winter waned, the promise of spring became overwhelming for my father and I, and for fathers long before us.

One late winter about a decade ago, some spring-spawned phantom possessed me, and I decided that I would like to plant a garden. I had never grown anything in my life, so I consulted with my father for advice, believing that with the accumulation of over sixty years under his belt he would be a wealth of old-time gardening wisdom.

He grunted in disdain at the question. "The most important thing you need to know about gardening, boy, is this: When it's time to work in that garden, *that's* when the fish are biting."

Not to be dissuaded, I started tomato and pepper plants by a window in the house, bought seeds for beans, squash, radish and cantaloupe. About early April, I announced that I'd be planting soon in the part of dad's back yard where I had tilled up four nice, long rows.

"Got to wait until after Easter," he said. "Everybody knows, you don't plant until after Easter."

I heeded his advice, and planted after Easter: A half-row of tomatoes, half-row of peppers, a full row of snap beans and the miscellaneous plants on the other two.

"Plant those tomatoes way up the stem," dad said. "They'll sprout roots and be stronger."

I thought about reminding him that two months before, he knew absolutely nothing about gardening other than having to work it instead of catching fish. My mom said dad's extent of gardening experience was that he'd dig a hole in the ground, throw in a few seeds and go fishing.

That garden was the most productive I have ever grown. It probably had much to do with the fact that I planted right in the spot dad used to cultivate his fishing worms. The soil there was so good and the winter so mild, in fact, we were still getting tomatoes the first frost at the end of the following February. We were so sick of snap beans by September that we started giving them all away. You didn't leave your car unlocked around our house when visiting, or you'd come back to find it full of snap beans. Growing fishing worms was dad's idea of gardening. In addition to having a never-ending supply for himself, he stocked the small stores around Charenton as well for extra cash.

The Old Man

When late season comes 'round again, Old Man Winter will know the diminishing of his days. But he also knows that he has lived and died this way for time uncounted, for all things are in the circle. Each death is but a chance for rebirth. The demise of winter is the earth's reminder that many circles remain unbroken.

There are domesticated white ducks in the bayou, swimming upstream against the wind, stark contrast to the muddy brown water. The bayou has been so low mud flats lie on its margins, pockets of water trapped within. Late one winter long, long before I was born, a bunch of then-young men could bear the cabin fever no longer and decided to go fishing during a brief spell of warm weather. My biological grandfather was among them. It's probably necessary to explain here that the people I refer to as my grandparents were biologically my great-uncle and great-aunt. Two brothers married two sisters, you see. Nicholas Stouff and Oral Rogers, my biological grandparents, died before I was born. Emile Stouff and Faye Rogers, the paternal grandparents I knew, had no children and adopted my father as their legal heir.

I'm told that Mr. Nick Sr. was something of a wanderer. Nick Sr. was proud of being a founding member of dozens of civic organizations in Ft. Worth and New Orleans, and when he opened his wallet a fanfold of charter membership cards as long as your arm would spill out. He seldom participated in them after that. Dad worked for him as a carpenter for a few years, but told me the old man was harder on him than he was on anybody else in the crew so it wouldn't appear he was showing any favoritism for his boy. Dad soon had enough of that and went back to the Rez.

The thing that Nick Sr. didn't know about fishing with Emile and his compatriots was that half the time they were serious about going catch a fish, but the other half of the time none of them could pass up a Jax or a Falstaff sign en route.

Upon being invited to participate in this "fishing trip" Nick Sr. promptly bought a new rod and reel and a fishing license. They left about noon (that was the other thing he didn't know about this gang of anglers) but five or six hours later, they were on their third or fourth Jax or Falstaff sign and Nick Sr. was getting pretty frustrated.

At that particular Jax or Falstaff sign, there was a bayou out back, so Nick Sr. grabbed his tackle and went down to the edge. His first cast with the new open-faced reel bird-nested, so completely tangled up it was beyond all hope. He retreated, I'm told, back to the bar and proceeded to cut the line out of his reel with a pocketknife, grumbling, "Spend money for a new rod, new reel, buy a fishing license, all to go beer-drinking."

"Don't matter if you're drinking or not," my grandpa shouted over to where Nick Sr. sat in the corner, grumbling and cutting line. "You still gotta buy a round when it's your turn."

January. Unseasonably warm for a time, with bursts of temperate weather countered by blasts of cold almost overnight. A halo moon rose above the earth one Saturday night, brilliant and humbling. The ring of ice crystals expanding outward from that bone-white disc in the sky reminded me again: Circles never end. Traditions do, unless you fight to maintain them, tooth and nail, to blood, to death.

I reclined on the front step, neck aching, back protesting, and watching the halo moon. If it were not for the intrusion of streetlights and neighborhood illuminations, it would have surely been more vivid than I could imagine. Science says it is caused by ice crystals in the atmosphere, viewed by the human eye at a 22-degree angle from the plane of the earth. Science attempts to demystify. Science fails in every instance, for knowing about ice crystals, angles and planes does not diminish the sheer wonder of that cosmic spectacle above.

Not that there is no place for science. In January, I am grateful for the efforts—sometimes fruitless, but mostly not—of meteorologists to let me know the temperature forecast, if there'll be rain or a hard freeze which would rip and snap the brittle old pipes under the house. In January, science is comforting, but it cannot sway the wonder and magic of the natural world in all its awe-inspiring magnificence.

The funeral dirges of December fading from hearing, wasting from memory, January's frigid air brings promises that the circle is never broken. Only men die. Winters come and go as they have all time, and will continue long after humanity is a speck of afterthought within the soil of the earth's skin.

The halo moon above me moved across the arc of heaven, and the ring expanded away from it, fading as the angle of its passage changed, altered beyond the capacity of 22 degrees from the plane of the earth to view with human eyes. It is warm out, but in two days a northern breath will cause the mercury to plunge, and I huddle against January in the house. I do not resent January like I once did. I cannot resent any part of the circle that has brought me at last to the place I have always wanted to be.

January, and the dog's coat has grown thick again, the cat scurries around the house chasing shadows, tail upright, back arched, seeming to tiptoe a fraction of an inch above the coldness of the oak floor. On a Sunday afternoon sitting in the living room, a bird's shriek cut the quiet: *Kee-ree! Kee-ree!* So loud it was, we thought it was in the house, but as it continued to resound its message, we looked all through rooms filled with decades and found only coalescing memories. While the *Kee-ree! Kee-ree*! continued I opened the front door and silence became absolute.

I never saw that January messenger but I know its name. *Kich.* It came early this year. Usually it would perch in the fig tree in March or so, giving me its message which I do not understand. I do not know what it came in January to tell me. My father's people said *kich* would foretell the coming of visitors, of rain, of danger, of death. But I do not know which sounds have which meanings, and a January coming must bear some meaning of significance.

Mottled-brown birds and halo moons. Science and magic. Alligator teeth and turquoise. Electronics and newsprint. These are the halves of January through which I make my way. Is it any wonder that, at times, I am overwhelmed by the duality? Must seek divinity of water to cleanse and renew myself?

Halo moons and messengers from the past. Friend, cold, rain or death. I do not know what they mean in January. It has all been taken from me. I am bereft. I am half-handed and nearly blind. Someone stole my eyes shortly after I was born. Not the eyes in my head, rather the eyes *in* my head. The eyes that can see January, open front doors and catch a glimpse of *kich*, distill prophecy from halo moons. I used to have them. But long ago, at the hands of Spanish or French swords and Carlisle Indian school teachers, descendants were blinded. Taught not to see. Made *ashamed* to see.

Sometimes my sight returns to me, and January seems to help. In the brown deadness of the winter lifescape surrounding me, a flash of movement, a scurry of flight, alerts that my eyes may see clearly again in time. The halo moon, so far above me as I propped myself there on my elbows, may move as a scientific principle a distance away from the degree of plane, but the message it brought is as purposeful as that of *kich.*

I look forward to learning the meaning behind it. Perhaps in January. Or February. Maybe so late as June. It doesn't matter. Only that I know it is there, waiting.

At last the halo is gone, though the moon continues her white-faced trek across the arc of the sky. Regretful, I go back into the house and lock the door against a night left dark and impenetrable. There are whispers of winter in the house, and I touch the thermostat to chase them away. Nestled onto the sofa, the cat comes and snuggles the flat of her head against my arm, purring softly, inaudibly, discernible by feel only.

Messages in January. I can only await them. I can only look ahead for them. Halo moons and shrieking mottled-brown birds. Whatever they forebode, time will tell. Carlisle teachers, swords, gun-wielding turn-of-the-century sheriffs cannot sway them. Some things persist. Sometimes it doesn't matter if you believe in something or not, so long as something believes in *you.*

Though my back ached and my eyes were strained, pushed beyond their means, driving through the January night gave me a sense of quiet solitude, and I purposefully chose roads that held little other traffic. It made me feel like I was alone in the whole wide world.

The friends and like-hearted souls which surround me are precious gems, but on less-traveled roads on dark nights, the streaking glimpses of all my relations, all my known and unmet kin alike, open a hollow pit in my heart, a longing which cannot be satisfied by those around me. Perhaps this is why they claw their way into these words so often, demanding to be heard, refusing forgetfulness. Nature, it is said, abhors a vacuum. In this, what Thomas McGuane called the longest silence, the quietude of a noisy, quarrelsome world fades to black. The longest silences are those between awakenings.

Ahead, the headlights of my pickup are twin sabers, thrusting, paleo-spearpoints skewing the night and sending it flurrying for cover. On a night like this, before I was born, my parents were answering the telephone call that a dearly loved member of the family was dying. As they sped through the darkness, a huge white bird suddenly flashed in the headlights, swooping at them, larger than they could imagine, up over the cab, then swept away into the darkness as the illumination of the car passed. When they arrived, their relation was dead.

Night reveals such things, and in the high-speed passing of the truck through a lightless landscape, I am reminded that to everything there is a balance. There can be no day without night, the old adage goes. No gargantuan wings flash through the headlights, but shapes streak by, fluttering out of control, and vanish behind me, like relations died one January night before I could reach them.

There are silences in a life, moments when not even the beat of our hearts pounding in our ears or the voices of all those we surround ourselves with can be heard. These are the lonely silences, and the longest of these are intolerable to most of us. We scrape and fight for the next scuffle, desperate for the promised conflagration, because the long silence makes us feel empty and solitary.

The road leads me to water, and I am not surprised, though I had not planned it. Under a half-moon, the shimmering surface of it seems to invite me to discover its many secrets. I rush down the road alongside it, glancing out the window at it, and the rumble of loneliness strikes hard deep within, dwarves with cold iron hammers beating against my bones. If the water's murmur is indeed the voice of my father's fathers, then this silent stillness is the quietude of the peace they have gone to abide within. I dislike the Western notion of the dead lying wasting in the ground. I refuse and exorcise it. My relations flash by in nighttime excursions along empty roads. They sleep in quiet, still water and speak when it moves with the wind, the tide, the ebb and flow of the earth.

Yes, I am surrounded by boundless friendship and love, chasing away January's chill breath. They fill most of the pits, occupy most of the vacancies. No man could be richer than I in that way. Yet, none of us should allow those hollow places to be completely lost. On exhausted nighttime trips of weariness, it is proper to immerse myself for a few moments in the loneliness. They still live in the hollow places, in the night, the water and the wind and the long, lonely silences.

Were I to meet another traveler in the night, if it were ages ago when such things mattered, I would introduce myself by lineage. I am Nicholas Leonard Stouff Jr.'s son, whose father was Nicholas Leonard Stouff, who was a carpenter and general contractor. His father was Octave Pierre Stouff, who traveled by horse-drawn buggy to attend the opera in New Orleans once a year. His father was Jean Pierre Stouff, who came from France to work for Martial Sorrell overseeing his plantation. I am Lydia Gaudet Stouff's son, whose father was Edwin Gaudet who came from St. Martinville to farm near Charenton, and her mother was Eremise Abshire, who made the very best yellow cake in the world.

But such things don't matter in the world of daylight anymore. My grandfather had a key that I never saw, but it opened doors through which he could slip and visit people long gone. He took that key with him when he joined them for the last time. Without that key, I can only speed through the night and let the road, the night and the water open just a sliver in the door, enough to let me hear and see fragments.

The longest silence is the quiet of their voices, the reaching, the holding on. The longest silence is the absence of all my relations in this amok world, this calliope of dizzying confusion I make my way through day to day.

I stop the truck near the end of the water's expanse, and when I think of walking out to it, a lifetime of taught and perceived apprehensions conjure slight fear. Why are we afraid of the dark on some lonely road near silent water? Perhaps it's because we have filled all the holes, all the empty spaces, and we don't want them to be emptied again. They are too painful, perhaps, evoke too much loneliness.

I cling to that. If, after I join my relations for the last time, no one ever sits in the silence and feels the hollowness of my memory, how will I know I was ever loved? How will I be sure I ever really existed at all if not by the silent place left empty in someone's heart?

The truck door slams behind me and I push through tall grass to the water's edge. So still and quiet is the lake at my feet it seems unfathomable. I reach down and touch it with my forefinger, and circles expand outward through the rest of January and beyond, answering me, reminding me. There is no need to fear the darkness, and people make whatever monsters dwell within it, not by the night.

There in the longest of silences, I understand that it is natural and right to mourn the empty spaces. They do not displace the places that are filled, brimming over with cherished friends and treasured loved ones. But to all things there is a balance. Day and night. Open and closed. Emptiness and fulfillment. I could never have been this companion-rich but sometimes-melancholy man, standing on the edge of the water listening in the night, without the circles expanding out from the center.

The longest silence reaches back far, far behind me, and stretches out far ahead. It will not be forgotten, as long as these words continue to flow through the night, fluttering, out of control, glimpsed by passersby on lonely roads in January.

My grandmother, Faye Rogers Stouff, wrote: *The little bird would come close to the house and sing or chirp its messages that only an Indian could understand. Sometimes this little bird would make its nest in the screens, or on a wooden shutter. No one was allowed to touch the little bird's nest; it would leave if you did.*

There was a halo moon Saturday. A halo moon usually means the coming of rain. Sunday morning, *kich* sang to me, very close to the house. The sound my grandmother described in her writings, the one the bird made to foretell rain, was very much like the one I heard last weekend.

And Thursday morning, as rain fell in cold, stinging sheets at dawn, the voice cut through the deluge again: *Kuee suya! Kuee suya!* Very near the house, as if just outside the door.

In my grandmother's writings, she described this sound as a harbinger of good luck. So she had transcribed. Upon reading this, upon my being made aware of this, the little bird at once went silent. As if on queue. As if satisfied. As if its duty had been done.

Halo moons and little birds in January. I know them as surely as my own name. I know them as surely as Benjamin Paul did, who told my grandmother that one spring, he and his wife and sister were out picking berries along the shore of Grand Lake.

The cry came as a surprise, the cry of danger. Benjamin saw the little bird sitting high on a berry vine near where his sister was picking fruit, and he warned her not to pick there.

But since she did not believe the bird could be understood, she continued, and as she reached for the ground to pick a berry, a rattlesnake leaped from where it had been hidden in a tight coil beneath the vines.

Benjamin treated the frightened, quickly sickening girl with medicines he had learned from his grandmother, then at once took her to see a physician. The doctor in turn sent them back to the tribal medicine woman, saying he could not do better for her than they had already done. The sister recovered completely.

My grandmother also related that, if a flood were coming, the little bird would merely hover in the sky, silent, as if afraid to come down. She said the last time it was known to do this was, in fact, 1927, when Louisiana suffered it's worst flooding in recorded history.

There are fine lines, for me. Boundaries. Disturbances in faith and loyalty. I struggled long and vainly trying to discern the razor's edge between keeping oral lore sacred and private, and not letting it die. Some part of me still feels guilty when I put down the words here that were for thousands of years meant only for *Sheti imasha* ears. I sometimes feel I am a betrayer. Perhaps, I wonder at times, things should just be allowed to die, to fade away and be forgotten.

But *kich* has come to me every single spring for the past seven years, perching in the fig tree in the back. When the old fig tree died after more than a century of life, I feared *kich* would not return again. I had taken cuttings from the old tree shortly before its demise, one of which survived and is growing heartily in the front yard near the driveway. *Kich*' voice has come to me from the front of the house this January, and though I have not seen it, my heart knows I am hearing it from the waist-high prodigy of the old tree that died two years ago. When I go to the window or open the door, its call ceases and I see only the rain.

I believe the Creator of all things speak to each in their own way, in the words which they hear and understand the best. While this may raise the ire of the theological arrogant, I believe that the Creator speaks to me through black lake water, rushing wind, violent thunderstorms and little mottled-brown birds. I believe the Creator's name is as infinite as the vocalizations of the human spirit, and the perceptions that allow us to know his presence.

Taunte Pauline, according to my grandmother, said way back in the 1930s that *kich* no longer came to the Indians, perhaps knowing that "all the older Indians are gone who could talk to it." But my grandmother, who was not Chitimacha by blood but as wholly in spirit as any other, heard *kich* and spoke to it in our native language. In the more than 70 years she lived in this old house, she heard it and spoke to it, and I believe it comes back now and then to pay homage to her. I believe, in my heart of hearts, it has not forgotten her, and the voice with which it rings to me is given in honor of the friendship they shared. It honors me by speaking, and though I don't know the words to reply, I understand its purpose, if not its literal meaning.

Many years ago, the Conquistadors landed at Grand Lake, at the shell beach that is now a boat landing, and tried to come ashore. The *nata* of the Chitimacha forbade them, but they tried anyway, and the Chitimacha beat them back. The Spaniards retreated, only to return in allegiance with the Oumas nation, and were victorious over the Chitimacha. Later, the French accused the Chitimacha of murdering a priest named Fr. Cosme, while he and his men slept in camp. That resulted in a war which lasted many years, until the chief, Framboise, signed an agreement with Gov. Bienville ending the hostilities. It has been suggested in recent scholarly circles that the murder of Fr. Cosme was actually carried about by the Natchez nation in retribution because Cosme fathered a son by a Natchez woman. As it happens, the only survivor of the massacre was a Natchez slave, who immediately reported the incident to Bienville and accused the Chitimacha of the crime.

That was in the early 1700s, and the Chitimacha disappear from the historical record until 1883, when historian Albert S. Gatschet visited, and later in 1907 when John R. Swanton came. It is believed that during that time, the tribe stayed close to itself in the swamps around Charenton, shunning all contact with outsiders, and they come out of that historical blackout in 1883 having largely taken

European names and many western ways. Adapt or die. But many still clung to tradition, and because of them, many of those traditions persist today.

My grandmother arrived here in 1926, and was taught these things by Benjamin Paul and her mother-in-law, Delphine Stouff. She was taught the language, the art of basketry and the medicines. She was told of *kich* and *Neka sama* and much, much more. Ben Paul died in 1935 and Delphine in 1940, and for the many decades that followed, only a white woman who had some Osage in her but could not trace it definitively, held onto all those secrets, all those prophecies, all those magics. On bright spring days, she would listen to the call of a little bird, speak back to it in Chitimacha, and until her death in 1997, was its sole companion.

I can only guess what it told her, what she spoke to it. I can only imagine the conversations they held in perfunctory, abbreviated and difficult exchanges. But I know that they spoke, she and that ancestral little bird, and today it comes and speaks to me, and though I don't know how to reply, it speaks anyway. I believe it tells me how it loved her. How it misses her voice, the proud posture of her stature, the lilt of her laugh.

In this, at least, we understand each other beyond the barriers of language. In this, at least, we are the same.

Halo moons and messenger birds in January. Her footsteps still fall upon the floors of the house late at night. She straightens picture frames and touches split river cane under darkness. *Kich* comes to speak to both of us, because some part of her is still here with me. We trade stories of her, memories without words.

How we miss her. How we love her. How I wonder, after I have left this world to join all my relations, who will *kich* speak to then?

People of the Lake

After Crawfish brought the earth up from beneath the waters and the land was formed, the Creator took the dried mud and formed it into human beings.

He made three mud figures, and fired them under the sun for different durations: The first he fired the least, and it became the White Man. The second he fired the most, and this was the Black Man. The third he fired somewhere in between, and this became the Red Man. These he placed in different corners of the land that now dissected the oceans, and eventually they sought each other out, made war, made love, killed each other and bore children. They settled each other's countries and fished each other's waters, and while Crawfish worked and the rivers labored, the mud-made men were unknowingly pulling down heaven and lifting up catastrophe.

This is the beginning of the third flood. It is the one that will wipe clean the land of *Sheti imasha* where invasion could not.

The second deluge was Noah's flood. It happened to my father's people too, because the flood was global; the Creator is God and God is the Creator, though most Christians seem to think they've been insulted when reminded of this. Forewarned, my ancestors made a giant clay pot and they all climbed into it as the waters rose. Within this clay pot—fired like their bodies in the sun—they persisted, awaiting the flood to subside. A rattlesnake, nearly drowned, begged them to let him into the pot, but fearful, my ancestors refused. The rattlesnake promised them it would not bite them, and brokenhearted over the snake's plight, they let it into the pot, where it survived Noah's flood with them. So grateful was the snake he promised that he would never bite a Chitimacha for the rest of all time. Unfortunately, the cottonmouth water moccasin made no such arrangement.

My mother's people called themselves Acadians. Exiled from the Nova Scotia land Crawfish made for them, they sought out the other Frenchmen in Louisiana and settled here. They settled near water, seeking grace. Like the Chitimacha, they were people of water. People who live on and with water know it, and it knows them.

A natural affinity between Cajuns and the Chitimachas must have been uneasy at times, but largely firm. Water joins and bonds. The Acadians brought with them the skiff and the bateau, and from the Indians they learned how to fell cypress to make the dugout canoe. Before iron tools, this was accomplished by setting the inside of the log afire, using mud to direct and control the direction of the burn. Adapting the dugout canoe, the Acadians developed the pirogue, that most elegant and wily of bayou and swamp vessels.

They also farmed, something my father's people did little of. In the basin, in those days before "civilization" was shoved in, food was plentiful. It was easy to throw out a trap in the morning and empty it of garfish and catfish for lunch, then repeat the process for supper. But Edwin and Eremise Gaudet, my maternal grandparents, farmed the land near Charenton for one of the major landholders. Though they died poor, cheated by way of English monetary systems that were a mystery to a solely French-speaking couple, I don't know that they were ever unhappy. They later lived in a tiny house on Willow Street in Franklin. Edwin kept an old car in the garage that hadn't run in years, if not decades. Next to the garage was a chicken yard, and when the time was right, Edwin would kill a chicken for cooking. There were always fresh yard eggs.

Eremise Abshire Gaudet made hot, thick black coffee by dripping boiling water through the grinds a tablespoon at a time, serving it in tiny demitasse cups. She also made a yellow cake, no sugary icing, but all her grandchildren loved it. They spoke French to each other, my grandparents, mother and her siblings, and very little English. I never learned French, because in the days before Cajun cooking and culture became a national sensation—thus beginning its destruction—speaking Cajun French was an embarrassment, something to be ashamed of. Thus the language barrier prevented me from ever being very close to them, something I regret mightily.

Old man winter's grip suddenly reaches out, firm again, icicle fingers which burn flesh and freeze marrow.

Here, in January, time seems to slow to a meandering ice flow, expanding like frozen water, growing outward into infinity. The days are growing longer, but the chill has saturated deep into the earth, safe and hidden from the few warming rays of the sun.

It was in February that my father was born in 1924, in the colder latitudes of Ft. Worth, Texas. Abandoned early by his natural father, he was rapidly thrust into the role of man of the family as he grew up, feeling inwardly responsible for his mother and his little brother. He matured on the streets of Ft. Worth, then a city no larger than Lafayette, street brawling in January and looking forward to spring when he could escape to lake water. By the time he was five, the depression was in full swing, and in every January that followed, he kicked and scuffled his way through a poor city child's life.

Perhaps it was in January that he made his first trip to Louisiana. It took three days by car back then, on roads that were little better than trails, mending flat tires and pouring quarts and quarts of oil into belching, exhausted engines. It was sometime in the 1930s, that much I know, and he stayed in an old house on the reservation that was, by then, some 90 years old. He stayed with his grandmother, Delphine, who would not allow dogs in the house, a truly despicable crime in her culture. Once, he recalled to me, an old hound slipped into the house unnoticed, and when Delphine saw him, she snatched up a cat o' nine tails, each tail tipped with a lead pellet, and Dad said after that he was so terrified of the old woman his only comments to her for the rest of the visit consisted of, "Yes, ma'am," "No ma'am," and "Thank you, ma'am."

It would be after his military service that he returned for good. In December of 1947, he married my mom. They exchanged vows in that same old house of Delphine's, though she was gone to her Creator by then, and my grandparents lived there. In Januarys to follow, they spent many happy days living for a time in that old house until they moved just next door to another, but they were always there, sharing within it, and in time, my uncertain feet scampered over its oak floors and turned from toddler to teen to grown man. Now I sit here in January and listen for old dogs sneaking into the house, the sound of wedding vows, the padding of tiny feet.

When Delphine, in her later years, grew weary of late visitors, she would make a point of getting her clock from the bedroom and winding it. Everyone in the family knew this was a signal it was time for them to go home. In January, I listen for the winding of clocks, and sometimes, in the longest silences, I think I might hear them.

January, and last night a brass candleholder toppled from a kitchen shelf for no apparent reason, and broke at the weld. The cat is startled sometimes, though I cannot discern why. As the mercury changes, the house groans and creaks, timbers moving, building pressure against each other, storing energy, until the strain is too much and they move suddenly with a loud *Snap!* Over time, they settle back into position again, relaxing, remembering winding clocks and padding feet in January.

At no time am I closer, more wrapped in the cloak and sanctuary of this old house, than winter. My outdoor activities decline, and I shield myself within its snapping, popping walls for warmth. I see crown-molding joints slowly open over the days of January, watch them gradually close up again, sometimes until they bulge with strain. The house breathes, in January, inhales and exhales, its heart beats and its blood flows. Sometimes, I feel like a symbiot, living within a living host, feeding off it, returning its needs in my own way.

Can a house die? I wonder this, sometimes, in January. The sag of a roofline, the peeling of paint from walls, the thin crack in sheet rock spidering up out of the baseboard. It's glass eyes stare out at January, and one or two of the frames have small fractures in them, cataracts threatening blindness. Years ago the back porch rotted and nearly killed me as I fell when it collapsed. I tore it down and rebuilt it, but could I have been extracting a cancer from a body?

There are times when January makes me think it is tired, grown dim and thin. It tells me it is tired. It tells me it's lived a good life, it's seen some wonderful and some horrible things, and it's time to be done. It reminds me that the bayou behind it once ran clear and full of fish, but now it is black and nothing lives there. It tells me stories about when the family would come from all over and they'd set up a dozen tables in the backyard and cook food and laugh and laugh and laugh. It shows me how the women gathered to make baskets and speak words that weren't English, and the men whittled cypress knees into life forms. Doors were taken down from its innards, placed on sawhorses to lay out the dead. Children were born in its bedrooms. It says, in January, that without my love for it, there would be no need to go on.

So I find cypress and antique Douglas fir, and I rebuild its bones, shore up its liver, heart and muscle. I insulate its lungs to keep the breath within it, keep the chill of January from its marrow. So long as it moves, snaps and pops as the mercury changes, I know that it is alive for another January, another chapter in my life.

In the quietest moments, when the heater is not running and the television is off, when we are alone inside, I wonder what would happen if I woke up one morning and found that it had died during the night? That it was only wood and sheetrock and nails, no more than the individuality of its parts, no sum, no total? If it stops snapping and popping, draws a final breath with the expansion of a crown molding joint, exhales one last time? The silence would be unbearable. The emptiness would be harrowing.

Nothing lasts forever. Not January. Not winter. Not even old family houses. I can only hope that it will outlive me, but then, who will walk its floors and listen in the night for winding clocks and tiny feet? Who could possible live here in January and know that their own parents were wed in these rooms, flakes of dead skin from their own toddler feet are still imbedded in the grain of the oak, understand the meaning behind a first grade math flash card found behind a baseboard? If they removed a piece of facing from the old cypress window in the living room and found, penciled on the joist, "E.A. Stouff, 1940" and directly beneath, "R. Stouff, 1998," would they understand the Februarys and the winters of endurance saturated in those walls?

January. Wrapped within walls for warmth. Spring is coming. Sunlight will warm the roof, limber old aching bones of cypress beams, cease the arthritic noises of age. I'll come home late in the evening from work, or from a pond, and shelter myself inside. For as long as there is life within, as long as wild unfettered magic whips through its windows and doors, I'll listen. As long as the clock is never allowed to wind down.

Days in the life of a man whose life is flowing with water. They round bends in the current, struggle against snags and sometimes calm to motionless, still and black, tranquil. It is no easy thing to be born of water, to have it saturate the very essence of being. To be far from it is unbearable, to be detached unthinkable. I have never known fast-running mountain streams or trout water, but I have read

Middleton and McGuane and Geirach describe them. I know how they feel and the depth of them, so I think I understand that whatever waters we immerse ourselves in are equally special, whether they be clear, fast and cold, or warm, green-black and still. My home waters, these native waters, were the lifeblood of my father's people for millennia. Floating along them in wooden bateaus or skiffs, offering cork poppers or feathered streamers off the leader of a fly rod may be a detachment from my grandfathers, hunting fish with spear and arrow, but in our essence we are the same.

Winters here are mild by comparison to the northeast. Those infrequent dips of mercury into the twenties are uncomfortable, but we are blessed to have temperate conditions most of the year. Still, in February, I am longing for warm water, for bass and bluegill, for green cypress and shrieking eagles. I have been bound to these wonderful walls for too long, and much as I love them, need them, I require the surge of lake water in my veins. Dreams of Grande Avoille Cove filter into my sleep like tides; in waking hours, if I close my eyes, I see its stands of second-growth cypress, water lapping at their trunks. Though I pay attention to conversations, laugh with friends, commune with acquaintances, there is always Grande Avoille Cove behind my thoughts. I am always aware of it, cognizant of the distance I stand from it, I know which direction it lies without thinking about it, and I sense its presence day and night.

Cok'tangi it was called a century ago. *Pond lily worship place.* A small bay on the greater system of lakes which have been dissected by the Atchafalaya Basin Protection Levee, Grande Avoille Cove was so renamed by the Spanish conquistadors after their word for the flat-topped pond lily which grew in abundance there. These lilies, some big around as a car radiator, grew from the hard shallow bottoms along the cove, drops of lake water sometimes resting atop their waxy dinner-plate skin in beads like jewels. It was a haven for bass, lurking between the lily stems, and more than once an unfortunate bird perched on a lily pad would fall prey to the tremendous splash of a largemouth.

When my father and I fished there, we would cast yellow and black cork poppers between the lilies, and without many pauses, the bass or bull bream would attack these with ravenous glee. To coax these fish out of the lilies with old fiberglass fly rods was challenging, and we often lost them to broken leaders twisted around a clump of lily stems, muddy murk coming up in a cloud from the disturbed lake bed. The mud comes from deposits laid down by the Mississippi River over thousands of years, mud which came from far, far north, perhaps partially from trout streams and cold mountain water. Though I never considered such things as a boy, I know now that I am fishing the same water as Maclean and

Middleton, swept down to us here in the delta in the same way I am breathing air that was once breathed by Jesus Christ and Crazy Horse. All things are circular. All things are connected.

Entering Grande Avoille cove from the channel that was dug to provide soil for the levee system, the south shore was once the central religious place of the entire Chitimacha nation. My grandfathers would come there to honor the Creator. In the early part of the 20th century, the reef of shell bank the Chitimacha built from the shoreline was dredged for its value in shell, and skeletons tumbled out into the lake water. These are the bones of medicine men and chiefs, of Honored and Nobles, of grandfathers and grandmothers. The only solace I have is that they at least remained on *Cok'tangi.* Others of my ancestors have not fared so well.

But it is February, and Grand Avoille Cove is shallow and muddy, the intruding sediment showing above water in many places, a result of the damnable interruption of the natural flow of water by the levee system. Even if I were to brave the cold ride, the boat would never find passage to the cove's backwaters. Back there where Sawmill Bayou was once filled with thousands of harvested cypress and tupelo logs, ready to be floated out to one of the many sawmills that once dotted a map of St. Mary Parish. Winter restricts me in so many ways. There are no cold-water fish to pursue here. It is too shallow for crappie, our sac-au-lait, and there are no trout. The largemouth and the bluegill are lethargic in the cold depths of Lake Fausse Point or the channel itself.

I satisfy my need for water, for fish, on warmer days at landlocked ponds not influenced by the flow of sediment and the muddy tides of snowmelt far, far north. It is enough, for the moment in February, to be close to water, but Grande Avoille Cove lurks behind my eyelids, floats in the fluid between the back of my brain and skull.

The connection some human beings make with home waters is profound. There are those who are born on those waters, and there are those who have come by them later in life. When a man or woman finds home water, the recognition and realization of its truth is powerful and cannot be forsaken.

We are, I believe, the sum total of all those who have gone before us. A part of each of us is given down by our ancestors, who have in some way shaped each following generation. Because of this, I believe that those who long for water, need to be near it, hear it, feel its flow, have been ancestrally connected with water for generations. When I look behind the eyes of people who see water as no more than an elemental aspect of nature, something to wash in, boat in, drink or flush the toilet, I believe these people are descended from inland forebears, people detached from the ocean, lake, stream or pond.

I cannot disparage them. In the same way that I long for water each moment of my existence, others find divinity along desert dunes rolling with tumbleweed and cactus, or cold, dry mountains, or dense forest woodlands. It has been posited that cats, for example, act in domestication much as their wild forebears did. A housecat who prefers lazing at the top of the stair was descended strongly from felines who lived perhaps on craggy cliffs, or stalked high bluffs. A cat that prefers to nestle in under a sofa, or hide behind a chair, may be an offspring result of a lineage of caves and deadfalls, hollow logs and steep overhangs.

People, though we choose to deny it, are biological creatures that carry those same tendencies with them. There are those of us who are fastened at the navel to mountains, those to desert, those to tundra and savanna, and those to water.

My father was probably the most pure artist I have ever known. His art was not lofty. It was not thought provoking. The things he made were so elegant in their simplicity that they skirted conceptions of art. As an artist, my father was Everyman.

He was an artist with wood, first and foremost, but he was also a magician of music, a silversmith, a stonecutter, and most of all, a fisherman. There was no presumption about his art. It was beautiful without complication, and it was all connected one to the other. He made no apologies for it, and was never required to. The art he sent out into the world flourished and lifted his name to heights he never longed for nor ever really became comfortable with.

That workshop was a wonderland of dusty chaos. About the same size as the house, it had a dirt floor, and when Louisiana rains continued for weeks on end, tiny rivulets would snake through it, miniature versions of Bayou Teche. There were two small doors on two sides, and one large double-door that he would swing open and let air circulate in the hot summer months.

Everything was covered in a layer of dust. Now and then he would take an electric blower and kick up a small storm of sawdust that would drift out of the big double doors and blow away. A table saw and band saw were the most prominent tools, but dozens of hand power tools and hundreds of hand tools lie everywhere. To the unenlightened, it looked like a complete mess, but he knew where everything was and could walk to it without hesitation. One wall contained a dozen and a half Stanley planes, from low angle blocks to big jointer and rabbet planes. There were chisels from quarter-inch to timber framing, fifteen or twenty Disston hand saws in every variety, numerous tools whose purpose I cannot fathom even today. Tucked up in the roof trusses were old boat windshields, big saltwater fishing rods, my old wooden rocking horse, a baby bed and dad's treasured stash of spalted soft maple.

Here he sat when the fishing was impossible, on a tall stool at the bench, and fashioned bolo ties, carvings, turquoise rings, nearly anything that could be made by hand. He made a wall-to-wall and floor-to-ceiling entertainment center for a friend at work, and he carved a Garden of Eden scene with tiny animals smaller than dimes, many of which he dropped and lost on the dirt floor to be remade amidst a flurry of cussing.

I would hide in the shop while he was working, and on cue, he would shout, "Where's that Tiger?" and come find me. No matter how well I hid, behind the band saw, in a cabinet, under a boat tarp, he always found me because I always let go a giggle when he shouted, "Where's that Tiger?"

"Tiger" was not my official nickname. It was what Wilmer Joseph called me. Mr. Wilmer ran an establishment just off the reservation. It was what the locals called "a bajoon." He was African-American, a big, hulking man with the disposition of a lamb. Though it was marginally a grocery store, mostly it was a bar, and dad would go there to buy King Edward cigars, invariably having a Jax or two. No children were allowed behind the counter except me. As soon as dad and I walked in, Mr. Wilmer would yell, "Come on back here, Tiger, and let's see what we can find for you!" It was usually a pack of candy cigarettes or a root beer. The black children looked from the other side of the counter at me angrily and enviously, and I felt bad, but Mr. Wilmer would pitch them a pack of Now or Laters. Wilmer Joseph's place was one of the businesses which sold dad's fishing worms.

Though dad built boats like no one else in south Louisiana did, with his own design particulars derived from a natural eye for the form and function of small craft. Though he made silver and turquoise and abalone jewelry which found its way across the world, and though he could play blues guitar like a delta bluesman, and make violins, the depth of his artistry was most apparent and most private in fishing. Here again, he made no apologies for being a bait fisherman.

In some faraway world he had never visited, the bait fisherman is scorned, eyed with disdain along the long narrow taper of a bamboo fly rod. The bait fisherman, in circles where rainbow and brown trout are elevated to some higher existence, the bait angler is the lowliest of fishermen. Only the fly is worthy of the trout, at its extreme the dry fly, and the trout the only prize worth pursuing. If my father ever fished trout in a cold, fast-moving river, he never told me about it. He was a bait fisherman, yes, but the fly was omnipresent. When the particular essence of his art manifested itself on days chosen only by itself and the water, the fly rod would emerge and, like a sorcerer conjuring a storm, he made art that required no trout streams, no rainbows, no browns, but which would surely have pleased them. The waters in which he fished—those primordial cypress and tupelo swamps of Louisiana—were thick with narrowly spaced trunks rising from the green-black waters. The opportunity to cast a fly from a boat was rare, but when it presented itself, the chance was taken.

An old Heddon fiberglass fly rod with Martin reel would emerge from under the spray rail of the boat, and he would free a popping bug from the hook keeper. The Martin would shriek as he stripped out the line and, like a maestro conducting an orchestra, he began to cast. I would sit there watching him in wonder. The bait fisherman was productive, but the fly fisherman was an artist. The line grew life of its own, curling, arcing, stretching far back behind him and, with a subtle flick, sped forward and lay itself over the water straight as an arrow, the little popper settling in last at the end of the leader.

Like the bait fisherman, the loftier angler may also demean my father's preferred quarry. In the 1940s, he would complain bitterly that the largemouth bass would not leave his bluegill bait alone long enough for him to catch a suitable supply of slab-sized goggle-eye and chinquapin for my mother to fry up for supper. The largemouth bass, prized in these waters like the trout is in more northern latitudes, was decidedly beneath the bream to my father. Perhaps it was because he was not very interested in fighting to land a largemouth, though in later years he would fish for them purposefully, as if the battle was part of the struggle against his fading youth. The bream was more to his liking because it was not a fish of brute force, a water-ripping juggernaut mindlessly attacking everything in its path. The bluegill was, in fact, among the cornerstones at the origin of his art: Resourceful, intelligent, and abundant. At the risk of raising the ire of the trout angler, the bluegill is south Louisiana's brown trout, in my father's eyes more worthy of being caught by a true fisherman, and let the brutish bass fishermen have their largemouth. He was not enchanted by the struggle. Bluegill were not only feisty and perfect for the pan, they were so abundant that taking them was no scar to the natural resources he treasured. In fact, he considered he was doing the bass fisherman a favor by catching them.

Fishing bream with the fly rod was exciting for both of us. I would leave my cork and hooked worm in the water, forgotten, watching him. Sometimes I got bites and did not realize it until I felt the rod being tugged out of my hands by a big bluegill seeking to escape with it. Dad put the fly here, whipped it back ever so gently. Then he put it within six inches of the previous spot, twitched it a few times, back over his shoulder, six inches farther, and repeated the whole process, every six inches in a fan, until he had covered every half-foot of a likely spot. When the bluegill took the fly it was like a firecracker in the water, and the line would leap tight, the old rod would curl and the Martin would scream. Before long, a bull bluegill was in the boat, and the casting begun anew. Now and then he would hook a bass, and the real fight would seem to go on forever. My fondest memory is when, on his back swing, a bass leaped and took the fly out of the air. He landed it.

It was in that little wooden bateau that my father had built, that art, water and fire were made known to me. He said, when he built it, "That's it. It doesn't get any better than this." That was two years before I was born. He made a few more for other people, but this was the last one for himself. It outlived him. It'll probably outlive me. I learned a lot of things in that boat, without even realizing it. About him. About boats. About me. We'd paddle around—he'd paddle, anyway—and fish all day. I'd get cranky and tired by mid-afternoon, and we'd go home, and it was always a relief to me to touch dry land again, but I remember how he looked. As if he left something, some part of himself, back here. No matter how tired he was, he always took the time to make sure every drop of water was out of the boat, that it was clean and dry. "Always take care of her, and she'll always get you home." I never forgot that. But he wasn't just talking about boats. It was an analogy, I guess. Though he didn't know it. In the old days, the old Indians used to sit around and tell these long stories to teach the young ones life lessons. Like Jesus and his Parables. In modern times, dad told modern parables, and though I never really knew what I was learning at the time, sooner or later the lesson would be clear to me. Taking care of things. Taking care of things you care for. Do it, and they'll never let you down.

I learned so many things in that boat. My dad always said, "That lake will never hurt a Chitimacha. It knows us. People who live on water, with water, know it, and it knows them. That lake, it'll stand up on its hind legs and eat boats. But it will never harm a Chitimacha. That's its promise to us." And it never did. There were times when I swore we were dead, when storms would come up so fast and so fierce the lake would seem like it was boiling. And he'd get us out, alive, in that old boat. We should have died, by all right and truth. But we didn't. The lake made a promise never to harm any of our people.

Out there, promises mean something. They're absolute. Inviolable. Back in town, at work, in the subdivisions, on the concrete streets and in the metal buildings, they're ghosts. They mean nothing to most people because they don't really mean them when they give them. And they don't mean them because all they've ever known themselves are broken promises…mostly the ones they made to themselves. There are lots of folks in the world who build lots of things, but few people can build a boat. It's science, art, mysticism and surrealism all at once. It began for him out of necessity. He couldn't afford anything else. Not even a trailer. He built this boat light enough so that he could pick it up by himself and put it in the back of his pickup truck. It was years before he could afford a trailer to haul it around on. He cherished it and adored it, but it arose from beneath his hands out of necessity. Spartan practicality. He worked every day at the plant, dawn to dusk, worked evenings and weekends fixing boats for other people, making crafts, to afford the basic things in life for me and my mom. In his spare time—what little he had—he built that boat and took me to the lake.

Time passed, as time is apt to do, and I quit fishing for more than a decade. Other things, things I deemed more important—though they weren't—occupied my spare time. Most of my tackle rusted and deteriorated. Pursuing fast cars, girls and keeping up with the Joneses, I spent more than ten years never wetting a line or taking a bream to hand. Over that time, my best fishing pal moved away and was replaced by another, who moved away as well, and Dad retired.

I remember the day everything changed, everything came full circle. It was a golden dusk in late fall, before the grip of winter had come but the heat of summer had faded. I had gone over to my parents' house for something or another, and noticed Dad's car was absent, the boat shed was open and empty. Walking along the path to the bayou, through the natural arch between bright green junipers, browning cypress and evergreen oaks, I could see a silhouette in the last hours of the day blazing out in gossamer hues of reds and oranges. The sun conjured shimmering wraiths of bright white, unleashed silver magic, on the unmoving bayou surface. Glimmering light sketched the shape of that old bateau, tied off to a cypress beyond the edge of the bank; the old man, straw fishing hat, still-powerful shoulders and a handkerchief dangling from a back pocket; four fishing rods, thin black shadows, propped up on the gunwales, motionless. A halo of shipwrecked sunbeams fringed everything, but nothing moved. Not the boat, not the cypress needles, not even the old man, save for his head, which slowly panned from side to side, as he watched the dusk overtaking the day, a day spent as he wanted to spend it, in an old wooden boat on the water.

"Hi, pop," I said quietly, as if my voice would somehow shatter the vision, send it raining into pieces like a broken windowpane. The years I had not fished, and that he had spent fishing alone, accumulated in the tree limbs, scattered across the clouds and sank into the motionless water of the Teche.

The outline of the straw hat tilted, but he didn't look back, kept his gaze fixed on the rays fanning out from that brilliant eternal flame in the west. "Whatcha say, boy?" he answered kindly.

At the edge of the bayou at my feet, the water might just as well have been ice it was so still. "Caught anything?"

"A few cats and one little perch," he said. "Tide's not moving much."

"Slow day," I observed.

"Slow day," he agreed, but I knew, somehow, at some level I had until then forgotten, that though maybe the fishing was slow, a slow day was precisely what he wanted, what he watched fading across the horizon of cypress peaks down the bayou.

I sat on a stump and we didn't talk anymore, we just watched that slow day pass into night. Years and years of disconnection fell away like the leaves which autumn claims. I was aware that while the dusk was communal between us, the only thing separating us was my seat on dry land and his on the water. A chasm of years began to close along with that day. The edge of the sun dipped lower, finally vanished behind the tree line. Orange, pink and billowy white brush strokes swept across the sky; tiny specks which were distant birds climbed high winds on their flight south, and I remembered the wonder of a slow day on the water and never forgot again.

When traveling in a boat in unfamiliar waters, it is always wise to look behind. To see if the wake is muddy, if thunder squalls are sneaking up at unawares, if the path behind is firmly in mind so that the return to the beginning of all things will be charted.

I am haunted by waters, Norman Maclean ended that most-revered of memoirs in which water was integral to a life. Perhaps, when life has largely looped behind me and I look back again on the search for that eternal flame, these lakes and bayous and rivers will haunt me as well. But for now, on this day, on this watch, waters enchant me, bring me on journeys a thousand years past and, in their grace, bring me closer than I can ever be to my Creator.

This is how it appears to me looking aft. It is not so much a boat or a fishing story as it is autobiographical mutterings under my breath alongside a pond or on the bench seat of a bateau.

This is how it all happened. This is the view from amidships.

Circles

o o o o o o o o o o o o o o o o o o o o o o o o o o o o o o o o

What is life? It is the flash of a firefly in the night. It is the breath of a buffalo in the wintertime. It is the little shadow which runs across the grass and loses itself in the sunset.

—Crowfoot, Blackfoot warrior and orator

The Feather

Nestled into the crook of my arm and extending to my palm, the feather weighed a thousand pounds.

Our lives are the sum not only of all our ancestors but also all the memories, perceptions and images in the minds of the people who knew us. How we see ourselves is moot—it is the pallet on the canvas of the earth that defines who we are.

On the half-full slate of my memories, in colors growing dim but still alive, he kneels with arms outstretched, on the floor of the old house that he built. I stand on the sofa with toddler's feet made all the more uncertain by large, black-rimmed glasses that I had worn since I was two years old. There was no need for courage—I leap, physically and in faith. He catches me and we laugh, and the laughter is the stroke of the brush, swirling, laying down the colors of memory.

A thousand years later, the feather I cradled like an infant weighed upon me as if the earth were in my arms. For the first thirty years of my life, I denied my blood, ignored my heritage, much to my father's pain and sadness. Only in the last few years have I felt a stir of fires long gone cold, heard the whispers of my ancestors, and have taken some small interest in the other half of me that I hid for so long. So silently, I cursed the white part of me for its weakness, beseeching the Chitimacha part of me to lend its strength to carrying this totem that once sailed on the wing of an eagle across the heavens. From the moment it had been placed into my hands it was a Goliath, and I am no David.

The brush dabs oils and whisks them across the canvas—a Kay guitar, older than I, rests across his lap. Under his fingers, the dry wood and cold steel strings come alive. Fingers so large and scarred from decades of cutting marble, throwing bags of carbon black onto railroad trains and working wood, metal and stone, you'd never believe they could create beauty, but from those fingers magic flowed. The Kay resonated, and he sang, and his fingers were lightning, the chords born and gone so quickly they hardly existed at all.

Still the canvas fills, and he tells me about the old folks. Family, friends, secrets. People he knew and people he never met. The tales come from his own memories, and in his perceptions they are defined.

From his fingers, silver and turquoise turned from natural wonders to man-made art. From his tongue history and tall tales drifted to the ears of so many that went away from him changed.

With the eagle feather in my arms, the people come to be in their best suits and dresses, with solemn faces at first—they come to me and they always let slip a smile as they share with me the painting in their own minds. They tell me stories and I take them and put them into my own painting, adding them to my perceptions, but with every telling the feather grows larger and heavier until I fear I will shriek, scream from the burden.

Our family minister, our dear friend, tells his stories. The choir flanks him and he clutches the Holy Bible. He has lost a truest friend, but he raises again the laughter they shared so many times, and those gathered with us to say goodbye also laugh, wild silver magic which fans out in waves across the cold wooden pews.

Then the man I call my brother tells us how they were driving from one of the sacred places, how he tells my father that he has always known there was another world just on the edge of the one he sees, but when he looked, it evaded his eyes. He waits for the laughter, the ridicule, but the old man, grown frail and tired, says my brother is one of the Lost Ones. He knows this because he, too, was one of them once. They have been swept too far from the earth, out of the circle, but something in their souls longs for return.

My brother sings the old songs now, the old music and the old words. He burns sage and cedar, fans the smoke with an eagle feature, and I marvel at how easily he handles it. Why isn't his feather as heavy as mine? Behind him, our father rests. The medicine bag around his neck, the abalone bolo tie, pipe and feather in his hands are stark contrasts to the crisp blue suit and white shirt. My brother, cowboy boots and jeans, long black hair in braids and the words and music are a study in contradiction.

But as the aromas of the sage and the cedar drift across me, I understand. Our sleeping father with his blue suit and feather; our minister and nearly 30-year friend holding the Holy Bible; my brother with the words and music and cowboy boots and jeans, they part the fog and though they cannot lift it for me, I glimpse the path.

The feather in my hands is ethereal now, wispy, a cloud. It is so light, so unemcumbering I hardly know it is there. There are no windows, but I long to look out, to see if there is rain, for I sense the eventide I have long known was coming has finally arrived. And it was then that I know it was the Chitimacha part of me that buckled under the burden of that feather, and it was that blood coursing through my veins that cursed its weight. And I knew, at last, that it was the white part of me that lent strength to the load, and when the two became at last one, the toil was over.

Do we forgive our fathers in our age, or in theirs?[1] I have nothing to forgive. Nothing to regret. My father led me as he led my brother, pointing to the path but waiting at the foot. Under this new sun I walk the land of my family, and my ancestors reach up through the earth and with their fingertips touch the soles of my feet. They only whisper to me now, but I know that one day I will hear them clearly.

I believe the dead do sing, and our father sings now, as a child, at the feet of his ancestors, ancestors from North America and from Europe, and they celebrate the peace he has passed on to me.

My father gave me so much. More than I ever knew. He was always there to catch me when I leaped. Now I stand again on toddler's feet, unbalanced and uncertain, to leap into the rest of my life, but not without him. He is always with me, and one day, when the sun of this new day sets at last, I too shall be a babe at the feet of my ancestors, and we'll sing, he and I, forever.

Change is seldom easy. We are often so afraid we rebel against it, despite the promise that it may, in fact, be of benefit. We tend to cling to the status quo desperately, obsessively.

But sometimes, change is overwhelming, a locomotive, unstoppable. We think we are strong, but we are not. We are most often weak as old twine, brittle as window glass in old houses. Change overpowers us, sweeps us up and carries us away kicking and screaming.

---

1. A debt to Dick Lourie's poem "Forgiving Our Fathers" as interpreted in the Sherman Alexie and Chris Eyre film "Smoke Signals" is gratefully acknowledged.

Some twenty years ago, I sat cross-legged and uncomfortably under a sky with an impossible number of stars atop a desert mesa. Kachinas danced around me, and in days past, to witness this as an outsider would have meant certain death. It was only by the personal voucher of the people I was visiting that I was allowed into this circle, to see this thousands-year old event. There, as the Kachinas danced in masks terrifying and beautiful, I was painfully aware of the other spectators, the jet-black hair braided or free, the tawny skin, and the centuries of sorrow.

I could no more identify with these people than they could with me. I was not one of them. I was not even one of the like-hearted people. How could I? Sure, I grew up on a reservation, just like them. In that technicality, I was that invisible entity, the reservation Indian. But there were always two cars under the garage, new clothes for school, food on the table and a television in the den. Perhaps my father from the same recycled lumber as the house had built the garage, and the cars were at least a decade old, and perhaps the new clothes were not brand names or the food premium. There was only English in our words, bibles on the shelf and at the edge of it all, talk among the grownups of things I could not understand.

There were the occasional admonitions: *Be proud of your heritage.* That advice made me fall apart like ashes. Like ashes from the King Edward cigar hanging from his lips, sending out smoke signals from its burning tip. I had no idea what it meant. Mere words, as meaningless as an alien tongue. I grew up with the Superfriends and Scooby Doo, on Charlie Brown and John Wayne. What pivot, what crux or connection did I have with those words?

Older, later, my perception of the words grew distorted. Indians I saw were caricatures. Either dumb as a stump or radicals. Billy Jack. Tonto. *F Troop* and *Texas Across the River.* I wanted nothing to do with it. My blinders were permanent, an outgrowth of my confusion.

I look into the mirror and do not see the people I sat with while the Kachinas danced. This hair is too light, and in the summer sun it turns dirty blonde. This face is not angular enough, these eyes don't carry enough sadness. Who am I to equate myself with them? By what right? I have never been turned away from a barbershop, a grocery store, a church. I went shopping in town and got toys for Christmas. I have never known hunger, bigotry or neglect.

There is a photo somewhere, a newspaper clipping. I have not seen it in years, but I am sure it lurks, dusty and yellow, in a closet or drawer at my mother's house. I am reluctant to go find it, fearing that it will not be as I recall. Or perhaps I am afraid it will.

In the photo, I walk beside my dad and a host of other Indians. We are marching on the state capital in the early 1970s, perhaps as early as 1969, to demand rights, equality and justice for our people. In the photo, my dad, the chief, is in buckskin and a headdress, and I have my own tiny little fringed buckskins, big black horn-rimmed glasses and hair as blond as sunshine. Marching for Indian rights.

And yet, change overpowers us. Change is like a sniper in ambush. It comes unbidden and unwelcome, uninvited and unwanted.

I fear I can never sit with Hopi again. Not just my physical appearance sets me apart. I have not their experience or their spirits. Today, I look in the mirror. Everything has changed. What I thought I knew is now doubt. What I thought I believed is now myth. Who I thought I am is now a stranger.

Half of me is alive and well and living in the present. The other is sleeping and dreaming in the past, on the brink of wakefulness, at the precipice of nightmare. I would push it away if I could. Change is frightening, a black storm churning across the ocean toward a tiny sailboat. I do not want it. I am afraid of it.

A journey has begun. I do not know to what distant shores it will carry me. But I can think of nothing else to do but ride with the tide of change. Like the Phoenix, I fear I have become a child of fire.

How could I know that I was never turned away from barbershop or grocer or church because my parents protected me from them? How could I know that I never felt the heavy hand of oppression, because they knew where it lay in its den and guided me away from it? I have been oppressed, and never even knew it.

Turquoise and silver. Teeth and bones. Beads and feathers. Owls and death, east wind and life. Cedar and sage. Past and present. Panthers and wolves.

Day to day, as I make my way through a life turned someone else's, eyes fall upon the alligator tooth hanging from the silver chain around my neck, and I can see the blankness in those stares, the silent confusion, the centuries of preconception and forced forgetfulness. Some of their eyes I can read: *Who is this? Where is the person I knew? Why is he being so different? Why can't he just stay the person I've always known?* And I know then that I have been, until this day, the culmination of United States Indian policy—no longer extermination, but absorption. Absorbed culturally, spiritually, linguistically. Destruction by sponge. We never went away. We just hid in the shadows.

I sat with my brother in my mother's home. I told him the things I have written here, and more. He hit me so hard I felt I would collapse. Not physically, but spiritually. In his words was the hidden message he would not speak: *You have betrayed your people for your entire life. Now you have to make a choice.*

Dreams are doorways, and they open all around me. To step through them is a greater challenge than I have ever faced.

But what else can I do, when the voices of a thousand ancestors beg me to remember them? To speak aloud their names?

Aunt Mary's Wolf

We all have our ghosts. Not in the haunted sense, or even in the manner of intangible spirits of long dead persons, floating through the air. But in one way or another, we all have our ghosts. They are the ghosts of ancestors, of indiscretion, of regret and joy. Our ghosts are the spirits of who we are.

My people had a story about Aunt Mary's wolf. Aunt Mary died shortly before my grandmother arrived here in 1926. The elders told my grandmother that in the weeks before Aunt Mary died, family and friends began seeing a wolf. It would stroll through the reservation, across Aunt Clara's yard, then Bayou Teche, and vanish somewhere toward Grande Lake, the ancestral home and heart of the Chitimacha.

Aunt Mary was wolf clan, they said. The wolf was her guardian spirit. It was her ghost. Everybody on the reservation could see it, hear it howling. But nobody from outside could see it, though they could hear its cries.

The night Aunt Mary died, the elders said, the wolf didn't cross the lot. It went into the house and sat on Aunt Mary's deathbed. She put her hand on its head and they sat that way for a time. Then the wolf left, across the land to swim Bayou Teche, and then to Grande Lake, never to appear again. Nobody from off the reservation saw it, but they heard the howl when Aunt Mary died.

These are my ghosts. Can you see them? Across Lake Fausse Pointe, when we were teenagers, we saw lights. All of us saw them. Lights always in the same place, almost every time we camped there, lights dancing above the trees, sometimes in the trees, sometimes appearing to shine from the water. One night we dared shine a spotlight back at the apparitions. They promptly disappeared but within moments returned, halfway across the lake and moving toward us, fast. We made a hasty retreat, but as we did, we saw the lights were hovering just above the water, paused at the shore we had just fled.

What did we call that night? What answered the signal of that electric lamp, coming to shore as if it were dying of loneliness?

My father's people knew those lights. They knew of them long before Aunt Mary died, long before there was anybody who couldn't see her wolf. My grandmother wrote that a small group of Chitimacha was steaming clams on the shores of Grande Lake when a white deer appeared from the water. The Indians killed, cooked and ate it. Then, one by one, they arose, picked up their children and walked into the lake until they disappeared. It is said they all live in huts under the lake water. Sometimes, their spirits can be seen as dancing lights on the lake.

They also knew *Neka sama,* the "new devil" and feared it. It moved through the forest, making horrible noises as it went. It emerged from the fire to take children sometimes, so youngsters were never allowed to play close to the hearth.

Do you see my ghosts? My grandmother lived over seventy years of her life in the old house I live in now. How many friendships, marriages, even families endure that long? When the call came to me early that morning, when my dad's voice cracked and trembled over the telephone, "Old woman went home," beams in that house shifted just a fraction of an inch one way or the other; nails unseated themselves; flecks of paint lifted from walls and fell to the floor. That house had enveloped her for seven decades, had tucked her into bed at night, locked doors against intruders, shut windows against the cold. The house embraced her and told her goodbye at the same time. From that day forward, picture frames would never hang straight in that house again.

These are my ghosts. They don't wail or rattle cups. They don't knock on tabletops or steal trinkets. They exist only in names. When my father was a carpenter, he marked his tools with the letters NIX. He learned that trick from his father, who carried the same first name, Nicholas. It was easy and quick to take a file and cut the letters NIX into a wood handled hammer or handsaw, or any other tool. When he built anything, he put those letters on it. Nobody puts their names on anything anymore. It's a vanished tradition, just putting your name on something, to show your pride in your workmanship. Our descendants will have no ghosts, because we have no names.

As we rush through our lives, we are only vaguely aware of the empty space inside of us. The space where our ghosts belong. We try to fill that burning emptiness with material things, with money, sex, alcohol, drugs. We walk through our ghosts without seeing them, though sometimes their tears stick to our skin and we carry them for a little while with us, not knowing why we are suddenly so sad and so cold.

We are not isolated. We are not alone. No matter how we miss our fathers, mothers, grandparents, friends, our one true love. No mater what toil life throws, we are not alone. We carry our ghosts with us, if we would but try to see them. For better or for worse, we can see them if we try.

Perhaps one day I will lay my head to rest in that old house and a wolf, or a panther, will come to lead me home. Perhaps one night I'll start a fire on the stove, or open the front door on my way out, and *Neka sama* will be there, slavering jaws wide, to swallow me whole. Perhaps one day, dancing lights will swirl around my boat like sprites, and lead me to a lake from a thousand years past.

Can you see my ghosts? Or are my ghosts like Aunt Mary's wolf?

The Summer People

I was driving to Morgan City everyday, working at *The Daily Review*. During the summer, the heat was overwhelming. Sometimes, for a change of scenery and to escape the heat radiating from the four-lane highway, I would drive home to Charenton through the villages of Ricohoc, Verdunville and Centerville. One day, as I was passing just outside of Ricohoc, I noticed the old man.

He was sitting on the porch of a small house, comfortable on the bench seat from an old Chevy. He was African-American and wore glasses, his hair salted. As I passed, he lifted a wrinkled old arm in a friendly wave.

I was moving too fast and thinking too slow to return the wave in time for him to see it. I felt guilty, and I thought about turning around and passing again just to return the wave, but it was hot, my air-conditioner didn't work, so I kept going toward the comforts of a cool home waiting.

That summer, waves of heat would radiate from the concrete, squiggly layers of distortion which tricked the eye like in old movies where the oasis arises from the desert, but like the foot of the rainbow, it can never be reached. Lawns, once green and plush, withered and browned. The next morning, I purposely took the slower route to work again, and as my car approached, the old man lifted his arm to wave. I tooted the horn and waved back. The windows, I noticed, were open wide, doors ajar in hopes of a cool breeze, hopes I am sure were in vain.

There are people we don't notice. As we scurry to and fro in our cars very often we do not notice people. We don't see them because we are too busy rushing through our lives, or perhaps we develop a selective blindness. After I saw the old man, I started to think of him as one of "the summer people" from a story by Shirley Jackson.

If we would but look, we would see. Them. The summer people. Sitting on old brown rocking or straight-backed kitchen chairs, perhaps the bench seat from a long-since rusted away Chevrolet, under wooden porches. I began passing that way more often, never failing to wave, and never failing to receive a wave. I always told myself that next time I would stop and tell the old man hello, talk about how hot it was, ask if he ever did any fishing, and if I could muster the courage, ask if I could take his picture in black and white.

Daily I noticed small details: an old stovetop clothes iron on the windowsill, holding up the stick of wood that propped open the window. A few tattered clothes on a wire in the backyard—did he have a wife? I never saw anyone else, just him; sitting on his bench seat, arm out lifted. I could never quite tell if he was smiling as he waved, but I'm sure that he was. I noticed that the house was green, what paint remained, and one of the corner posts of the porch was askew, leaning precariously towards the highway.

I wondered what it was like to sit on that porch with him, to perhaps wave to a child, riding in the backseat of an air-conditioned car, who places a chocolate-smeared hand on the windshield to prop himself up and stare back through the windshield glass which separates two distinct, non-merging worlds.

One day, one very ordinary day, I was on my way to work and when I passed, I was already prepared to blow the horn and wave, but when the house rushed up at me from the distance, the porch was empty. My finger went limp on the horn button; my left arm paused and retreated in mid-wave. That afternoon, I passed back, hopeful, pleading even, but the porch was still empty.

Over the night, I wondered about the old man. Had he gone on a trip? Fallen ill? If so, did he have anyone that checked on him from time to time? I had a vision, terrifying not because of the fear of sickness but by its sheer loneliness, of him lying in that house, perhaps near death, with no one to call upon. I resolved that I would stop on my way to work.

The cosmos moves in ways that defy our comprehension. Sometimes, pieces of life's mechanism seem to snap into place, and often they form geometrics that we wish they had not. I arrived at the house and pulled over, just outside the driveway. The car seat was empty, the windows were shut and I could see shiny new nails binding them closed. Heavy board barred the front door. New weeds leaped skyward, the only living things flourishing in the heat.

I got out of the car and stood there for a while, just at the edge of the driveway. I knew he was gone. I didn't step foot into the yard, knowing somehow that I didn't have the right to approach in his death what I had never managed to find the time to do in his life. The house seemed so barren, so in despair and mourning, that I felt like an unwelcome intruder, and I shuffled back to the car and drove away.

I thought then that I would not drive that way anymore, that I didn't want to see that empty, forlorn porch, didn't want to witness what would happen to that house now. My windows were open to gather the rushing air, but the sky suddenly blackened, and rain, cold as the grave, suddenly ripped in sheets across the landscape like grim specters.

Photographs are magic. Mirrors, peepholes into the past. Photographs are, if you think about it, an instant of time captured into a static prison, held within to be relived when needed.

My grandmother left behind albums and albums of photos. Stacked, they would reach me to my waist. I keep them in a safe place and, now and then, take them out and leaf though the gummy, cellophane-wrapped pages as the instants, the encapsulated moments in time leap out to me from the near and distant past alike.

Grainy, grayscale vistas, these are time machines. The shutter snaps, and in one press of a button, an instant is frozen, a two-dimensional canvas of paper sealed with layers of emulsion. The Kodak Brownie or Polaroid Land aims, focuses and a millisecond becomes eternal. It is no wonder that some cultures suspected the camera could steal their spirits.

Among the many photos my grandmother left me, she scrawled notes on some in that earthy, perfunctory script of hers. Many are humorous, some are merely names, and many others are mysteriously unmarked.

There is one photo. It shows my house, my grandparents' house. There are windows in the top floor, dormers that are no longer there. Off to the left of the picture on a tiny three-by-three inch square of paper with wavy-sheared edges, I can see a trellis holding prolific muscadine grapes. My grandmother is at the forefront of the photograph. She looks to be perhaps twenty-two or so years old, a pretty girl I barely recognize but know instinctively that this is my kindly, gray-haired Ma Faye that I spent so many happy days with. She is teetering on one leg, as if she is about to fall, but the camera has frozen her in mid-flight. Off to the right, there is another woman I do not know, and she is holding her hand over her mouth to stifle a laugh at my grandmother's plight. A hand, not Ma Faye's, has penned in the framed margin of this photo, "What were you and Effie doing?"

I do not know who Effie is. Judging by the appearance of the house and my grandmother's youth, I estimate the photo was taken in the early 1930s. But the photo leaves me puzzled. Who was Effie? What caused my grandmother to teeter so on one leg? Who snapped the photo?

There is another. In it, I am about ten years old. It is Christmas. I am wearing a straw cowboy hat and drawing a toy six-shooter on my grandfather, whose back is turned to me. His lips are in mid-syllable, and he is unaware that he has suddenly become an outlaw who must be brought to justice by the good sheriff. My father is to the right, smiling, either in response to my grandfather's story or my draw of the gun.

This image I can add dimension to. I was there. I can, If I think hard enough, remember the sights and sounds and the smells, the laughter and tearing of bright-colored Christmas wrap, of that long ago day.

But I was not there when granny was teetering on one leg, about to fall, and Effie was laughing at her predicament. I sometimes wish I could grasp the corners of the frame to pull it open, raise it like a window, to reveal the panorama of that world from 1930-something in its entirety. If I could but poke my head through that tiny window into the past and look around, perhaps it would be like starting a recording, and the frozen events would unfold. Granny would fall down and giggle with Effie, or she'd just barely catch herself and still giggle with Effie, and maybe I could look behind me and see whose finger touched the button on the camera that saved that mysterious, wonderful moment for me to wonder about sixty years later. It would be hot, Louisiana summer, and the smell of honeysuckle, muscadine grapes and magnolia blossoms would be in the air.

"What were you and Effie doing?" someone wondered. There are other photos, of course. A picture of a big brown dog looking forlornly at the camera, and Ma Faye has written, "Waiting for her treat," but no more. What was this big brown dog's name? Did she pad quietly through the house at night while the people were sleeping, guarding them? Did she scamper after butterflies in the yard? Was she buried somewhere behind the house where I know many of the pets my grandparents owned were interred?

Some photos are fading. Their once crisp, toned details have blurred to shadow, ghostly faces stare out at me as they slip into darkness. Somehow, the eyes seem to persist the longest, the windows to the soul. The paper has turned acid and is burning away the portraits, the emulsion is tired and weary, and the photo is like a senile old man, losing its memory of that instant in time. One day, perhaps when I am old, I will open that album and only a blank sheet of paper will greet me, its story lost.

What were you and Effie doing? I doubt I shall ever know. But the photo, and those with it, are treasures. For the slight glimpses, the unanswered questions they pose, they are worth their weight in gold. I will never know what granny and Effie were doing, but as long as I have that photo, as long as it remembers that day filled with the giggles of two young girls six decades ago, and the scents and the summer heat, then for awhile at least a happy moment, the briefest instant in their lives, will survive.

My father's people used to be called "the Vanishing American." I don't think that's true anymore. The Vanishing American has completely vanished, and those who are full blood only appear as squiggly zones of distortion, like a highway in the distance under a hot sun.

The rest, like me, are like the wizard behind the curtain. We pull levers and buttons, but Toto always draws aside the curtain to reveal the part he wants to see, ignoring the rest.

Some people turn the things that make them feel guilty invisible, Ralph Ellison pointed out. We exist on the edge of chaos, in one of the thin places. It's fine to see us on television, selling trinkets, riding bareback with Kevin Costner. Or dressed in uniforms and business suits at casinos, dealing blackjack and driving courtesy buses. But the moment we appear in reality, unabridged, we turn invisible. We no longer conform, we are no longer comfortable. Eagle feathers and alligator teeth aren't funny, offensive or insulting, they simply do not exist.

I know this is true because for thirty years of my life I invoked the same invisibility on others. It is my other half's only true magic. But sometimes, it doesn't matter if you believe in something or not, if something believes in you.

Now, in a life turned somebody else's, I see eyes look through me, away from me, against me. I am slightly more tangible than my full-blood brothers and sisters because I have lived and existed in America for long enough that they can't make me invisible so easily. Like sipping from a bottle of poison every day, I have developed a tolerance, and I punch through their magic with the fist of familiarity. But I am no longer, I know, completely seen.

I tell my stories every day. But telling stories is sometimes painful. Day to day, I hear the unspoken, *Oh, no, not another Indian story,* and a part of me rages with hurricane-force winds, while another part withers and dies.

People liked me better, I think, when I was completely visible. I was easier to swallow when I only shared their conversations about computers, movies, books and cars. Turning invisible makes people nervous. I guess it's hard to talk to someone when you can't see him or her anymore.

It's amazing, really. I'm just as real and substantial as I was a year ago, and sometimes, I'm still that way, until I mention a Jim Northrup joke or a Sherman Alexie passage. Then I fade out, like Captain Kirk in the transporter beam, I get all fuzzy and insubstantial to my listener and they squint their eyes to see me. It's not their fault, of course. They are merely products of our culture. A culture of destruction by sponge.

But sometimes, when you overfill a sponge, some of it leaks back out. There are millions of us invisible. I don't know how many of us are completely visible like I used to be, or how many more are teetering on the edge of visibility like I am now. If I could find a doorway that would accept my key, the key of my grandfather's magic, I'd slip inside of it and visit people who could actually see me.

Sometimes, it doesn't matter if you believe in something or not, if something believes in *you.*

I wonder, though, if I would be more visible if no one I know today had known me before. If I am more visible in the morning before the alligator tooth on a silver chain or the string of turquoise encircles my neck.

A few weeks ago, I went to the cemetery to visit the graves of my family, seeking kinship. They told me many stories, those cold headstones. Stories of invisibility and mass; of cyclical time and bell-shaped curves; of science, doorways and ghosts.

I am a child of the storm—wind, rain and lightning. I'll keep telling my stories. Nothing, I think, can stop that. They come living, like blistering rain, like blue lightning from a thunderhead. Perhaps the rain will cause a tree of understanding to grow; perhaps the lightning will burn away a friend. But stories leap into my throat, claw their way past my teeth and all I have to do is open my mouth and they are there.

After all, when the workday is done, when the routines of the job are finished, when the people who know and don't know me are gone, I make my way home. To the house that an ancestor built, that my grandmother spent 70 years of her life in. There are stories in that house—in the cigarette burns on the kitchen floor, in the drops of blood on cypress joists from a misplaced hammer blow, in the whispers of windy drafts through loose-fitting windows. I gather them up and save them for ears that will hear, that want and need to hear.

Raintree

I awoke Sunday morning to the sound of thunder.

Raising my head just enough to look out the curtains, the drizzle outside was hardly enough to disturb me, but the thunder and occasional flash of lightning promised me that this was only the beginning.

I fell back to my pillow for a few moments, listening to the rumbling. When a drizzle becomes a rain, then a downpour, you can feel the air move from the space the water has taken as it falls. I got up, made coffee, then moved through the house, opening windows and doors, letting the displaced air rush inside. I turned on no lights, no television, no radio. The murmur of the rain on the roof went unchallenged.

On my way back to the living room, I glanced at the wall in the back room where I have a collection of photos. They are all black and white, grayscale moments gone by, and my attention was drawn to one.

While my grandmother was on this earth, she kept this photo safely guarded. It is a seemingly simple photo, well composed, obviously old: A canal, into which a massive cypress tree has fallen. Sometimes in the 1930s, a stranger drove up into the yard of this same old house.

"I think you should have this," he said, and presented my grandparents with the photo I would look at on a rainy Sunday morning 70 years later.

The man explained that he was a photographer, and he had taken this photo in 1927. He said he knew the Chitimacha recognized four trees which marked the boundaries of the nation. He said this tree had been the rain tree, for each of the four held certain properties. In time of drought, the Chitimacha would go to this tree, and in some manner invoke the power that moves through the world, touch a limb of it to the water, and rain would come. When the tree had fallen, the photographer somehow received word of it and went out to document its demise, the last of its kind.

He went on to say that when he developed the negative and printed the picture, his first view of it was with the long edge on horizontal. It immediately caught his attention that there were figures in the reflections of the tree in the water, which he showed my grandparents.

I looked at those figures that morning. The skeptical, logical mind of a 21st century man knows they are likely illusions, odd refraction of the light in the ripples of the canal waters. A lifetime of wrapping the comforting quilt of practicality around me dismisses this photo as fancy. But sometimes, in the quietest moments, a lifetime of conviction crumbles, the blinders fall away, and I can see spirits in the waves, joined hand in hand, dancing around the fallen tree. At times they are distant, doubtable. At others, they are undeniable.

"I think you should have this," he said, and he gave my grandparents a handful of sticks. He said he took them from the tree the day he made that photo. "One more thing. Something you have to know. It was drizzling when I took that photo. The tree had fallen sometime the day before. It kept on raining, for a long, long time. That was in 1927," he reminded them, and without another word, got into his car and left.

In 1927, south Louisiana experienced the worst flood in recorded history.

Thunder rumbles, a celestial chariot rolling through the clouds. I take the photo with me, along with a steaming cup of coffee, to my chair. I turn it sideways. I see spirits in the waves, clearly, at least three of them, hand in hand, dancing. Back in 1908, ethnologist John Swanton was told about the last tree. He was told that a steamboat tied off to it, and in so doing, broke a branch off which fell into the water, and it immediately began to rain.

Outside, the rain has become a drizzle again. There will be no flood, but the colors of the trees are saturated and given depth by the rain, and they seem more real than yesterday. I wonder if somewhere, at some forgotten spot along a bayou, there is enough power left in the dead wood out there to bring more rain. Sadly, I wonder if that spot has been washed away by the current, or is scarred by ATV tires, or plowed into rows.

And suddenly, without warning, I feel cheated. Robbed. Sometime long ago, someone decided that my generation should not know the melodies and words sung around that tree. The only power that moves through my life now is the electricity humming through wires in the house. The only power I know is in a seventy-year-old photograph, which sometimes I doubt.

I am angry, because someone decided I should not know how to dance.

Rain fell all day.

There's nothing better than driving for thinking, short of a boat. Sometimes, it's just not possible to set to the water, so when I need to sort through the puzzle pieces, I take to the road. With only the radio to keep me company, I let the voices drifting through the speakers guide my mood, my thoughts.

A season of change, of chaos and of many, many fears. Winter ended a chapter, spring opened another, and as I look back at the book of my life, realizing there are fewer pages ahead than behind, I wonder were the road will lead.

On the road, green highway signs rush toward me, seem to narrowly miss, then vanish behind, their destinations on the off-roads remaining undiscovered. Is it death that is bothering me? I wonder as the truck races north, no destination in mind, no idea when I would get there or when I might return, if ever. My piddling in the workshop has received unexpected praise from those who have seen it, and with it the remark, *Your dad would be so proud,* but also the puzzling question, *Why didn't you try this before?* The unvoiced question really is: *Why didn't you try this before he died?*

It is a question I ask myself often, and the only answer I can supply is that I was too stubborn. Like many offspring, I wanted only to find my own way, make my own mark. Yes, I think I actively denied anything that was his simply because it was his, not my own.

So you're trying to be Indian now? That is the other question. My answer is always the same: *No, I just stopped trying not to be.*

The road rushes on, and I follow. Hunger begins to gnaw at my stomach, like the questions chewing on my conscience, so I pull into a drive-thru and order a cheeseburger, fries and drink. The pretty cashier in an ill-fitting uniform smiles at me, but the smile is hollow, the same smile she has used for dozens of cars ahead of me and dozens more to follow. I try to smile back, but I see my face in the reflection of the glass, and I realize it is just as empty.

The cashier is floating. She stands on carpet, which rests on concrete. I sit in the truck, rolling on rubber tires, which ride on concrete. There are people who spend the majority of their lives on concrete, their feet never touching the land, and when they do, they only complain about the mud, or the dust on their smartly polished shoes, or ants. I know the prison. I lived there for a long, long time.

I got a shiny new stereo for Christmas when I was an adolescent. I don't know how many boats he had to repair or how much jewelry he had to make to pay for it, but I asked him for a few extra dollars for a small cabinet to put it in. "Why don't you make one? I have some good plywood I've been saving." I remember I thought this was ridiculous, going through all the trouble of making a stereo stand when they had them at the department store. He gave me the money, it was never about the money no matter how hard-earned, but the chance he offered me went untaken. The chance for freedom. To do something for myself without relying on someone else. To stop floating and touch the earth.

The food goes uneaten, my appetite gone. I point the truck to the road again and rush toward the clouds ahead. I search the folds and pillows of blackening tufts, looking for a thunderbird. There's freedom just down the road, I can sense it. I pass someone walking along the service road next to the highway, casually strolling, as if in no particular hurry, no place behind and none ahead, only the road and the storm brewing ahead. I imagine he might be Kartophilos, doomed to walk the earth until Judgment Day. Sometimes I feel like that. Only wandering, until I reach the storm.

I stop at a signal light where my road and another intersect. A crossroads. It was at a place very like this that Robert Johnson allegedly sold his soul. The decisions made here are watched closely by Ol' Scratch himself. The clouds have overtaken me, blackened the sky before, above and behind me. When the light changes, I turn for home. On the way, I pass the walker again, and I wonder if the road really does go both ways.

The storm and I race home. When I arrive, the house welcomes me with the cheery face made by its windows, door and gables. I open the workshop windows and doors, and the smell of the rain approaching is magic. Chance and Mocha come to the shop, nubby tails wagging, and I give them both an ear rub and a bacon treat.

In the fig tree, a mottled-brown bird shrieks the same two syllables over and over: *Kee-ree! Kee-ree!* I know the messenger, but I do not understand the message.

Freedom. Roads. The bird stops its lament, and silence pervades for a time, broken all at once by the first sheets of cool, fresh rain.

Dreams

Sometimes, when darkness falls and the wind sings swirling sonnets along the eaves, dancing with the gables and romancing the pillars, the house stirs.

As the mercury changes, the house moves, like an old man with creaking bones, and I listen to it find new comfort. Oak and cypress and pine slide against each other, grumbling, but at last it settles in to sleep, perchance to dream?

It does dream, sometimes. It dreams, as all living things must, to remain sane. It dreams of the things it has seen, the people it has known. It dreams of children, their uncertain footsteps padding along its wood floors, knees scraping on the planks when they fell. It dreams of those same children, old and fragile, tenderly searching their way through the darkness at night with failing vision. It dreams of the things it has seen. Window-glass eyes, shuttered brows looked out on picnics and muscadine vines growing on long trellises. It saw sunlit gardens brimming with tomatoes and beans and corn; on murder and innocent blood; on fevers and pneumonia; on bedroom doors taken down from its innards, set upon potato crates to hold the dead while candles burn tobacco and cedar; it gazed, across the canvas of its life, upon the circles of those whom it held within, roof firm against the rain, walls solid against the wind, doors locked against fear.

A house that was built of things living, by living things, occupied and loved by living people, must surely be alive, in its own way. The essence of life exists in the rafters and joists of its bones, in its flesh and muscle. So it is in everything where power moves.

Sometimes, in the spring, a tiny mottled-brown bird would perch in the fig tree in the back yard and shriek *Kee-ree! Kee-ree!* Over and over. When this old house was built, the old folks said that little bird was called *kich* and it would come and speak to our people, foretell rain, warn of enemies, sometimes even predict death.

But now there's nobody to understand *kich.* Nobody to make baskets. Nobody to cook woman's potatoes or split river cane. In the fitful slumber and dreams of the house, the bayou out back runs clear and full of fish. It remembers when the family would come from all over and they'd set up a dozen tables in the backyard and cook food and laugh and laugh and laugh. The women gathered to make baskets and speak words that weren't English, and the men whittled cypress into oars and paddles. Sometimes two or three families occupied its little rooms, but as the years passed, one by one they left and never returned. My grandmother lived 70 years of her life within its walls, and for 20 of those she was its sole occupant, perhaps for the first time since it was built. Now I am its only tenant, and it seems, at times, to dream of bygone days.

Sometimes it moves in its sleep, reacts to its dreams, and a door opens or a stair tread creaks. Its dreams expand from it like a wave far out at sea, growing, until they crash down on me and scatter me across the beach, and I am left to search the sand for the pieces of myself, never quite finding them all.

Sometimes, dreams are wiser than waking, Black Elk said.

In my dreams—our dreams—I see my grandmother sitting in its folds, making beadwork, weaving baskets, cooking sweet potato pie as only she could. I can see her stop, suddenly, her hands unmoving on the strands of river cane or wooden spoon at the stove, cocking her head, straining to hear.

Listen! Do you hear it? It's in the fig tree.

Perhaps she didn't understand the message, but she believed in it. Just as she believed in the life within that old house, so entwined and one with her own. Yes, a house can be alive, and it can die. But not so long as it is believed in. Not so long as it is loved.

When spring comes, and the fig tree sprouts buds which will grow into emerald leaves, I'll watch, and listen. I may not understand the message, either, but as long as someone is left to believe, the messenger will return. This spring, and the next, and the next, and each spring for as long as I am alive to listen for it. I know, in my soul of souls, that for the rest of my life, that old house will wrap its walls around me, cover me with its roof, and hold its doors firm against any fears. As long as someone is left to love it, life will persist within old rafters, joists and floorboards.

And so it is, in everything where power moves.

Chill air stung my skin as the boat made its way down a maze of winding bayous. There was little to see, really, and I found myself grateful that our guide knew his way for I would have been hopelessly lost within minutes of our departure from the landing.

We were on our way to see a piece of history. My history, and your history.

A local resident had told me about a place he knew of. By description, it was prehistoric. I contacted the Chitimacha Cultural Department, and after a little wrangling with schedules, the four of us went out in the boat, not knowing what to expect, not even sure it was a site that had already been documented.

It emerged from a bank of the bayou, a long finger of white clamshell. Much larger than I had thought it would be.

Clamshell crunched under the bow of the boat as aluminum touched the mound. We disboarded and already fragments of pottery strewn across the bank caught our attention. Most were plain, unadorned, indicating a recently recent timeframe. Later discoveries of shards pointed to a much older era.

We climbed the first, gentle slope of the mound and above, in places where the roots of trees and the burrowing of animals were more prominent, the significance of the site became clear.

At first it was a splinter here, a section there. But the more we looked, the more we found. Ancestors, human beings who once walked the earth and laughed under the cypress and slept under the same stars as you and I, their bones unearthed by the movement of nature. We had found a burial mound.

Of the four of us, two were Chitimacha, and we offered tobacco to each ancestor whose remains were exposed. We touched none, disturbed none, but the tobacco sprinkled freely, abundantly, until it was clear there would not be enough to honor them all.

Farther down the finger of the site, we climbed an incredibly high slope to the top of what must have been the pinnacle of the mound. There, in the center of the apex was a huge pit. Bottles were scattered about, garbage, signs of modern intrusion and an unspeakable, bitter truth.

Someone had been here before us. Someone who had excavated a large section of the mound in search of...what? There is no gold here. No jewels. No buried pirate treasure. What could they have hoped to find there on that isolated bank?

I don't know. But I know what they did find. Perhaps a few pottery shards for them to show to their friends and brag over the barbecue pit on Sunday afternoon while drinking more beer. Maybe to frame and hang on the wall of a living room next to the television set. But that's not all. I am sure they "found" the scant remains of human beings in that forlorn pit.

We surveyed the rest of the mound, and the euphoria of discovery and our plans to contact state archaeologists veiled the truer feelings inside me. When we finally left, hours later, I looked back at the old place, and it was in my mind's eye no longer a white ribbon of shell, but a long bone, unearthed and dishonored. Then the anger began to set in, and the anger was fanned by mourning into a tsunami of rage.

What, do you think, would anyone feel if they went to any cemetery around here and found a huge pit, the perimeter strewn with trash? How would they feel? Violated? Dishonored? Furious? They would curse the filthy grave robbers, vow that God would punish them for their sins against the dead, ban them to the deepest realms of hell.

Yet, if someone digs into the apex of a 1,500-year-old Chitimacha burial site, we don't consider it the same thing, somehow. Why is that? Because it's from the past, and the past is somehow not important? Because it is disconnected from us? Because we cannot make a personal connection in our minds and our hearts to the people buried there?

Or is it because, in some fashion or another, the bones pulled from the pit are still today not quite human? Not quite equal? Not, to be blunt, as good as the rest of us?

Am I only part human being, then? Is that part of me that finds its way back to the people who built and buried their dead in that mound not human and not worthy of the same respect, honor and dignity that my other ancestors buried in the church cemeteries are due?

Atop that mound, in the sight of our ancestors, the two of us who were Chitimacha were appalled and stricken. The two of us who were white were just as appalled and stricken at the indecency of what had been done.

This is why Native nations such as ourselves so jealously guard our cultural heritage. This is why any time something is discovered someone must be notified. This is why highways go out of the way to avoid a burial ground. Just think of the terms we use to describe them: Burial ground, not cemetery. Very cold, very sterile, a descriptive phrase with no emotion attached. Not quite human. Not quite as good as the rest of us.

There are wonderful people who, like our guide that day, wish to see such places protected and unviolated. Unraped. But there are far too many more who see our old place, our special, sacred places, as some amusement park for their enjoyment, something to be picked through for souvenirs and trinkets.

So I sit in the living room that night and I swallow down the rage like hot coal, feel it burning down my throat, where it lodges just next to my heart. I feel not quite human. Not quite as good as everybody else. Perhaps in a few centuries someone will find where my bones lay and poke through them in search of treasures or conversation pieces. Perhaps the silver Navajo ring on my skeletal finger will be that special prize they search for among the graves.

Or maybe somebody will poke through your bones, through your ancestors' or your children's bones.

The Chitimacha Nation jealously guards its heritage locations because of just what I'm describing. Looters, grave robbers and pot hunters. The shame of us has forced us into clandestine secrecy.

Hell walks the earth. And it carries a shovel.

Boundaries

It had been long—far too long—since I had been on the water. Thinking of people present and others sorely missed, I took my dad's boat out of storage, cleaned her up, took Mocha with me and we went to the lake.

Though undiscovered seas beckon, I'll always be a creature of the lake. As *Sheti imasha,* "people of the lake," my spirit courses with its currents, laps at the margins of its banks and lurks dark and still beneath its waves. There, I can forget the many boundaries that shackle me.

Sometimes I get rammed along the cattle shoot, propelled and pushed and elbowed into the singular facelessness of the crowd, and I forget where to find peace. Boundaries close in. It has been…what? A year? Yes, a year, I think, since I've been to the lake, and other than a November sailing trip, on the water at all.

Mocha didn't enjoy the boat ride much, but I was in sheer delight. The wind was up, and the lake was restless, choppy waves battering the bottom of the 40-year-old bateau that had found its way along this same channel so many, many times before I was born, and after. We came into the lake riding with the crests of the waves, moving over them and collapsing down, and the oak frames of the boat groaned but, true to the craftsmanship of the builder, never failed.

The dog wrapped herself around my feet throughout the trip, frightened but at once delighted. I pointed the bow toward Cotton Canal weaving between white fishing buoys, bobbing in the sway like storm-tossed castaways. Mocha whined at the constant battering. I felt sorry for her, so I turned around and headed back to the lake's threshold.

Now moving against the crests slamming into the bow, the boat trembled and shuddered, but remained fast. I idled out, giving the dog a brief respite from the overwhelming experience, and allowing myself a bit more time to savor it. Storm clouds menaced, but kept their peace, at least on that day.

The lake is a mirror of the souls of its people. It may display fitful frustration atop, but far within its deepest layers is an area which is devoid of oxygen, where no microscopic organisms can devour the things that rest in the darkness below. Like the souls of its people, like the locked rooms within, unchanged by the momentum of time, preserved by the merciless regret that chimes with things longed to be forgotten. Between the crests above and the unmoving, perpetual layer beneath lies the zone where they mingle, attempt to coalesce, but usually only create chaos.

Out of the lake, I throttle up to visit the more protected waters of Grand Avoille Cove. The propeller churns mud, but the calmer waters persuade Mocha to sit up and look around, nostrils flaring as she tries to sort through the varying, unfamiliar scents sweeping past her as the boat cuts through the afternoon air. In the rear of the cove, I idle down Sawmill Bayou, remembering: A goggle-eye caught here, a mess of chinquapin there, the choupique I hooked when I was six that scared the daylights out of me. There were no boundaries then, and the world was a great, wide openness to a young dreamer. At the mouth of the bayou, a thousand logs of timber lie sunken. I navigate around them, but the engine skeg bumps the outer reaches of one of the logs left there in the 1920s, when the lumber industry collapsed overnight. I ventured too close. I have been away too long, begun to forget the secrets lying here.

But then, not far into the canal, steel cable with blue barrels tied to them loom up; a rusty metal gate is padlocked closed with gallows' chains. Signs forbid entrance. I feel cheated. For eight millennia my grandfathers walked these banks, fished these streams, my grandmothers collected pond lilies and woman's potatoes and clams here. Now steel and barrels and red paint forbid me the ground where their footsteps displaced just a shred of their souls; lock me out of the waters where they lowered their cupped hands to drink, kneeling at the edge. Mocha whines, sensing my dismay, but I pat her neck gently and she sits down again, panting.

No matter. Such is but a symptom of the malady. The Reaper's toll for forgetfulness. When the spirit becomes property and free-flowing waters become possessions, I know my time has passed, just as surely as those who have come here before. Such is the legacy left to me.

So I steer the boat in a tight arc and idle away, careful now to veer farther out from the sunken timbers, careful to avoid the submerged pilings my dad warned me about all my life, and just before the propeller begins to churn up the mud again I throttle to full, and the boat lifts itself outward, upward, barely touching the water now, and I skim the surface of the cove in exit.

Out of the cove, I turn toward home, and the battering of the bow puts the dog back at my feet, but I push the boat, hard. She flies, then, just a little wooden bateau, a man, and a dog, wanderers all; but she flies, crashing from top of crest to top of crest, for the wind has risen again. I push her, hard, as if by sheer speed and mechanical horsepower I can break through boundaries seen and unseen, and she flies; my paddle is jarred from its niche along the gunwale, surprises Mocha as it tumbles and rattles along the floorboards; the anchor at the end of a line under the deck leaps out and rolls against the forward bench, but I throttle up just a little more, and the motor screams, throwing a long fantail to either side, and the boat's nose lowers just a tad more and the wind wails in my ears and I glance behind, leaving the cove and the lake a distant turmoil behind it, but the boundaries remain.

And then we are home, I am bringing the boat back onto the trailer, then I am bringing us back and Mocha is whining and yelping with joy over being out of the boat. Then we are home, and I put the boat back under the tarps and the dog in the back yard. The wanderers are held captive again by fence and plastic, and by life.

But then we are home, and I have only been gone for an hour or so, but I am exhausted. I lie down on the couch, and Patches nuzzles under my left arm. Then we are home, and I slip into its embrace as I always do, but the smell of the lake still is in my lungs, the wind is still in my hair, and the larger voices are still calling, though distant now, subdued, whispers. As I drift off to sleep, I promise myself that I shall not wait so long next time to go back.

I sleep, and dream of things far below, preserved, which no steel cable, iron fences or red paint can ever destroy. Dream of the things that I bump now and then when I start to forget about them, the gentle reminders they offer me. Some things refuse to be forgotten. Some things fight to live on, struggling against the boundaries of possession and disbelief, if only in memory.

Here at the Beginning of All Things

o o o o o o o o o o o o o o o o o o o o o o o o o o o o o o o o o

"A wee child toddling in a wonder world, I prefer to their dogma my excursions into the natural gardens where the voice of the Great Spirit is heard in the twittering of birds, the rippling of mighty waters, and the sweet breathing of flowers. If this is Paganism, then at present, at least, I am a Pagan."

—Zitkala-Sa

March

In March, I long for spring and obsess about my tackle.

I spend long nights, with cold permeating the 160-year-old house, tying perfection loops in the butts of leaders, treating lines, sorting flies by color, size or intention. The boxes in my tackle bag are organized, removed, shuffled, and returned in another configuration. Each rod is cleaned and shined to a spectacular luster, reels oiled and rod tubes dusted. Outside, cold rain crashes down in sheets.

Hidden inside my home, I long for *Cok'tangi* relentlessly. My feet have for too long ached on concrete, my eyes assailed by fluorescent lights endlessly. It's a need that few understand. When I talk to friends without water behind their eyes of my need to go fishing, they don't understand that it's not catching fish that I need, though that's part of it. It's the smell of Spanish moss and purple irises, the scent of alligator nests and egrets. It's the comforting feel of a wooden boat beneath me, drifting obediently along Sawmill Bayou, recalling its many secrets and its countless moments. I need lake water around me, surrounding me like a spiritual host. I need to hear *Neka sama* pounding and whistling in the distance of the cypress stands. Though I fear that ancestral spirit, hearing it each season affirms that it is still there, surviving against disbelief, extant against the notions that have abandoned those without water behind their eyes. Even in my imaginative mind's eye, I cannot conjure the magic of standing on river-smoothed rock, water rushing cold and clear past my knees, surrounded by fir and pines. But I can know that when I turn west into Grand Avoille Cove, there is a, when the water is low enough, the remains of a huge cypress barge along the southern shoreline. In the 1940s, my father took many of the beams that made up its bulk to add to the materials in constructing the home I grew up in.

I know that, as I idle along that ancient shoreline where the shell was removed and the dead disturbed, I'll come upon a small canal which runs shallow and winding into the swamp and the eventual cane fields beyond, though I have never been able to navigate it that far. I have never known its name, but it is Susan's Canal to me now, for my better half considers it her favorite locale on Grand Avoille Cove. I know that if I pass Susan's Canal and I must swing wide to avoid the broken cypress stump at the point, I will find three other small canals to the rear of the cove. Then I'll come to Sawmill Bayou, where a thousand logs of cypress and tupelo lay submerged, left there when the logging industry collapsed overnight. They hold bass and bream, the occasional carp as well. I am reminded that, beyond those ancient submerged timbers is the small canal on the north side of the cove where I heard *Neka sama* crashing and whistling the spring before.

I cannot imagine headwaters or pools in trout streams, but I can see Bayou Phillip, where dozens of small shell mounds still poke whitely out of the mud, forgotten home sites of Chitimacha centuries ago. I can follow the cut that leaves Grand Avoille a bit farther and end up in Lake Fausse Pointe, *Sheti*, or part of it before the levee dissected and dismembered it into northern and southern waters. I know that Cotton Canal is there, and Peach Coulee and Bayou Jean Lewis, where Martial Sorrell brought in munitions and arms to support the Confederacy. I know that finger of cypress trees is Cotton Point, and the one farther still is Eagle Point, and I know that there are sandbars and sunken logs to be avoided with great care.

The literature of home waters is a creel full of memories and moments.

It is a book I read of my own writing during winter. I fill my eyes with the memories of others, too, understanding their need of water if not the spirit of the waters they immerse within. I know the longing.

There is comfort in knowing that *Sheti* and *Cok'tangi* are there, waiting for me to return. In the spring and summer, when I drift on their faces and find myself in the company of bass fishermen from Morgan City or Lafayette, anglers from the city or out of state, I wonder if Grande Avoille Cove holds me closer, relishes our kinship. Like anyone who reveres home waters, I sometimes resent the intrusion of others on my sacred places, but I cannot deny them entrance. I am content that my feet, my spirit, at least, have been here for eight millennia. I am secure in the words my father told me: *That lake will never hurt a Chitimacha. That's its promise to us.*

But there are iron gates midway down Sawmill Bayou, and wooden signs protest that the shores of *Cok'tangi* are private, controlled by hunting clubs and "preserves." These same shores are littered with refuse and trash, and I wonder, what do they seek to preserve? No one can own free-flowing waters, but I don't challenge their dubious legal claims to my heritage. Treaties, it should be recalled, are seldom fair, but Indians usually honor them.

Everywhere I look along the cove and the lake, signs accost me. Signs forbidding, signs warning, signs threatening. In the fall, gunfire rips open the silences, hunters bagging ducks or deer. Sometimes I spy them, and they look back at me, resentful that I am present, fishing the waters beside their leases and preserves. If men could practice greed without legal limitations, there would be no venue of community beyond our front doors.

Signs challenge my claims to the Creator. Signs tell me I have no business here, no rights, no purpose. Fading and peeling paint offer phone numbers I can call and, for a monetary fee, join the ranks of those who have nailed the signs into cypress trees. My claims to *Cok'tangi* are meaningless because they are not notarized and stamped with a seal. If I want to know my Creator, the signs say in unwritten commandment, go to church. This is not a church. This is a preserve for shooting ducks and deer with shotguns and high-powered rifles.

For a fee, they'll give me the combination to the padlock locking the gate that blocks Sawmill Bayou. I do not bother to tell them that my fees have been paid in blood. Conquistadors paid my entry to Sawmill bayou with swords, French colonists guaranteed my access with gallows nooses. If I join one of the hunting clubs on Lake Fausse Pointe, I can go sit without being bothered on the shell mound of an old village, or spread tobacco over the graves of those who came before me, for a price. My price has been paid with the murder of infants.

But I don't challenge them. I guide the boat along those waters which legislation and court documents have not denied me. Government, of, by and for the people, by treaty. One day, I fear I'll arrive at Grand Avoille and find the whole cove has been barricaded by a fence with combination padlocks on gates, signs posted with phone numbers I can call to gain membership.

Perhaps that's what I loathe so much about winter. That in my absence, I have lost everything to the fence-makers and sign-posters.

But when winter gets intolerable like this, I spend a lot of time obsessing over my fishing tackle. It gets to me, after awhile. I can't stand the cabin fever any longer, the walls are closing in on me, and the bleary winter landscape outside gives me a headache. So I obsess over my fishing tackle, waiting for spring.

There's a certain list of things anglers usually do in winter to their fishing tackle, but I have taken it far beyond those seasonal maintenance tasks. I think I spend more time with my tackle during winter than I do all during the warm months.

I clean fly lines and treat them with line dressing; I oil reels and polish the graphite and bamboo rods to a blinding luster (you need sunglasses, polarized, to look at my fly rods in February); I scrub cork grips with warm water, a little soap and a mild dish pad. Then I go to put them in the rod racks. I like to put the two-piece rods in the back, because the rod tubes are taller, and the three-piece rods in the front, so it makes a neat kind of ascending formation in the rod racks. Then I try to organize them by weight, length, graphite or bamboo, favorites, brand, color, action, date of acquisition, number of fish caught, rainy days used, sunny days used, location (pond, lake or bay), mood, atmospheric conditions and karma.

Then it's time to organize my tackle bag. I have been searching for the perfect tackle bag for a year now, one to carry my fly gear. I have gone through three already, and none were satisfactory. They were usually too small, with too few pouches and dividers, too narrow, too wide, too tall or too short.

Well, I finally found the perfect fly fishing tackle bag: It's black leather, with many pouches and dividers, just the right size, and never mind that it has the label "SONY" on it. It's a tackle bag, and don't forget it, ya folla?

I love my new tackle bag, and I obsess over it at the coffee table. Inside are two divided sections in the main compartment. My two favorite reels and extra spools go to the left, my fly boxes to the right. Now, before the fly boxes go in there, they must be obsessed over in their own right. It would never do to have haphazard fly boxes. So of the three boxes in the center, they are organized by poppers, by color, by streamers, by subsurface, by terrestrials, by size and by Stonehenge auras.

On the front of the bag is a zippered compartment with little slots in it, like for holding camera lenses or filters, if this weren't a tackle bag, of course. I use these to hold various sizes of leaders, line dressing pads, bug spray and the like. Each side of the bag has another zippered compartment, one side holds a flask and the other is as yet awaiting fulfillment. Inside the lid, a perfect spot of netting with a zipper holds my pliers and other tools.

The final compartment, to the back of the bag, holds two small fly boxes full of streamers. These are subsurface flies made from interesting materials such as rabbit fur, dear hair, elk hair, tinsel, metal beads, dinner spoons, electrical tape, Christmas lights and Timex watch parts. Streamers are my favorite bass fishing flies, because Ol' Bigmouth loves them.

My tackle bag thus organized, I put it away, only to retrieve it a day or two later when it occurs to me that perhaps the two small boxes might fit better in the side pouch, and the pliers and tools might be more easily accessible in the front pouch, while the reels could go on the right of the center section, since I'm right handed, and the other boxes to the left. A few days later still, I decide I don't like this arrangement, and put it all back like it was.

I change all my fly lines once a year. This is not a time to be around me. No matter how hard I try, no matter the method, I cannot get fly line out of the package and onto a reel spool without creating a tangled mess. To further complicate things, fly line must be put on the reel in a certain order, a certain end of it to the reel, otherwise your line is backwards and won't cast. They put little stickers on the line reading "THIS END TO REEL" which invariably fall off before I open the box, so I have to guess which end to put on the reel first. Usually I guess wrong, and have to take if off and flip it around, resulting in another 100-foot mess.

Patches thinks changing fly line is an invitation to play in the tangled, green mess on the floor, but once the cussin' starts, she figures it's safer to go hide behind the washing machine.

Then I have to make loops in the ends (the *proper* ends) of the lines, so that I don't have to tie on leaders when I need to because my vision has gotten so horrid. When this is done, I must tie loops in the butts of all my leaders, and unrolling a leader out of the package is even *more* fun than unrolling fly line, because it's so thin and tightly-wound, resulting in more fitful conniptions. Still, a loop-to-loop connection is easier than tying a nail knot on the water in 15-mph wind, I can promise.

So on the less than frigid days, I dress up warmly and go to a pond to test my obsessive behavior results. I went not long ago with a little six-foot fly rod I had been dying to try out. A small rod for fishing in close quarters, like narrow canals or between cypress trees from the boat. As I was trying it out, a spin fisherman nearby came over and asked, "What do you catch with that thing?"

"Oh, I've caught everything from bass to catfish," I say, the little six-footer whipping line like a sorcerer's wand.

"Really?"

"Yup," I say, proudly. "There are many folks who fish redfish and speckled trout with a fly rod, too."

He looked at me, frowned, and said, "That's not true." And then walked off without another word.

I wanted to argue my case, but since I wasn't, in fact, catching a dadblamed thing at the time, it is rather hard to prove that you can, in fact, catch fish on a fly rod, even redfish and speckled trout. Instead, I resisted the urge to cast a No. 4 wooly bugger at his retreating head, and just kept thrashing the water angrily.

But when it's too cold to even go play in a pond, I sit home and obsess. I am determined to be ready when winter breaks and spring peeks around the corner. I want nothing left to chance, nothing unprepared. When spring comes, I am going to leap forward, armed to the teeth with organized, well-oiled, perfectly cleaned fishing tackle. With my luck, the first warm day, I'll throw my bags into the boat, take off for the lake, and only realize once I get there that I forgot to bring a rod.

I've made very few winter fishing trips in my lifetime, despite the fact that I live in the deep south. People in Maine and the like admire us, thinking we're like Florida residents who can fish year-around. But while we can, indeed, fish every month of the year, we seldom do.

It was only this winter that I braved the elements and went to a pond, surprised to find that fish do bite in the cold, though sparingly. I managed three or four small bass in air temperature of 45 degrees, which was pleasant enough if I dressed appropriately. Running an olive wooly bugger slow and deep was the only thing that resulted in a few catches on my six-foot five-weight whip. I was having trouble getting a good hookset with such slow action, and lost two of the fish right at the bank. The little bass in that pond always run straight at me when I hook up, forcing me to scramble to strip in line before they throw the hook. They know this, of course, that's why they do it.

The wooly bugger is the paradox of fly fishing. It is perhaps the most universal fly, appealing to all species from trout to panfish, largemouth to smallmouth. What, exactly, a fish thinks a wooly bugger is remains a mystery which has confounded anglers for generations. Some say a crawfish, others believe it looks like some pupae life stage.

Olive is my favorite color for a wooly bugger. I like them in about size six, unweighted for shallow water, weighted when the fish are hanging deep and still.

It is versatile and productive. After the wooly bugger must come the Clouser minnow. Also a multi-species target, Bob Clouser's little dumbbell-eyed creation is a sure thing on bass and, in the smaller sizes, panfish. Crappie love them, too.

Only a year into my return to fly fishing, in a locale where fly fishing is frowned upon or ridiculed, I am still learning all that I can via internet and print. It is a slow, laborious process. When my father and I fly fished—genuinely fly fished, not jigging with a fly rod—we had braided, plastic-coated line and automatic reels on Heddon fiberglass rods, with untapered mono leaders. Lately, reading all the Internet discussion boards mostly populated by northern fly anglers I have realized that I am, it has become painfully obvious, the epitome of the vulgar angler.

Though I raise my hackles when I am surrounded by Philistines on the pond who have no respect or dignity in their pursuits of noble fish, when I sit at home on cold winter nights and read the Internet bulletin boards, I realize I am not so lofty as I would like to believe.

I wear no waders, no fishing vest. Waders are useless to me here in the swamps of south Louisiana, for their use would result in little more than sinking three feet into mud, suctioned without escape until some bait casting angler comes along to rescue me. With my luck, my would-be savior would be a Philistine I chastised on a pond somewhere, and he remembers me. Instead of executing my rescue, he will pluck me in the head with Texas rigged worms.

Fishing vests have no use to me, since I use no waders. I keep a small tackle bag with me on the bank of the pond, or in the boat, and all my fly gear is in there. It is compact and light, and serves me well, even though it was designed and sold as a baitcasting tackle bag. I keep no flies on the band of my fedora, either. I paid $40 for that fedora, I ain't about to go sticking hooks in it. A $40 hat may not sound like much to the purists, but it's a good night at the waterin' hole to me.

I do not use float tubes on the ponds around here. Float tubes are little more than a billboard advertising a free meal for alligators. I do not use pontoon boats, either, because I am fearful a ten-foot gator might mistake it for another challenging his claim to the territory.

My waders are knee-high mud boots, known locally as "Cajun Nikes" and available at any department store, the black ones with red soles like commercial fishermen use. These are only necessary for trekking to the pond through a muddy sugar cane field, where sometimes I have to run quickly to avoid crop dusters.

My tackle is budget-conscious as well. Among my graphite and cane rods exists the essence of the price-saving angler. The most I have ever paid for a rod was $150, and that for a restored cane rod. My flies come from Wal-Mart or the Internet, because in south Louisiana there are few fly shops, and the nearest to me is New Orleans, more than two hours away. This little Indian off the Rez avoids New Orleans like small pox blankets.

I do not tie. What little time I am allowed to pursue my fishing I intend to use to fish. It is worth it to me to purchase flies and use my time for being on the water. I am too busy to tie. I am a newsman, I cover meetings three nights a week usually. Tying does not relax me, fishing relaxes me. No offense to tiers! But given a choice between tying flies and buying them, I'll chock up the dough. It's easier on my eyes.

Add to this long list of vulgarities the ultimate insult: All this is used to fly fish for bass and bream. I've never seen a trout in my life, and sometimes I doubt they truly exist, a sort of Shangri-La of fishing. The El Dorado of angling. The Brigadoon of...well, you get the idea. Trout, to a south Louisiana fisherman, are speckled and they do not live in streams.

When I fish out of a boat, it is a twelve-foot wooden bateau my father built two years before I was born. The sparkly bass boats pass me by without notice, their 150-horsepower engines screaming, their drivers' faces all intensity and concentration and determination to go to the lake and relax, and everyone else better get the hell out of the way. Many times have I been swamped by these boats that come up upon me in a tidal wave of wake, the fisherman throwing lures the size of toaster ovens, and screaming, *"Catching anything?"*

But it occurs to me that to the gentleman angler of the fabled North, I am as much a Philistine as the sparkly bass boat anglers I so demean in my own waters. Were I to join a Montana fly fisherman on the river, I would probably put my waders on backwards. I have only a vague idea of hook and leader sizes. I wouldn't know a #12 Coachman if I backcast one into my earlobe. When I buy flies, I look at them and say, "That looks about right." When I buy knotless leaders (necessary because of my fading eyesight) I have to use a conversion chart to figure out the "pounds test" at the tippet from all that 1x, 2x, 3x nonsense.

I am, after all, the kid who learned how to fly fish with a fiberglass Heddon and Martin automatic reel. I am quite proud of the progress I have made thus far. I now know that "action" in a rod is defined as "the amount of flippity-floppity movement in the tip when you shake it." I now understand the rod weight system, defined further as "a bass'll break that one" and "a bass won't break that one." And best of all, I now realize that a "fly box" is a tackle box with Styrofoam in it.

None of my crude ignorance detracts from my enjoyment of fly fishing, of course. I have a little class. I have never put live bait on the end of a fly leader. Okay, there was that one time the bull bream were chomping down on caterpillars falling from a maple tree...but there are no witnesses so I cannot be convicted in any court in the land.

Around my part of south Louisiana, I often run into anglers who claim to fly fish. I nearly invariably learn that their idea of fly fishing is using a fly rod with a leader of long mono, a bobber, and a hook with a shiner impaled on it to jig for sac-au-lait (that's "crappie" for the bluebloods). When I do encounter the rare fisherman who uses a fly rod like I do, it is like meeting a long lost friend.

I have never owned, cast or laid eyes on a Hardy or Winston product. I suspect they are as mythical as rainbow trout. I did see an Orvis combo at a shooter's store in Lafayette once, as part of a going out of business sale. I watch the fly fishing shows on television, further lowering me into the bowels of vulgarity.

All of which leaves me in a predicament. While I am probably the Philistine of the fabled North, I am the blueblood snob of the deep South, considered aloof and downright foolish. I am told I cannot catch bream or bass on a fly rod. I am told that I would catch a lot more with conventional tackle. I am told that there are probably laws in this state against fly fishing.

But I plod on anyway, because like the simpleton I am, I enjoy my fly fishing more than any other type of angling I have ever done. Just last December, as I was casting at bass in a shallow pond, another vehicle pulled up on the road nearby. The driver got out and opened the trunk, pulled out a seven-foot heavy action bass rod with a Zebco 202 on it, loaded with what looked to be thirty-pound line, and a white five-gallon bucket. Gleefully he marched over to the pond, sat his bucket down on the ground bottom up, parked his behind on it, and proceeded to throw a two-ounce spinner bait with three blades at the water.

"I sure would like to try that one day," he yelled over at me. I didn't hear the very last few words, because at that exact moment his spinner bait hit the water and the splash was deafening.

"It's a lot of fun," I said, without much enthusiasm.

"Looks like it!" he said. Just retrieving his lure, the heavy action rod was bent over. "You using shiners or worms?"

I turned around and went home to sulk. A vulgar angler in a land of Philistines, I am doomed to the obscurity of eccentricity forever.

It makes winter a bit more bearable to have a sense of humor about it, I guess. As long as I don't go stark raving mad, laughing gleefully while casting at the television set while *In Search of Fly Water* is playing. Then they'll come lock me up in a padded room, and the spring fishing will be shot.

A lifelong fan of fishing shows on television, particularly Bill Dance, I felt like a true vulgar angler when watching them after I returned to fly fishing. Then I learned that there were fly fishing shows and eagerly tuned them in on weekend mornings.

It didn't take me long to realize I was outgunned and outclassed. In an entire season of watching fly fishing shows on television, I never saw a largemouth or a bluegill one single time. I never saw a lake, even. All I saw were trout, salmon, bonefish in streams, rivers and somewhere south of Florida. I saw Alaskan fishing, Bahaman fishing, New Zealand fishing. I saw Karen Graham hook into a gigantic Chinook, I think it was, and though Karen looked positively nymph-like fighting the fish in to her guide's outstretched net, the entire episode left me decidedly nonplused.

To fly fish in warm water, I still turn to Bill Dance and the Lindners. What a bass or a bluegill responds to in spin tackle can be converted to fly tackle, with the possible exception of plastic worms. I know people have made streamer versions of plastic worms, but I haven't had any luck with them. I get no help on warm water fishing from *Trout Unlimited Television* or *Flyfishing the World.* Locations with largemouth bass, apparently, are not part of the world as fly fishing television show producers know it. This mediocre geographical vision keeps me going back to Bill and Hank Parker.

But I learn enough on the 'Net or from the tube to keep me going. In winter, when February restricts me from the water, I drink my morning coffee and watch the television fishing shows, of either variety. I read the bulletin boards, happy in the knowledge that in a month, two at most, I'll be fishing merrily while the bluebloods are still digging out from the snow.

For now, though, it's February and I window shop online, because there are no fly shops in Philistine. Cabelas and the like are my best friends. Were I fly fishing before the Internet revolution, I probably would have given up by now, because the local sporting goods store does not stock fly rods. In fact, not even the local Wal-Mart carries those pre-packaged, cellophane-wrapped $19.95 fly fishing combos by Shakespeare or Daiwa. Sage rods? Forget it. The fly fishing section at my local Wal-Mart, much as it pains me to shop there, is one vertical row of poppers, a combo box of black ants, gnats and wooly buggers, and, if I'm lucky, a few fly lines, always weight-forward floating eights. There are usually knotless leaders, though, thank goodness, and in the fall when these go to the clearance rack I stock up for the next season. Reels? Ha. Not even a Martin automatic in sight. Not even a plastic Daiwa. I can go to the sporting goods store in Lafayette and pick up a decent reel, but they don't sell any rods and have about the same as Wal-Mart in flies and lines. What's the sense in selling decent reels but no rods? It is because, they tell me at the counter, nobody fly fishes down here. They only keep it in stock for the tourists.

Thus February is shopless, save for the broadband wonderland at my fingertips. All my rods were purchased online, either through a retailer or Ebay. Long live Ebay. All but two of my bamboo rods came from Ebay, bless their money-grubbing little souls. I would be lost without Ebay and Cabelas. I cannot, as the bulletin boards all advise, cast a rod before I purchase it. I must take my chances, and so far, have not returned one due to dissatisfaction of any kind. I do my research first. My rods are decidedly moderately priced, a step above inexpensive. The graphites range from $89 to $150. The canes no more than $150, all refurbished production rods except one nine-foot Granger Victory which came to me as a special gift from a friend. I paid $75 for a refurb Horrocks-Ibbotson single-tip eight-and-a-half footer which casts like a dream. Oh, when I strike it rich, I'll get an A.J. Thramer or a Harry Boyd, to be certain, maybe a couple of them, but for now, Ebay rules.

Existing as a fly fisherman in a land dominated by spinning and casting rods is far worse than simply being a fisherman. Harry Middleton, through Albert's words, lamented the tragedy of being an angler and the outcast it makes one. But fishing with a fly rod in south Louisiana, while not unheard of, is rare enough to be considered odd.

When a spin fisherman tells about his weekend expeditions, and the boatload of crappie or bull bream, the eight-pound bass from a farm pond, people listen with rapt attention, their hands twitching as they work the handle of a reel unconsciously. They can feel the pull of a big bass on 20-lb. line to which a spinnerbait has been tied. Their eyes dart up and back down in a graceful arch, following the bend of the rod with envy.

But mention that same bass was caught on a fly rod and you are viewed with suspicion if not out right disbelief. *Everybody* knows fly rods are fragile things that only eight-inch trout can be caught on. A bass will break a fly rod with a shrug. Now, ultralight spinning tackle, that's a whole different story, of course. That takes the skill and finesse of the angler to succeed in landing a lunker. No such talent will suffice with a fly rod. It just isn't possible.

I almost gave up my bragging rights after several of these blank stares. After a great weekend catch, over lunch with co-workers, the disbelief became palatable, and sourly so. When I turned to cane rods, it was like the gates of politeness were slammed shut with a loud clang. A fly rod of modern graphite technological wonder might land a small, skinny bass if you get lucky. But bamboo? Not in a million years.

Sometimes I long for locales where appearing at the edge of water with a fly rod is as commonplace as seeing the paperboy pass. The condescending smirks get tiresome. The only salvation is to catch many fish right in front of the smirking eyes. This is not always possible, of course. If I get too proud and mighty about it, I usually catch nothing while my detractors are tearing them up with buzzbaits. "Try that with a fly rod!" they yell with glee.

There are moments, though. Casting a No. 6 Clouser to the brush pile and tenderly walking it over sticks, twigs and limbs, with that marvelous magic that Clousers abound, and snatching out a nice bass in places even a plastic worm couldn't reach. Oh, not that there aren't hang-ups. But when such a small trifle miracle does happen, it is extraordinarily satisfying. Too bad there's never anyone else around to see it.

My girlfriend has decided she would like to take up fly fishing in the spring, should it ever really get here. I am eager but reluctant to teach her. Of course, the idea of having a fly fishing girlfriend really appeals to me. She's my best fishing pal in general, but if she used a fly rod, I'd have to adore her even more. Still, I am afraid that the bad habits I have picked up in casting, having no true instruction, will be transferred to her, and I am reluctant to do that because I know how much they frustrate me. But worst of all, I am not at all pleased about indoctrinating her into a life of disdain, putting a fly rod into her hand and making her an outcast and a reprobate like me. She has been my only saving grace thus far. I might be a fly fisherman, people think, but at least my girl keeps me somewhat grounded in reality.

People believe in my neurosis because it isn't enough that I practice fly fishing in a land of Philistines, but because I have the gall to write about it in the local newspaper. Rather than secluding myself like some sort of miscreant, the angling version of a sexual offender, to conduct my sordid affairs out of sight of decent folks, I not only carry out my vile crimes in public, but write about them in my twice-weekly column on occasion. There are two kinds of people who dislike these topics: Those who despise fishing in general, and those who despise fly fishing particularly.

"Enough about fishing!" the first group says. "I want to read about your pets, or your house."

"No more fly fishing!" the second group will cry foul. "I want to read about Rapala minnows and Jitterbugs and quarter-ounce spinner baits with willow leaf blades!"

But I do so anyway, pounding out a column now and then about fishing largemouth in small ponds with four-weight rods, leaving half my audience entirely confused and the other half disgusted. In February, these words tend to rear their despicable heads more often, showing their toothy, gnarled faces from beneath the brim of a beaten fedora dropped too many times into a pond. When the cabin fever gets too intense, the only thing better than watching fishing shows on television is writing about fishing. My readers never understand that it keeps me sane. Oh, some do, I guess. Some even realize that if there's any small appeal to my writing at all, it's that it comes from the heart, and whatever's in my heart at the time is what I feel like writing about right then and there.

When I first became interested in bamboo rods, a good friend of mine, whose family owns a sporting goods store, gleefully told me about how they had thrown away dozens, maybe hundreds, of bamboo rods. They were stacked, he said, like kindling in the store. In corners, on shelves, in the rafters of the roof. But when fiberglass rods hit the scene, cheap and tough as nails, customers started buying them by the bushels. Room for these technological, fish-busting breakthroughs had to be made. So the old bamboo rods were thrown into the trash bin. South Bends, Heddons, Montagues, probably a few Grangers and Leonards, too. It is, at least, good to know that those fiberglass rods would one day suffer the same fate to graphite, a poetic if not quite satisfying justice.

The same fate often befell automatic reels. I miss automatic reels. I cut my teeth on them, but some sort of snobbery exists regarding them, to which I have fallen prey. I haven't touched an automatic reel since a young teenager, but I miss the wonderful whizzing sound of their spools spinning line back onto itself when I touched the trigger. When I hook into a good fish that runs straight at me, while I'm trying to get him on the reel fruitlessly, I really miss automatic reels. Other than their weight, I see no good reason to not use them, but I don't. I am in enough hot water as a fly fisherman already.

When I buy a new rod, or a nice large-arbor reel, I show them to my friends, who "Oooh" and "Ahhhh" over them, but I know that they are only being polite. They have absolutely no idea what it is they are looking at other than a "fishing pole" with rare exceptions. I have a close friend who is a fellow wood worker, and he greatly appreciates bamboo rods because of their craftsmanship. I have another friend who is as devout a fisherman as me, and he appreciates fly rods because of their finesse and delicacy though he doesn't fish with one. But none are really cognizant of the satisfaction of owning a new fly rod that casts well despite my amateur efforts and will bring in bluegill and the occasional lunker bass. I spent an hour explaining, or attempting to explain, to one friend why a fly reel does not have a 3:1 retrieve. I don't think he ever completely got it.

There are clubs in Louisiana for fly fisherman, but all save one are too far for me to make weeknight meetings with my schedule as a journalist. The closer one, unfortunately, meets on the same night monthly which I have a government meeting on my beat. I can't attend, so I can't rub shoulders with people who understand my misery, who hide in closets to line their rods or bravely announce their sins to all who will listen. I created a web site for Louisiana fly fishing once, desperate to fellowship with the rest of the congregation, but it was not very successful. There is one such site on the Internet that has made it pretty well, but it still feels like some site of ill-repute which parents block out of their Internet browsers so that their kids can't find out what goes on inside.

With all this oppressive bigotry, I have to wonder sometimes why I subject myself to such misery. Of course, the romantic reasons are that fly fishing is so much more pleasing, elegant and satisfying, but I know that's a bunch of baloney. That I am a sadist at heart can be the only explanation. I have always attached myself to the disreputable, evidenced by my dislike of commercial beers in favor of microbreweries, complete disinterest in football or any other sport, preference for wooden boats, and neurotic pets. Fly fishing is merely an extension of this condition. I can self-flagellate myself victoriously and catch a few bass in the process, a talent that has escaped even the greatest of history's so-called martyrs.

My father taught me how to fly fish at a young age, unaware of the outcast life he would doom me to. We fished fly rods as they should be fished, at least down south. Most use them as jigging poles for bream or crappie. We actually fished with backing, line and leader, even if said leader was only a six-foot length of eight-pound mono. I am sure that if he knew the prejudice I would encounter later in life due to my instruction in fly fishing he would not have refrained. It was something I had to know, akin to the fact that I am Indian, Cajun, short, bespectacled and tend to fight my weight constantly. Fly fishing was just another obstacle I would have to overcome in life.

If the bluebloods could see the bass my father landed on that whippy, willow-o-the-wisp fiberglass fly rod! Fish destined to become legends. Fish that live on in my memory, though they were caught thirty years ago, seen through bulging, wide eyes of a child. Each is imprinted in my recollections, the mighty splash of them fighting the pull of that rod in the old man's hand, his joyous expression as he concentrated like a man intent on raising demons. I cannot recall what kind of bicycle I had, or what color it was, or the swing set they tell me was in the back yard, but I remember every bass taken on a fly rod on Grande Avoille Cove. Were I to visit a therapist, and be asked about my childhood as the old cliché demands, I would speak only of largemouth bass, bull bream and fiberglass fly rods.

We fished spin tackle, too. Most of the time, in fact. I think the fly rods were brought out when it was time for a little magic in our lives. I think the fly rods were truly magic wands. We used them, the old man and his boy, when we needed to spit in the face of conformity. To say that we may be Indians off the reservation, husband of and son of a Cajun wife and mother in a time before Justin Wilson popularized the culture, but we excel at what we are. We may be vagabonds, miscreants and rascals, but we damn sure catch fish.

As a grown man, I watch the clock and as soon as it releases me from the office, rush home, grab rod and bag, and head for the water. During 2003, I fished every single day the weather allowed, without exception. I nearly changed my voting registration to a pond where the bluegills are feisty and the bass moreso. My girlfriend is remarkably tolerant and actually encouraging of my obsession and no man could ask for more in a woman. On weekends, we were nearly always in the boat, coming home without a nibble at times, having succeeded greatly at others. We would fish past sparkly bass boats which cost more than my house, and cast the same bemused, demeaning looks right back at their occupants. We are not so lofty as to disparage anglers merely for their equipment. But a condescending smirk is best answered in return.

So in March, I swing to and fro from melancholy to giddiness with the nearness of spring. A fearless warrior who stands just a few inches too short among his peers, I race forward nonetheless each spring and challenge their grins with the whip of the wand.

The second week of March brought daily rains. I sit in the old house, one hundred and sixty years of relations surrounding me, and stare out at an already brown landscape deepened to saturation. Cold rain, showering in spasms, drizzling in doldrums, relaxing and building up to pour again, keep me inside. Surrounded by the warmth of cypress in the old house, I watch March pass without fanfare.

There are only two places in the world I feel at home: Here, in this old house built by Chief Alexander Darden in about 1840, and *Cok'tangi.* No matter where I am in the world, I always feel them. I have not traveled extensively or far. Once to Arizona, once to North Carolina, a handful of trips to Texas and Oklahoma.

At any give point, I could slowly turn and scan the horizon, and knew when I was facing home and Grande Avoille Cove. A glance at a map confirmed it: They are like beacons, both, sirens guiding me back to sacred fires and native waters.

Harry Middleton talked about peeling back the layers of time in a stream, revealing its essence below. It doesn't take cold running water to do that, though. When I cast my line into Lake Fausse Pointe, where my people lived for eight thousand years, it vanishes some few inches below the surface, the obscuring perspective of the water making it seemed to dart off at an odd angle from the intersection of the water's margin. As if reality has somehow been twisted, all folded up and compounded. I imagine I am connecting a bridge with something through the line, and the point where it seems to bend at a sharp, unnatural angle is the boundary between this world and the one gone by. I cannot see all my relations dead before I was born, and I can no longer see my father sitting in his wooden bateau casting yellow poppers. Just as I cannot see beyond that unnatural angle in the line, where it fades into murky oblivion. There is the transition point, the gate. When I cast my line into those waters, I am touching the past, both hidden from easy view.

I have cast into the Pearl River near New Orleans, and into the Gulf of Mexico. I have let my line sink into farm ponds. There is a shadowy reflection of home waters there. But when I cast into Lake Fausse Point or the greater system of lakes that once were before the levee, I am reaching as much into those green-black, impenetrable waters for fish as I am for visions. Somewhere, down there where the line has shot off at an impossible juncture, where it fades away from sight, it is surely touching last year, last decade, a century ago, a thousand years passed. I listen and feel for the millennia gone by like a kid with an old crystal radio, searching for invisible radio signals in the air.

It's odd that I only really think of these things in winter, staring at the cold rain from behind windowpanes that are now so old and brittle they crack with the changing temperatures and must be replaced. The windowpanes have ripples in them horizontally, decades of settling. If that old house would stand long enough, and I would live until then, they would eventually settle into puddles of glass. They say that in some of the oldest cathedrals of Europe, the glass must be flipped now and then to keep it from settling, because glass is not really solid. It is a very viscous liquid. When I have the panes replaced, they are crystal clear and dead flat. I cannot see the world outside in March as well through their clarity. The distortion of old window panes reveals more. Things on the peripheral can never been seen dead-on. They must be viewed askance. Seeing winter is best through old window glass.

It is comforting to be surrounded by water when it rains. Though I may fuss about having to go out in it, particularly when it is so cold, having so much water near is relaxing and soothing. Outside the window, Bayou Teche is frantic with falling rain, its surface blistering and pocked with drops from the deluge. It runs muddy and dark, rising slowly to meet spring in greeting.

So I warm myself with strong, thick Cajun coffee, keep my feet socked against the chill of the hardwood floors. Since January 31, I have fished twice, after a yearlong excess of fishing each day, even under lightning storms. Lightning I can brave, cold I cannot. I hope to one-day catch a rainbow trout, but it will surely be in July during a warm spell. For now, though, I am at least content to be indoors, looking out at cold rain, and knowing spring is near. Were the sun shining brightly but the mercury down low, the misery would be unbearable. At least when it's raining *and* cold, I know there is no chance of slipping to the pond and must come to grips with that fact.

On Becoming a Reprobate

It's true that I have wasted a perfectly good life. Lots of people do it besides Dave Ames. I have seen them, or at least, heard about them. Some people waste a perfectly good life to drugs, alcohol, gambling, womanizing, manizing or obsession with Alec Baldwin.

Years ago. I was quite a decent fellow. I was respectable though no blueblood; I was relatively well-dressed and drove a bright red Mustang with a fast engine. I could talk about politics, entertainment, science, religion and even good cigars. In those days, I was pleasant company and smiled a lot, was known for my keen wit and good sense of humor, though I was not above the occasional tasteful but off-color joke now and then.

I was Mr. Responsibility. I took great pride in my work, whether in radio or newspaper. I was a great proponent of professionalism, journalistic ethics and Freedom of the Press. I was climbing the ladder of success.

But then I caught a fish again.

Now I unashamedly rip off ideas from other writers, such as this one. But when someone points out something which rings true, and I see so much of that truth in my own eyes when I look in the mirror, I figure I have already sunk to the lowest depths of despair anyway, so a little plagiarism can't make things any worse.

Sure, I was having a great time, advancing my career and position in the community. But then, after something like a decade, though it may be shorter or longer, I don't really remember anymore, I caught a fish again. At that point exactly, my life turned to decadence, futility and complete failure.

Nothing else really matters. The bright red Mustang is gone, replaced by a pickup truck for carrying my tackle and towing the boat. I can sit and smile politely when talking about decent, polite things, but my conversation efforts usually fail quickly. I can get into about four exchanges with someone about the next election, the war in Iraq or Michael Jackson before the conversation digresses into:

"Which one of the presidential candidates is a fisherman?"

"Do they have bass in the Euphrates river?

"Is there a fishing pond in Neverland?"

I used to be sensitive about my scarce remaining hair. I struggled in keeping it neat, and I didn't wear hats, believing that hats promote baldness, a condition with which I am becoming acquainted quickly. I hated to be seen with messed-up hair. I was the same about my clothes. I had to have khaki slacks neatly pressed and spotless, my shirts immaculate.

But then I caught a fish again after a decade, more or less. Now I leave the pond and go to a city council meeting or a date with my girl to the casino with my hair matted into a crater-like shape from my fedora. I wear jeans which are hopelessly crumpled below the knees and slightly wet from wearing mud boots and wading a bit too deep, and shirts with cockleburs stuck to the back like a porcupine, as well as numerous fuzzy dimples from errant hooks getting caught in them and ripped out with a pair of pliers. People often comment, "Does something smell fishy to you?" These are usually not political observations.

And do I care? Not one bit. I tell myself all such concerns are meaningless. Do the fish care how I dress or what my hairdo looks like? Of course not. Why should I care what "people" think? I happily neglect all reason and obligation, merrily prance to the next fishing hole like a madcap sorcerer, long-brimmed hat shading my face, fly rod waving in the air like a wizard's staff, tackle bag flopping at my side like a satchel full of medicinal concoctions and voodoo charms.

It's but one symptom of a good life going down the toilet for the pursuit of fish. The aforementioned lady friend has stated that it's probably a good thing that I don't have an addiction to more serious improprieties. Wasting my life to fishing is not, at least, immoral, illegal or unconstitutional. Unsociable, yes, perhaps downright ornery, but not imprisonable offenses, save perhaps institutions for the fishingly insane.

I have learned to be jealous and possessive. Time was when I kept an open-door policy at home, even passed out my keys to a few close friends. I would share anything, good scotch, cigars, books, music, theatrical tickets, with good friends. Now I violently guard my best fishing spots with a determination similar to a badger guarding her nest of offspring. When someone I've known and trusted and been through life, death and other pitfalls with asks me, "Where'd you go fishing today?" I either launch into a fit of indignant rage and kick them out of the house or become moodily silent until they get the message of having worn out their welcome.

On the contrary, if someone tells me they have a good fishing spot, I pester them ceaselessly until they finally break down in exhausted tears and give me the longitude and latitude of the fishing hole in question, along with their own GPS unit to find it. Free from me at last with this divulgence, they pack up their families and move to Katmandu.

I practice diversion tactics. I regularly fish very well-seen, public spots which I know don't even hold minnows, just so everyone can see me on a certain date and time, then write a column about the monster bass I catch out of these places at said date and time. Confusion to the enemy, you see. When I am fishing one of my true honey holes, I park the truck eight miles away and, if I hear another vehicle approaching, immediately fall down and lay flat on the ground until it passes, even if I have a fish on the line. If I'm in the boat, I hide behind trees and fish through the branches, an exceedingly difficult task with a fly rod.

Fishing has turned me into a No. 1 First Class Grade A USDA-Inspected Reprobate, a hermit and a paranoid conspiracy theorist. I am convinced that anyone who is friendly with me is trying to steal my fly rods or find out where the big bass are. I am sure, in my dementia, that if someone offers some small act of kindness, they are only wondering what color Clouser minnows work best in April north of the levee in the basin on overcast days.

There are fears involved in all this. That one day I'll be homeless, having neglected paying the bills and have been evicted from home and sanctuary, to live in cardboard boxes behind the nearest tackle store, scrounging through the garbage bin not for food but discarded fishing flies, piecing together broken rods with duct tape.

I am, even at this early stage, becoming much like Elias Wonder, the crazy old Sioux mentioned here last week. Harry Middleton describes one of Elias' many encounters with lightning, having been struck dozens of times in his life.

Beware. My company may one-day be as dangerous to your health as Elias Wonder's. I'd hate for anybody else to get hurt due to my newfound status as a fishing reprobate.

Harry's Bright Country

Of all the outdoors writers I have read, Harry Middleton touches me most.

I enjoy outdoors writing, particularly about fishing, of course, and fly fishing most of all. But Harry Middleton struck a chord deep in my soul which resonated with truth. I think of the truth of Harry Middleton much in February.

I've passed a few of his books on to others who I thought would enjoy them, and mostly, they didn't, to my initial astonishment. Over time, I began to understand why.

Middleton is tragic and saturated with despair. Collectively, his books are unit volumes of an autobiography memorializing the deaths of those he loved, his own battles with chronic depression, the pitfalls of his life and the one thing that kept him sane, kept him hopeful and alive: Fishing and cold mountains waters.

In this regard, Middleton strikes me as more honest than any other writer I have known.

They are not fly fishing books. They are memoirs of a life made bearable by fly fishing, and even the fishing was only an extension of the being where the fish exist. His was a life of toils, and the purest joy he ever knew was on the water. Growing up with Albert, Emerson and Elias Wonder was the happiest time of his life. Few such times would follow. In "The Bright Country" he draws a double-edged and striking blade of metaphor: The bright country is both the mountain waters he returns to when he can, and the clearing of his mind after his psychiatrist finally finds the right medication to subdue his depression. The bright country, to Harry, is living a life without despair, at least for a little while.

It is impossible to miss the love with which he describes the characters that move in and out of his words and his life, like flotsam passing boulders on the river. Harry speaks of all of them with affection and childish wonder. Like any person struggling with something like chronic depression, Harry reached out to people nearly as much as he did to trout from the opposite end of that little Winston rod. He is a man I would very much like to have known and fished with.

It is a further tragedy that Harry died an untimely death, before his books were well-known, and the heartache of his demise is intensified knowing he was working on a garbage truck night shift to feed his family. It has been speculated that Middleton died thinking his life's work of writing had gone largely unnoticed.

I don't think so. I think Middleton wrote more for himself than for the public. Certainly, there is the desire of any person who writes to be read, to be accepted and appreciated. But Middleton's chronicles of his life were more of a purging, a thrashing battle with his own demons, than any intention of authoring an outdoors bestseller. In his writing, he probably found solace second only to those magical waters of Starlight Creek. I know how that feels.

And that's why I like Middleton more than any other writer: He is as human as the rest of us, perhaps moreso in his very misery. We've all had moments of despair, and if Harry's life was mostly defined by it, then the joy he found in his fishing must have been tenfold any you and I have ever found. To all things there is a balance. The Creator of all things does not take away without giving in return. He gave Harry Middleton a bright country in the darkness. And without the darkness, without Harry's words to us in exploration of it, the bright country would seem far less magical.

I don't think Harry died unhappy. I would like to believe he left this world with a loving family and a creel full of bittersweet but cherished memories. Harry Middleton doesn't strike me as the kind of man who would cease struggling, riding the back of a garbage truck, doing what he had to do to provide for his family, perhaps battling with his depression and other demons again. He had survived too much already to be beaten down by that. From the moment he saw his childhood friend blown to bits by a grenade, the spiraling descent of Harry Middleton was his gauntlet in life. I think he braved it and conquered it. Despair didn't bring Harry Middleton to his grave, a failing heart did. Perhaps his heart had suffered more than its share, but Harry beat the despair. That's heroism.

Yes, I think Harry was, in his thoughts, fishing with Albert and Emerson and Elias Wonder. I think that if someone saw him pass by the night of his death, clutching the back of that garbage truck, and looked into his eyes, they would have seen the bright country unfolding there, mountains lifting up like sudden creation, streams and rivers cutting across them, blind trout rising to the fly, bagpipes crooning in the distance, and a fake parrot shouting "Ollie Ollie Oxen Free!"

I think, or at least will choose to believe, that when his heart succumbed, Harry was in his mind writing their stories, his story, and he existed in that very fine and private sanctuary, the bright country of words and cold mountain waters behind his eyes.

Fishing Fancies

Worst of winter, and a young man's thoughts invariably turn to but one thing. The exuberance of youth rears up, eager, ready to shed the coats and gloves and fleece, anxious for and demanding spring. The house has closed in for too long, grown smaller with each passing winter month.

Now, since I don't have any young men available to me to write this, you'll have to settle for a rapidly approaching middle-aged man's thoughts. It's not the age, as Indiana Jones pointed out, it's the mileage.

That one thing, of course, is fishing.

Okay, maybe not just fishing. Some young men think of hunting, too. I'm not a hunter, haven't been since I got my first BB gun, when I promptly went off into the back yard and killed a cardinal. Yes, shame of it all, a cardinal. I was only about ten, I guess. Dad just looked at me with this sad, disappointed expression and said nothing. He was no longer a hunter, had not been for decades. It was, I realize now, a lesson he knew I had to learn. I felt so horrible I never shot another thing. After that, my shooting was limited to cans and paper bulls eye targets.

You may wonder what the difference is between shooting a cardinal and catching a fish. All I can say is there *is* a difference. I don't know what, but there is. Anyway, when temperatures get warmer, my thoughts prematurely turn to fishing. I understand that daytime temps in the high 60s or low 70s is what they call "Indian summer." I don't quite know why they call it that. Since it isn't really summer at all, just a deceptively alluring spell of warm weather until the next frigid blast, are they implying that Indians are deceptive? I think "Indian summer" is an ethnic slur, that's what I think. On the other hand, I've known a few deceptive Indians in my time, so there you go.

With thoughts of fishing in my head these days, my television often turns to that most dreaded, most reviled of television programming, that which sends wives and girlfriends into fits of depression or rage like no other, except perhaps the Super Bowl, and that is the fishing shows. In my younger days all we really had to watch was Jerry McGinnis and Bill Dance. They are the grandpappys of fishing show hosts. With their wonderful southern drawls and expert advice, they created the whole genre, much to the chagrin of many a wife or girlfriend who secretly dreamed of having him assassinated. Bill Dance could catch fish in a pothole on the street, and show you just the right technique.

Today, with so many sporting channels on cable, there are tons of fishing shows. Sometimes, in winter, I sit in my recliner, fishing pole in hand, and cast lures at the television screen. No, not really. But I do start cleaning and oiling my gear, changing line, sharpening hooks and organizing my tackle box.

Organizing a tackle box is an exercise in futility unlike any other known to man. It has been said that organizing a tackle box is what drove many a good man to madness. When guys fish together, they are always looking at each other's tackle boxes. They rarely comment on it, such as, "Man, that's a really well-organized tackle box," or anything like that, because to do so would be gauche. But there is a certain amount of envy to seeing someone else with a very organized tackle box. Doing so is something like wrestling three dozen scorpions in a coffee can. I don't care how hard you try, how careful you are, you *will* get a hook in your finger when organizing a tackle box. There are also the various mysterious things one finds. Certain types of plastic or rubber on some spinner baits, over time, turn to this taffy-like googe which, when you pick up the bait from the box, stretches into infinity. No matter what you try on it, the remaining googe is stuck to the tray forever. Many fisherman buy new tackle boxes just because their old ones have gotten so full of taffy-like googe all their baits stick to the trays and they can't fish with anything but bread crumbs.

But the well-ordered tackle box is googe-free, and is categorized: Topwater bass baits on the first tray; sinking on the next; bream or crappie baits (I don't mean baits that are junk, I mean *sac-au-lait* baits) on the next, and so forth. I often wonder why, in the south, Cajuns call that certain species of fish *"sac-au-lait"* or "sack of milk" when, up north, they call them "crappie." There's a certain disparity of imagery there that nauseates the mind.

In my tackle box, I have a large assortment of flies. Some of them are permanently stuck when they landed on the taffy-like googe thinking it was a Now Or Later candy, but most are for fishing with. My dad and I used to fly fish for bream and sometimes bass. I still have his old fly rod and the one he bought me when I was a kid. Dad could tear up a nest of bream or a big bass with a fly rod. I was not quite so good. In fact, when I got my own boat and my best friend and I would go fishing I tried fly-fishing. Once. After that, he refused to get into the boat with me unless I left the fly rod home. I don't know what he was so concerned about. He made it back with both ears the first time.

Fly-fishing brings up images of guys in waders wearing strange vests and floppy fishing hats full of flies standing in a fast-moving river casting for trout. The interesting thing is that these guys wear those hats forever, because all those little hooks have caught their scalps and they can't take the hat off anymore without surgery. It's not very common to see anyone fly fishing in south Louisiana, in fact, I've never actually *seen* anyone do so but me and Dad, though now and then someone *tells* me they do so. But there is certain elegance, a certain artistry, to fly fishing that fascinates me. Heck, just keeping from hooking yourself in the seat of the pants on your back swing is a science all its own.

Fishing requires courtesy, too. Dad taught me that very well. I remember when I was very young, we were fishing out on the lake, and some character in a huge fiberglass bass boat with a 150 horsepower engine passed by. Seeing us there, I'm sure he thought, "Old grit with his boy, little homemade wooden boat, ancient outboard engine, this guy knows this lake and knows where the fish are," so he zoomed in about fifty yards ahead of us. He dropped a trolling motor that was bigger than our outboard into the water with a huge splash, operating it with a foot pedal, and threw a bass bait out big as my shoe. Dad calmly put up his tackle, started the engine and brought us to another spot far away.

Ten minutes later, here comes Mr. Professional Angler, and he pulls in ahead of us again. "Put on your life jacket," Dad said, and started the engine.

We took off straight across the lake, right at an area where Dad had warned me a million times there was a huge sand bar. The little bateau breezed right over it, but the bass boat which was now pursuing us blazed behind and suddenly stopped on a dime, firmly stuck in the sand. Dad circled back around, gave a friendly wave to the fussing and cussing Mr. Professional Angler, and we went back to undisturbed fishing.

Fishermen, you see, can be quite ruthless, too. There's more spiritual powers in the world than we are aware of, and they usually go unnoticed until they come up and slap us upside the head in retribution for some indiscretion or another.

In this particular case, I think I'm paying a penance for heresy against the spirituality of fishing.

It started in my neck, a kind of dull ache. Now, having been told repeatedly throughout my life that I have a "stiff neck" I paid little attention to it. But the ache slowly spread into my arms, down my torso and finally culminated in my toes. Not satisfied, it proceeded north until even my scalp was permeated by a low frequency, throbbing ache.

There were no other flu-like symptoms associated, other than some slight congestion. Therefore, I suspect I was being made to suffer retribution for sins committed earlier in the weekend.

Saturday morning, I was up before sunrise, cleaning and oiling my fishing rods and reels, and organizing my tackle box. I had organized my tackle box a week before, but decided it could use a bit more. Now, nobody wants a Martha Stewart-organized tackle box, though fishermen often get tips as to where the best fishing spots are, what time, and if they're biting, so I guess that could be considered insider trading.

After that, I spent about four hours riding around in the truck looking at the water in different places, gauging its quality, temperature and likelihood of producing fish. Every boat landing I went to was chock full of fishermen's vehicles and boat trailers. The thought of fishing during a convention has never appealed to me. I don't like fishing in a crowd. I don't like seeing another fisherman across the lake from me. It disturbs my spiritual experience, so to speak. Also, I don't know my way around the basin like I should, having almost exclusively fished south of the levee my whole life.

But here's where the penance thing comes in. When I was about fourteen years old dad gave me my first boat. It was a twelve-foot bateau my grandfather had built, powered by a 7½-horsepower Wizard outboard which was so old the compression was fading, so it might have been about a five-hoss. The fuel tank was built in, wrapped around the flywheel, and I had to carry a gas can in the boat because it took two fills to get to Lake Fausse Pointe, another to run about finding good fishing spots, and two more to get back. The throttle was a lever which slid across the face of the motor, and there was only one gear: Go. You could go forward by pointing the motor forward, but to go backwards you had to spin it completely around.

When a teen, my best friend and I were coming back from the lake, a trip which took well over an hour, and only takes me about 10 minutes from my house today. We came out from under the old bridge across the canal that runs from the Charenton floodgates to Bayou Teche, right into the path of the most enormous barge I'd ever seen in my life. It looked like a giant, rusty wall pushing through the water, straight at us.

Now, we were probably fifty or sixty yards away, but knowing that my little Wizard hadn't enough gumption to escape should we get caught in the huge broil of water the barge was pushing, my friend turned to me and screamed, "Beach it!"

"Aye-aye, captain!" I shouted back, forgetting that I was in fact the captain here. I aimed the bow at the bank and putt-putted as quickly as one can putt-putt into it until the boat was firmly grounded.

A big tug pulls water away from the shore when it passes. Well, the spot we grounded at was soon high and dry, and we watched the big barge and tug pass in terror. The captain of the tug looked down at us from his pilothouse with a decidedly amazed look of, "Well, I'm glad I won't be picking them out of the props," and we waved timidly. He waved back but we all looked pretty stunned.

Not long after that, I saved up enough money for half of a more modern outboard. I say half, because Dad paid the other half. It was a Mercury 9.8 horsepower, so I was now 4.8 horses ahead. The trip to the lake was cut to about thirty-five minutes, and we could do it on a three-gallon tank of gas, there and back with room to spare. Within a year, the electronic ignition went out, and I had about $50, so Dad paid the balance, which I think was $150. A few months after that, the carb needed rebuilding, and I was broke, so Dad paid that, too. His frustrated comment at that point was, "Dang, boy, I could keep you in New Orleans call girls cheaper than I can outboard motors!"

The point to all this is that when I was a young man, I was quite willing to face long tedious trips to the lake with an outboard of unpredictable reliability, collisions with enormous barges, and my father's wrath to keep fishing. Nowadays, I clean my rods and reels, organize my tackle box in a way that would make Lynette Jennings proud, but I spend the day riding around in the truck looking for good, safe and unpopulated fishing water. So I went home and brooded, my shiny clean rods and reels and immaculately organized tackle box sitting in the corner looking dejected.

That's why I think I came down with this mysterious illness. By the middle of the night Sunday, I was aching from head to toe. My fingernails hurt. My ponytail hurt. I have never ached so much. My head felt like an enormous barge was running through it, sucking all the water off the bank, and my stomach felt like a mud flat. I went home from work each afternoon and laid on the sofa, groaning miserably, drifting in an out of sleep after taking a handful of Tylenol, dreaming of fishing trips from days gone by.

Lying there on the couch in one of my more lucid moments, I spied my fishing gear in the corner. I thought, "You know, if I just picked up one of those rods, stuck a piece of Kraft cheese on it and went to the bayou, threw it in, I'd probably appease the gods of fishing penance and get to feeling better." Instead, I took more Tylenol and went back to sleep, dreaming of angry goggle-eye biting my toes like piranha.

I have heard that many old-timers refuse to introduce young people to fishing because they fear they will burn in fire and brimstone for eternity as punishment for corrupting a young person's life. Perhaps there's some truth in that. Despite those feel-good, warm and fuzzy ads they used to run in magazines about "Bring A Kid Fishing" and "Get Kids Hooked On Fishing Not On Drugs" it may actually be a mark of doom to do so.

Now it's Wednesday morning, and I'm starting to feel a bit better, though only a bit. I think that, with the weatherman forecasting cold and rain, the penance may be over. There's no sense in forcing one to pay penance when it's too cold and rainy to go fish anyway. However, that leads me to the inevitable conclusion that come the first warm, dry spell, I will be obliged to fish without hesitation. I'll probably get hopelessly lost somewhere in the Atchafalaya basin, running around in my boat until I run out of gas, waiting to be rescued by some fisherman who will laugh his head off at me.

Last weekend, it got cold. And it didn't even get close to what they predicted. "They" being the meteorologists on television and the 'Net. They are called "meteorologists" because the phrase "fortune teller" was already in use by women with foot-long gold earrings, heads wrapped in four yards of pink fabric, and patchwork dresses. Meteorology, in my book, is like divining or palm reading. Actually, I think I believe in divining and palm reading a little more.

But it was still mind-numbing, teeth-shattering cold, in my book. And pal, when it gets cold enough to shatter teeth, that's cold.

I have a friend in Nova Scotia who insists on sending me pictures of fun in the snow over there, where they get excited when it gets up to minus 8 degrees. Kids on sleighs, iced-in boats (my friend is a naval architect) and the like. Every time I see one I just get colder.

Since I was keeping two sick kids over the weekend, I was pretty much housebound. Not that I would have ventured outdoors anyway unless absolutely necessary. It was absolutely necessary at bedtime Friday and Saturday and in the morning when I woke up, to go turn off the water all the way at the road and back on again in the morning. I don't take any chances anymore in this old house. But my driveway is about 300 feet long, and trudging up there in the biting, bitter wind to close or open the shutoff valve makes me feel like I'd died and gone to Nova Scotia. That would be my penance for a rotten life, I imagine. Eternity in Nova Scotia with no socks.

Sitting around Sunday, when the temperature actually almost nudged 60 degrees, a friend and me were discussing things we could do that afternoon. Suggestions from my friend included going to eat out somewhere, or other activities that involved leaving the house.

"You mean out *there*?" I asked, pointing to the barren tundra outside the windows.

"Well, yes, you have to go *out* to eat *out*."

"Like, *out* the front door?"

"Right. That's the definition of *out*."

"*Brrrrrrrrrrrrrrrrrrrrrrr!*" I said.

I hate winter.

I did have to go out and check on Mocha and the puppies, which was bad enough. Also, I noticed that Patches' favorite spot in the house this weekend was up at the top of the stairs. I went up there at one point and realized why. All the heat my heater is generating into the living room goes up the stairs. This really ticked me off at first, wasting all that heat on the stairs, and realizing that the dadgum cat is smarter than I am. Then I decided to make the best of it and sat down on the top stair to rub Patches behind the ear for about three hours. If I could have gotten comfortable, I would have brought up my portable television, or the sofa to take a nap.

Now we're getting upper 60s and maybe 70 or so during the days this week. That's the screwiest thing I ever heard of. Who thinks up the weather around here, anyway? It's a wonder we don't all go batty with this kind of weather. You don't know how to dress one day to the next, so you have to check the Weather Channel in the morning, and invariably, have to sit through 14 commercials and the forecasts for Toledo, Moscow, New Jersey and Istanbul before they get around to telling you what you really want to know, which is the expected high temperature or low temperature for your region. Of course, all you get here is the forecast for New Iberia, twenty miles away and slightly more north, which I guess the Weather Channel figures is close enough. I don't think it's close enough. In fact, I think I will demand they install a weather monitoring station in my front yard, so I can be dadgum sure what the prediction is when I walk out the front door. If I have to sit through slick advertising for devices that fold your shirts, cleaners made with orange that are guaranteed to take off any greasy mess, as well as the Formica on your kitchen counter, and the weather forecast for Beijing, by thunder I deserve my own weather station in the front yard.

Counting the days down to spring, that's what I'm doing. It's difficult, since nobody is ever very sure when spring will come, of course. The "first day of spring" you see on calendars and that they announce in the news is hogwash. Groundhog's Day is hogwash, too. Spring comes whenever the heck it feels like it, and winter leaves whenever it gets good and ready to. Neither give much of a hoot about groundhogs or calendars. Groundhogs sometimes come out of their holes and immediately freeze to death, but you never see that on the evening news.

My friend in Nova Scotia reminds me that our Cajun ancestors came from around those parts. I told him that, seeing the pictures he's been sending me of winter around there, I know why the heck they left. I suggested he should have left with them. I also wish our Cajun ancestors had settled in the Florida Keys. Not only would the weather be warmer, but we'd get all that tourism, too. Not to mention, Cuban cigars.

But I am grateful that it has not been so cold as to burst pipes. There's few things more unpleasant than fixing burst pipes in 30 degree weather, under the house, on the cold ground, with a dog licking you in the face. I did not, of course, insulate this summer as I promised I would last spring. And the spring before that. And the spring before that...c'mon, there was a boat to be built!

Which is, by the way, sitting under the garage looking abandoned. I keep promising it, "This spring. We'll be back in the water this spring," but I don't think it believes me.

Somehow, I don't think I believe myself.

Amidships, March

March flies through, riding the winds of seasons, the changing of the face of the world yet again.

The last week of the month, and temperatures are pleasant, though rain threatens vaguely. There are green sprouts on the fig tree in the front yard, but of course, fig trees are notoriously misleading regarding the arrival of spring. I watch the pecan trees, much more wary and timid about setting forth tender new growth.

In March, I watch the season unfold through the brittle window glass eyes of the house, grown distorted with horizontal lines in the panes. The grass in the yard is mostly brown and growing slowly, though patches of clover sprout like green mounds of spring here and there. In a few weeks, white flowers will turn the clover into pincushion-like celebrations of the nearness of winter's demise.

As I sit and watch March gather choirs to sing of spring, I look through those rippling window panes and marvel that I am seeing the same bayou bank I explored and grew to love as a boy. A man's life, measured from birth to where he now stands amidships, has been written on these same few acres and that wonderful flow of water beyond.

It was in March that I overhead my father say, for some reason I still don't know, that he'd just as soon pack up and move away. He was angry about something, I still don't know what, and I was about 10, suffering over what I overheard, not realizing the emptiness of the threat. I sulked along Bayou Teche, close to tears, wondering where we would be, what would become of us, if there would be water nearby. Perhaps that was what disturbed me most about dad's unintended and insincere threat to move us…that there would be no water to watch flow by, coming from unknown headwaters and making way to undiscovered countries far ahead. I thought he might take us to Ft. Worth, where much of the family had fled for jobs and opportunity long ago, escaping the reservation and all its fruitless, hollow emptiness. My boyish vision of Ft. Worth was a dry, dusty place devoid of water. No greater misery could be imagined.

Of course, we didn't move, and I never asked my father what it was that made him so angry that day. It was unnecessary. Sometimes, in March, when the air warmed and the rain held itself in restraint, I'd hop on Nancy, my Shetland pony, or in later years, my quarter horse Kate, and ride the brown cane fields around Charenton alone. Mine was a childhood of solitude, but I was never lonely, never really longed for friendships because I was so surrounded by those four old people and their powerful presence. I wonder, as I look back now on those March bayouside forays and horseback rides, if children who grow up in solitude have less apprehension of the long silences and more fear of crowds and noise. I know I do not like crowds, I feel confined and suffocating in them, the nerves in my skin buzzing with the instinct to get away. Riding through brown cane fields in March on Kate's back, crowds and noise and thoughts of escape from either were completely unknown.

It's not that I was completely friendless in March, but there was only one that I can recall who was close. Otherwise, March was solitary and comforting. No kick the can, no baseball, and no sleepovers. In March, I huddled under blankets late into the night reading Black Beauty and explored Bayou Teche days, a few hundred yards of it, anyway, but there was more there to find than any basketball court or chalked-in pattern of hopscotch could ever offer. Armadillo holes were mysterious and dangerous, for I had read somewhere that the animals carried leprosy. There was an abandoned water well near the old camp that Uncle Fred had lived in, and dad warned me many times to stay away from it, though he had covered it up, there was still a chance of catastrophe.

A big cypress tree stood in the bayou a dozen feet from the bank, and rows of thickly growing knees bridged the two. If I was careful and the water not too high, I could negotiate across the cypress knees to the tree, where I had nailed a couple of old boards to sit on and watch the water move through, coursing between the knees. Now and then I'd spot small sunfish, orange-breasted and wide-eyed, chasing minnows. I would dip tadpoles from tiny pools of isolated water with an aquarium net, or survey a nest of sparrows in the limbs above me.

I wonder sometimes, in March, what person I would have become if there had been different lands to explore, away from water, expanding the solitary nature of childhood. On the steps up the stairway of my life, I have mostly stood alone as those who were my world left to join the Creator, reluctant even to accept the support of those who remained, knowing that in time attrition would leave me completely abandoned. When I think of that day, I think of a boy in March, sitting on boards nailed to a cypress tree, watching sunfish and tadpoles, and I wonder how I might find that sense of safety and wonder again, bereft as I am and will become.

But it is March, and the weather is warming and the year is unfolding like creation all over again. In a few weeks it will be time to load the boat and go to the lake, where I'll feel complete once again. I have been bound to these wonderful walls for too long, and much as I love them, need them, I require the surge of lake water in my veins. Dreams of Lake Fausse Pointe filter into my sleep like tides; in waking hours, if I close my eyes, I see its stands of second-growth cypress, water lapping at their trunks. Though I pay attention to conversations, laugh with friends, commune with acquaintances, there is always lake water behind my thoughts. I am always aware of it, cognizant of the distance I stand from it, I know which direction it lies without thinking about it, and I sense its presence day and night. It lurks behind my eyelids, floats in the fluid between the back of my brain and skull.

It's odd that I really mostly think of these things at the margin of seasons, staring at March from behind windowpanes that are now so old and brittle they crack with the changing temperatures and must be replaced. The windowpanes have ripples in them horizontally, decades of settling. If that old house would stand long enough, and I would live until then, they would eventually settle into puddles of glass. They say that in some of the oldest cathedrals of Europe, the glass must be flipped now and then to keep it from settling, because glass is not really solid. It is a very viscous liquid. When I have the panes replaced, they are crystal clear and dead flat. I cannot see the world outside in March as well through their clarity. The distortion of old windowpanes reveals more. Things on the peripheral can never been seen dead-on. They must be viewed askance. Seeing March is best through old window glass, like sitting on cypress boards watching sunfish and tadpoles in the water, which swim away or vanish with the fading dusk, like childhood, like the safety and surrounding embraces of the truest hearts in a life.

Yes, it's March. There's an easy way to tell if it's March, in case you're not sure, other than looking at the calendar.

The best, most surefire way of determining if it's March is to keep your eye on folks like me. If you see us lurching down the street like some bizarre marionette, it's March. If you talk to us for eight minutes without stop about your recent trip to the doctor and the various maladies he said you are suffering, and we say, "Huh?" at the end of your dissertation, it's March. Most of all, if you are with one of us at a restaurant and tell the waitress, "I think I'll have the fried fish," and we suddenly slaver from the mouth, tremble convulsively, our eyes bug out like an amok dragonfly and suddenly fall face first into our potato soup, well, it's surely got to be March.

That's what happens in March to fishermen. The spring is so near, but not quite there yet, and we're about to go stark raving mad with anticipation. It's been a short, mild winter really, but even in such cases, it takes its toll on us.

If you go shopping with one of us, and we walk into the store and say, "If you need me, I'll be in sporting goods," and rush away before you can protest, it must be March. If you are following behind us on the road in our vehicles, and we suddenly swerve crazily, slam on the brakes and pull over to the side of the road, the driver's side door flies open and we leap out, jump the ditch near the shoulder, race across a pasture to see if the water in the pond we just spotted is muddy or clear, it must be March.

If you call our homes and we pick up the phone and say, "Yes, I'd love to!" it must be March and we thought that nobody would dare call us for any other reason than to go fishing. If you reply that you were only calling to inquire about our health, we'll slam the phone down and never answer your calls again until July, at least.

Don't make road trips with us in March. A trip that takes an hour will take four, because we simply must take every side road, byway and dirt trail we see to look for fishing holes. Don't try to engage us in conversation about world events, religious issues, film, music, pets, computers, bad hair days or just about any other topic, because we'll only reply, "Yes, that's all fine and dandy, but where are they biting and on what?"

Expect no sense of responsibility from us, either. If the sun is shining, there is no threat of rain in the immediate forecast, the temperature is moderately warm and you have invited us to your annual extravagant get-together with free food, drinks, door prizes and chocolate cake, don't expect us to attend. If our children were getting married on a day such as the one described, we'd have to send our regrets, and if a daughter were involved, recruit someone to give her away at the altar.

This is what March does to an angler. Some people get "spring cleaning" fits in March. So do we. We clean our tackle, our boats, our lines, our bilges. Some people say spring makes them feel "frisky." Fishermen have no time for "frisky" in March. Frisky is relevant only when it's raining cats, dogs and pitchforks outside and there is no hope whatsoever of donning a wet suit with scuba gear and going to spear the stupid fish.

In March, church congregation numbers drop drastically on Sundays when the weather is clear and fine. Fishermen will remind you that John was, after all, a fisherman and Jesus did a bit of angling in His own day, too. Fishermen take this as gospel that fishingness is next to godliness. This is evidenced by the number of so-called "angling widows" sitting in the pews.

One of my best friends is a minister who also owned a bass boat and loved to fish when he lived around here. We called him "Preacher With A Boat." The theory was, you wake up on Sunday morning, the sun is shining, the birds are singing and the bass are biting. You skip church and head out for the lake. But you forgot about…*Preacher With A Boat!* Here he comes, zooming across the lake, a Bible in one hand and a Zebco 333 in the other, and he says, in true Psalms style:

All of you anglers get it wrong
Fishing trips take half as long
When you've met:
Preacher With A BOAT!

He thought it was pretty funny, but then, he was always in church on Sundays in March, too.

This particular parson, one of my best friends in the world, used to fish with a Snagless Sally. If you don't know what a Snagless Sally is, let's just say it's a fishing lure that looks like nothing which ever lived in the entire biological history of planet Earth, aquatic or terrestrial, and gets snagged on almost every cast. But my friend had remarkable faith in his Snagless Sally, even though he never caught a fish on it. It's that sort of faith that I admire, in preachers and in fishermen. It's probably also why preachers make dedicated anglers: It requires absolute faith, a trait required of ministers, to purchase a bass boat, outfit it with hardware and tackle, dump it into the water, take off on a 30-mile trip into the Atchafalaya River Basin without the foggiest idea of how you'll ever find your way back before dark, without hitting a log and knocking your outboard motor into the drink, risking snakebite and thunderstorms—to blindly cast a Snagless Sally into water you can't see four inches down into in the hopes that a fish will bite it. The ultimate expression of this faith is that whatever bites will be a bass, not a choupique.

So it's March, and we fishermen are gearing up, shining the boats, checking our bilge pumps and trolling motors, oiling our reels and organizing our tackle. We put $30 worth of gas and oil into the tank, $12 worth of drinks and snacks into the ice chest. We drive 48 miles to a lake, wait impatiently in line to put the boat over, fire up 175 horsepower V-6 engines with more torque than our pickup trucks, blast across the water throwing a rooster tail 85 feet from side to side—all to try to get an animal with a brain the size of a BB to bite a hook on what appears to be a translucent worm that swallowed a bottle of gold glitter, or a concoction of feathers, deer hair and lead wire that's supposed to represent a mayfly. And we wonder, who exactly has the BB-sized brains?

No matter. It's March, and we aren't using our brains much anyway.

Desperate for water, but aware that the Atchafalaya River Basin had yet to clear up its muddy flow, I grabbed a couple rods after work and headed to a pond.

A cold front had passed through over the weekend, but it only dipped temperatures down into the mid-forties. I thought perhaps there might still be a fish willing to strike, if I held my mouth just right. Upon arriving at the pond, I started setting up on the tailgate of the truck. I use an Okuma soft tackle back pack, which I simply adore, and I have managed to adapt it to carrying a couple of rod tubes by lowering the butts into the lower side-pocket and using the strap midway up the pack. It holds four plastic tackle boxes below, not true fly boxes but they work great for me. I can keep all my knotless leaders in little pouches, and there are multitudes of spots to tuck cleaning pads, bug spray, pliers and the like. I keep four reels in a shaving bag in the upper compartment of the Okuma pack.

I assembled my seven-weight nine-foot South Bend cane, realizing that March is a great time for the bigger bass, and I knew there were some lunkers in this little pond. While looping the leader to the fly line, a young fella pulled up on a four-wheeler, his chocolate lab huffing alongside.

"Going fishing?" he asked.

"Well, I'm going casting," I said with a smile, though I was hoping I didn't appear overly friendly. I had only about an hour of daylight left. "You never know, really."

"Oh," he said, clearly disappointed. "I was going to let the dog swim, but I'll find someplace else."

I found this show of courtesy refreshing. "It's big enough," I said. "You can let her swim on one side, I'll fish the other."

"No, really," he said. "I'll go find another spot. I don't want to mess you up. I brought a rod out here one day and every time I'd cast, she's go after it. I gave up pretty quick."

With a smile and a wave, he and the dog meandered down the road in search of other water. I wish everyone were as polite.

Rigged up now, I shouldered the back pack and put on my Stetson. South Bend in one hand, I walked the fifty yards to the pond. The wind was breezy, making me grateful I had rigged the big cane rod, though I had a six-and-a-half foot graphite four-weight in its tube in the back pack if things calmed down.

There are few things I enjoy more about fishing than casting a bamboo fly rod. I am no purist: I have graphites and canes. But I find I can cast farther and better with bamboo, and though the weight of a nine-footer wears on my casting arm after a while, it's pure delight for me. My cane rods are decidedly production vintage: Grangers, South Bends, better grade Montagues. All reworked with modern guides and spacing. If I break one on a big bass, well, I'll cry a little, but far less than if I broke a Leonard or a Thramer.

Over the winter, I had stocked up on flies through Ebay, since I don't tie. I have found that bass love flies not intended for their big mouths. In this particular case, I had on the leader an Atlantic salmon fly, I'm guessing size six, and on my third cast, a twitch of the line suddenly was followed by a giant pull. I lifted, the South Bend curved over, and I was sure I had a respectable bass on.

About a minute later, he broke the surface, and I saw it was a big, dark bluegill, a good one pounder. A one pound bass would not have fought nearly so well. Though he would have been a blast on the four-weight, the South Bend still gave me a thrill. After taking a couple pictures, I let him back into his pond. The fight in a bluegill will always amaze me.

I worked my way around the pond, casting the salmon fly, which was adorned with mostly silvery feather and a splash of red and yellow. Dusk was nearing, and the world one moment was bright and washed out, the next golden and saturated, as if reanimated. Near the far side of the pond, the line twitched four times in rapid succession, and several minutes later a three-pound bass met my thumb. No Atlantic salmon, but then, Louisiana folks can't be choosy.

I caught three very small bass, all half as big as the bluegill, over the next few moments as the day faded across that westward horizon, splashing dragonfire across the scant few clouds. A half hour before dark, the pond was suddenly full of rising fish, and I quickly put a popper on, my all-time favorite, the Accardo "Spook," which brought in three more pound-and-a-half bass.

The temperature was dropping, and I was in short sleeves, the sun was so low now I could see my fly only barely. I dismantled the rod and dried it, put it in its sock and tube. I found a silver flask in the Okuma bag, sat down on the bank and watched the fish rising, unmolested by me, chocolate labs or fire-breathing dragons somewhere over the curvature of the earth to the west. Somewhere behind and to the north of me, Atlantic salmon would be rushing up cold rivers when the time comes, and somewhere else, anglers not so unlike myself are donning waders and chasing rainbows and browns in their favorite streams. To the south, battles with redfish and black drum are taking epic proportions in the retellings.

In the final moments of the day, before I made the walk back to the truck and home, I thought of my father again. Last chief of my people's nation, he was perhaps also the last of the rank of Chitimacha known as the Suns, the lineage from which the chief was chosen. I thought of all the things the he had given me: Love, a safe and happy home, wisdom and boundless vision. But perhaps the thing that will follow me with the most devotion, until the end of my days, is this pursuit of fish with the rod, and this soft, solitary silence of distant fire at the end of the day.

At the end of March, I took my "spring vacation," as it were. I usually take off in the spring and the fall to take advantage of the best fishing of the year. Allegedly, that is.

My cousin, Jim Ray, and his son Christopher would be joining me after driving in from Ft. Worth, Texas, on Wednesday. Jim joined me for my fall vacation last year, wherein our generation of the Stouffs committed to spending more time together. We also resurrected the venerable old family tradition of referring to each other as "boy." That was the way it was in our family: The males of the next generation were always "Boy" as in, "Hand me that box of worms, boy," and though we are of the same generation, Jim and I had nobody else to call "boy" so we had to improvise…

Aunt Jimmie was married to my father's only brother, Ray. Uncle Ray died when I was 13. He was 51. My cousin, Jim Ray, was named after both of them. Jim is 18 years my senior, and over the course of our lives, this would be the first time we'd really ever had any one-on-one time during a visit.

So Jim being a fisherman and me being a fisherman, we set about fishing Tuesday morning. I had taken out dad's bateau, cleaned and gassed it up. Our first hole, out of Charenton Beach, proved fruitless, so we quickly abandoned it and went to Grand Avoille Cove on the north side of the levee, where we picked up a few small fish. Discouraged, we picked up, went had some lunch, and returned to Grand Avoille Cove on the south side of the levee, where we picked up a few more rare fish and gave it up.

Reminiscing was the best part of our fishing trips. We both laughed as we recalled how the men in our family were fond of the word "boy." No matter how old we got, we were always "boy." It was, "How about some coffee, boy?" or "That's a good-looking shirt you got on, boy." It was never a term of disparagement, it was just the way it was: They were "boy" to their parents, we were "boy" to them.

Jim being older than I, he has both more memories of the family and more clear recollections of things my memory has grown fuzzy over. It was great to hear his stories, share mine, and receive confirmations, corrections or additions.

Wednesday we fished from the bank at a few of my special ponds, but the weather was so dadgum hot we didn't enjoy ourselves much and the fish refused to cooperate.

We did manage to get in some fly fishing though. Imagine my surprise when Jim brought out his fly rod and I saw it was a sweet old fiberglass rod with a Garcia automatic reel on it. The story went something like this:

The Texas Stouffs were visiting the Charenton Stouffs, and of course, the menfolk and the "boys" went fishing. Dad pulled a fly rod out and handed it to Jim, and said, "See what you can do with that, boy."

After some instruction casting on the lawn, they fished fly rods most of the day. Dad put up the fly rod after the first trip, but let Jim use it the other days again.

When the Texas Stouffs were packing up to go home, Dad handed Jim the fly rod. "Take that and see if you can do anything with it back home, boy."

Somebody must have cut an onion upwind of me when Jim told that story, 'cuz my eyes kinda teared up.

While popping around from pond to pond Wednesday, we stopped in at a couple stores to pick up a soft drink to fight off the heat, and had lunch at Polito's. A bunch of you kind people stopped by to chat and meet my cuz, and when we finally got back to the fishing, Jim noted that it seemed I had finally found my place in the world. I agreed that I had, and it was in no small part because of the kindness, generosity and support of all you folks who faithfully follow the dribble I ramble out on in the newspaper twice a week. While sometimes I get the uneasy feeling I might actually be John Boy Walton with a pony tail, sans cheek mole, well, I guess there are worse things I could be.

Thursday was our most interesting fishing day. We managed to find some clean water, and were throwing plastic worms to nearly no avail for a few hours. Then Jim changed from a "watermelon chartreuse" colored worm to a dark blue one, and bam! Fish on. Fish on, by the way, in an area I had just covered thoroughly. He also caught three more in that same spot, so of course, I switched worms and we had a fairly productive afternoon, but by the time the heat was so oppressive we headed home after landing and releasing about 12 pass and eight bream. Yes, the bream, though small, were even taking the plastic worms.

That night, just before dark, we fished one of my favorite ponds. Jim took one corner and I took an area with a patch of willows. We were working fly rods. I caught a couple bass near the willows.

"Why don't you come over here and join me, boy?" I said.

"No, that's okay," Jim said, though he hadn't gotten a single strike yet. "I'll just stick it out over here."

Bam, bam, bam, three more little bass. As I was unhooking the third, I said, "I ain't gonna beg you, boy."

"It's okay," Jim said. "I'm sure there's fish over here."

Bam, bam. Two more fish.

"Move over, boy, and give me some room," Jim said.

The Stouffs went home Friday morning. While my aunt was visiting with my mom, I asked her to go through all my grandmother's photo albums and identify those people she knew by writing the name on them. It was very helpful, and I was very grateful. She asked me for one photo: Uncle Ray, perhaps 20 years old, holding a guitar. I gladly gave it to her. It's more hers than mine anyway.

I got a little melancholy Friday, and I was tired. I spent most of the day dozing in and out, laying on the couch with the television on. Late in the afternoon I went out to clean up the old boat, and it occurred to me that the boat, two years older than I am, had carried Jim before it had carried me, to some fishing spot or another and returned him safely home. Now, here it was, more than 40 years later, cleaned up, ready for its cover, and again it had carried the Stouff boys out to the fishing holes and safely home flawlessly. It has carried me and my son. There's a lesson there. There's a spirit there I don't know if anyone else can truly understand, but I hope so.

Standing there, my palm on the deck, relishing the warmth of the fir, someone must have cut another onion upwind, because I got to feeling teary-eyed again. Silently, I thanked the old boat for carrying us to *Sheti* this week, for every safe return throughout our lives together. I got to missing my dad something awful, but under my palm, the grain of the wood was like veins, and the life that flowed within them was uninterrupted.

Many times in my life I would regret that I was born so late. That I was 13 when Uncle Ray died, rather than perhaps 20-something. That Jim and I didn't fish our first fly rods together. That all the old folks, the ones he knew so well but were mostly gone by the time I came around, don't exist in my memories.

But as I've said before, the cornerstone of my life, the most important lessons I learned and the most vivid, cherished memories I have, were most often born during a few moments in that small wooden boat. It's a good thing to know that cornerstone is still there, and treasures are still being born from it.

I covered it and tied down the tarp securely. There under the blue plastic weave, its shape was clear if the details were obscured. Much like my memories. Jim and I vowed that we'd visit each other more often. Get back to the way it used to be, when the family made annual visits. We are, after all, the last of our generation of the Stouff boys, and though we both have sons to carry on the name, we can only hope that some day, within some small moment, they'll fish fly rods from a little wooden boat somewhere out there in what is, for us, Eden, and tell stories about us after we're gone, catch bass, complain about the heat, and learn something about themselves, the world, and legacy.

Who knows, they might even call each other "boy" in bittersweet tribute...

It is worth pointing out that of the five brothers in our grandfathers' generation, all moved away from the reservation in search of opportunity and to flee oppression. Only Emile Anatole Stouff remained, though working far and wide. The rest relocated, mostly to Ft. Worth and New Orleans, one in California. Time was when the Ft. Worth Stouffs would visit the Charenton Stouffs annually and vice versa. My dad's only brother, Ray Lanier Stouff, died when I was 12 years old.

This time around, Jim and I had a proper boy-calling recipient, that being Christopher. Makes no difference that Christopher is 24-years-old. In our family, we are "boy" to our forebears forever, no matter the age. It's not a term of disrespect, disparagement or demeaning. It's just the way it is.

Jim had, on our fall visit, expressed his regret that his kids (he also has two girls) had not experienced the beauty and the wonder of the Atchafalaya Basin like he had when he was growing up. A fishing trip was required on all visits of the Ft. Worth Stouffs to the reservation, and Jim shared many stories with me of those boyhood excursions. He had pledged to make sure his children are no longer so deprived.

Monday morning I set out to start the fishing, and was doing quite well until mid-morning when that nasty little storm front came through. It caught me on the lake, and I had to tie up under the cypress canopy to wait it out. And as is typical of the days following a weather front, the fish displayed no more of the enthusiastic biting that I had experienced early Monday morning. Catching so much as a skinny sunfish was an exercise akin to carving Mt. Rushmore.

Tuesday and Wednesday were excruciatingly and frustratingly unproductive. The Ft. Worth Stouffs arrived late Wednesday evening, and on Thursday we were on the water. I had not seen Chris since he was something like age eight. He told me his goal for the entire trip was to catch four fish. Just four. I thought just maybe we could arrange that, but it would be marginal.

Chris was also informed of the "boy tradition" in our family, much to his initial dismay. When you're 24-years-old, on your way through a successful career in the information technology field, and making your first trip to Louisiana in a bunch of years, the last thing you want to be referred to as is "boy."

So whenever I had the opportunity, I'd say something like, "Hand me my hat, boy," and Chris would steam. But by the end of the second day, if asked for something, he'd note, "I guess that *is* the boy's job." Settling into the groove, you see.

We lost perhaps $50 worth of tackle to lure-eating trees. These are those peculiar varieties if trees which are magnetic, and their magnetism is so strong, they'll divert a cast lure from its path from a dozen yards away, pulling it into an arc, upward, and wrapping the lure and line around a branch precisely six inches farther than you can reach even when standing on the boat deck with a long paddle.

Thus began three days of the nearly fruitless pursuit of fish. I kept thinking the next day would be the day we'd get into them, they'd be over the effects of the storm front, but alas, it was a no-go. Oh, that's not to say we didn't pick up the odd fish here and there, and Chris actually doubled his goal with eight fish over three days. Jim and I did perhaps a dozen each. All in all, a disappointing expedition entirely.

But in the end, that was the only disappointment. It was a fine and pleasant thing to renew my acquaintance with the boy, and visit with Jim again. During our time on the water, I took the time to re-introduce the boy to the ancestral homeland of *Sheti imasha*, people of the lake. We visited the ancient worship place, and Peach Coulee. I showed him the river and Lake Fausse Pointe. We saw alligators and red-tailed hawks. It was obvious the boy was humbled and at once invigorated by his native waters, and the resonance of them tugged at something deep within him, awakened thousands-year-old memories he has yet to recall. He will.

If the one version of our people's origins is to be believed, when we left Natchez we took with us a torch from the sacred fire which burned at Grand Village night and day, year upon year, without ever extinguishing. We carried that fire here, to these magnificent swamps and marshes and prairies, to tend it as faithfully as our Natchez kin did to the north.

It is unknown when the sacred fire went cold; probably some time after the conquistadors arrived in their galleons on Grand Lake, sparking the first of the wars which would follow and lead to the virtual disappearance of the people of the lake for many, many decades. During that time, those people took immigrant names, imported religion, but still clung to the memory of the fire out there somewhere on *Sheti*, no longer giving off its light and heat and promise, but as alive and bright in the heart and soul of those who tended it as it always had been.

My life has been etched upon the search for that flame. While I know I shall never find the burning brand that marked the exodus from Natchez, the settling of the villages along the coast and river basin, I search for its memory and the resonance of its presence. The boy, perhaps surprising himself, felt that distant fire, and a link was established last week that I do not think shall ever be broken. Jim Ray fulfilled his pledge. He brought the first of his children back to where it all began, planted a seed which will flourish.

And us old timers, Jim and I, spent the Sunday evening before I had to come back to work and the Ft. Worth Stouffs were to set back upon the trail that will return them home, fishing a small pond alone. It was near dusk, and fish were rising somewhat reluctantly under the full moon which was moving across the sky.

Dusk. My favorite time of day. We brought the fly rods to hand and whisked line across clear water. I landed one nice four-pounder, three more small bass, and Jim took to hand four or five respectable fish as well. The sun turned into a gigantic, red-orange eye as it retreated into the western horizon; the eternal, sacred flame which remains with us. The moon, silver-white, cast long streaks of wild magic across the pond, providing just enough illumination that we caught a few more fish on surface poppers before the mosquitoes forced us to retreat.

Monday morning, I returned to work and the Stouffs returned to Ft. Worth. I felt nearly as if history was once again repeating itself: Nine decades ago, the exodus from the reservation began, though one remained, tending a flame of the heart. Over the years, some returned and continue to return, answering the call of fire, the beckoning of water. That, at least, will continue it seems.

Mine is a world of fire, and of water. Mine is a world of what has happened, and what will yet be. Fire and water. Resonance and callings of the soul. I never knew what was being handed down to me without my knowledge, without even my consent. But the flickering ember I saw in the boy's eyes reminds me again that there is, after all, no place like home.

But the long and short of it is, we had a durn good time on my vacation.

There were, of course, a few misadventures other than not catching many fish. I have become accustomed to not catching many fish. In my younger days, I caught fish constantly and abundantly. I think I caught my lifetime share of fish in the first 20 years of my existence, and have since been put on a budget. Of course, that's why they call it "fishing" and not "catching."

I spent six days in the boat, my cousin Jim and his son Chris spent three. That's a lot of time in any boat, particularly with the cost of gasoline nowadays. Since we roamed far and wide in search of receptive fish, every morning began with the requisite fill-up. Standing at the gas pump, watching the "total sale" number spin and spin and spin until we all felt queasy and weak in the knees. OPEC members, in addition to their other character flaws, are Public Enemy Number 1 to fishermen this spring.

The cousins, living in the Ft. Worth area, have a handful of waters to fish in within reasonable driving distance, and the entire fishing, boating, jetski, swimming and sailing population converges on these lakes whenever possible. So trying to fish in their area, they tell me, is a crowded, demanding proposition at best. Chris had caught one largemouth, his only fish in general, before coming to Louisiana.

The first morning in the boat, he commented with grinning wonder, "I didn't know there was this much water in the world!" This was only having seen Lake Fausse Pointe thus far, so there was a lot more water yet to see, particularly when we went to the river. The problem was, there seemed to be a lot of water, but north winds had pushed much of it out, so it was shallow in lots of places south of the levee, and up into the trees north of the levee, neither situation conducive to good fishing.

Then there were those lure-eating trees. Like clover, hackberries, crabgrass and red ants, lure-eating trees have become one of the top pests in Louisiana. Nature has evolved these trees to exert magnetic force outward, snatching lures midflight into their limbs, wherein they twist around 17 branches, six times each, and the hook lodges into the tree trunk deeper and more firmly than you could ever hope to hook a fish.

I was using light tackle, as was Chris, but Jim was using 25-pound "Spiderwire", a braided fishing line with which he just pulled down the lure-eating trees that gobbled up his lures. While Chris and I would say, "Durnit, I'm in the tree again," Jim would merely yell, "Timber!" in warning that a massive tupelo was about to be uprooted by Spiderwire.

We are all, of course, excellent at casting when there are no lure-eating trees nearby, so please, do not cast a shadow—pardon the pun—upon our technical abilities.

When not engaged in epic battles of Gilgamesh proportions with lure-eating trees, we were largely biteless. The front that came through Monday gave the fish a serious case of lockjaw. However, I did catch my first two sac-au-lait in my life, something I have never purposely fished for until now.

It was difficult to translate, though. A sac-au-lait in the French is a crappie away from Acadiana. Then, it can be pronounced "crappie" or "crahppie" depending on how sensitive you might be to the metaphorical imagery the word conjures. This perhaps is why our Cajun forebears chose to call them sac-au-lait, "sack of milk," rather than something rather disgusting.

At one point, I became desperate enough to turn to the Internet fishing reports for help. I found that one particular fellow was catching big fish in northern Lake Fausse Pointe, so I emailed him with a desperate plea for help:

"Dear (name withheld to protect the angler):

"Where are you catching all those monster fish? Are there any lure-eating trees nearby?

"Thank you."

I got a response giving me the place, and we shot off there the next morning. However, those north winds we had talked about had pushed a great deal of water out of this particular canal, and the fish were gone with it. So much for the World Wide Waste.

We began scouting various locations, but the situation was the same everywhere we went. Some places, the proliferation of lure-eating trees was so great we cast for half an hour and never got a lure into the water, so retreated before we ran into any boat-eating trees as well.

When Saturday afternoon rolled around, and we were all out in the boat, tired, with aching backs, knees and egoes, we all just kinda looked at each other and said, "Okay, I've had enough." So we went home and retired from fishing for the duration, save for one trip to a pond which was fairly productive.

All in all, though, it was an excellent vacation. Chris had a total of eight fish, so he realized an 800 percent advance. I figure that the total number of fish caught in the week, divided by the number of lures lost to lure-eating trees, gasoline and drinks and snacks, cost us about $10 each.

I made a big pot of crawfish stew Sunday, believing that was the closest we'd get to that fish fry we were all hoping would happen eventually. I could have fried the crawfish to make it a little closer, but figured I'd just aggravate myself.

The Stouffs went home Monday and I came back to work. I got quite a bit of sun over the week, and folks were saying, "Wow, you really look like an Indian now!"

So I guess the time spent on the water wasn't a total waste. However, I am now on a vendetta against lure-eating trees. I am hoping they have some value to the lumber industry, or perhaps some other commercial application. I plan to secure my retirement as well as rid the world of a dangerous pest in the process.

First, though, I have to go get a spool of Spiderwire.

The Box

One rainy weekend, I set about cleaning up and organizing my dad's old tackle box. That tackle box frightens me even today. When I was a kid, there were some things I was never allowed to fiddle with: electrical outlets, knives, matches, power tools, the gas space heater and Dad's tackle box. The common denominator there is that severe injury would likely result. Dad had an aluminum box, which would open across the middle of the top, and three layers of trays would spread out on hinges when the lids were lowered to the sides. Inside was, in my youth, a wonderland of amazing fishing dreams. Once I made the mistake of reaching for a fascinating looking bass lure, and the lid snapped closed so quickly I nearly lost a finger. I think I was in my late twenties before I was allowed to touch that tackle box, and then only under direct and overwhelming scrutiny.

But I cleaned it up that weekend, and sorted through the dozens of lures, flies, hooks, popping bugs and everything else in there. Some of these lures were clearly designed to catch fishermen, not fish. If I were a fish, I'd swim like all get-out in terror of one particular lure I found in there: school bus yellow with bulging red eyes, the body striped vertically in blue, hinged in the middle, with four sharp treble hooks, an aluminum lip, and something inside it that rattled. It certainly didn't look like anything I would eat if I were a fish. How many minnows or shad rattle when they swim? I've never heard a minnow or a shad rattle. If this were the case, fishermen could put a baby rattle on the end of their lines and catch bass. A rattlesnake too near the water would be history.

Also in the tackle box were five floating Rapala minnows. Dad's favorite top-water lure was the floating Rapala. He gave me a Rapala once, with the stern warning, "That one's yours. The ones in my tackle box are mine. Got it?" I got it, clearly enough.

There must have been three dozen flies, mostly little popping bugs. Not a spinner bait or soft-bodied jig anywhere. Dad didn't believe in them. He apparently believed in bulging red eyed, vertically striped in blue, hinged in the middle, with four sharp treble hooks, aluminum lipped, and something inside that rattled lures, but not spinner baits or soft jigs. I actually suspect somebody gave him that lure and he just kept it in there in the same way someone gives you a sweater or tie you absolutely despise but you wear it anyway to keep from hurting any feelings.

It put me in mind to happier days. Days when a twelve-foot wooden bateau my grandfather had made, with a decided twist in the frame somewhere in the middle, powered by a Wizard outboard that was low on compression, meant nothing but pure joy for a young fisherman. I named the boat *Gandalf*, because it was only by some kind of sorcery that it kept getting us home every time my fishing pal and me went out. I even painted the name on the bow. We'd head out every Saturday morning when the weather permitted and stay out there until dusk, sometimes barely getting home before dark. Once we were fishing way back in Sawmill Bayou—before some malcontent came along and put up a fence and gate—and got stuck on a log or cypress knee under the boat. We grabbed our paddles and paddled furiously, but the boat only spun around in circles until we were exhausted and short of breaths. Finally my pal had the bright idea to walk to the front of the boat with me, thus displacing the weight forward, and we slid right off the log.

Fishing has been defined as "a jerk on one end of a line waiting for a jerk on the other end." I think we proved it that day.

Our greatest nightmare was choupique. If you're not familiar with them, a choupique (pronounced shoe-pick, or bowfin away from Acadiana) is a fish that has changed little from the age of the dinosaurs and, unfortunately, did not go extinct with them. They are more eel than fish, if you ask me, and love the bait we fish bream with. Choupique are actually demons, because when you hook one they try to take you to Hades. They dive straight down into the mud and burrow in. Fighting a choupique is terrifying on six-pound line. I've caught choupique which could give Wes Craven nightmares.

My pal hooked into a choupique on Lake Fausse Pointe one wonderful summer, and the fish pulled our boat a couple hundred yards. All we could do was hang on and ride it out. I am sure we looked rather funny, towed along the lake by a monster choupique, grimacing like kids on the roller coaster at Astroworld. Finally the fish straightened out the hook and, to our great relief, was gone. We took about an hour-long breather, discussing philosophically whether that was indeed a choupique or the Loch Ness monster.

In a particularly adventurous mood on one trip, we took the old bateau and the feeble Wizard from my house on the reservation all the way to the lake and clear across it. This took four tanks of gas and about two hours. On the way back, I hit a log or something and sheared a pin in the prop. A shear pin is a small piece of metal that allows the engine shaft to drive the prop around, so if you hit something, the pin breaks and you don't ruin the shaft. This was in the days prior to the modern slip clutch. I had no spare shear pins, and it was so close to dark we barely had time to make it home even if we were still underway. This was in the days before cell phones, and there was no hope of rescue. I found a big old catfish hook and with a pair of pliers cut the curved part and the eyelet off, and using that as a shear pin, we made it home just after dark. It was then that Dad decided I was old enough for a new outboard.

That big old aluminum tackle box sits in that room of the house which, when renovated, will include a cabinet for storing my collection of antique firearms, fishing gear, maps, boat plans and a desk for my laptop computer and tying flies.

It's a work in progress, like the rest of the house, but the room is a sort of small alcove off the living room, about eight by twelve, with windows on two of its three sides. It will be perfect for a place I can write, do odd jobs like oiling my reels or cleaning a gun, or tying fishing flies. It will also be a sort of conservatory.

The old aluminum tackle box is rounded on the corners, like a loaf of bread, but much bigger, and the sheet metal is dappled with a texture. You unclip the lid on each side, and it separates down the middle and the two halves open outward with a slight shriek of metal on metal. Inside are rows of trays stacked three high which also expand outward on hinges, revealing lots of individual tackle storage units and a larger space beneath.

I take it out, sometimes, and study it carefully. When I was a kid, that tackle box was many things to me. It was a symbol of being a grown-up: A grown-up sized tackle box marked the entrance to a whole world of grown-up privileges and perks, without cognizance of the responsibilities entailed. It was also a wonderland of things I was seldom allowed to tinker with, mysterious fishing lures that would emerge only out on the lake, and a plethora of unknown objects which I could only glimpse while the lids were open and the trays sprawled outward.

I had my own tackle box, I remember, a little yellow plastic one that was about a foot long, six inches wide and five inches tall. It held a few hooks, a half dozen lead weights, a couple of corks and some lures which had seen better days that dad had donated to my collection, and I prized them all greatly. When dad opened his tackle box, I opened mine, whether I needed anything or not from it.

Today his old box sits in the room which will be my "piddling room," along with his nine-foot, five-weight fiberglass fly rod and Martin automatic reel. The burgundy finish has speckled and grayed, and the reel is chipped and greasy. The line, once yellow and flawless, is crackled and dry. But if I wind the external disc and merely touch the release, it whirls and sings, pulling line in as if it were brand new. It is a sound I know so well. I don't use automatic reels anymore, but they still hold a warm spot in my heart.

Sometimes I open the tackle box and finger through its contents: old wooden Heddon Lucky 13's, badly chewed up Rapala Floating Minnows and oodles of fly poppers, their feathers long disintegrated and their rubber legs melted away like the years. There are Jitterbugs, many of them, and I can recall their strange movement atop the water, slowly retrieved on the line with a jerky, side-to-side motion that often drove the largemouth bass wild. There are large bass poppers, a single Snagless Sally which I don't recall him ever using, and huge lures which I can't identify the make or model of, but seem to be the size of a Cuban cigar.

At the bottom of the box, in the larger space, he always kept spare Johnson Century or Citation reels. We always fished with Johnson Reels, Citation or Century. There was also always a spare fly reel, too, just in case. I had my own fly rod, which I never quite mastered but became reasonably proficient with my the time I put it away as a late teen.

He kept a smaller box for the tackle he used most, to be stashed at easy reach under the deck of the boat. I have it, too, but it came along after I was a grown man, and I have no connection to it. No tether or lifeline. His spincast fishing tackle I still use, most of it, though a dozen old reels lay in a box at home, common ones as well as brands of which I've never heard.

A red-and-white Heddon Lucky 13 catches my eye, and I pick it up. The hooks are rusty, and the body is marred by a great many tiny pricks, teeth marks of largemouth bass. If I could recall the exact number of fish taken on each lure in that box, I would guess they'd fill the living room from floor to ceiling. There are a thousand fish swimming around in that old aluminum tackle box, taken under a thousand cypress or tupelo branches, from behind a thousand sunken logs, aside a thousand weed beds and nearby a thousand flat-topped pond lilies. There are dozens of oatmeal creme pies inside there, too, the only snack we'd bring with us on the water. Lurking somewhere under the expanded trays between the metal hinges is a small boy and his aging father. The boy was born late in the man's life, an only child at that, knowing no sports, no baseball or football, only a tackle box full of lake water, cypress trees, shell mounds, broken pottery, bluegill, bass and safety.

If I turned the box over and spilled its contents onto the oak floor, not only would the Heddons and the poppers and the Johnson reels tumble out, but so would eight cottomouth snakes which ran us out of Peach Coulee one day, intent on getting at the fish we had in the livewell. If I shook the box to free anything stuck to the black innards, an old Hildebrandt straight-shank spinner might dislodge, along with a catfish that must have easily gone 40 pounds, which we chased around the lake for half an hour before it broke the line on a cypress knee. If I brush the insides of the box with my fingertips, I might stir the dust of memory, recollection of something I had forgotten and can't recall now.

But I don't turn it over, don't shake it or brush it. The fanned trays and open lids are enough, for there is a world of water contained in the bottom of that old aluminum box. Sometimes I feel like all of a lifetime could fit in there, does fit in there, like a treasure chest, or a hope box. Most of a lifetime is rattling around inside that old box, bumping against its component memories and events. I don't use the box; I don't use the fly rod, either, fearing that something might happen to either of them and I'll lose all my memories somehow. Such things as memories can't be bought, they can't be remade. In the house, in the greater sanctuary like a secret box inside a secret box, they're safe from forgetfulness.

Instead, I take my new graphite flyrod out of its canvas case while standing on the bank of a pond somewhere nearby and connect the ferrules of the two-piece rod. I strip out line, inspect the knot of the fly line to the seven-foot leader and the condition of the chartreuse popper with white rubber legs and black fuzz on the tail. Thinking of the child in the box and the old man to be somewhere on the stream winding ahead, I lift the rod and the line whips back, pushing through air which Abraham breathed in and Black Elk exhaled, then snaps forward and stretches out before me. A few false casts later the line is laid straight, leader out, and the popper is let still near a clump of submerged brush, submerged like the days gone down from my youth.

A bluegill rushes out of the brush and boils water around the fly, and the line snaps taut, and the rod bends, and for a moment, at least, he's standing over my shoulder, just behind, just out of my sight, and the circle comes 'round to where it began yet again.

Sacred Fires

After Crawfish made my world, and after the Creator peopled it, things began to change rapidly.

By the time the change was still far from complete, I was born into it. An Indian-Cajun, only child, son of Suns. My father was the last traditional chief of the tribe, and our first elected chairman. When he wasn't taking care of tribal business he was working at Columbian Chemicals where he breathed carbon black all day long and could not keep a car for more than three years before it rusted out. When not fishing in his spare time, he repaired fiberglass boats, made

Native American crafts, which involved much cutting of stone, built wooden boats and smoked King Edward cigars. The emphysema was inevitable.

As early as I can remember, we fished. Dad was never into sports. He grew up in a world defined by the Great Depression, on the streets of Ft. Worth, Texas, where his father had fled the poverty and hopelessness of the reservation to pursue dreams. Nicholas Leonard Stouff Sr. never stopped pursuing dreams, and eventually those dreams led him far away from his wife and two sons. Perhaps dad threw a ball to Uncle Ray to entertain him as a boy, perhaps they played a few games of softball on the streets of Ft. Worth, but by the time I came along, ball playing was only time away from fishing.

He came to the reservation only once as a teen. I don't know what he found here, don't know how to define it. It's something that can only be felt, perceived, but never described because it surpasses language. Dad was drafted to serve in the Army, and he went to Germany. He never saw action, though he always claimed that the Germans surrendered the day he was supposed to go fight. During his tenure, he was promoted to corporal. While working a cleanup detail in the yards, he noticed a scrap of paper the detail had missed, picked it up and threw it away. A lieutenant saw him and *poof*! Back to private first class. He was thankful for it.

While in Germany, he challenged himself to swim across the Danube. The current was so strong, he made the opposite bank exhausted, out of breath, and three miles downstream. He had to walk six miles back upstream to make it back to his unit. After the German surrender, dad was invited by his commanding officer to visit Dachau, but he declined.

When the war was over, he went back to Ft. Worth, spent a little time with his mother, and promptly moved to the reservation, never to live anywhere else again.

At the precipice of the Atchafalaya Basin from the protection levee at Charenton, the Beach is a destroyed Chitimacha village site. My father's people used the clamshell *rangia*, which thrives in brackish water, as cement. It was the Indian's concrete. Studies by anthropologists have suggested that it would take approximately 350,000 of the half-dollar sized clams to equal the nutritional value of one average deer. But the additional benefit of the clam was the material it provided for construction.

Dr. Jon Gibson, professor of anthropology and the premiere archaeologist in south Louisiana, told me once that I should think like folks have always thought. I was pursuing a degree in archaeology at the University of Southwestern Louisiana, with visions of graduate degrees and field work, never realized. But Jon Gibson made that impression on me early: People do what they've always done. Just differently.

If basket load after basket load of *rangia* shell is dumped along a lake shore or a bayou bank, as the Chitimacha did in hundreds upon hundreds of areas around their ancestral territory, Gibson said, "That keeps your feet out of the mud when you're at home. And it's sure easy to see a big ol' black cottonmouth crawling on that white shell going after one of your young 'uns."

People do what they have always done. Just differently.

The beach was the site of *Ama'tpan na'mu*, and a huge village it was. When the war with the French ended and the Chitimacha retreated into the swamps of Louisiana to vanish culturally and historically until about 1883, the village site—and incorporated burials—were leveled, and a huge dance hall constructed. It was the hot spot of west St. Mary Parish for many decades.

Dad was playing in Franklin in a band, a half-breed living it up with his Gibson guitar and singing country-western and blues, on the site of his Indian ancestors. This is adaptation as evolution intended.

A tiny little woman, jet-black haired and not weighing a hundred pounds soaking wet walked across the floor, and my father barked at her over the microphone. Yes, barked. This was 1947 in south Louisiana, what do you expect? She was furious. Several months later, Lydia Marie Gaudet married him.

"I found that woman working for old man Edwin, cutting cane with a cane knife out in the fields," he used to say, which would infuriate my mother all over again. Several months after my father died, she'd somberly tell the story, "He found me working for my daddy, cutting cane with a cane knife out in the fields."

Nonetheless, those early days were hard for them. Dad fished the lakes commercially, pulling seines and, when times were hardest, picking moss. He did carpentry work, and eventually found gainful employment as a stone cutter at St. Mary Granite in Franklin, until taking a position at Cities Service carbon black plant in Bayou Sale.

I was not born until 1964, during the rage of Hurricane Hilda. After all those years of marriage and no children forthcoming, my father's mother asked him, "Don't you think you and Lee ought to be...you know..."

"I dunno," Dad shook his head sadly. "I'm starting to think I might need some outside help, ma."

That ended the conversation abruptly. Nonetheless, I arrived riding the storm swell of a hurricane. Sherman Alexie once observed that there are some children who aren't really children at all, they're pillars of fire that burn everything they touch. And there are some children who are children of ash, and fall apart if you touch them.

I was a child of water, and wind.

Last Coup

Not far from home is a small pond I've been fishing regularly since last April when I first discovered it.

Nestled into a subdivision project, on the fringes of the area under development, it was hardly, if ever, visited by anyone other than me. Perhaps two acres and only about four foot deep, it was a magical, secret place, not far from the main highway but far enough to be unnoticed by those passing in cars. That was to end before long.

We came to be friends, this little pond and I. Full of small bass and the occasional respectable big boy, I could count on it for nearly guaranteed catches only five minutes from home. The fish were bold and brazen, unaccustomed to tackle, and they struck at my offerings with a zeal I had seldom experienced before. Even writing about it, I carefully concealed the location of my little sanctuary, but knew it would only be a matter of time before my secret would be out. Now and then, the errant jogger or four-wheeler rider would pass nearby and notice me.

But until this spring, this little pond and I had a perfect secret between us, a cherished, treasured thing to be turned over in the mind late at night and savored. I would go there after long days at work, desperate for peace, and the small bass would answer my plea eagerly, almost obligingly. In a year of fishing it, I learned its unseen contours, its moods and its personality. Few guests were ever invited to accompany me: Cousins from out of state, the most trusted of best friends, my girl. People I knew would hold this secret place to heart.

I guess I caught hundreds of small bass there, and a dozen or more very nice fish, a handful of true trophies. I often wondered if I had caught the same fish more than once, but near dusk on warm summer nights, the frenzied risings on the pond's surface verified for me that my little pond was abuzz with life. All were native largemouth, and all were isolated to this lonely pond on the edge of the subdivision's steady, relentless encroach. I used to stand there on the bank and watch the cars stream by to the west, aware of the creeping advance of utilities, concrete and manicured lawns to the east. These little fish gave me such joy, and I sensed a brotherhood with them. Their little pond reminded me of the reservation, the surrounding of it by industrialization and greed, and each struggling, frantic largemouth that I brought to hand reminded me too much of myself to not respect and empathize with it.

We shared quite a year, that little pond, its fish, and I. I could throw my bag and a couple rod tubes into the truck and be there in minutes, and the bass responded to my presence almost as if they knew it was a game, a counting of coup. They'd nip at my Clousers, roll at my muddlers, toying with me. They'd savagely attack my poppers and rubber spiders, bending my rod and making my reel sing. They'd ignore anything I offered some days, strike at the line-leader knot on others, just to infuriate me. I'd finally bring them to the terrestrial world, unhook them gently as I could, thank them for the coup, and release them. We knew each other as well as old friends, and when I'd pack my bag and tubes and walk away to the truck when the light was gone, they'd splash and strike in the darkness behind me, almost as if in farewell.

Or at least that's the way I like to imagine it. But in the end I betrayed them. In the end, I doomed that little pond and its occupants.

Of course people saw me. Of course they noted my rod, my tackle bag. There weren't many passing near enough, but word spread. The property is private, but the landowner cares nothing of who fishes there and who doesn't. This spring, my little pond has been overrun with anglers. Each time I pass there, there are people there, throwing tackle, with white five-gallon buckets or ice chests nearby. I know what they are doing. I know what they are holding inside.

There is the anger, that my sanctuary has been taken, but perhaps that just greed. There is regret, that I don't have that place, those childish, innocent large-mouth, to count coup with when I wish.

But worst of all is the guilt. The gnawing guilt that rests bent and cold in ice chests and five-gallon buckets, staring glassy-eyed and dead into a sky which will turn orange with dusk each night, prompting the fitful risings, the joyful striking at insects and minnows, but never to be seen again.

I find myself wishing I had never found it, never gone there, and those friends of mine would still be unmolested, unencumbered, free. When I can get there alone now, the strikes are rare, the rises infrequent. I cast and cast, hoping to feel redemption, even forgiveness, at the end of the tippet, but all I hook is regret. Where once I looked over this pond in the last moments of the day and I saw a microcosm of the magic of all earth's life, now I see only waste and greed. What estranged companions may still lurk, lonely and wary, in those scant few feet of water may see my offering pass them by, but turn away from it, betrayed.

Perhaps I'm making too much of it all. Sometimes I sound even to myself like a crybaby and a whiner. I have an entire river basin to fish, places to explore, waters enough for a lifetime. I'll never see them all, never cast into them all, never know all the occupants beneath them.

Still, the guilt chews at my bones with icy teeth. What I treasured most I destroyed without intending it. The path to hell is so paved. The delusion I cultivated and molded is being carried away in five-gallon buckets and ice chests, and there's nothing I can do to defend it.

The funny thing is, now, so quiet and still, the little pond feels even more like the reservation than before. It seems so much a reflection of a time I did not live, but exist within still. So quiet and still, the joy and magic of it evaporated, sliced down, mined, relocated, murdered and raped.

Soon I'll stop trying to go there, stop searching it with long lines and longing heart. I can't bear it much longer. In days long gone, my people thanked their kills for the sustenance provided to their families. In this way, the animal's spirit was appeased and the Creator knew the goodness of the hunter's heart. Perhaps, in this same way, I can ask for forgiveness of this little pond and its occupants.

It's the vanishings that hurt most. The ancient old growth cypress stands, the dried-up marshes and swamps, the dammed and gated canals; the absence of the wild muscadines, the yellow finches, black panthers and fragrant irises. And the ways of a life, of a people, of a man, who have no more place in this world anymore than a lonely, shallow pond dying one bucketful at a time.

May. Hummingbirds visit the feeder on my front porch, almost unreal they are, like fairies photographed against backlit aspens.

Their wings a blurred flurry, they poke their long beaks into the feeder's outlets, drinking long and savoringly of spring. The cat watches them, and I believe she can hear the dizzying flutter of their nearly invisible wings. When the breezes of May leap up suddenly, they drift alight slightly, but maintain their inertia.

Perhaps it was in May that a boy, rotund and bespectacled, set out to build a tree house in a big oak in the back yard. Borrowing a hammer and some old pallet lumber from my father, I nailed a haphazard, dangerous platform into the crook of two huge branches, some dozen feet off the ground. It was unstable and precarious, and my father made me abandon it, but he built me a small clubhouse in the back yard. I sat in there many times, surrounded by the smell of creosote posts which framed it to hold the corrugated metal walls, and never dismayed over the fact that there was no club. I was its sole member, the solitary occupant of this clubhouse, but with a box of dominoes or a stack of comic books, it was a sanctuary.

One of the many outbuildings around my grandparents' house was my grandfather's wood working shop, and he had a big old lathe in there. He'd turn wooden things, the manner of which I don't recall, and would let me sit on the bench with a small pocket knife and a piece of cypress to whittle things which invariably turned out to be toothpicks. Sometimes he would work on leather in his other shop, with punches and dyes, and he'd give me some scraps to toy with, which I'd turn into nonsensical items of wonder, valuable only to me, but I'd store them in my special club house for safekeeping.

In May, there would be festive gatherings of family for barbecues and crawfish boils, fish fries and cookouts. We'd all gather on the homemade picnic table with bench seats dad had made near the cinder block barbecue pit, the men would cook and fuss with the meat, the women would conjure bowls of bright yellow potato salad, sweet-smelling pork and beans. The children would scamper here and there, imagining we were super heroes or The Six Million Dollar Man, petting the horses or exploring the bayou side. The big pecan tree near the picnic table would bear gallons of fruit in the coming months, which I'd crack with pliers and nibble on during summer vacation.

Before the days of waste pickup, there was a big trash heap in the back of the yard which dad would burn regularly, but the accumulation of ash, metal and broken bottle glass had grown to huge proportions. Nearby, the horse stables were double-stalled, but in the years after the horses were sold I kept my first boat in one side, assorted junk in the other. My father's boat stayed in the boatshed connected to his workshop.

He built a 35-foot camp boat, a bateau hull with a large cabin on it. It took him many years to complete in his spare time, and during it's construction, before the hull planking was on, I'd explore its skeletal form, balancing awkwardly as a larger child does, on its ribs and keel. Its frames and chines were oozing brown Weldwood glue and speckled with galvanized nails. Sawdust lay in the lap joints and miters, to be slowly washed away by wind and rain. As the hull went on, it took form, and for years I'd sit on its bow deck, there in the yard, and imagine it sliding effortlessly through green-black lake water. More years passed, and the cabin took shape, then the aft deck and the interior details.

One memorable May, dad and a few of my uncles took a dozen or two round wooden fence posts and laid them out crossways in front of the boat. Slowly, laboriously, they rolled the big hull down to Bayou Teche in this way, over the fence posts, rushing those cleared astern back forward to continue the slow, steady trek to water. There it sat for another space of time until the outboard was installed, and I'd go down to the bayou and walk its rails, stand on its aft deck and wait for the journeys to begin. I'd bring folding chairs from the yard and sit on the back deck catching catfish and small bream.

There was, in May, talk of ghosts, like most times of the year among my kinfolk. I never feared them. I had no reason. They were only family, departed but still with us, as is our way. On the few acres of land that my parents and grandparents occupied, there were spirits in the crevices of trees, looking down from branches where shaky, abandoned tree houses were rotting away. They left murky footprints along the muddy edge of the bayou, and sifted through ashes in the burn piles, looking for memories. The echo of them reverberated in old barns where the chickens, cows and hogs were once kept, along the fence row of fallen posts and rusting barbed wire, between the forgotten bricks of walkways uncovered when digging for fishing worms or plowing the garden. I knew from an early age that I would never truly be alone.

There was a big rain cistern near the barn at my grandparents' house, and though I was forbidden to drink from it since it had been unused for decades, now and then I would crack open the faucet and sip when no one was looking. It was cool and fresh despite the disuse, and the taste of it conjured memories I had not lived, of May before piped-in water, before humming electrical wires and ringing phones. Like the old rabbit cages near the cistern, memories, falling into disrepair, their cypress frames separating at the joints, the wire rusting, legs collapsing. Like the old Sea King outboard motor under the back porch, its red paint bubbling and bursting with boils of rust, its prop long vanished; like the three or four passe partout in the barn, their teeth huge and ravenous and threatening. Memories of May before I was born seeped into my skin like cool cistern water, disused but still vibrant.

In May, all those outbuildings are gone save one small shop my grandfather used for his smaller crafts, which is my woodshed today. The yard looks barren and lonely. When I walk its measure, I try to distinguish the memories in my mind that I lived from those I drank from old rain cisterns and stirred from the dust of old chicken pens. The different between the two is becoming increasingly vague. They have coalesced, become singular. Though there are no rows and rows of flower pots on the back patio anymore, no muscadine arbor near the front porch, no pump house for the well water, no cistern and no brown rabbits, they exist as surely as the old people that tended them for all those decades. He in his straw hat and checkered shirt, massive of frame even at his age, wrestling with mending fences; her, always elegant and graceful, pulling clothes from the line, watering irises, calling for me to help her carry the basket and stay away from that dangerous old cistern.

May, and there are things to be remembered. Never let fade. Never surrendered. I walk the unoccupied lawn, resurrecting old sheds and workshops, conjuring rabbit pens and brick walkways from the silent earth. In May, remembering is like the taste of sweet sugar water to hummingbirds, and I suspend myself between the memories lived and those forged before I was born.

There ought to be a law.

A constitutional provision. An amendment. Something to keep bad weather restricted from weekends.

The preceding month and a half had been murder for me in terms of work. Finally seeing light at the end of the tunnel, I was so looking forward to a weekend of relaxation with a fly rod, chasing bream and bass out in the basin.

But the weatherman had a sad story to tell. A huge band of thunderstorms and associated cold front was on its way, don't you know, and there was an eighty percent chance of rain on Saturday and Sunday, with winds in the fifteen mile per hour range.

This put me in severely bad humor. To make myself feel better, I went and bought a bunch of tackle. I put all this in my bags and immediately realized I didn't have enough money left to pay the electrical bill. This is not uncommon for me. A man's got to have his priorities.

Between rainstorms on Saturday, I worked a bit on my boat and sulked. I kept checking the radar on the television, and the storm front was just getting bigger instead of diminishing. Later in the day, the forecast began calling for twenty-five mile per hour winds Sunday! Completely disgusted at this point, I just gave up the ghost.

I spent Sunday morning puttering around the shop and yard, but suddenly something occurred to me. There was hardly any breeze at all. In fact, the sky was overcast, and though temperatures had dropped a few degrees, not at all a bad day for fishing. I waited until early afternoon, decided the weatherman was a complete idiot, and headed out in the boat.

I arrived at a small canal off an industrial waterway, dodging huge, long barges and tugboats along the way. The water looked cleaner than I expected it to, but no sooner had a No. 6 Clouser hit the surface than a ripping gale of northwest wind pushed the entire boat into an overhanging clump of tree limbs. It took me five minutes to work myself out of the grasping branches, fighting the wind, and by the time I freed myself, I narrowly managed to capture my rod, which was still tangled in clutching limbs, before it went overboard. But I also noticed the boat was full of caterpillars after the incident, and promptly found a San Juan worm to let the wind place any spot possible except one that was wet.

Thus began a stubborn two hours of fishing in the wind. Trying to cast, light a cigarette, sip Diet Coke, mend line, keep the boat on course and out of the trees, set hooks on strikes, all this amounted to an exercise in futility which knows no comparison. I ended up resorting to spin tackle, which offered little improvement in strategic advantage. I did manage a few fish, though, and my girlfriend caught a few more than I did.

On the way out, the game warden stopped me to check for a fire extinguisher in the boat, and my fishing license. I offered up my license and showed him the extinguisher, noting that a fire didn't have a snowball's chance in hell in this wind. He also wanted to check the livewell. He probably didn't understand why I was laughing so hard when I opened it up for his perusal.

It was late evening by then, and the temperature was dropping. The ride home was invigorating, which is a macho way of saying it was cold as tarnation. It was one of those times when you just don't know if you want to cruise at low speed to cut down on the biting cold, or just open her up and get it over with. By the time I got the boat trailered, home, cleaned and stored away, I felt like I had been fishing all day, though it had only been a few hours. I collapsed to the sofa, exhausted, and turned on the tube, which was still on The Weather Channel, and the weatherman was promising, "It'll be a great weekend next time, sunny skies and no rain!"

I threw the remote at him and told him where he could tie his hackle.

There ought to be a law. No bad weather on weekends, and no predictions of great weather a week in advance after a weekend of torture. Don't think there's someone up there controlling the weather? Ha. There is, and he plays indoor sports.

There Were Giants In The Earth In Those Days

I sit, sometimes, and look out at the bayou running behind my house, marking the northern border of the reservation.

Bayou Teche, my father's people said, was created many generations ago when a huge snake attacked the Chitimacha Nation. It was so large its tail was at Port Barre, La., and its head near Morgan City at the junction with the Atchafalaya River.

Many warriors tried to destroy it. Many died. It took a massive effort of all the tribe's strongest men to slay the great serpent. It's great body lay there and decomposed, and water sought out the spot where it had compressed the earth in its death throes, forming the small channel. My father's people called it "teche" meaning "snake."

Geologists tell us that Bayou Teche was a former channel of the Mississippi River, that great wonder of rivers, which fanned across the Louisiana coast for millennia, creating the land upon which I now live. I do not doubt them. The Vermilion and Atchafalaya rivers were once channels of the Mississippi, we are told. I do not doubt this either.

But I likewise do not doubt that my father's people fought and killed a giant snake, or that the mighty Mississippi flowed down the course of the channel. The two are not mutually exclusive.

It is the inability to believe which astounds me sometimes, as I walk along the water's edge, watching small bream strike at bugs and chase minnows. I stand on the dock away from the bayou bank and watch the current take debris downstream, and I know an epic struggle took place where I cast my gaze. Spears and arrows whistled through the air, the shouts of warriors, the fearful shrieks of women and children. It's great head, diamond-shaped and tough, held eyes which fed upon chaos.

But it is far easier to believe in inanimate forces, the natural movements of the earth and its waters. I know that science can be comforting because people want to be comforted, want to apply order and definition to the world around them, to their lives. To believe that a miles-long snake carved out the channel of Bayou Teche takes away order, introduces uncertainty, conjures fear and danger.

Did a living, breathing serpent of flesh and blood attack the Chitimacha nation? In the collective consciousness of its people it did. In each village, around the campfires as the young listened in wide-eyed amazement, it did. In the generational memory of each passing on of the story, it did. Descartian reductionism seeks to lift the veil, reveal the wizard behind the curtain, and in so doing takes away the wonder of looking out at Bayou Teche and seeing a mind's-eye view of heroism, replacing, reducing it to the haphazard, mindless movement of water.

"There were giants in the earth in those days," we are reminded. Perhaps we study the skeletons of those giants in natural history museums, on educational channel documentaries of paleontological digs, and apply order, definition and Latin names to them. In so doing, the simple statement, "There were giants in the earth in those days," loses all its wonder, grows fat and cumbersome with elaboration. A world, which has grown so distant, so estranged from wonder, is a world turned two-dimensional. A world made anorexic and dull.

I want the wonder back. I have a plan to rescue it. I will one day take the boat from Port Barre to Morgan City. I will ride the spine of the great snake from tail to fang, noting where its vital organs might have fallen, where Chitimacha warriors might have concentrated their spears and arrows. I'll cross the Wax Lake Outlet that now intersects the Teche and make my way onward, until I reach the river, and hear the great rasping of its nostrils, the flick of its tongue.

Some of us refuse to shed the wonder. It doesn't matter how deeply we reduce it. It doesn't matter, because we choose to believe in it. We refuse to let go the wide-eyed gazes around campfires. We refuse to view this meandering, beautiful waterway as nothing more than an accident. The great villages of shell banks, with children playing along the water's edge, men pulling fish nets and traps, women making baskets, may be gone, but the memory of them survives with a giant snake and epic battles.

What can be so wrong with believing in a little wonder, of giants in the earth, and heroic struggles of humanity?

The Building of Boats

o o o o o o o o o o o o o o o o o o o o o o o o o o o o o o o o o o o o

"She floats upon the river of his thoughts."

—*Longfellow*

A Bateau, First and Foremost

My father was at his most content on the water. In 1962, two years before I was born, he constructed a twelve-foot bateau. Oak frames, Douglas fir plywood and a Mercury 9.8 horsepower outboard. His world was complete. He intentionally made it light enough that he could pick it up by himself and put it into the back of his pickup. He couldn't afford a boat trailer.

When I was about five, he took me fishing with my grandfather, Emile Anatole Stouff. During the quiet conversation out there on Lake Fausse Pointe, that part of *Sheti* which had been divided from Grande Lake by the Atchafalaya Basin Protection Levee, dad mentioned that the boat had a one-quarter inch plywood bottom.

Emile threw a conniption. "I can't *believe* you brought that baby out here on this lake in a boat with only a quarter-inch bottom! This lake *eats* boats, dammit!"

And so admonished, he took the boat home, laminated another three-eighths of plywood over the bottom, robbed the piggy bank, and bought a boat trailer, since the vessel was now too heavy to manhandle. This apparently appeased Emile, because the subject of dad taking me fishing never was brought up again.

The building of boats—and there were many—was inevitable. He was born of water, and the waters coursed through him. A boat is the medium by which men stranded by their Creator on the dry land return to the waters. A boat is a bridge, therefore, into grace, though tenuous. Man can never truly be one with the water. He may swim in it, or he may float along in this craft, feeling as near to it as he may be allowed, but in the end, we are still prisoners of the air we must breathe to live.

Yet a boat and water are only the beginning of an epic novel. Should it end there, the story would be but half-told. The boat also brings man closer to the terrestrial. To understand this, you have to see a man like my father but once. To see him, pressing at the water with a cypress paddle, moving the boat slowly, somehow ethereal, though a gauntlet of cypress trees, their knobby knees spiking from the water, Spanish moss draping them. To understand the purpose of a boat requires more than appreciation of its functionality. A boat, to some people, is merely a vehicle. It is a means to an end. It is not, in itself, a part of the destination, a component of the reward. For some, the boat is objectified, separate, apart from the boater.

For a man like my father, the boat is a facet of the whole.

There were many boats, all of wood. Even as early as 1962, fiberglass might have been an alternative, had he been able to afford it. But it was always wood, save for one aluminum boat he owned and disliked terribly. I am not sure why he even acquired it, but he used it very little and eventually it went to our family minister.

Perhaps due to growing up in a small wooden boat, I have no more tolerance for fiberglass or aluminum than my father did. I actually used the sixteen-footer more than dad did, but soon developed a bitter distaste for it as well. It was long and narrow, noisy, cold and lifeless. Powered by a thirty-five Mercury, it definitely made good speed to the lake, but once there, it was like fishing while riding in a coffee can. The lapping of the water against the aluminum was a tinny, reverberating sound which the lake itself seemed to shrink away from, much less the fish. If I dropped a pocketknife or bumped a gunwale with a paddle, the sound was irritating and bone grating. The feel of it was cold, even in summer.

That's not to disparage people who like fiberglass or aluminum boats. A boat, by its very nature, is a rare and wonderful thing. Yet wood has life. The feel and warmth of brightly varnished wood is quiet, contemplative and somehow sentient. Even painted, wood feels more attuned to the water in which it rests. A wooden boat was made of living things, save for its screws, nails and fittings. Its majority bulk is breathing, moving wood. Composite materials insulate us from the spirit of the waters—wood transfers it, a conduit, a medium. It's like listening to the sermon in a sound proof box.

To understand the love of a wooden boat is an epiphany. Many people who have ridden for the first time in one of my boats have been in awe of the feel of it, the warmth, life and glow of it. To understand that love is to float lazily along between the cypress and tupelo, when the lake water is so smooth it reflects in detail an endless sky. It is to touch a paddle to the water and feel a wooden craft respond without complaint; to cut through swells conjured by thunderheads, hear the oak and cypress groan and protest but remain fast, as if determined to bring its guest safely home no matter the cost.

That little boat is now forty-two years old, and solid as the day it was built, patient with my short comings, tolerant of my lack of mastery. It always brings me home because I always take care of it. It is no Whitehall, was never documented by Chapelle and there is probably not another like it extant. I sometimes wonder what will happen to it when I am gone. I hope that I can instill the same values in my sons that my father gave me, that they'll take care of it, that it will always bring them home. Perhaps they'll pass it on to their grandchildren.

The love of a wooden boat is a pure one. It is the love of art, craft, science and a bit of mysticism, all wrapped up into one rare and wonderful thing we too simply call a boat. It is far more. It is a conduit between the water and the terrestrial. Between its frames, floating along the rivers, in the cypress swamps, on the lakes, we are as near to balance as is possible.

Though there were often a dozen fiberglass boats in the yard awaiting repair, dad did that for money, for school clothes, things needed in the house, and of course, fishing costs. He worked on them and repaired them soundly, but they were, in the end, merely means to a greater end.

I can recall two other boats my father built: a thirty-five foot cabin cruiser on the same design lines as the little bateau, and a sixteen-foot version he made for someone else. The cabin cruiser was constructed over the course of a decade in the yard. My best school days friend and I would leap from its incomplete bow, pretending to be super heroes. When the boat was finally done, a couple of my uncles came and, using round fence posts, moved the big boat the one hundred and fifty yards to Bayou Teche.

They lifted the boat with jacks and placed a dozen round fence posts under the flat bottom. With a mighty heaving and pushing, they rolled the boat forward. As fence posts cleared after, they would pick them up and run them around to the front of the boat so its roll toward the water would continue. It was slow, laborious, but inch by inch, the big boat made it to the bayou and grace.

We emerged from the channel into the lake proper early on a Saturday morning. I was still yawning, but full of anticipation of a great day of fishing, the two of us. Dad sat at the stern, his straw hat flapping in the wind, guiding the boat across the water, and I sat forward, holding the bowline.

A mist, a quilt of illusion, covered the lake and it seemed we were moving through a thin layer of cloud rather than water, but the sun peeking over the cypress trees was already burning it away. Dad brought the boat into a deep cove and stopped the engine, letting us drift toward the trees while we switched seats.

I was maybe seven, eight. I could bait my own hook by that time, something I was very proud of. I had a difficult time, still, casting it into the water and not into the trees, but I kept trying. There were oatmeal crème pies in the little ice chest and drinks. I always had to bring oatmeal crème pies when fishing, it was a prerequisite.

Nick Stouff was not into sports, so consequently neither was I. We spent all our best times on that lake, the one our ancestors called *Sheti*, in that old boat which wasn't so old at the time. Whenever I think of him, I think of that old boat first and foremost.

That day, he was particularly attentive to the weather. "Got to watch it out here," he said a million times to me. A billion times. "That lake will rise up on its hind legs and eat boats." But it would never hurt a Chitimacha, he said. That was an ancestral promise.

That day, though, a summer squall formed north of the lake, so quickly and so mysteriously that it took him completely by surprise. We were fishing on the north side of the lake, in the trees, and he couldn't see the horizon to note the approaching storm. Within brief moments after he said, "Pick up, it's time to go," the wind had reached out for us, the sun had hidden behind black clouds, and the lake was coiling upon itself to strike, like a serpent.

The old Mercury fired up on command, and he pointed the stern toward the channel that would lead us safely home. But we were far across the lake, and the water was a lunatic genie freed from a thousand years of imprisonment. We catapulted into the fray, making for the channel.

I had donned my life jacket at his order, and clung tightly to the bowline with one hand and the seat with the other. The boat, only twelve-feet long and with low sides, flung itself into the storm. Beyond the crest of every growing wave, it slammed down into the valley between them hard, jarring me, but there was little spray over the rails. Then it would climb the next, and as I looked southward, toward the channel, my heart sank at the number of waves between here and there, and the ferocity with which they were growing.

The lake raged that day. If I live to be a hundred years old, I'll never forget the fury with which it raged, as if it were saying, *Never forget that I am the master. I was here before your grandfathers ever touched these lands. I have been dammed, re-directed and your levee cuts through my heart, but never, ever forget, with one breath of my wind, one fall of my waves, I can send you far, far beneath me.*

I looked back only once. Dad clutched the starboard rail with his right hand and the tiller arm of the motor with the other. All his knuckles were white. His face was a mask of intense concentration, and the muscles in the arm that guided the motor were tight springs wound to the hilt as he grappled between the sheer exertion of keeping the boat from flipping or being deluged with water, and the delicacy and finesse of guiding it along the specific course he demanded.

Looking at him like that, I saw fear on my father's face for the first and only time in my life. I could hear that warning in my head above the roar of the wind and the crash of the waves and the steady scream of the outboard: *That lake will rise up on its hind legs and eat boats.* And it was doing just that.

Halfway across the lake, the waves had swollen so massively that, in the valleys between them, we could only see walls of water surrounding us. Dad would gun the Mercury then, climb the slope of a wave at full-throttle, and just at the crest before the boat slammed down, he'd pull the throttle back and let it follow the down slope of the swell as gently as possible...then, at the bottom, he'd repeat the entire process.

The rain had come by then, drenching us. Sometimes, no matter how dad tried, the lake refused to be predicted, and it would throw up a wave out of symmetry, alter its shape just a tad, and the boat would crash into it: I heard the sound of creaking frames, tackle boxes and fishing poles and paddles leaping across the inner deck, the feel of my bones rattled inside me with the impact.

We were coming up the slope of one swell, the Mercury screaming like a banshee, when suddenly a huge log emerged from the green-black water. Dad wrenched the motor around, which sent the boat climbing the slope sideways, and it crested the wave that way, and I was sure we would capsize then, but he slowed the engine back to idle for just a split second—just enough to let the bow swing back forward, then spun the throttle to full as hard as he could, and the boat righted itself at once. The log passed so near to us I could have reached out and touched it. It was half as big as the boat, and would have come straight through the hull if we had hit it.

Then, all at once, the channel was there.

The waves subsided somewhat at the mouth, but he kept pushing forward, until we were deeper within the channel, and at last the water had settled to a moderate chop. I glanced behind, and he was glancing behind as well, and out the mouth of the channel, the lake was rising, rising up on its hind legs, raging in the throes of chaos.

And as *Sheti* continued its fury, I knew the promise had been kept. Like a parent after scolding a child, it whispered gently: *I will never harm your people. I may remind you of my power, but I will never harm Sheti imasha…*

We got home that day, tired, frightened, but alive. At the house, he dismissed me to go inside, get out of the rain, warm myself—he would take care of things. I walked to the house, but stopped short of the front door and went back to the boatshed where he had just put the boat.

I found another sponge and dry rag, and began helping remove all water from inside the boat. New words were in my mind now, words he had also repeated to me a million times: "Take care of her, and she'll always get you home." And we didn't say a word, he and I, while we cleaned and dried that wooden boat in the shed that day.

We didn't talk about taking care of things, or lakes that rise up on their hind legs, or promises. Especially promises. For there had been three promises kept that day, I realized so many, many years later. The promise of taking care of things, and they'll be there for you. The promise of that ancestral lake to my people.

And most of all, the promise that if we remember, if we store them in that special place close to our bones, no modern trinket can replace true treasure.

There were half-dozen fishing poles in Pa Biz's workshops, and a couple of tackle boxes. He had a boat with a 1957 Wizard seven and a half on it, both of which would be mine eventually, and a decrepit old Montgomery Wards Sea King under the back porch. Other than the fishing trip with dad and me where he thew a conniption about the quarter-inch boat bottom, I don't recall him ever going fishing in my lifetime. I am told he was quite the fisherman in earlier days, not quite my father's caliber, but passable. Perhaps the crippled leg slowed him down as he aged.

When that big cabin boat was built, every other weekend the Stouff family would climb aboard and dad would navigate us down Bayou Teche to the cut which led to the borrow pit beside the levee. That cut ended up at Lake Fausse Pointe, where we'd spend the whole day, sometimes on the lake proper, tied up to a big cypress tree, sometimes in Grand Avoille Cove, *Co'ktangi.* On one such outing, my grandmother, in her late sixties by then, fell overboard. Dad was about to jump in after her, but she promptly stood up in the waist deep water, holding a long, muddy piece of wood, shouting, "Look what I found!" We were never sure what it was: About four feet long, cypress, obviously intended as some kind of tool or jig.

I don't recall ever staying overnight. Dad wanted to, but the women folk did not. I would have loved to do so, there in that home built cabin boat. There were four bunks, and I could have slept on the floorboard. But we never did. Instead, we moored to a cypress tree and we fished with corks and worms, or dad would pull the bateau behind the cabin boat and he and I would depart for a few hours. In the afternoon, the men would drink beer, but never so much as to disregard safety. We watched owls perch in the trees.

When I was a kid, not many people fished Lake Fausse Pointe. Dad wanted to keep it that way. He told me we were fishing at the North Pole, and if I was careful, I might see Santa. If anyone asked me where my dad and me went fishing, I told them the North Pole, and I'm sure they wondered if I had a condition of some kind.

Once I became a teenager, I begged long and loudly enough that my father let me take out the cabin boat with some friends, and we stayed overnight. On the way home, though, we struck a log and made a bread loaf sized hole in the bottom just above the curve of the bow. By throttling the engine up to full, I was able to keep her nose high enough to make it home. Then I had to tell my father.

Luck was with me that day. Dad was building the Baptist church in Charenton with the minister, Rev. Bobby Hodnett. I went to the church to tell him what happened. He turned bright red, but no fountain of expletives followed. By the time he got home, his anger had faded and over the next weekend he fixed the boat. We sold it shortly thereafter.

The last boat I remember my father building was when I was a teenager. It was a sixteen-foot version of our little bateau. By that time, I was trusted enough to take the bateau out on my own on rare occasions. My grandfather's 1957 Wizard outboard on my boat had caused us considerable trouble at one point when my best fishing pal and I were dying to get to the lake. Dad worked on it and worked on it, but could not get it running. I begged to take his boat, and in the end, I received a vote of what I considered half-trust: He took the Mercury off and put it on my boat.

With this increase in horsepower of about five, my boat moved a bit faster and pulled to the right much harder. By the time we reached the lake, my left arm hurt badly from trying to keep a straight course. But we fished, and that was what mattered. Upon returning home, boat full of bream, dad had the Wizard running again, and it was another year before we had more trouble with it.

That time, he said, "Take my boat."

I did, and there were no mishaps. But dad bought me my own Mercury 9.8 that week. I think spending the money was preferable to allowing me the use of his boat by far.

I would like to say I hovered over him and watched, learned, became familiar with the task of building that last boat. I would like to say I learned a lot from that last project. I did not. I watched it come to shape on my way to the Mustang that carried me to town for girls and movies and friends. One day I returned home and it was gone, away to its new owner, and my father cleaned up his tools and put them away as a boat builder for the last time. I learned that within a few years it was gone, fallen into rot from neglect, treated like an aluminum or fiberglass boat.

People came from all over the state for boats from his shop. Bateaus almost exclusively, though he built some pirogues as well. Rev. Bobby Hodnett, as near and dear as any family to us, said, "Your father could see what was right with a boat. He had the eye. He could look at it, and by instinct tell you what was right and what was wrong, what would work and what would not." That, I think, is the instinct that comes from being people of the lake.

Richard Bode wrote in *First You Have to Row A Little Boat,* "The truth is that I already know as much about my fate as I need to know. The day will come when I will die. So the only matter of consequence before me is what I will do with my allotted time. I can remain on shore, paralyzed with fear, or I can raise my sails and dip and soar in the breeze.

"I was the beneficiary of their collective genius. This boat, an amalgam of mechanics and music, was the highest gift within their power to pass down the ages to me. When I knew that, I also knew the truth about creation. Many lives, going back thousands of years, had gone into the making of my sloop, just as many lives, going back into time unknown, had gone into making of me."

I built no boats with my father. It is my only major regret. I built two boats, eventually, and will build again, and a more minor but no less significant regret is that he did not see me do it, or see the result. But in the building of boats, the legacy out there in the swamp, the flame I am searching for, burns on.

While I feel fortunate that I have done all that I needed in the proper perspective, a few things remain, a few opportunities missed. One of those was building a boat with my father.

A good friend of mine and his step-dad built a boat which I had been hearing about during the construction. I went by the see it.

There it was, sitting on the trailer, not quite done, all shiny aluminum, just a little touch up work to be finished. But by thunder, it looked like a boat, and pretty yar, too. If a boat has good lines, seems to exude agility and speed, it is yar. They slid his Mercury outboard on it, and it suddenly became a thing to be reckoned with. My dad owned nothing but Mercury in his life. "Take care of it, and it'll always get you home," he would say. "It's like a Swiss watch." At five years old, I had no idea what a Swiss watch was, or what it had to do with the black, gleaming chromed 1963 Merc 110 on the transom of the boat, but the fact that it always started on the second crank and it always got us home made the proper impression on me.

He said the same thing about the boat itself. In retrospect, I think I grew up in that boat. I can't imagine having become who I am today without that little wooden boat. I used to joke that if somebody would have come up to us on the lake with a gun and said to my dad, "Either the boat goes or the kid does," I'd have drowned.

He built it two years before I was born, and after that built a few more for other people, but other than a big houseboat, that was the last for himself. For us. He tended to that boat meticulously, making sure every drop of water was out of the corners where ribs met chines and battens. "Take care of it, and it'll always gets you home."

I talked for years about him showing me how to build a boat. Of course, something always got in the way, something far less important in hindsight was far more pressing then. After he retired, he would spend his days on the lake, or just behind the house in the bayou with that boat. I began to see it as a cornerstone of our lives together. That and the workshop. The old house had been replaced with a new one, the furniture changed, cars were sold and different ones parked under the garage. But that workshop was always there and the boat was always there, always waiting quietly, always ready to go when we were, when he was.

Early, he would move us around the lake with the paddles he had made himself. Later, an electric trolling motor took up most of the work. While I was struggling to untangle my fishing line from a tree limb, he'd pick out a spot the size of a dime and place his lure exactly on it.

I remember the feel of it so well. How it would slide effortlessly through the water, me on the front bench seat, him at the motor in the rear. Turning, accelerating, decelerating, on mirror-smooth water or waves, that boat became part of the water, coalesced with it.

"Respect that lake," he said time and time again. "That lake will get up on its hind legs and eat boats. But it won't hurt a Chitimacha, as long as you respect it. The lake knows us." I remember exactly the way the boat would bob ever so gently as we fished our way along through the cypress, him paddling with one hand, casting with the other. I remember each time at the end of the day, when I was tired and sore and cranky, how he'd start the Mercury and point the bow toward home, and how when we disboarded at the landing to my great relief, he always looked sad, mournful, like he had left a part of himself somewhere behind.

When his health began to fail, when he could no longer draw the breath needed to handle the boat in and out of the water, it sat in the shed and waited. He could still work in the shop, making violins and Native crafts, and I would now and then talk to him about building a boat, but it just never happened.

Still later, when the shop itself became his lost sanctuary, and he moved his craft making into the spare room of the house, when the oxygen machine arrived to become a permanent fixture, I said he could sit outside under the garage and tell me what to do. He always agreed, but...there's always "but", isn't there?

One weekend, my cousin was visiting from Texas. We decided to go fishing, but the Mercury wouldn't start. It had sat up for too long. We worked on it all day, dad out there with us, short of breath, haggard and pale in the heat, but passionate about getting the engine to fire. It was his Mercury, after all, and for it to not run was both unthinkable and abominable. By the end of the day, by tweaking it in the spots only he knew about, it was purring contentedly on the transom, and he was more than satisfied.

Sitting around the living room that night, the fishing trip abandoned for it was then too late, I mentioned how when he did show me how to build a boat, I could put the plans on my laptop computer and save them for the future. It sounded like a great idea.

Then one day he was gone. Gone, and there was no boat.

I built one, eventually. I took the dimensions off his and replicated as best I could. It wasn't bad, but it wasn't his. Meanwhile, I retrieved that beloved old boat from the shed and, over the following year, carefully revitalized it. Thirty-eight years of paint came off and was replaced by new varnish. The hull was smoothed, faired and repainted, the seats replaced. A new stainless steel rubrail and a new outboard finished it off. The old Mercury is still there, awaiting its own restoration.

This weekend, I rolled the boat out and began the final steps to return it to the water. Bring it home. A wooden boat will die out of water, as I will die away from home for too long. Its bones will grow brittle and break, its skin shrink and shred. It is as much a part of the water as I am a part of the land and the lake here.

So I wrote all this for my friend. Not for my dad, or for me. The pride in my friend's work is evident, the caring and attention he expressed in the construction of his boat is clear. It will serve him well, for it was built with a passion that seldom exists in the world any longer, and that is a sad, miserable loss.

But most importantly, he has an experience I missed, and one I hope he'll treasure forever. Every time he steps into that boat, every moment he spends in it on the water—in that great sanctuary—he will remember the two of them building it, forming its lines and curves from raw materials, pouring not only their skill and sweat into it, but their hearts as well. You can tell a boat that was built that one from one that was just built, just utilitarian, just an object.

There are lots of people in the world who build lots of things, including boats, but the best boats are those built like his and my dad's.

Take care of it, and it'll always get you home.

The First Boat

I think I accidentally built a boat one weekend.

Well, not all of a boat. Maybe just under half of a boat. But anyway, it all happened by accident.

Building a boat by accident is a lot like getting pregnant by accident. You pretty much know the process involved toward the final result, but it's a maybe-it-will, maybe-it-won't kind of venture. You just kinda hope for the best.

It all started out as a whim. A flight of fancy. A wild hair. I had been thinking about it for years. What I wanted to do was duplicate the boat I inherited from my father. I don't need another boat, but I was curious to see if I could do it. They say that talent like that skips a generation—it that's the case, my son will build a boat and I'll end up with firewood.

The original boat is a 12-foot bateau, wood, constructed in 1962. My dad had been building boats for years, but when he built this one, he said to himself, "That's it, it don't get no better than this." Dad's boat was intentional. Mine is accidental. It started with an accidental trip to the building supply store. Making an accidental trip to the building supply store is like making an accidental trip to Mexico City on your way to church. One accident generally leads to another, of course, and I proceeded to accidentally buy enough fir framing and plywood to accidentally load into the truck and take home.

Now, what I intended to do during all this was finish painting the front trim of the house. But what I ended up doing was using dad's boat as a guide, taking measurements. I had seen him build enough boats to remember many of the basic steps, those being in rough order:

1. Cut wood to various necessary lengths to build the ribs and other framework.
2. Test each individual piece for proper fit before gluing.
3. Lay ribs out and join to chines and sheer to form the hull shape.

Of course, it's not my style to mimic, even a master, so I applied my own individuality to the process so that the accidental boat would be distinctly mine.

1. Cut wood to various necessary lengths.
2. Test each individual piece for fit before gluing.
3. Recut one third of the pieces that were too long.
4. Recut another one third that were too short.
5. Lay ribs out and join to chines and sheer to form the hull shape.
6. Realize that I have no idea what order the ribs go in from fore to aft, so go back and measure the originals to figure it out.

Next I intended to cut the grass over the weekend, but on my way to the lawnmower, I accidentally started drawing out the transom on the plywood. Dad's transom was two inches thick, but he never intended more than a ten horsepower engine on it. I opted for three layers of plywood, for a total of two and a quarter inches, to accommodate the fifteen horsepower outboard I have, with more bracing to the sides, bottom and deck.

This took most of the day, but by nightfall I had accidentally framed the ribs and joined them to the chines, and the think looked something like the upside down skeleton of a dinosaur. I then intentionally went to bed.

Sunday I intended to take it easy. I was going to wash the truck, have dinner with my mom, and spend the afternoon watching the tube or something. But at daybreak, I accidentally picked up a saw instead of the water hose, and began shaping the newly glued transom to fit. As it turns out, the only thing I did which I intended to do was have dinner with my mom, and after that, on my way to the sofa at home for a nap, I took a wrong turn and ended up back in the workshop.

Without intending to, I ran the sheers along the ribs and mounted the transom. Before I knew it, the shape of a boat had emerged and as I was walking past the workshop on my way to supper, I suddenly saw it.

There it was. Skeletal, bare, but it looked like a boat. It was like finding an abandoned car in the desert. I had to sit down for a minute and wonder how it got there. It was then that I realized I had made a mistake. Despite all my best intentions to paint the trim, wash the truck and cut the grass, I had accidentally started building a boat. Curious, I took a closer look and was impressed. The fits were okay, not perfect, but okay. The joints were fairly tight, though they could have been tighter, but it was all an accident, remember? It actually looked like a naked version of dad's boat, with was sitting a few feet away, looking jealous.

I'm sure the neighbors think I'm accident-prone. I guess I am—building a boat under the workshop while half the trim on the house is blue and the rest is green, with a dirty truck in the drive, weeds sprouting in the lawn and some serious napping gone unattended.

The time has come. This weekend we set sail. Well, not sail, exactly. My new homemade wooden bateau does not come equipped with a sail. A Johnson 15 horsepower outboard, not a sail, will power it. But you get the idea.

I won't be smashing a bottle of champagne over the bow, either. Perhaps a bottle of Diet Coke, but not champagne.

After a couple of months of piddling with it in my spare time, I'm ready to launch. The bottom paint should be good and hardened, and we'll negotiate it onto the trailer, drop it in the bayou and determine the following:

1. Whether or not it floats. I'm reasonably certain it does, because I left it uncovered recently during a rainstorm, and it held water. Therefore, using the Law of Reversible Situations In Boatbuilding By A Rank Amateur, if it holds water in, it should hold water out, right?

2. Whether or not it floats level. I did my best to construct the boat straight and fair. However, I was dismayed to be told by another boatbuilder recently that, "It's not that it needs to be level, it needs to be plane." I have no idea what plane means. I have decided the fella must have thought I was building an aircraft, not a boat.

3. Whether or not the transom will support the weight and torque of the motor. I don't think this will be a problem, either. After the construction was done, but before the epoxy and paint, I nudged my truck up to the front of the boat, which was sitting on the frame which rested on saw horses, and just barely touched the bumper to the bow so it wouldn't move forward. I then went behind the boat, scooted up the garage wall, and proceeded to kick the pecan out of the transom. I kicked it hard as I could. Upon inspection, I found no sign of structural damage, so I kicked it harder a few more times, and still so sign of problems.

4. Lastly, whether or not it drives straight. The first boat given to me was a wooden bateau and it was slightly askew on the bottom, so it always pulled to the

right. Driving it with an outboard was like driving a car in need of a front-end alignment. It was exhausting, but it sure built up the biceps.

I'm eager to get it into the water. All told, if I add up the total hours I have invested, I could probably build another in under a month. I'm already preparing to do this, in fact, this one a cedar-planked pond boat. I've got a waist-high stack of cedar that's just crying to be a boat. I keep arguing with it, telling it that it's going to be a cedar box, but it won't listen. Cedar is stubborn that way.

I built a lot of stuff in wood. But none give me greater joy than a boat. There's just something about building a boat, something more satisfying, something more real, and right. Especially for someone who grew up on the water, whose ancestors were lake people for thousands of years. For people like us, there is no greater sense of belonging.

Boats have been a part of human culture since the beginning. Noah, the first boatbuilder on record, for example, built one heckuva boat. It is not known whether or not Noah kicked the pecan out of his boat, but it supported the weight of all those rhinos and elephants and all, so we have to assume he did a pretty good job. And he was an amateur, like me. The Titanic, by comparison, was built by professionals.

I will, of course, be wearing a life jacket. It's just good boating principle. Oh, and I'll be on vacation when I launch, so don't worry if you don't hear from me. I'll probably be fishing. Or something. And one more thing, if you see any smoke rising from behind my house next week, don't worry about that either. I might be burning a little firewood over my vacation. Roasting marshmallows and hot dogs, picking off the flecks of epoxy and paint before eating them, of course. Just don't ask me how the launch went.

Well, I did it. Sunday morning, I woke up and made a pot of coffee. I sat down to watch Norm Abrams, check my email and let Patches stretch and yawn in my lap for a little while.

Norm was building a really cool side cabinet, about the size of a side table, but with shelves and a door. I really liked it, but I knew I had many other things to get done, so after the coffee was gone, and Patches was sufficiently stretched and yawned, I put on my work clothes and headed for the shop.

Now, here's the way it happened. I want out of the back door of the shop with the bag of dog food to give Chance some breakfast, and as I glanced to the right, I saw the boat.

There it was, on the trailer, ready to go. I was going to do it Monday. But it just seemed right. I made careful plans. The idea of losing my new Johnson outboard if the boat's transom decided to abandon ship didn't make me very happy, no matter how much kicking the pecan out of it I had done. So I came up with an ingenious plan. I attached a long, sturdy rope to the engine, and at the end of that, about ten feet of string, and at the end of that, an empty milk jug, tightly closed. Therefore, should the motor decide to take a swim, the jug would float and I'd be able to find it and pull it back to the surface, assuming I survived the entire incident.

Now, the idea of losing the engine brought to mind the prospect of losing myself overboard, so I found my best lifejacket, made sure the fit was proper and so forth, and loaded it into the boat, too. A paddle made the expedition complete.

I didn't tell anyone I was doing it. I didn't want to get anyone nervous, and I didn't want an audience. People keep asking me if I've tried out the boat yet, and I just kinda kick at the ground with the toe of my shoe, put my hands in my pockets and mumble something about being so dadgum busy these days, and it's been so hot, and what with all the trouble in Iraq going on, well, you know...

I drove it to the boat slip behind my mom's house and, being very careful to avoid detection, backed the trailered boat into the water. I pushed the boat out, keeping a good grip on the bowline, and climbed aboard.

Initial inspection revealed a small leak astern. I had kinda expected something like that. It could be fixed. After a few minutes, though, the wood swelled up and the leak stopped.

Now it was time. I guess I wandered around the length of that 12-foot boat several times, theoretically looking for more leaks, structural stress, etc. I knew I was just putting off the inevitable. Finally, I positioned the milk jug and line so that it would flow out if need be, donned my life jacket and fired up the motor.

Off we went, my new boat, lifejacket, milk jug, paddle and I, just idling along. I checked for more leaks, found none, checked for stress problems, still found nothing. I brought it up to half-throttle. No problems. So bracing myself, I hit the gas.

Up and down the bayou we went, fast then slow, turning, putting as much stress on the transom as I could and guess what? She held together.

My neighbor, cutting grass in his back yard, caught my eye and I waved my arms triumphantly. He waved back. I must have looked like some kind of gleeful idiot, but I didn't care. The boat was in the water, and the outboard and me were pretty much out of the water, and that's all that mattered. She held together.

So I really don't know what everybody was worried about. I knew I would be okay. I knew it all along. Ah, ye of little faith.

I've been considering building a pirogue for some time now, a trial run so to speak. I have a pirogue that my dad built, hanging in my garage, that I can take the dimensions and lines from. However, the thought of a pirogue gives me a shudder.

Back many years ago, my fishing buddy and I decided we wanted to fish some of the ponds we couldn't get to with the boat and trailer, so we loaded dad's pirogue into the truck and went drop it into an appealing pond.

Now, entering a pirogue is the first step in a series of harrowing experiences. The first person has to board and make their way to the back seat, walking in this vessel which, despite the fact that you know it is 14 feet long and 30 inches across, has just taken on all the characteristics of a log in a river. It rolls and bucks, threatening to plunge you into the pond, until all you can do is drop to your knees and pray for your life, which amazingly stabilizes the pirogue, so you crawl to the back seat as carefully as you can.

Then the second person has to enter, but now your weight in the stern has further destabilized the pirogue and watching him get to the front seat, turn around and sit down is rather like watching a man on a high-wire. At last you're all settled in, and you realize you left the tackle box on the bank, and have to decide whether to go back for it or just fish with whatever tackle is already on the rod. We decided to use what we had.

However, the beer had made its way to the middle of the pirogue. It's important to note that my friend remembered the beer, but forgot the tackle box. Go figure. A man's gotta have his priorities. I do not drink beer if I am boating, but I don't disdain those who do, if they remain sober. But whoever said, "Beer and boating don't mix," undoubtedly had a bad experience with a pirogue. It wasn't so much the drinking of the beer that caused the problems, it was the reaching back to the middle of the vessel to open the ice chest, retrieve a beer, close the ice chest and return to a semi-upright position without causing a major maritime disaster.

The first cast was mine. I reared back and pitched my lure as I normally would, which sent the pirogue into spasms of rolling and lurching so much that water spilled in over the side, ruining the ham sandwiches and chips. My pal's cast was a little better, having learned from my misfortune.

So along we fished, and finally, my friend's cork suddenly shot off across the surface of the water.

He looked at me. I looked at him.

"What should I do?" he asked.

"I dunno," I admitted.

"Should I jerk?"

"Don't you *dare,*" I warned. Just talking about it was making the pirogue start to roll.

"But we're here to fish," he protested.

"I know that, but if you jerk, what's gonna happen?"

He jerked anyway, and the pirogue rolled, water slopped in, and my shoes were soaked.

"I thought you weren't going to jerk?" I yelled.

"It's okay," he said. "I missed him, anyway."

"Jerk," I said, but he thought I was still complaining about his fishing-in-a-pirogue technique. "You ready to go home?"

"Yeah."

"I got some fish in the freezer," I noted.

"Sounds good to me."

So we went home and thawed out fish and fried them for supper. I haven't been in a pirogue since. But that's fine. That doesn't have to stop me from building them. I see folks comment on pirogues they have built on the web sites that offer plans. "Great boat! So light! Can go anywhere in it! I love my pirogue!"

I just shake my head in wonder. But then, there are people in the world who throw themselves out of perfectly good airplanes; people who climb rocks straight up without ropes; people who bungee jump and people who wrestle alligators. I'm sure to people like these, fishing from a vessel that has all the characteristics of a greased eel is child's play.

So I guess I'll build a pirogue, and if it comes out okay, I'll give it to some poor fool as quickly as I can. They, you understand, will have to test it out. I can build 'em, but nobody says I have to use them.

I will require a signed waiver of liability, however, in much the same way as if I gave someone a full-grown anaconda, a Ford Pinto, or a rocket launcher with a hair trigger.

Well, here it is the middle of the summer, and I still haven't started another boat.

No mahogany runabout is taking shape under the garage. No pirogue is rising atop sawhorses in the shop. Not even a rubber ducky in a bathtub is to be seen anywhere around my place.

I walked into a meeting I had to cover the other night, and someone inside saw me coming and said, "Here comes the boatbuilder!" I was grateful for the comment, but I started to realize then that I just barely qualify for that description.

Sure, I've built one boat, and I guess that qualifies me as a boatbuilder. But despite my vows earlier in the year, I still haven't started a new one.

Oh, my intentions were always good. But I think I've gone about the whole thing the wrong way. My first boat, you may recall, was built accidentally. I was about to do something else, and the next thing I knew I was building a boat. But this time, I *planned* to build one, and nothing's happening.

I told you, I get distracted. So I decided maybe to try reverse psychology on myself. I started to remodel the living room of the house. No boat emerged. I took up the task of cleaning out the storage building in the back yard. No boat was forthcoming. I built a patio behind the shop. Still not a boat to be seen.

Obviously, that wasn't working. So I went to the wood shed and picked out the best cypress I had to frame up the boat with and put it in the shop, leaning against the table saw. It sat there for three weeks. During that time, I started a nightstand at the request of a friend, put an air-conditioner in the shop (hey, this is *Louisiana*, for Pete's sake!) and built a new back porch on the house. After three weeks, I put the cypress back in the woodshed.

I dunno. I've had the plans for the runabout for over a year now. It's a 15-foot outboard model that the designer calls Zip, but I'll name it something else, like *Cheesehead* or *Patches II* or *Oops!* There's a 1958 Mercury 40-horsepower outboard for it in the garage, a classic old engine with enough chrome to blind you.

I think I'm intimidated. I never considered myself a "boatbuilder", I thought more that I was a "jackleg" as they call it, a "shadetree boatbuilder." Now, having been publicly called a boatbuilder, I'm like Peter Beagle's piano player who's in the middle of a magnificent concerto when he suddenly starts thinking, "How, exactly, am I doing this? What is the procedure? What will I do next?" and then, suddenly, he can't play anymore. I've thought too much, and worked myself into a corner of inaction.

So to make myself feel better, I read about boat building. Books about *real* boatbuilders; issues of *Wooden Boat* magazine; Internet articles and sites, and anything else I can get my hands on. I go to the boat building discussion boards on the Web and ask dumb questions about framing, planking, painting and so forth. I am in serious danger of becoming an armchair boatbuilder.

But I take solace in the fact that I am, apparently, not the only one. There are, according to *Wooden Boat*, about 8,000 wooden boats in the United States, from rowboats to yachts. That number is derived from state vessel registration records, classic boat society memberships and so forth, and does not include the unregistered bateaus, skiffs, rowboats and the like. So figure maybe 12,000, oh, give it 15,000 wooden boats left in the country.

But the circulation of *Wooden Boat* is 110,000! Only *Boating* magazine has more subscribers, at 200,000. So that means (using my usual fuzzy logic) that if you subtract the 15,000 total boats in the country, there are 95,000 people out there who either have an unregistered wooden boat, or are building one, or just enjoy reading about them.

I'm in good company, then.

Ah, well. Sooner or later, it'll happen. Building a boat is kinda like falling in love. You can't make it happen, it just does, whether you want it to or not. That's why, I'll bet, people who build or own wooden boats, or even just enjoy reading about them, are so obsessed. Like love, wooden boats are things of obsession, jealousy and heartache. They give you enormous satisfaction one moment and excruciating agony the next. They cannot, however, divorce you. Worst they can do is sink. They sometimes take you with them when they sink, though, so I guess that does make it rather like a divorce after all.

So I imagine one day, I'll head out to cut the grass and suddenly find myself with boat frames in the shop. I hope so, anyway. With my luck, I'll have it done and ready for the water in, say, January, and it'll be something like 20 degrees below zero and a blizzard outside, so I'll have to wait until spring to try it out. But no matter. At least it'll be done.

The Second Boat

This weekend, on Sunday, I decided with total conviction that I would not become a "gonna-do."

If you're not quite sure what a "gonna-do" is let me explain. In Native American culture, we are all quite familiar with the Wannabe tribe of Indians. Make that, the Wanna-be tribe. Those who "want to be" Indian because they respect and admire us so much. These members go on "vision quests" with grizzled old Indians to gain enlightenment into their souls, find their spirit guardian, learn their true names, all for the meager fee of $5,000.

A "gonna-do" is similar. It's the kind of person who says, "I'm gonna do this," and "I'm gonna do that," and end up never doing anything. I was in severe danger of becoming not an armchair boatbuilder, as I reflected earlier, but a "gonna-do."

So Sunday, I pulled out the plans and patterns for the mahogany runabout and set them in the shop. During the week, a buddy of mine who is good with outboard motors and had read my column lamenting my lack of boat building, emailed me and said, "I tell you what, I'll get that old 40 (horsepower) Mercury running if you agree to get started on the boat. How does that sound?"

Sounded like a deal to me, and I said so. So I hauled the 1957 Mercury Mark 55 E—"E" meaning "electric start", isn't that clever?—into the shop and onto a stand, where it sits awaiting my friend's arrival.

I found some good cypress and my carbon paper. Now, this isn't just any carbon paper, you understand. Most of us are used to carbon paper that we used to use to copy a letter on a typewriter. Remember typewriters? But this carbon paper is two-feet wide by 16 feet long, for making boat patterns. I was starting with a small piece: the breasthook.

Herein lies one of the difficulties of boat building in south Louisiana in that we have different names for everything in a boat. See, down here, we call the braces that run the width of the boat "ribs". Makes sense to me. But the proper term is "frames." The long pieces of wood that join the ribs to the bottom on both sides we call the "bottom stringers" but the proper term is "chines." The similar pieces of wood that join the sides to the top gunwale and deck we call the "top stringers" but the correct name is "sheer." The piece of wood at the front of the boat where the bottom, sides and deck all meet in Cajun lingo is the "head-block" but the boatbuilding term is "breasthook."

So I copied the pattern onto a three-quarter-inch piece of cypress and got to it. Now, you understand that a boat is not a piece of furniture. I built most of my furniture "Shaker style" which means clean, crisp lines and *no* fancy curves. I don't like curves, save the feminine variety. But a boat is a compilation of curves converging on various bevels arranged at different angles that come together to create this thing we simply call a "boat."

All these curvy pieces require me to use my band saw. Now, I think I'm a passable woodworker, and I've mastered all my tools. Except the band saw. If you have never seen a band saw, picture a sewing machine with a thin, sharp blade but about five times bigger, and you've got a general idea. Real boat shops have a similar tool called "the ship's saw" which is an enormous band saw about the size of a pickup truck and a blade about as wide as your hand. This would not even *fit* in my shop, so I have a band saw.

My earlier attempts at cutting curves on the band saw ended up in the trash can quickly enough that nobody would see how bad they were. I think the waste pickup people accidentally let one spill out of the dumpster one morning, though, because I saw them at the road laughing so hard they couldn't breathe.

After several vain attempts at cutting the breasthook on the band saw, and wasting enough cypress to make you wanna cry (this is known as a "wanna-cry" or a situation that makes you desire to shed tears) I called a friend of mine who is pretty good with similar tools.

"Am I just a complete and utter moron, or what?" I asked bitterly.

"That depends on the subject," he said. No, not really. I explained my difficulties, and we had a long discussion about the band saw, in which he patiently and kindly reassured me that my band saw was a great tool, and the chances are the factory-supplied blade was probably inferior, the saw itself was probably not set up and adjusted properly, and that he was sure it was a quality tool and it just needed some tinkering and practice and a better blade to make competent curves.

I learned later that when he hung up the phone with me, his wife asked, "What was wrong with Roger? He sounded upset."

To which my friend replied, "His band saw is a piece of junk."

"But that's not what you told him," the wife pointed out.

"I know, but sometimes you just gotta tell people what they want to hear."

He was just kidding, really. However, just for reference, "gotta-tell" is a situation where you must say something whether it is true or not. Like when your girlfriend or wife asks, "Do you think I'm gaining weight?"

In the end, and a trash can full of lumber later, I finally realized that using the band saw requires psychic powers.

I adjusted the saw by the book, and still messed up everything. But somewhere along the line, I started to realize that you have to *predict* where the blade is going to go *before* it actually goes there. This feat of psychic power applied, my curves started getting competent and lo! I stood there at last, the day shot to tarnation, my nerves frayed to shreds, but with a completed breasthook in my hands! Jean Dixon and Edgar Cayce should have been boat builders.

I had a barbecue at the house that evening, and I proudly showed my breasthook to everyone that came by, whether they were interested or not. I said, "This will be a boat someday," showing them the 20-inch by 9-inch triangular piece of wood. Someone remarked that it looked like a boomerang and wanted to throw it to see if it would come back, but I refused and asked them to please leave the premises before I called the cops.

So I am, officially, no longer a "gonna-do." I have started building the boat I have been talking about for seven months now. I have a breasthook. It's a good breasthook. As breasthooks go, it's a work of art, I think. I may submit a photo of my breasthook to *WoodenBoat* magazine, with a caption: "Apprentice boatbuilder Roger Stouff, Louisiana, built this breasthook for a mahogany runabout replica in a remarkable seven months, and has plans to build at least one set of frames over the upcoming seven months. He hopes to have the runabout completed by the year 2056."

Monday, I actually got into the shop and built the "transom knee!" That's the part of the boat that...oh, never mind. I'm too tired to explain it.

There are several great moments in the building of a boat. The first is called the "laying of the keel." That's when you...well, lay the keel. In the old days, this was cause for a party. However, in the old days, when there was no television, no Internet, no printing press, no radio, in those days the dog shedding was cause for a party, so there you go.

The next great moment in building a boat is turning over the hull. You must understand that most boat hulls are built upside down on a frame, then must be turned right side up to continue construction.

I had finally gotten the hull of my 14-foot 4-inch runabout epoxied and the bottom painted with three coats of bottom paint, and it was time to do the turning. I had two pals come over one Saturday morning, and we set about the task.

Now, turning over a 14-foot hull doesn't seem like a big deal, but for three guys, it's kinda awkward. One of us had to get underneath to remove the building frame while the other two held it up and chatted about the weather, football, the latest episode of *Ally McBeal,* whatever.

Of course, we faced the problem of the actual turning. I was fearful that turning it on its side would put too much stress on the frames and the plywood and crack one or both. So a great meeting of the minds then took place to determine exactly what to do.

It was obvious three guys couldn't turn the boat in mid-air. Other ideas came up.

"What if we run some two-by-fours from here to there and there to here," said one. "Then we could turn it on those."

"But that won't distribute the weight evenly across the space-time continuum," said the other. "That would probably cause a minor temporal rift, or at worst, a gravitational flux that would be irreversible."

None of us liked the idea of gravitational fluxes or temporal rifts, especially of the irreversible variety, so we scratched that idea. "How about if we run the two-by-fours this way, instead of that way?"

"Definite warp field distortion," one of us pointed out. "The dilithium crystals would fracture."

Now, all this time, I'm wondering how the heck the Egyptians moved 10-ton blocks of rock to build the pyramids and this one man down in Florida, I think, built a huge castle-like thing of gigantic blocks of coral all by himself, but three guys couldn't turn over a 350-pound wooden boat hull without resorting to witchcraft. Luckily, it was too early in the morning for beer, or the job might never have gotten done.

"Look, if we pick it up, take the building form out, walk it into the yard, we can then rent a crane, put straps under it, turn it over, set it back down, then put it back in the garage."

Nobody thought this was a good idea, since there were no cranes readily available in the neighborhood, and everybody knew I didn't have the money to rent a crane anyway.

Finally, one of the guys went inside to get a Diet Coke and came back and said, "Okay, the strongest part of the boat is the transom, right?"

That's where the engine mounts on the boat, and we agreed that is was, indeed, the strongest part of the boat.

"So we just pick it up, move it out into the yard, set the transom end down, roll it over on the transom, then set it down right side up."

The two remaining geniuses in this operation looked at each other, looked back at the idea-giver, then looked back at each other and said, "How did *he* think of that?"

It must have been the Diet Coke. A little Nutrasweet has a tendency to kick-start even the most troubled brain. Of course, in the long run, it causes memory loss, so there you go.

But it worked like a charm. A round of back-patting, congratulations and handshaking ensued, after which everybody stood back and admired our work. Not so much the construction, but merely the fact that three guys, one of which turned out to be something of an idiot-savant, had actually accomplished something on the order of the building of the pyramids.

Now, the point to all this is that the guy who came up with the brilliant strategy read my column of a couple weeks ago regarding my trip sailing, and my notion that I might build a 22-foot wooden sailboat one day.

Not long after that, I received the following email:

Hello there, Popeye,

Just one thing...when it comes time to "flip" the 22 ft. wooden sail boat...ah, I'm gonna be out of town that day-week-year but if you need some advice, feel free to call.

You know who.

Golly. With an attitude like that, the pyramids would *never* have gotten built.

Isn't it amazing how some people always just love to put a fly in the ointment?

As of this writing, I have virtually completed the actual construction of my boat. By that I mean the woodwork itself is done, with just a little detailing here and there to go. All that is left is painting and varnishing, mounting the hardware and engine, and awaaaaaaaay we go.

This Mardi Gras, when I had some folks over at the house to watch the Chitimacha Tribal parade, the boat was, of course, a center of interest. One person, however, had the nerve to ask the following question:

"Will it float?"

I was incredulous. Will it *float?* What kind of question is that? Isn't that what boats *do,* they *float?* If it doesn't float, it's not a boat, it's a brick.

Then it occurred to me that the question wasn't nearly so philosophical. The inquiry was not whether or not the object was, in fact, a boat, which by definition floats, but rather, was my craftsmanship up to par enough that it would, in fact, behave like a boat and not a brick.

Now I turned from incredulous to cranky. If I didn't think it would float, I wouldn't call it a boat, would I? I'd call it a brick. "Yes, this is my brick," I'd say to guests. "It's 14-foot four-inches long, made of cypress and mahogany plywood, and will be powered by a 40-horsepower Mercury outboard, straight to the bottom of the bayou."

Will it float. Jeesh.

But the unfortunate thing is that this simple, insulting question now has me second-guessing myself. Whereas before I was so confident in the quality of its construction, now I'm starting to wonder about little things.

Did I spread enough glue on the places where the sides and bottom butt together? Did I put enough screws? Will the cypress hold the screws? Come to that, are the frames solid enough, glued and fastened properly? Will the transom support the weight of the engine? How about that one screw that I put into the stem to hold the planking in place, the one that stripped out, so I dipped it in epoxy to give it some grip? Will it hold, or will the planking peel off like an orange skin?

Some people ought to just keep their mouths shut, you know?

Now that I'm less than a month from launching, pending any major disasters and good weather prevailing, there's a nagging doubt in my head, thanks to the question. Will it float?

When I built my first boat, which was a flat-bottom bateau, I put off launching it for nearly four months. When I finally got the courage to do so, it went this way: I took a length of chain, about 12 feet, and used a padlock to attach it to the engine. At the other end of the chain I tied about 20 feet of nylon twine, and on the end of that, I tied a milk jug with the lid firmly tightened. All this I coiled into the back of the boat.

So should the worst come to pass, and the boat fell apart on me, things would happen this way: The boat would sink. The milk jug would rise to the surface like a cork, marking the exact location of the engine. I could then pull up the nylon twine to the end of the chain and, with luck, at least retrieve a $2,000 outboard. That was the theory, anyway.

The boat didn't sink. It didn't fall apart, either. I felt kinda foolish for having gone through all that nonsense. I felt a little more foolish for having on two life vests, too, but nobody noticed. Nobody noticed, by the way, because I made sure that nobody was around to witness the event.

So here I am, a month or two away from launching this new boat, and apprehension is settling in.

You know, you build a piece of furniture, say a book shelf, and you know if it's going to work or not right away. If it stands up straight without falling over, if the shelves are all pretty level, if it doesn't come to pieces when you move it around the shop, chances are, it's functional. With a boat, how do you know until you get it into the water? Nobody comes up to you when you're building an armoire and asks, "Will the doors open? Will the drawers slide? Will the hanger rod break?" But build a boat, and everybody gets antsy.

"Fill it up with the water hose and see if any water comes out," someone said. I politely asked them to leave the premises before I called the cops.

"Beat it with a rubber mallet and see if anything comes apart," someone noted. I suggested testing the mallet on their head.

I had originally planned a proper launching, complete with a bottle of champagne to break over the stem (can you hear the questions now? "What if you break the bottle over the bow and the boat splits in half?")

But now, thanks to some Doubting Thomases, I have decided that I shall find the most secluded, out-of-the-way boat ramp available, and will launch all by myself. That will be the "unofficial launch." If all goes well, I'll hold the "official launch" later. I think I still have that chain, twine and milk jug.

One thing's for certain: If everything goes right, and it is in fact a boat and not a brick, and if the person who cast such doubts into my mind ever says, "Hey, when you gonna take me for a ride," my rubber mallet will get some use after all.

My extra vacation of that year went something like this:

Saturday: Not much of anything except rest.

Sunday: A buddy and I mounted the engine on the back of the boat. Found out the transom was too thick for the motor clamp. Improvised. Successfully mounted!

Later that afternoon, filled a barrel with water and started the engine. Ran like a Swiss watch. It did not, however, pump water. Something's wrong with the water pump. Getting that sinking feeling.

Monday: Bring the lower unit to the shop. There doesn't appear to be anything wrong with it.

Tuesday: Install the lower unit back, at the shop, where I brought boat and engine. Put it over in the Franklin Canal and ran it on the trailer. Pumping water now. Must have been a slight misalignment. Success!

Get home that afternoon, the control cables for the shift and throttle, which I've been looking for all over the country, are waiting for me via mail. Installed those.

Wednesday: More fine-tuning to the engine. The controls, where they mount on the engine, are impacting the transom when I turn the steering wheel. Take it down and make some modifications to the transom. Success again.

Thursday: I can't put it off any longer. I call my neighbor who has volunteered to come with me for the unofficial launch. He walks over and I say:

"I've got an idea, why don't you take it out, run it, and I'll just stay here and wait. Let me know how it goes."

"Get in the truck and let's go," he says.

So we take it down to the reservation boat landing, and drop her in. Another neighbor joined us.

This is, you understand, the moment of truth. The hour of decision. For 10 months, since I first laid a length of cypress to the band saw to cut the first piece of many to follow, this is the culmination of all those hours of assembly, gluing, driving screws, painting, cussing, moaning, crying, screaming. This is, after all, when we find out if it is a boat or a brick.

I am pleased to report that it is, in fact, a boat.

I climbed aboard and started the engine. Ran great, *and* pumped water. Let it warm up for awhile. I checked under the deck. No leaks. Checked under the front cockpit floorboards. No leaks. Checked under the rear cockpit floorboards. No leaks. Checked in the motor well. Still no leaks. A boat, not a brick.

"Naysayers," I mumbled to myself. "Ye of little faith. They all need a swift kick in the transom."

But now the time has come. It's far more than whether or not it leaks. How will it run? Will it hold together? Will my craftsmanship be up to par?

I put the engine into reverse, and back the boat out of the slip. Varnished mahogany decks gleam in the sunlight, chrome cleats flash sundogs under the afternoon skies. The engine both purrs and clatters, the characteristic sound of an antique outboard.

This is the moment. I admit, I am frightened. This is why I had a private launch before I have a more public one. But the moment is now.

I shift into forward. The engine idles down, nearly dies. *Need to adjust the carbs,* I think. I throttle it up just enough to keep it running. I brace myself, one hand on the wheel, the other on the throttle lever. Slowly I push it up.

The engine accelerates. The stern of the boat dips low, and I hear the cavitation around the prop. I move the throttle up to about half. The boat's nose looks toward the apex of the horizon for a moment, then settles in.

I move down Bayou Teche this way for a couple minutes, then turn it around and head back the other way. This time, the throttle goes all the way.

There are moments, my friends, which we remember for all our days. Other memories fade, other moments diminish. It's exciting, if you're a boat owner, to take out a new boat for the first time. To see what it'll do. Run it through its paces, all that.

Arch Davis once said, "Never to land on an island, from a boat of one's own building, is to miss one of life's great moments." I landed on no island that Thursday afternoon, but I understand what Davis meant.

The boat squatted under the sudden power of the engine and the nose angled upward. The stern wiggled a little bit as she tried to get her sea-legs. The prop churned great boiling swells in the water. Then, as if she suddenly realized that *this* was what she was made for, that this was her true element—not the building form in the garage nor the trailer on which she was carried—the boat leaped forward, nose still up, and the engine roared as it, too, seemed to catch the water and push mightily against it.

As we accelerated, the wiggle in the stern ceased, and the boat dropped her nose, low on her haunches now, and we sped off down the bayou, throwing a rooster tail behind, parting the black-green water as we went slicing through it.

I doubt I'll ever forget that moment. In the midst of the sheer glee, I realized that I had actually done something. This concoction, this conjuring of wood, glue, screws and dreams had a life at last. She glided over the water, straight and sure, and did all that a boat is supposed to do. I had done something, and I didn't have to take a socially acceptable, government-stamped and accredited class to tell me how to do it. My pains and tribulations had culminated into this.

I sped by my two friends at the dock, and gave them the thumbs up as they took photos and digital movies of my triumph.

Ten months at the saws, with the brushes, mixing the epoxies, correcting mistakes, moaning over those I could not fix. Ten months of wondering if I had lost my mind: Who was I to think I could do this? By what manner of arrogance did I suppose that I could construct a boat, something that is science, art, magic and surrealism all mixed up in one little package? Me, who never paid attention when my dad was building boats. Me, who just made a few pieces of furniture, all nice and square.

I lived a bit more life that Thursday afternoon. A bit more memory to cherish in my old age. I won't be sitting on the shore getting old.

Now, you know it couldn't have been as serious as all that.

Here's what I didn't tell you about my vacation last week, and the launching of the boat. Here's the other side of things.

While I was over at Bayou Marine having the lower unit remounted, there was an older gentleman there and a younger guy. Both were admiring the boat, and the younger guy remarked, "Man, that's quite a restoration. How old is that boat?"

To which the proprietor said, "That boat's brand new!"

The younger guy didn't believe it. "Just ask the man," the proprietor said.

"Is it?" the younger asked the elder man standing there minding his own business.

"I dunno, ask him," the gentleman said, jabbing his thumb at the grinning me.

It was quite a compliment, you understand, to be considered a restoration in the first place, an even greater compliment when it's really a new build. I was considerably smug and proud.

In the next place, I mentioned Wednesday that the transom was too thick for the engine clamp to fit. This was my mistake. The designs called for two layers of three-quarter inch plywood. I wanted a planked wood transom, I made mine from two layers of seven-eighths inch cypress. That gave me a grand total of one and three-quarter inches. However, to achieve the herringbone look on the transom, I laminated a layer of three-eighths inch mahogany ply over it, giving me a grand total of two-and-one-eighths. Lesson one: The designer knew what he was doing, don't mess with it. Lesson two: If you *do* mess with it, remember to deduct the difference from the total.

Friday morning I had to be in New Iberia, with the boat at 9 a.m. to have it inspected by the Department of Wildlife and Fisheries. I made sure I had the proper, functional lightning, the fire extinguisher, air horn, all that stuff. I trailered the boat to New Iberia, and the agent there raved and raved over it, which was very nice, and I got my inspection decal and went home.

By afternoon, it was raining cats, dogs and General George Armstrong Custers outside. No boating today, so I politely threw a hissy fit and retired for the evening.

Saturday morning, the weather was foul, but it wasn't raining. So I was at the launch and in the water by 6 a.m. This is called obsession. I had to be out there. I ran the boat up and down the bayou for about 20 minutes, then the first drops of rain began, so it was back to the boat ramp and home. Another polite hissy fit.

So it was Sunday before I got back into the water. This time, I got brave, and decided I would take it all the way to the lake and back. I would, I reasoned, call for help on my cell phone if anything went wrong.

Halfway to the lake, I realized I had forgotten my cell phone in the truck. Ah, well. Too far to turn back, so I motored along nervously.

But things went great, and I made it safely there and back. I made a few trips up and down the bayou from the reservation boat landing, and I got to tell you, folks, the stares I got from the people I passed all that day were amusing.

Though I couldn't hear what was being said or thought, I pretty much can guess from their facial expressions:

"What the heck is *that*?"

"Whoa, what a classic!"

"What a geek. Get a fiberglass boat, ya bum."

"Hey, I haven't seen one of those in 40 years!"

"Get a haircut, ya hippy."

"Did they make Mercury's that long ago? Do they run on gasoline? Or steam?"

"Hey, look, it's the *African Queen.*"

"Isn't that the boat from *On Golden Pond?*"

"Where's the electric trolling motor? How ya gonna bass fish outta that without an electric trolling motor?"

"Is he lost?"

"Is he crazy?"

"Is he a cheesehead?"

"Betcha it rots in a year."

"Betcha it falls apart in rough water. All dem wood boats do."

"Wonder if it's really aluminum painted to look like wood?"

And so on, and so forth. Maybe my imagination is running away with me, a little. Doesn't matter. Just as long as she turns heads.

I have future boats named. I want to build a bateau on the design my dad made, but a bit larger, perhaps 14 to 16 feet. It will be named *Nix* in his honor. When I get sufficiently skilled, I will build a large cruising boat, probably sail, probably designed on the lines of the Norwegian kosterbat *Elly*, but I will name her *Wanderer* in tribute.

This boat? I dunno yet. I had originally said I would name it *Done.* You know, as in "completed," because that's what I've been saying for 10 months: When the boat's done I'll...After I get the boat done, we'll...Wait until the boat's done and you can...etc. So it just seemed like it should be named *Done.* I then decided I was suffering from lack of oxygen or inhaling too many epoxy fumes, and that it was a cheesy name.

We'll see. I have a name floating around in my head which could serve as a precursor to that large cruiser *Wanderer* but I haven't made up my mind yet.

Meanwhile, see ya around the lake!

One wonders why one spent 10 months building a boat when one never goes out in it.

Since launching, I have been out in my new mahogany runabout exactly three times. That includes the initial launch. Rain, other obligations and general all-around laziness have thus far kept the boat under the garage, covered with a tarp. It is covered with a tarp to keep it from getting dirty and dusty, so it is quite shiny and clean under the tarp, where nobody can see it.

One wonders why I went through all that effort. I fear I may be one of those strange types of people I have heard about, those who love to build boats but do not use them. This would not be surprising, because when it comes to strange types of people, I usually have a membership.

What's the use of building a boat if you don't use it? I talk about it a lot. Anyone who gets within earshot of me might hear:

"Yup, launched my boat finally."

"Really! How did it go?"

"Great. Runs nice, handles great, the works."

"Bet you've been enjoying it, huh?"

"Go jump off a cliff," I say, and stalk off angrily.

Now and then somebody will come over, and I'll take the tarp off the boat and show it to them. They generally compliment and rave. I am always humble and appreciative. Until they ask if it's a) a head-turner on the water b) a babe magnet on the water or c) a real speed demon on the water.

"Go jump off a cliff," I say, and stalk off angrily.

I go out and buff it sometimes, to get all the fingerprints off from people coming over and touching it under the garage. I clean the little yellow drops of carpenter bee gunk—I really don't want to know what that stuff is—that drops on it from the nest of them in the garage rafters. But I don't go out in it.

I tell myself, every weekend, "I'm going to go ride in the boat this weekend." Every weekend, I do not. What's up with that? I tell myself that it's because my registration decal and numbers had not come in from Wildlife and Fisheries yet. However, my registration did come in last weekend, so I'm sure I'm just making excuses.

It may be fear. I don't want to get it scratched. I don't want to get it dirty. How can you use a boat if you don't want it to get it scratched and dirty? Boats get that way. However, my reluctance to subject it to that has proven that it is not a boat, nor a brick, it is an oversized coffee table. I think I should just make little legs for it, put it in the living room and serve coffee to my guests from it. With very good coasters, of course, to prevent any cup rings from developing on the varnish. *That* would be intolerable.

Speaking of registration, you don't know how it broke my heart to put that big, ugly decal on the hull. And I will have to get custom lettering for the numbers, because I refuse to keep those incredibly nasty store-bought block number decals on it. In many states, there are exclusions for hull decals on classic boats, but not here. It's like putting a bumper sticker that reads "My Other Car Is A Junk, Too" on your Mercedes.

Just last Sunday, I decided I was going out. I spent a leisurely hour or so getting everything ready. I pulled her out into the yard. I checked the fuel in both tanks. I checked the oil. I even started the engine briefly to make sure nothing strange had happened while the boat was napping. I loaded a small ice chest with Diet Coke. I checked the lights on the trailer. Everything was ready to rumble.

Just as I was putting the ice chest into the boat, black clouds rolled in like chariots, the trees starting bending over to kiss the ground under gale-force winds, and the rain came down like hallelujah, brethren. I barely got the boat inside the garage again before I was soaked to the bone. I spent the next hour standing at the front door, looking out at the rain whipping like mad outside, fussing loudly and wondering why I didn't build an Ark instead. Admittedly, an adequate supply of quality gopher wood is hard to come by these days, but cypress might be a reasonable substitute. I also haven't the faintest idea how long a cubit is. My Stanley tape measure does not read in cubits.

Of course, a half-hour before dusk the sun was shining, the wind was gone and birds were chirping.

"Go jump off a cliff," I said to the sun, birds and absent wind, and stalked off angrily.

Well, it could be worse. I could have been out on the lake when the storm started. That would have been bad. So I guess my guardian spirit was looking out for me after all. Just my luck: My guardian spirit can manipulate the weather enough to bring it on before I depart, but does not have enough stroke to keep the skies clear completely.

Figures. I not only don't get to use the boat, but I'm stuck with a second-rate guardian spirit, too.

It seems that I have been having gremlins lately. Gremlins break things. That's where the old story came from, particularly among World Wars I and II fighter and bomber pilots who couldn't explain why things kept going wrong with their planes.

I have been having a whole herd of gremlins lately. In the first place, having recently had the threads repaired in one of the spark plug sockets of my 1958 Mercury outboard motor, as I reported to you earlier, I went to the boat landing and put over. I got exactly 19 feet when another plug socket stripped out. Back to the landing.

Then my coffee pot died during the night. Then my DVD player succumbed. As far as the boat goes, on the way out to the lake, trailering the boat behind the truck, I decided that the old outboard had exactly three chances left. I realize that with an engine that old, it will take some time to get the bugs worked out. The breakdown that day leaves two chances.

I also found that one of the spark plug wires had fried to a black crisp inside the distributor socket. This is not a good thing, either. So new plug wires are in order as well. Do I consider that one chance or two?

Pricing outboard motors is enough to make your eyes cross and your brain go numb. Talk about sticker shock. You could buy a compact car or a small house for what outboard motors cost. It's a lawnmower on a boat, that's all. Think about it: an engine that drives a shaft which turns blades or a propeller, which is near about the same thing. Why is it you can get a lawn mower for a reasonable price but an outboard engine costs a princely sum?

I think it's because there is a difference in the intentions. A lawn mower is for work. An outboard is for play. Anything that costs too much and which you would have to work at using would cause the peasantry—that's us, those who have to cut grass—to rise up in revolt. It's like if a mop cost $200. Or a bottle of dishwashing liquid cost $50.

An outboard, on the other hand, is a purely recreational item unless you're a commercial fisherman or something. In that case, all you're having to do is pay too much for the equipment you need for your work because of the recreational users. Because it's something designed for fun, though, outboard manufacturers believe they can overcharge for them. And they are right, because most people go out and pay a king's ransom for an outboard motor, which many of them then hit a log or something with and knock the lower unit off.

But what really boggles my mind are these jet ski things. Now, not to sound like an old fuddy-duddy or anything, but if there every was a more obnoxious, troublesome, profane and irritating device made than a jet ski, I don't want to know about it.

I apologize in advance if you are a jet ski fan, but look at it from my point of view, if you can. Riding a jet ski is like strapping yourself to the back of the space shuttle rocket boosters and lighting the fuse, except you're on the water. There I am, fishing quietly, enjoying my commune with nature, and the next thing you know, this guy on a jet ski comes screaming by. The trees shrink away in terror, the fish dig down into the mud, and the wake nearly pitches me out of the boat. Not long ago, there was a news story about a guy riding a jet ski and he was killed by a head-on collision with a duck that had the unfortunate luck to be flying in the opposite direction along the same course. Any device that will kill you by being hit in the head with a duck is nuts. Ducks are pretty quick birds when it comes to flying. They can change direction in a heartbeat. But when a jet ski comes rocketing at a duck at 56 mph, there's only disaster waiting to happen. By the way, the duck didn't make it, either.

But I was talking about outboards. Now that I've made all the jet ski fans mad, let's go back to outboards. I have a 15-horsepower outboard for my small bateau, it's a year 2000 model, and it performs without a glitch or a gremlin. It cost me $2,000. My 1958 Mercury 40-horsepower cost $285, plus another couple hundred in repairs and parts. If it ceases breaking down in the next few weeks, I may have a grand total of $600 in it. However, my 15-horse never breaks down. So what you are paying for is reliability. There's a concept. Instead of making a product that doesn't break down and charge a reasonable price for it, you are being charged for not having it break down. You are, in effect, being charged for quality. Does that make a lick of sense? Remember when we *expected* quality?

Weed trimmers. Oh, now there's a quality machine. I go through about one weed trimmer a year. A weed trimmer is the same principle as a lawn mower and an outboard: a motor which drives a shaft which spins a piece of monofilament fishing line, which I suppose makes it closer kin to an outboard than a lawnmower. But the weed trimmer is perhaps the most unreliable, cantankerous and annoying piece of machinery in existence, second only to the jet ski. There's nothing more aggravating than a weed trimmer that won't operate after you've mowed the lawn, and if you're like me and don't mow the lawn until the dogs go missing, then you're left with this jungle growth along the edge of the house, fence, around the trees and under the porch, while everything else is nicely mowed. Because of this, I think I should do the trimming first, then mow the lawn. That way, if the trimmer proves to be nonfunctional, I can just forget the whole thing and go take a nap.

At least, though, the likelihood of getting hit in the head with a duck while weed trimming is slight.

Come to that, the chance of getting hit in the head with a duck in my boat is pretty slight too, because the dadblamed thing doesn't run long enough to give me the opportunity.

Well, I guess you could call it a debut.

It wasn't all the pomp and circumstance of a debutante ball, I'm afraid. But me and the boat made our public debut this weekend.

A bunch of folks from the office and some of their associated friends and offspring went out to Lake Fausse Pointe Park Saturday, and some of us brought our boats.

There's so many people around the park you couldn't swing a cat by the tail without hitting somebody. I don't like crowds, and I like crowds with $25,000 boats built like battering rams even less. Crowds with jet skis are something like hell on earth.

Saturday morning, I gassed up the boat and threw in an ice chest full of—I swear!—Diet Coke. I left my tarp covering on the boat and snugged it down good, to try to keep some of the dust off the vessel, since I had decided to take the levee road to the park.

It was an interesting ride, dodging potholes and the occasional mud hole, but I made it from my house to the park in about half an hour. Once at the park, I pulled up at the ramp and uncovered the boat, readying to get underway and meet up with my associates. Well, it took me another half hour to get the boat into the water, because everybody that came by had to stop and admire it. I'm not boasting, you understand, just being a good little journalist and reporting the facts as they occurred.

"Boy, you don't see many of those anymore!"

"How old is that boat?"

"Must have taken a lot to restore it."

"Does it leak much?" This one drew a long comment from me, of course.

Finally I was in the water and cranked up the engine. Remembering all the trouble I have been experiencing with this 1958 Mercury outboard over the past couple months, you will understand that I was deservingly apprehensive. I idled down the winding canals at the camp and met up with my comrades. After some pleasantries and further complimentary remarks, we headed out for the lake proper.

Debbie got the first ride, since she's the boss' wife and thus has executive privilege. We followed another guy, Joey, who also brought his 22-foot long aluminum hulled bateau with a 115 horsepower Evinrude, out of the park and into the lake.

There was a brisk breeze, and the lake was kinda choppy. There were also more boats around than I could have ever possibly imagined. Nonetheless, we took off across the lake toward a wide canal.

The boat was battering heavily on the choppy waves, in a kind of rat-a-tat-tat pounding. I leaned over and told Debbie over the roar of the engine and the clattering of the hull on the waves, "Well, I guess we'll find out how good a boat builder I am, eh?"

"Oh," Debbie said, holding her sun visor on her head.

Now, when someone says "Oh," in answer to a statement like that, it can have several meanings. People say "Oh," like that because they're leaving off the rest of the sentence, which could be:

"Oh, it'll be all right, I'm confident in your abilities as a craftsman."

Or, "Oh, we're gonna die, aren't we?"

The chop got steadily worse, as I tried to explain to Deb that a sharp vee-bowed boat slices through waves very well, and that I had reinforced the 3/8-inch bottom with epoxy, and that there were longitudinal stringers—battens—running across the length of the bottom spaced closely together.

"Oh," Deb said.

This could mean, "Oh, I feel better now," or it could mean, "Oh, we're gonna die, aren't we?"

But we made it to the channel without incident, and the other boat proceeded to accommodate the skiers and boarders. I was just cruising. While my boat could have been constructed for skier-pulling, I chose not to build in that functionality. So me and Deb just cruised up and down the bayou for a time, admiring the scenery and trying to avoid other boaters who were about to run aground because they were staring at us in my mahogany runabout. I felt like shouting, "No, it doesn't leak!"

I took on another passenger then, and all together we cruised and the others skied for over three hours, before we headed back to the big lake and just kinda beached the boats' bows and relaxed under the shade of a willow tree for a time. The only dreadful moment in the whole experience was when, as we were leaving to head back to the park, I bumped the other boat. The old Mercury has controls with two levers as opposed to the newer single-lever controls. Mine has one to throttle and one to shift. While backing out, I was watching where I was going astern, reached out to shift into forward, but grabbed the throttle lever by mistake and *bam!* Luckily, there was only a slight scuff on my boat, and Joey's wasn't even marked. The only real damage done was to my ego, which suffered a nearly fatal injury.

We idled back to the park and after a time cooling off, me and Vanessa, our esteemed managing editor and another pal went to load up my boat so I could make the trip home.

What amazes me is the extreme paranoia *other* people exhibit over my boat. My cohort in loading the boat went through great pains to make sure it didn't touch the dock when we arrived. Then, as we were loading, he actually jumped overboard to make sure it didn't rub anything on the trailer or anything else.

"It's okay," I said. "Really, it's just a boat."

"No, it's a work of art," he said.

"No, it's a boat," I repeated. "It's going to get dinged up."

"No, it's a piece of artwork," he said.

We went back and forth like this for a while before I finally gave up. That's not to imply that I didn't appreciate the compliment, but the problem is, if I start to believing that way, I'll never have the nerve to take the boat out of the garage.

We went back to the gathering spot and relaxed for a while, socializing, before it was time to cover up the boat again and head down the levee for home. I was tired, a little sunburnt, and ready for a trip to the waterin' hole. The trip home was uneventful, thank goodness. Upon arrival, I slid the boat into the garage and counted my blessings. Aside from a bump into Joey's boat, I had survived without engine failure, structural failure, jet ski attack, rainstorms and running aground while gawking at the scenery, looking for Indian mounds.

So that was my unofficial debut. I promise, the official launching and naming ceremony will be held soon. I plan to get my mom to break a bottle of champagne over the bow. On the other hand, that might be a little too uppity for a little Indian off the Rez's boat, so it may be a bottle of beer.

One thing's for certain: I'll have to explain to somebody that, in order to break a bottle over the bow of a boat to christen it, you have to actually *hit* the boat with the bottle. This may cause the person to faint. But that's what the rest of the beer is for.

For Labor Day, had I not been feeling badly, and had the weather not been uncooperative, I was going to take the boat out.

Now, I hadn't really stopped to think about how foolish this idea was. On Labor Day, everybody that has a boat is out in it. Even if they have nowhere to go and nothing to do when they get there, they go out in their boats. Anybody who owns anything that will float throws in an ice chest and does their best to make sure they do not labor all day.

I fortunately was dissuaded by the rain, but from my window I could see the people in the bayou. Mostly it was the jet skis. Man, I tell you, they were tearing up the water. The bayou was smoking with these 60 mph modified snowmobiles running up and down the way, somebody mounted on them like thoroughbred horse jockeys.

This put me in a better mood. The last thing I wanted to do was be running around in my mahogany runabout, doing about 30 mph, while jet skis were passing me by left and right doing 50 or 60 mph. They sound like bees buzzing by you when they pass, and the people on them try to wave, but you can tell by the looks on their faces they only want you to *think* they're having a good time. In fact, they're scared out of their skulls, those that suddenly realize that they are blazing at 60 mph on a craft about the size of a carousel horse and with no brakes. This is the definition of suddenly getting religion.

"*Whhheeeeeeeeeeeee*!" they scream when they pass me by. That's what I *thought* they were saying, anyway. After listening closely, though, I realized that they are in fact screaming, "*Pleeeeeeaaaaaaaaaase*!" and I suspect the entire sentence, without the distortion of speed, roar of engine and wind, would be, "Please get me off this crazy thing!"

Having remarked to someone recently about my dislike of personal watercraft, I was told, "Oh, you're just an old fuddy."

I was severely taken aback by this statement. Me? An old fuddy? I am not! Listen, I explained, I used to drag race on Northwest Boulevard when I was a teen (the statute of limitations is up on that, I hope) and I used to do doughnuts on the levee in my Mustang. But somewhere along the line, I grew some semblance of sense and realized that these things were about as intelligent as racing a mockingbird on a bicycle while driving down U.S. 90 at 5 p.m.

I'm not suggesting, of course, that people who like jet skis have no sense. No, I believe they are victims of slick advertising campaigns. The makers and retailers of jet skis make them look so downright fun and sexy, people just seem to fall into this hypnotic state and start mumbling, "Yes, master, buy a 60 mph contraption and go rocketing down Bayou Teche with it, yes, master, I am your obedient servant," and they go buy one for $10,000. This is slick advertising of the worst kind.

Old fuddy? Not. Just because I like my boats wooden and moving somewhere below the speed of sound in performance, that doesn't make me an old fuddy by any stretch of the imagination. I have no desire to reach mach one on the water. I have no desire to imitate Chuck Yeager on Bayou Teche.

You wanna ride a 60 mph runaway penny rocket, go right ahead. I'll not be calling you a young whippersnapper. Just give me and my old-fashioned wooden boat a wide berth when you see us coming, or one of us will undoubtedly be embarking on a desperate search for a surgeon to remove the other's vessel from our—well, you get the idea.

Old fuddy. Hrmph.

This does not mean that some people, who might be old fuddies, don't get aggravated with the sound of my outboard as I pass them by doing 30 mph. "Whippersnapper," they probably mumble under their breaths. "Speed-kook." These people are usually in pirogues or rowboats and have yet to discover the steam engine.

People think I'm a snot, because of these opinions. I am not. I also think flying is stupid. The entire idea of flying is stupid, and just because a couple of brothers in North Carolina did it everybody fell for the slick advertising and started doing it, too. I've flown twice in my life, under protest the second time. I also hate telephones. I look forward to the day, like no other, when I can free myself of telephones. No phone in the house, no cell phone, retired from work and away from business phones. You want to reach me, send a smoke signal from a burning jet ski. I hate telephones.

This does not make me a snot, or an old fuddy. It just makes me cranky. Jet skis make me cranky. Junk mail makes me cranky. Telephones make me cranky.

Perhaps I'm being too harsh, though. I am glad that recreational jet ski users have found some way to get their kicks, really. It makes me happy to see someone having a good time, even if they are exceeding the recommended g-forces that a human being should be able to stand. It makes me smile to know that someone is enjoying the rush of a 60 mph fiberglass bullet down a narrow waterway like Slim Pickens riding the nuclear bomb in *Dr. Strangelove.* I should be more understanding, I know. I should be more broad-minded about the fact that folks are different, and we express such differences in our likes, dislikes and such, and that should not be cause for crankiness.

Don't take it personally, please. I'm quitting the Diet Coke. Maybe those jet skis remind me too much of a Diet Coke can when I see them. The colors *are* often similar.

I'm feeling cranky again just thinking about it, so I better stop here, before a regalia of jet ski proponents stage a protest in the bayou behind my house. At least I still have a telephone to call for help.

I have learned how to make toast. Out of myself.

Sunday, I decided another trip to the lake was in order, this time for some serious fishing. How serious my fishing becomes largely depends on the fish, of course. If the fish are biting, it's pretty serious. If they're not, it's not very serious at all. Generally speaking, my fishing trips are not very serious.

I got dad's boat, loaded up my electric trolling motor and battery, rods and reels, and tackle box. I made sure my fishing license was valid and my boat registration was in the boat. I filled the fuel tank, checked the engine lower unit oil. Reminding myself that I hadn't seen the light of day on my legs since September, I found my sunscreen and put it on the kitchen table. I then borrowed a small ice chest from my neighbor, packed it with Diet Coke and fishing worms I had bought earlier, and headed out for the lake.

Once there, I was in seventh heaven. I love being on the lake, in a little wooden boat, throwing at perch. That's what my dad always called it. "Let's go throw at the perch today," he'd say to me. In the days before I developed any reasonable cognizance of mind, I pictured us sitting in the boat throwing things at the fish in the water: baseballs, rocks, sticks, chewing gum. But later I understood that what we were "throwing" was the bait. This bait must always be earthworms, my dad said, on a small, sharp hook attached to a straight-shanked spinner, with a tiny bobber.

So I started getting a bit warm, and I took off my shirt. I was already wearing my short pants, and had forgotten my sunglasses to ward off the glare from my legs. It was then I realized I had also forgotten the sunscreen on the kitchen table. As I wasn't about to turn around and go all the way home to get it, I reasoned that I'd just get a little sun and then put the shirt back on, cover the legs with a life jacket or something, and everything would be cool.

Well, I got severely distracted. First, because I was catching fish left and right. Every other cast brought in a fish. However, these fish averaged about the length of my index finger. You are pretty much guaranteed that when your cork goes under and you snatch back on the rod to set the hook, when the fish comes flying out of the water and slaps you in the face, it's too small to keep.

But I was catching oodles of them, and I started realizing that they were about the size of a potato chip. This reasoning made me consider that, just fried whole like that, they could be Perch Chips. I then decided this was a bad idea and continued throwing them back.

An alligator came to visit me, circling the boat for an hour or so, wondering what all the commotion was about. I tried to get close enough to take a picture with the digital camera, but he would have nothing of it, so I went back to catching potato chip perch.

It was, therefore, a few hours before I realized that when I brushed my arm against my legs, the nerve endings in my skin jumped up and down and yelled bloody murder.

By that time, it was too late. I was burnt. I put my shirt back on, covered my legs with the life jacket, and went home. I told you, I get distracted.

On the way back, the game warden came by and flashed his blue lights at me. I shut down the motor and started rummaging through the tackle box for my papers. "Good afternoon!" I shouted. "Got my papers right here!"

"No, that's okay," said Mr. Game Warden very courteously. "I just wanted to check out your boat."

I was stunned. "But I have my papers, got my fishing license, too, just give me a minute…"

"Don't worry about it," Mr. Game Warden said. "I see you have a current sticker. Tell me about this boat!"

I explained that my dad had made the boat in 1962, that I had just restored it, etc. He asked if I had ever been to the Madisonville Wooden Boat Festival, and I said I had, and I told him about the boat I am building which I may launch sometime in the next decade, and so forth. I was still looking for my papers during all this.

"Caught any fish?" he asked.

"Nothing worth keeping, but you're welcome to look," I said.

"No, that's okay, just wondering if you had any luck," Mr. Game Warden said. "Have a great day, and be careful!"

He motored off, and right then I found my registration papers, so I waved them in the air at him, but he wasn't looking. I was kinda disappointed. I really am proud of my registration papers.

By Monday, the tops of my legs were so badly burned I could barely walk. My shoulders and back were a little better, but not much. I had to go to the hospital board meeting that night, and of course, everyone I met had to grab my shoulder or slap me on the back in greeting. I screamed a lot that night. But it was okay, because in a hospital, people are used to screaming.

So I picked up some burn cream with aloe vera in it. "Put it in the refrigerator," the pharmacist told me. "Cool it down before you use it."

I thought this a fairly good idea. I learned that it was, in fact, a pharmacist's idea of a practical joke, for when I put a dab of it on my hand, straight out of the fridge, and applied it to my crawfish-red legs, I immediately turned into a ping-pong ball and went jumping up and down all over the living room screaming in shock. *Do not* let pharmacists do this to you. Cold burn cream on a sunburn is like getting shot with a frozen bazooka shell. By the time the cream warms up to your body temperature, you've bruised the top of your head on the ceiling multiple times and clipped your ears on the ceiling fan.

Now, one of the many quirks of the human body—mine seems to have more than normal people—is that when sunburn begins to heal, it also begins to itch. The tenderness is not gone yet, however, so you can't really scratch it without inflicting severe pain upon yourself and bruising your head again. So the cream has an anti-itch medication in it, too. Applying the cream—at room temperature!—requires waiting about 30 minutes before getting dressed, or your clothes stick to you in very unfashionable contortions. About 30 minutes after you get dressed, the cream has worn off and the pain and itching starts again.

Patches, by the way, didn't enjoy my sunburn episode any more than I did. Sitting there in my chair, suffering, she'd come near me and crouch, ready to leap into my lap.

"Touch me, and you're violin strings," I said in the most threatening voice I could manage.

She must have gotten the idea. She stayed on the sofa.

Reminder to me: Bring the stupid sunscreen *with you* next time, cheesehead.

When Longfellow wrote, "She floats upon the river of his thoughts," I was never really sure if he meant a boat, a woman, or both. But I am sure I know the passion that lingers behind either invocation.

The need to build a boat, as Ransome pointed out, is something which begins like a grass seed, so tiny and minute it is barely perceptible. It roots and sprouts, grows and spreads, and before long it overtakes everything in sight. Building a boat is to touch something so far back in the past of human existence it is unreachable in any other way. We may unearth Egyptian vessels from the sand, dive ancient shipwrecks, study the occasional Norse long boat, but we can never connect with that moment when, so long ago, a human being not so unlike us took to the water in some manner of vessel. Some say it was inflated animals skins, others just a log. It doesn't matter. What we sense is that need to leave the terrestrial and reach out for divinity, a spiritual commonality with that first distant ancestor to which all boat builders share descent.

Noah was the original recorded boat builder, and probably the master of it. There's not much I can say about Noah that the authors of the Old Testament and a million others have not said. Having received his boat building plans from God, rather than mail-order or the Internet, Noah probably did not suffer the occasional consternation of reading offsets, lofting and bending the sheer strake. Whether the ark was just a big floating box or a vessel with some style will never be known, unless that mysterious shadow in Turkey is ever fully studied.

Building boats defies logic. It must be undertaken with a certain measure of insanity. The notion of them is nearly unfathomable. That a pile of lumber sitting awaiting the saw could ever become something as elegant as a Whitehall, or race the wind like an Alden sloop, such precognizant vision requires a slight bit of madness. The purist will demand traditional construction, with traditional methods. While there are some things I am fussy about, I am not so purist as all that. In far less complicated days, people had the time to master the art of boat building from the felled tree to completed vessel. Such conditions have been murdered by a society which places too much importance on monetary goals. Therefore, I do not mind my power tools or plywood as they help me achieve something within what limited time this modern order allows me. Such boats remain far more animate than sparkly bass boats or aluminum hulls.

So I settled on a larger fishing boat, though not too large. It was time to build again. Time to bridge the gap between the dry land and legacy.

I have for years entertained the notion of building a large sailboat. There is something calling out there which, while not as powerful as that sacred flame somewhere in the swamp, tugs at me when the wind blows through my hair and the smell of salt air nips at my wanderlust. Maybe a big catboat, I think to myself, or perhaps a sloop. The notion of sailing the seven seas does not appeal to me at all, but I nurture a strong desire to sail up the East Coast and back. For now, though, the world around my home is world enough, more to understand and discover than I will ever live long enough to complete.

Around these parts, the premiere boat building materials are cypress and oak, readily available, though not in the quantity or quality as in the past. Little or no mahogany, fir or teak ever found its way into the construction of Louisiana boats, but cypress is perhaps one of the finest boat materials in the world. Old cypress, reclaimed from the demolition of houses and other structures, is a far superior wood to the new. When the lumber industry was thriving here, it thrived itself into extinction by cutting down every single old-growth cypress tree in the state. The cypress nearly went extinct with the industry, which shut down practically overnight. These old logs, thousands of which remain sunken in the muddy bottom of the basins and lakes, are prized wood for craftsmen and boat builders. There are in Grand Avoille Cove a thousand such logs, though some are tupelo, which were left there to sink when the lumber man departed, leaving behind a decimated landscape. These logs have claimed many an outboard.

Having collected antique cypress, as well as Douglas fir, for a few years now, I have a suitable stash for the boat. If it were not for fishing weather and cabin fever, I would have started already. But the *sac-au-lait* are moving into the shallows, the bass are getting active again, the bream—that most wonderful of fish—are popping at the very early hatches of spring bugs. The new boat will have to wait just a few more weeks. The fly rod is calling me. One cannot embark upon a project such as the building of a boat, be it a pirogue or a schooner, without reflection of the task about to be undertaken. The best place to reflect is in the cathedral of that spirit which makes building a boat far more meaningful than the practical use of it. The preparation of the spirit is vital, and the only way to do that is go to the water, seek its blessing, before making the presumption that a craft will be accepted and protected by it.

And that is the most perfect of excuses.

As a teenager, I stayed out of major trouble. I was never picked up by the police, never came home in a drunken stupor, never did drugs. My worst offense was skipping school one time, for which I was promptly nailed by the parents of myself and the other boys I went truant with. I made that mistake no more. I was never in trouble because, unlike today when juvenile delinquency is epidemic and the courts are overrun with teenage problems, I never worried once about the police, the sheriff or any robed judge. If I messed up, none of those distinguished gentlemen would ever see me in their halls, dad would see to that.

But with adolescence came a parting of ways with my father. It happens. We did not see eye-to-eye on many things. I cared little for my heritage back then, and sought only to be disassociated with the entire Indian thing. I wanted to be just like everyone else in town, and when I started in the newspaper business at the tender young age of fifteen, I saw that as my opportunity. I skipped college, kept working at the newspaper. By the time I was seventeen, I was covering city council meetings and the new mayor reportedly told someone that if he ever got hold of me he would wring my neck. It was pure joy. We're the best of friends today.

There were cars, and girls. I fell in love with the Ford Mustang and a girl or two. The Mustang was no less expensive than the girls in upkeep costs. Ask anyone who knew me then, and they'll say I was arrogant, stubborn and self-centered. I am no longer self-centered.

Dad and I could agree on nothing. If he said it was black, I said it was white. There was no gray. I wore my hair long, and this perturbed him greatly, but he never refused me. I tended to wreck cars fairly regularly, and this also perturbed him, rightly so. I also had a problem with money, because while I was enamored with this journalism thing, the pay was far below what dad thought I should be earning, and when I declined a full scholarship to college, his disappointment was tactile.

Particularly heartbreaking to both of us was that I followed none of his craft. No Indian crafts, no wood, no metal jewelry, nothing. All I knew how to do was write, and while I might have done that well, it was not truly art in the eyes of a man who struggled with English class throughout his education. He was far better in math, which I was not. I passed high school algebra with a "D" grade. He was constantly bailing me out financially, for I have never had nor will I ever it seems develop any financial aptitude. I also made many decisions in my life that completely annoyed or disappointed him. Our estrangement lasted about ten years.

Those days are not an evil which I wish to purge myself of. In retrospect, I have many fond memories of them. Few involve water, though, and perhaps that is where my course strayed to back countries where I should not have let myself go. Water was my grounding rod, my tether to what mattered. When I strayed from it, I was like Rabbit.

Rabbit was ordered by the Great Spirit to take some medicine to a little girl who was very ill. The Creator warned rabbit, "Do not wander or stray from the signs," but Rabbit did. In his haste to make up for lost time, he fell and split his lip on a sharp rock, a mark he would carry to this day. I split my lip on a sharp rock in the same way, by wandering too far from water.

I finally went to college when I was twenty-seven, on a tribal scholarship. I was married and had two children by then, and my prospects of further employment as a journalist were dismal. At the university, I met Dr. Jon Gibson in a class on cultural anthropology which did more to guide me back on course than anything ever could.

Before long I was fascinated with the history of the Americas and its indigenous people. And before long, I was asking questions of my father, which he gladly answered. And before long at all, we were friends again. Our remaining years together may not have been smooth as the lake at twilight on a warm summer morning, but they were once again those of a father and son.

Throughout my days, in many ways, I lived under his shadow. I was constantly asked if I was Nick Stouff's son, or even grandson. It was something with many offspring find necessary to rebel against. Dad never encouraged my writing interests, feeling I was headed for some unspecified doom, until three weeks before he went to his Creator.

He had a bad spell, and spent a few days in intensive care at the local hospital before being released. I had been back in the newspaper business for three years, my education stopped short by financial problems. While in the hospital, several people asked if dad was related to me, and they praised the work I have done at the newspaper, particularly my weekly column.

When he returned home, in those brief three weeks before he left for good, he said to me that he had never known I was so well thought of. He said he was surprised that so many people enjoyed my writing. He said, in so many words, that he was proud of me. The circle came around to where it began, and I think, if he had been in good health, we might well have boarded the little bateau and found our way to a secluded cove on the lake, to fish all the day, until the sun blazed like eternal fire across the horizon, forcing us at last to turn the bow toward home.

A good fishing boat must serve its user well in the environment where it is made to exist. In my world, the world Crawfish made for me, a good fishing boat must have certain characteristics already aptly defined by my father's boat.

It served him perfectly for its intended purpose; when he was not forced to travel more than a mile or two in protected waters to catch all the fish he could want to catch in a lifetime. This was what it was created for, not long trips into the basin, crossing in some cases thrashing rivers, in other cases open bays. A good fishing boat for him remains a good fishing boat for me, but the waterscape has changed. Now, because of the tinkering of man with the natural order of things, I must venture farther to find the same things which were at my father's back door.

In choosing such a vessel for building or simply as a purchase, there are always trade offs. To obtain better rough stability, I will have to compromise draft. Whereas my little bateau draws three or four inches of water, depending on its load, the Monk boat will probably draw ten. Some of the shallows I previously entered and fished without second thought may become inaccessible to me. To confront large swells without battering the bow, the good fishing boat I need today will have a sharp stem tapering to a semi-vee aft. Due to the distances I may travel, it will probably have to accommodate up to a fifty horsepower engine, still a far cry from the big sparkly bass boats, but a large engine nonetheless to someone accustomed to outboards no larger than fifteen horsepower.

It was decided that the boat would be equipped with two "riding seats" center, one for a passenger the other set behind the steering console mounted to starboard. Pedestal seats would be installed fore and aft on the sole, removable so they might be stashed away when not needed. There would also be a live well, stowage and a mount for a good electric trolling motor.

But a good fishing boat must also be pleasing to the eye. It must not be an aberration on the water, must not accost its surroundings, to be accepted by it. The outer hull, I decided, would be painted, perhaps white; but from the rub rail upward and inward it would largely be finished bright, with natural wood showing wherever possible. It must not reek of assembly line production; it must have the subtle imperfections that come with hand craftsmanship. A boat which is so smooth and slick as to be obviously manufactured by machines fits into the natural world as suitably as a football into a the ninth hole of the golf course. A blunt box will float, add a slight bevel to the bow and it will even travel relatively well under low power. But a boat must be fashioned to glide with the water, over it and through it, supported by the water like a cradle. It is an amazing and welcome coincidence that the lines which make such grace possible are also so pleasing to the human eye.

A good fishing boat should rest easy when the water is calm, not wander aimlessly like a simpleton. It should, likewise, follow the flow of the water obediently, stem forward, and not twist sideways like a miscreant log. When directed, it should turn without protest, and when requested, it should find a calm, quiet balance, still and silent, to allow an undisturbed lunch or naps under the cypress canopy. It must be well behaved and well mannered.

Only wood boasts such a fine pedigree. A good wooden fishing boat is all these things, and more. You may feel a little proud but also a little odd, perhaps even eccentric, putting over at the launch, surrounding by sparkly fiberglass bass boats and blunt-nosed bateaus or sharp-stemmed, nearly right-angled sides. You might even feel uncomfortable under the grins, the condescending smiles that seem to voice the owner's thoughts that you are too poor, too silly or too tacky to own a sparkly bass boat. Ignore these. They are only the wedges of a modern world that demeans anything which is not produced by that most marvelous of technologies, conformity. These wedges are driven to split and fracture the log which is individuality. I will never comprehend what delight people find in living on a street of identical houses, with identical cars in the garages and identical boats out on the lake, varying only perhaps in color or a brand decal glued to the side. But they do. It is some measure of excellence to be so generic. Distinctiveness, once the mark of a Renaissance man, are frowned upon or ridiculed because the distinct individual does not conform, and that is to be pitied. Such people insist on being insulated from everything which might make them believe there are things out there more important than money.

Most people spend the majority of their lives on concrete. They live in homes that are built on concrete slabs; they walk on cement sidewalks to their vehicles that ride on concrete highways to work. They spend their days in offices or factories built on concrete. On the weekends, they wish to "get away from it all" so they hook their boats to their vehicles, drive on concrete streets to a concrete boat launch, from which they step into a fiberglass or metal boat, spend the day fishing, and return home by the same route. Other than perhaps being splashed in the face by the tail of a fish, they have touched nothing of what they thought they were seeking at all.

Concrete, fiberglass and metal are insulators; they prevent the flow of speculation, observation and affinity. This is as it is intended. Should everyone in the world suddenly begin to tune themselves to the world as the Creator and Crawfish made it, economic doom would surely follow.

There was no concrete in my childhood. The driveway was clamshell, necessary only to keep the cars from bogging in the mud. The front yard was lined with juniper trees and two massive live oaks. There was a wild cherry near the old workshop, and in the back, all manner of cypress, oak and other trees grew along the bayou. Only at school or the downtown shopping district did I touch concrete. Even today, when walking along a sidewalk, if there is grass nearby, I'll step off to it. Concrete hurts my feet. It insulates me from my ancestors.

At the boat launch, putting my little bateau into the lake, I have received such grins and the obligatory comments. "Boy, that sure is a *big* boat," was one genius remark. "Think you can handle a boat that big?"

Or, "That is a scary little boat."

And, "How often do you have to bail it out in a day?"

For the record, the bateau has never leaked, save for a small transom spot which only manifested when it was thirty-nine years old, and promptly repaired. The myth that wooden boats invariably leak is a lie perpetrated by a world that promotes the equally vicious lie that composite and metal boats do not. Dad did put a layer of fiberglass over the bottom after the episode with my grandfather and the quarter-inch bottom, but this did nothing to change the feel, sound and character of it. Under the green coat of hull paint, the subtle grain of Douglas fir still speaks loudly that this is a wooden boat.

The other lie is that wooden boats are not long-lived. At forty-two years old, my father's boat contradicts this. Certainly, unlike modern boats, it cannot be left in the weather and expected to remain fast. It must be taken care of. The number one commandment of wooden boat ownership is, *Thou shall keep it dry.* This does not, of course, apply to large sea vessels that are constantly submerged in saltwater, which is a preservative. But freshwater is a boat's worst enemy. A little extra care negates the myth that wooden boats rot and die quickly. That extra care, in a world where things are as disposable as a plastic shopping bag, a Styrofoam coffee cup or a milk jug, seems to be some sort of insurmountable peak which only the eclectic such as myself will dare summit.

In my younger days, I admit to feeling a slight embarrassment at the boat launch putting over my little wooden boat. I felt, as intended, that I didn't make enough money, was not ambitious as I should be. I got over it and now simply smile back with the same demeaning glance at the sparkly bass boats.

While pulling up at the boat landing recently another gentleman was putting down his boat, so I waited politely until he was done, and as I was coming in to disboard, he said to me, "You sure don't see many of those anymore."

Thinking he meant wooden boats in general, I smiled with thanks and said, "Nope, sure don't."

"That's a Nick Stouff boat, isn't it?" he noted. I was surprised and grateful. While my father made many boats in his lifetime, mine is the only one that I know of surviving. But that others live on in memories such as those of the kind fellow at the landing that day makes my heart rejoice.

So the objective of a good fishing boat, one necessarily of wood for someone like myself, is the search for living creation. It is the essence of the Raintree and the medicine of grandmothers. It is little mottled brown birds and dugout canoes. A wooden fishing boat embodies all those things. It is a link not only to the waters, but to all those who came before us. When we reach home waters in a wooden boat, we are touching that which made us.

The lyfe so short, the craft so long to lerne.—Chaucer

Native Waters

o o o o o o o o o o o o o o o o o o o o o o o o o o o o o o

Many men go fishing all of their lives without knowing that it is not fish they are after.

—Henry David Thoreau

Bass Tournaments

One Friday afternoon I was off from work. I went to Polito's Cafe in Franklin for lunch with the office crew, scarfed down my food with a speed and accuracy which amazed my friends, had one cup of coffee, stood up and said, "See ya," and was headed for the Rez and the boat.

By Sunday, I was fishing in not one, but two BASS tournaments, though I had not intended to and was not a bit happy about it.

I was on the water by 2 p.m. Friday. I put over at the Charenton beach landing, and after hearing that the fishing wasn't too good right now, made a determination that I would try anyway.

It has been a plan I concocted over the winter: I would hit the water every weekend the weather permitted, and when the fishing started good, I'd be there. Many years in the past I waited too long. Not this year. Concocting such plans are the fisherman's method of maintaining a grip on sanity when the temperatures are too cold, the rain too wet and the house has compressed to the size of a shoe box.

So I fished and fished and fished and got nary a nibble. I saw nutria rats big enough to swallow a dog, staring at me from atop logs as if they were thinking, "What you want here, boy? This is our lake." The nutria is a member of the rodent family, imported from South American in the early part of the century to help control vegetation in a private landholder's ponds. A hurricane allowed it to escape, and today's estimates are that twenty million of the twenty pound rodents are running all over south Louisiana, destroying wetlands with their voracious appetite for vegetation. The state has a bounty on them to licensed hunters who bring in the tails to prove their kills.

Discouraged—and a little intimidated by those vicious looking nutria since I was unarmed—I went back to the landing. I ran into a guy I know there, and asked where he thought the fish might be biting. He said I had to go back of (I'm paraphrasing here) Boudreaux's pond, but I don't have to go around Taylor's Point anymore, and I need to cut across Bamboo Canal into Lake Worth at which point I'll be somewhere in the neighborhood of Lake Superior.

Since I had no idea Boudreaux even had a pond, and I had never been around Taylor's Point in the first place, I was completely lost without having even left the landing again. When I said I hadn't fished Grande Lake in fifteen years, there was just a sad shaking of the head and best wishes.

That was the end of Friday's trip and Saturday the weather was so dreary I didn't bother at all. But Sunday, the fever hit me like a ton of bricks again, and off I went to Lake Fausse Pointe with my fishing buddy.

Without realizing it, I was to spend the day fishing in not one, but two fishing tournaments.

I didn't know there were two fishing tournaments going on, or I might well have stayed home. But when we arrived at the lake, the sparkly bass boats were everywhere. I mean, there were so many you couldn't swing a cat by the tail without hitting one. Professional Anglers had overrun my favorite place on earth, and I was none too pleased about it.

I strongly considered turning right around and going home, but then thought, "I have been fishing this lake since I was four years old, by thunder," and then I thought, "My dad fished this lake for 40 years before that," and then I thought, "My ancestors have been fishing this lake for eight thousand years," so I decided to stay.

Let me tell you, it weren't a lot of fun. At times I was surrounded by Professional Anglers in their sparkly bass boats, each of which easily cost more than my truck, probably more than my house. I've never seen a more annoying contraption in my life than a sparkly bass boat. When they'd activate their bow-mounted, 100-pound thrust trolling motors with a roar like a diesel bulldozer, they'd actually cause a wake. Professional Anglers do not arrive at or leave a fishing spot quietly, either. They go from dead stop to full throttle at once and rocket out of the area like they're late for the Hank Parker show on television. Professional Anglers also throw baits the size of telephones with rods as thick as baseball bats. When they catch a fish, they horse it in like they're winching the boat onto the trailer, fling it into the boat with their rods, where the poor fish flops around in a frantic panic, knocking himself senseless on the fiberglass bulkheads. Then the Professional Angler measures it and either tosses it back or puts it in the livewell.

I simply do not understand the need for all this. Call me a Luddite if you wish, but remember when people fished to relax? Lazily drifting among the cypress and tupelo, watching the day pass slowly, without complication, casting for fish and living life to the fullest. None of these poor guys looked relaxed. They all looked like they were at work and the boss was doing an employee evaluation. I've never seen such intensity. It was like fishing in a shopping mall.

But I tried to be kind. As I was coming out of a canal, we passed a duo of anglers, one of whom had just caught a bass.

"I left that one there, just for you!" I said with a big, friendly smile.

"Yeah?" he said, all saturated with intensity and competitiveness. "Why didn't you leave a big one?"

Ungrateful heathens.

It was quite a sight to see, really. Surrounded by at one point five big, sparkly, noisy bassboats, there we were in my 42-year-old wooden bateau, 12-foot long, coasting along with my 10-pound thrust Minn Kota trolling motor, casting light and ultra-light tackle. I got many an odd look, and I'm sure most were wondering how long it would take me to get back to the weigh-in spot with that little 15-horsepower outboard. My greatest pleasure, though, was the looks on their faces as we disappeared down a shallow canal in my little boat, a place none of them could even consider going without divine intervention. As far as I know, the Holy Ghost does not grant the power of walking on water to Professional Anglers.

It must have been time for the weigh-in around 3 p.m. because all of a sudden it was like a buffalo stampede. All you heard was roar after roar after roar of V-6 outboard engines screaming across the lake, dozens of fantails kicking up behind them, Professional Anglers hunched down behind smoked-glass windshields with their baseball caps turned backwards and their Team Daiwa jackets zipped to their necks. I suddenly realized that wherever the weigh-in was happening, by most tournament rules, any live fish must be returned to the water. That means they were taking fish out of my lake and letting them go somewhere else. This did little for my already foul mood.

In the end, though, we got three bass and two bluegill, all of which were released, and when we were out of sight of the Professional Anglers, a great day. I didn't win either of the tournaments, of course, because I didn't even make it to the weigh-in. That's fine by me.

The spring fishing finally broke, and I am happy to say that I have also finally broken a decade-long case of being snakebit. That's like in gambling, when you just can't win anymore, it's called being snakebit. The same thing happens, I'm told, in fishing. I have been snakebit for years.

I'm afraid, though, that I have to owe it to the Internet. Technology, it seems, has reared its ugly head in fishing, and I'm none too happy about it, despite breaking my bad luck streak.

I've been resisting the urge to get into techno-fishing for years. I guess I'm too much of a traditionalist, like my old man. It wasn't until he got much older that he finally got an electric trolling motor. Before that, he'd paddle us around the lake all day without complaint. I still have that little Minn Kota trolling motor, and it still runs great, though it's a low-thrust model, kinda like me.

Over the years, I have also resisted the urge to purchase a fish-finder. You know, those electric doomaflotchies that give you a graphic representation of what's under the water's surface. There's something inherently wrong with that. Where's the sport? You might as well get scuba gear and go spear fishing, or just throw in a stick of dynamite and be done with the whole sordid business. Not only that, but I was always afraid the little black-and-white screen would suddenly fizzle, shudder and display the message, "Give it up and go home, ya bum."

Watching the fishing shows I hear a lot about fishfinders. There are now models that you can attach to the side of your boat just like a trolling motor. If you're fishing from a dock, you can just dangle it over the side. There are also wireless fish finders. You put a green plastic thing on your line like a bobber and throw it out, and it sends the display back to your unit on the boat or on shore. Please. What next? A robot that goes underwater and gets the fish for you while you nap in the shade?

But I was talking about the Internet. Yes, I have to admit, I read the fishing reports for Louisiana. For instance, I know if that the vast majority of freshwater anglers are not catching, I should not feel so bad. I also know that if the vast majority are mopping up on 'em, I need to feel quite bad.

Therefore it was quite a surprise to me when I read an Internet fishing report last week which said the fish are biting at Place A at Time B on Bait C, and this was just about as close to my back yard as possible without just opening the back door and throwing out a line. Grumbling that any self-respecting Luddite such as myself should have more dignity, I loaded up the boat after work and took off.

The information superhighway is a wonderful thing. I can find out if the fish are biting in Glascow, Scotland or Portland, Maine. I can find out if the weather is right to throw a dry fly in Argentina. I can also learn that the fish are biting out my back door, and sure enough, they were. A hook and worm under a bobber was all it took, and the big bluegill were coming in hand over foot. I let all the females go, since it's spawn time, and kept the big males. These were rod-bending, drag-stripping fish, not midgets. At the end of the two hours I had before sunset forced me back to the landing, I brought home 14 nice ones to be cleaned and stuck in the freezer.

I went back the next day, with my oldest son, and we caught exactly zilch. Notta. Nein. Nyet. Zero, my hero. Upon getting back home, I checked the Internet. Yup, they stopped biting, the reports said. This is getting too much like a fish finder, this Internet fishing report business. I am starting to fear that I'll log in to one of my favorite fishing reports sites one day and a page will come up that says, "Please wait, you are being redirected to our web page for Luddites." This is followed by another screen with big letters that say, "Sell your gear, it's going to be another 10 long years before you catch another fish, ya bum."

Now, Friday, without looking at the Internet, I headed out late in the afternoon. When I got to the boat landing, there was no room to park. I went to another nearby with the same results. I should have known better than to go fishing on Good Friday. The lake was so full of boats they looked like drowning bees all over the water, darting back and forth, jet skis screaming across the waves, anglers shaking their fists at the jet ski drivers. It didn't take me long to decide this was not where I wanted to be, so I put up the boat, threw my fly rod and box into the back of the truck with a few Diet Cokes on ice and headed to some ponds I know about.

There are no Internet reports that I know of for ponds. I have yet to see someone post that they caught a mess of 'em in the pond next to the Opelousas overpass or something like that. Most dedicated anglers are ashamed to admit they'll go fish in a pond off the highway. They're afraid their compatriots will laugh at them. One day on the lake I was having such miserable luck, I commented to my fishing buddy that I might as well go fishing in the highway ponds with the po' folks. Then I realized, I *am* po' folks, so the next day, there I was. I don't care. I've been laughed at for ten years now. Besides, at this particular pond I can catch little bream and the occasional keeper all day on the fly rod.

While I was there, a lady came by with her kids to just walk around and enjoy the day, and she said to me, "There's some big fish in there." She said she had hooked one a week or two ago that broke her line. I smiled politely, thinking this a fish story, since I had already pulled about 40 little perch out of the pond and thrown them back. I missed a couple hundred more because they were too small to get their little lips around the fly.

"You oughta go somewhere where you can really use that thing," she said, pointing to my fly rod. "You know, a river with trout in it or something."

I told her it was in my plans, one day. After awhile, her and the kids departed and I continued taking out little perch. I can do that all day. I fish for the fun, not the fight or the food, though both are nice. But a chartreuse popper on a five-weight flyrod in a pond full of little bluegill is fun as heck. It's one of the reasons I chose to go back to fly fishing in addition to my regular tackle. I'm not interested in impressing anyone, and if you saw some of my casts you'd know this is true, but I like the purity of it.

"Big ones in here," I grumbled, removing a tiny bream about three inches long from my popper. "Right."

I laid the line out next to a tree overhanging the pond. I had noticed the tree was full of caterpillars, and as they'd fall into the water when a breeze trembled the leaves of the tree, the fish would suck them up. Since I had nothing in the fly box that resembled a caterpillar, I didn't think it would do much good.

Suddenly I saw something flash green-white under the surface, the water boiled and erupted around my popper and a huge splash exploded. I pulled back on the rod, which promptly bent over until the tip nearly touched the reel, and something pulled back mightily then shot off toward deep water, promptly relieving itself of my fly in the process. Upon inspection, I saw that the hook was straightened right out.

If the lady with her kids is reading this, I want you to know, you were right! Boy, was she right. There's some big ones in that pond. And I didn't need no stinking Internet to tell me, just good ol' word of mouth, like it should be, and I don't need batteries.

It may seem odd, to people whom do not fish, or even to some whom do, that someone could make an adversary out of a fish.

While I've never found an adversary in a fish, though I've been fishing since I was old enough to hold a pole, the time apparently has come.

There is a pond I fish regularly, in which I mentioned sometime back that I was told there were some big ones. I verified this by hooking into something on my fly rod that bent the hook straight and escaped. A few days later, I hooked into him again. This time he took the fly like a rabid pit bull dog, darted across an open expanse of water and into a thicket of brush. I pulled back, cognizant of the fact that I was fighting this monster with a four-pound leader tip, and he freaked out a little. He changed direction at my pull, bent the rod over and the next thing I knew he pitched the fly out of the water so hard my leader wrapped around the tip of the rod, creating a nasty mess which took me half an hour to untangle.

Missing a big fish once is a tragic thing, but twice is complete devastation. I am sure it is the same fish, for he hit the fly when laid in precisely the same spot both times. The first time he hit a chartreuse popper with rubber legs; the second, he threw back at me a floating bee imitation.

He hangs out under a maple tree that, at least this time of year, is full of caterpillars. As the wind moves the limbs of the trees, sometimes the caterpillars fall off and immediately vanish as the fish gobble them up. Mostly it's little ones, but now and then, there's a cataclysmic boil of water marking the passing of my adversary. He's a sneaky, taunting devil, and I don't even know what species he is, but I'm guessing largemouth bass. Now and then, as I'm popping little bluegill out of the pond, he'll tease me by rolling at something just out of reach of my cast, or chasing a tiny bluegill across the top of the water. I see the bluegill skipping along in sheer terror trying to escape by growing wings and taking flight, but behind it, only a v-shaped rippling of the water's surface as the big fella pursues. The little bluegill rarely escapes.

In keeping with tradition, I have named him the General, after my now-absent temperamental and troublesome lawn mower, Gen. George Armstrong Custer, because, like both the mower and its namesake, he's crafty, sneaky, behaves like a bull in a china closet, and thinks he's going to outwit this Indian. That makes it personal, you see. It's now one-on-one. In so naming him, the General has become my archenemy, like the Goblin to Spiderman, like Lex Luthor to Superman, like the Joker to Batman. You get the idea.

The easily accessible ponds around these parts are heavily fished, mostly by perch-jerkers such as myself. The General must therefore be used to seeing a lot of red-and-white bobbers with worms or crickets or shiners thrown before him, and has learned to ignore them, having seen so many juvenile bluegill yanked into perdition by them. He also ignores, I can tell you because I tried, spinnerbaits, tube jigs and anything else I've thrown at him. He only goes after flies, and then only rarely. He doesn't like sinking flies, either, only floaters. I tried a hook with a caterpillar on it, live, but he's much too smart for that. I fed half a dozen caterpillars to bluegill before I gave up. The misery of it was that, while I was fishing my hooked caterpillar, he took one just four feet away that had fallen in. Smart aleck devil, he is.

It's easy for me to imagine the General in his pond, of which he must be the undisputed master. If there is a bigger fish intimidating him, I don't want to know about it. I can imagine him, lurking there under a tree, gills fanning gently, tail sweeping to and fro. Even the bigger bluegill avoid him, because they never know if the General's might be in a bad mood and they'll end up his lunch.

There was a third time that he bit, but I didn't realize it at the time. It was a month or so ago, when I first started fishing this particular spot. I had thrown out a fly when I was just re-learning to cast my rod, and snagged it on some limbs just below the surface. I tugged and negotiated, and there was suddenly a mighty tug back, which I thought at the time was the limb springing back, but there was also a churning of water around the brush. I wonder now if he wasn't trying to pick my fly off the limb? The General is way too smart.

I'll keep trying, but I wonder if I'll ever catch him? I can imagine myself, 80 years old or something, either still trying to land the General or too old to fish and talking about him to anybody that I can trap in a corner.

"Yep, sonny, the old General, he's one crafty sucker," I say.

"Uh, right, gramps, I heard this story..."

"Did I ever tell you about the time he stole my sandwich off the bank? Right there next to my tackle!"

"Yeah, heard that one too, 14 times."

"You getting smart with me, boy?"

Or maybe I'll land him one day. Maybe one day he'll slip up, forget the usual deceitful and sneaky way he takes a fly, and I'll fight him for hours and finally pull him up on the bank, both of us tired and weak.

What then? Put him back, of course. It's not about anything else. It's not about a fried fish supper. It's about who's smarter, me or the General. It's a contest of wits, and of will.

And that, I suppose, is what I enjoy most about fishing in the end. While it's certainly far better to catch than not, the fishing itself is what is so intriguing. Blindly presenting a lure or bait which hopefully a fish will find tempting. Trying to figure out what they might want when what I'm using isn't working. It's good to bring home some for the table, but a fish like the General deserves to live. Should I ever land him, he'll go free again, defeated but respected. Should I never bring him to the bank, he'll still be free, and I'll be defeated. I have no idea if the General might respect me regardless, but it doesn't matter. I'll respect myself for having tried.

Eden Lost

In my youth, no one but a few of us local went to Lake Fausse Pointe. It was rare that we ever saw another angler in the lake or the cove, and even then, it was usually another like us. But since the state opened Lake Fausse Pointe State Park in Iberia Parish, north part of the lake just before it makes an imaginary transition into Lake Dautrieve, my Eden has been overrun by the heathens.

They frustrate, confound and infuriate me. While I take great care to respect all boaters, the most important consideration of which is to *slow down* when passing another boater fishing or anything else so that my wake will cause as little disturbance as possible, the masses of sparkly boats on the lake today do not. Their drivers deem themselves king of the water, and they pass by with engines roaring, never caring about who might be broadside of their swells, not concerned who they might annoy.

They are everywhere on my lake now. Even the cove is packed with them. They are often rude when passed a friendly angler-to-angler hello or comment, so intent upon their competitive task that good manners is forgotten. They think nothing of zooming in a scant fifty yards ahead of us when we're fishing, or worse, fifty yards behind and quickly overtake and pass us with their huge electric trolling motors, never offering an apology. When fishing and I come upon another angler that I would like to pass quietly behind, I always ask permission. That does not imply that the other angler can forbid me, but I have never been forbidden. It is merely courtesy, a forgotten if not obsolete art.

It is a purely European phenomenon. Five hundred years ago, settlers and colonists touched the stems of their boats to this continent and largely saw only a resource to exploit. North America was so vast, so incomprehensibly big, it seemed to go on forever. The adulteration of Christianity had firmly planted the belief that man is holier than all things on the earth, and that all else is placed here to serve him. We are the overlords of dominion. Does not the Bible say that God gave man the world? It is only just, then, to use it. The Protestant work ethic demanded that trees be felled to clear the way for farms, to build cottages and towns which would grow to cities. It was not as if we could cut *all* the trees, or kill all the deer or catch all the fish. The world was too vast, and God always provides.

Europeans came to the Americas with the idea that it must be tamed. It was a crusade in the name of their religion. The wild forests, wild animals and wild Indians were an affront to God, and must be subdued to serve civilization. Man's place is to subdue the world, and the colonists promptly set about doing so, quite efficiently and effectively. A hundred thousand acres of hardwoods would hardly be missed if cut and burned to create farmland. The entire continent was covered with such forests.

I struggle with the violation, just as Maclean struggled with seeing his precious Montana home waters overrun by fly fishermen who gave not a rip about the Eden he grew up in. The enormous continent has dwindled in five centuries, and still the conquest must continue. They yell at each from one seat in their boats to the other. It is as unthinkable as yelling in the pews. They throw their trash overboard. This is a generalization, of course. I am sure there are sparkly boat anglers who are considerate and thoughtful. It's just that I have not yet encountered the species.

It as if there is a technological novel at work, a science-fiction tale. The state stocked my lakes with Florida largemouth bass, but nobody is catching them much. Though the anglers arrive equipped with graphic display fish finders, sounders, high-tech fishing lines and multi-ball bearing reels, catches are not increasing. Yet they keep coming back, putting more pressure on the lake, which it cannot survive.

It is said that trees once covered Easter Island. In the time that human beings lived there, trees were felled for the purposes trees are used. For generations, humans on that tiny island chopped trees as they needed them, and at some unfathomable moment, the last tree stood on Easter Island and a human being cut it down. I wonder, when he laid the blade to that final tree, did he know what he was doing to himself, to his people, but did it anyway?

So it is on the lake. They seem to be determined to fish it and fish it until the last fish has been caught. Then they'll come back for a time and fish it some more, until all hope is gone, and they'll migrate off to another Eden somewhere to tear apart the water with their massive engines. The state may stock the lake again, but this is only a stop gaps measure.

Yet I go on. I have a right to my legacy. The name of my people is written on these waters, though most have forgotten it. I do have to venture father afield now, out of my gardens and into foreign waters, but I will go. I have been cast out of Eden, but not by my Creator. The serpent himself has cast me out.

There were four trees that marked the boundaries of the Chitimacha nation, a territory that lay over about a third of the present-day state of Louisiana. One of these, the last, was the Raintree.

It is believed that each of the four trees possessed certain properties, but the other three remain a mystery. The last tree, the sacred tree, stood somewhere near

Bayou Portage until the current undermined its roots and it fell into the canal in 1927. It, at least, was a cypress, and the other three may have been as well, but we do not know.

According to both oral Chitimacha tradition and documentation by Bureau of American Ethnology researchers, if a limb from the Raintree was placed into water, rain would come. My great-grandmother, Delphine, was said to have been the last Chitimacha to use the tree for this purpose, successfully. It is interesting to note that when the bulk of the tree fell into Bayou Portage in 1927, Louisiana experienced the worst storm in recorded history. A photographer took pictures of the fallen tree, and was so stunned by the prints he brought them to the reservation and gave them to my grandparents. They clearly show spirits dancing hand-in-hand in the water. He also gave them three long branches that he took from the tree. They remain with me today. I have never tested them. Some things should not be tampered with in ignorance. There is great power in them even now, the power which permeated *Sheti* and which remains potent in places today.

Prior to 1839, the Atchafalaya River flow, where it became a tributary of the Mississippi, was partially blocked by a logjam that measured thirty miles. It was known as The Raft. In that year, the state undertook a massive project to clear The Raft, something that had been tried and failed many times before. But this time the state succeeded, increasing the flow of water down the Atchafalaya tremendously, deepening the channel and widening the lakes in some places. Perhaps this increase in flow is what undermined the Raintree.

Nevertheless, it is gone, save for a few limbs kept safe and dry in my house. I am thankful, at least, that it fell to some force of moving water, rather than the saw blades of loggers. Such an end would have been horrifying.

It was from cypress that the Creator taught my father's people to build the canoe. They were instructed to pack a ring of wet mud around the base of the tree, a couple of feet from the ground. Then they set a large fire around the roots and burned the tree until it fell over. The wet ring of mud prevented the fire from spreading into the higher areas of the trunk. Once the tree was felled, they used fire and mud to fashion the dugout canoe.

Cypress was as important to my ancestors on my father's side as it was on my mother's. It is a living wood, whether still rooted and tall, or fashioned into a boat or an oar. For the bow, we used Osage orange. From the black walnut tree we crushed the nuts and threw them into small ponds. A mild toxin in the nuts would stun the fish so they could be easily picked up from the dugout.

There were wild blueberries and muscadines everywhere in the basin, as well as other edible plants long forgotten. The flat-topped pond lily grew potato-like tubers deep in the mud, which the Chitimacha called "woman's potato" and the bright-green, stiff briar could be uprooted for small nodules that were ground into fine flour. The bloodweed was an excellent treatment for snakebite. Medicinal plant knowledge went to the grave with my grandmother by oath that she swore to Delphine. After treating a white man for snakebite in the 1960s, from which he fully recovered, several local doctors approached her to learn her methods. When she refused, the American Medical Association threatened to file charges against her for practicing medicine without a license. She never treated another person beside herself again, and all that wisdom, all those miracles, went to rest with her.

I have pages and pages of documents she left behind listing the various medicines and their uses. Unfortunately, all the specific plants are listed by their Chitimacha names, with no physical descriptions, making sure identification impossible. It is probably better that way.

May

Winds, blustery and persistent, lost en route to March, make their arrival at last on the doorstep of May. The trees dance with them, waters lurch back and forth beneath them.

This is May, when we stand at the graveside of winter and sing dirges, though there is always the knowledge that winter's passing is only cyclical, and it will return. In the pasture behind the house, blue wort, oxalis and white clover leap from the dry ground, because May hasn't brought the rains it promised. On the lake, the Louisiana irises, blue and purple and red to each their own, have already blossomed and faded.

Behind the house, I walk and search for signs of *bahjootah* while Mocha runs. I have not seen it for nearly three decades. It once grew wild behind my house, and when my grandmother lived there, she said it would cure any external malady or wound. She was taught this by her mother-in-law, Delphine, my great-grandmother. When my grandmother was diagnosed with throat cancer and given six months to live, she boiled the roots of *bahjootah* and drank the brew daily. The cancer vanished and she lived more than 20 years after that.

I helped her pick the plant in that pasture, where it grew just beyond the dripline of the old oak tree. I have never seen it again. I don't know it's Latin name or its taxonomy. When my grandmother was threatened with prison by local doctors because she refused to reveal her medicines after she saved the life of a boy from snakebite, she never used them again on anyone but herself. Delphine had made her promise she would not reveal the old ways to non-Indians, and she never did.

Sometimes when I walk the pasture looking for *bahjootah*, I know it is futile. I'll never find it. It has hidden itself. Perhaps it was always hidden, lying dormant there in the ground for decades, until my grandmother needed it. Perhaps it will rise if I should ever require it's magic. Such things defy the disbelief of a mind half-blinded by living outside the circle for most of my life.

But I walk the pasture and look anyway, glad to be away from the fluorescent lights that make my head throb, the computer screen which burns my eyes and the stiff shirt on my shoulders that grows tight and suffocating. There are days when the nonstop ringing of the phone is torture, the chatter of business words unintelligible, and the constant hum of traffic on the street outside like a beast, circling, stalking.

It is at such times that I feel like a stranger in a strange land, a totemic panther in a circus cage, pacing, back and forth behind iron bars, pacing, pacing, pacing. Such times I know that I was born a century two late. I stand out there sometimes in the basin, in the cathedral of my ancestors, and wonder what it looked like five centuries ago. Before there were chinaberry and chicken trees, before hydrillia and water hyacinth, red ants and nutria. Before the levees and weirs and locks and garbage scattered along the banks. When grandfathers used the roots of the black walnut tree to stun fish in shallow pools, and muscadine, blueberry and elderberry grew wild, nibbled upon by white deer. When my grandmothers sought out *bahjootah* to cure.

Long ago, the last of four trees which marked the boundaries of the Chitimacha nation fell, and an era passed on the crest of a mighty flood. It swept away more than a cypress we knew as the Raintree. When it fell that day, crashing into the water with the screaming crack of branches and sundering of trunk, a people passed into shadow along with it, only to return to the light a scant decade ago. The world I was born into was a world with no Raintree, but with the memory of it firmly in tow. My grandparents possessed branches taken from the Raintree when it fell. When I touched them, I felt some stir of power, like when hear someone calling you on a windy day from afar, barely audible, and you're not quite sure you heard it at all. I still have the branches, and when I touch them now, I hear them more clearly, but they are still distant.

They ask as they pass my desk, *What are you in such deep thought about?* but I only smile and answer something noncommittal. They wouldn't understand that the shoes are hurting my feet, the fluorescent lights are making me blind and the computer screen is sowing tumors in my brain and I have no *bahjootah* to cure myself. What doesn't kill you only makes you stronger. The clock ticks off the minutes and I feel prisoner to it; captive to some clicking, falsely uplifted god that believes it can dictate to me what I should do, what I should wear when I do it, when I can stop doing it, and when I'll have to do it again. I stopped wearing a wristwatch three years ago because it felt like iron shackles. If I could live in a world devoid of clocks and telephones, I would surely be free.

At last my master, that ticking dictator on the wall, releases me and I rush to the water. Sunlight eases the burning in my eyes and terra firma soothes the aching in my feet. I am far from concrete and telephones and flickering lights. If I look hard enough, if I put aside the recent memory of captivity, I can imagine I am here, in the past, a century ago, and there is, beyond that treeline where an eagle is watching me with sadness, nothing but more trees and more eagles, and an eventual ocean farther still. No buildings, no roads, no clocks and no utility poles stringing copper wires from one end of creation to the next. If I see no human trash bobbing at the water's edge, hear no traffic in the distance and perceive no concept of time, I can believe that this might have been how it was.

My father used to tell people that these rare and wonderful swamps and river basins were the Garden. "This was Eden," he would say, and people would laugh, but beneath the laughter was often the sneaking suspicion that perhaps the old man really meant what he said. Deeper still was the uneasy feeling that perhaps he was right.

I also wondered, back then. I thought the old man, who had a tendency toward sarcastic wit, spoke a bit out of turn. But as I sit in the vessel that is my life and look aft from amidships, I realize he was more correct than I ever knew. Eden was the confluence of rivers, and from that union the Garden sprang. Perhaps not the Eden of scripture, but in its very essence, it is a reflection.

Only here do I feel complete. Closer to my Creator, nearer my God to thee, than within any structure fashioned by men. It is for me a far greater affirmation of faith, of divinity, to read the waterlines at the trunks of trees, the marks of woodpeckers and the nests of eagles than Mark, Luke or John. It is a far greater rejuvenation of spirit to feel early morning mist on my cheeks, sunlight on my brow, to know currents and breezes and sweet-scented rain, than feel my back ache on wooden pews, stiff in the clothes of my betters, those I'm told are more just, more holy, more divine than I, timid under the fire and brimstone of the man behind the pulpit. Here, at least, I am never threatened with damnation, rather I can be uplifted by creation.

Because in the end, I learned more from a few moments in a small wooden boat than any school or tabernacle; in each essay about renovating this old house is the remnant of a huge cypress barge, half-sunken on the lake, but when the water is low you can see iron spikes outlining its shape, the enormous upper removed five decades ago by my father to become part of the house I grew up in; in each bluegill taken from beneath the branches of a cypress canopy is the Raintree, and deeper still in my green-black home waters lie a thousand secrets, a thousand memories I just haven't recalled yet, and still more secrets and memories to be found.

I can sit and wordlessly sing hymns surrounded by stained glass and dead mahogany; or I can listen to the melodies and music of the wind, the water lapping at the crevices of cypress trunks. I can be preached at about grace, or I can know it in the sailing wings of a hawk overhead, the screech of an owl, the gentle drift or raging torrent of rivers. I can rejoice in it, for as long as it still exists, and I think about how I could not see across Grande Lake as a child. I wonder what my children will not be able to see across when they are my age. What will they not be able to see at all, blinded by the present, blind to the past, deaf to all but the ringing of phones and the ticking of the overlord on the wall.

My father never tried to own creation, he only tried to revere it and learn from it. The words spoken to him and I from behind that pulpit speak of the same creation as testament, but without the commandment of dominion. Once, when I was very young, my grandfather and I sat in a patch of river cane where we were cutting the stalks for baskets. We harvested only enough of that patch to use, and it was there when we returned year after year. Until it was cleared for agricultural use, as were all the other patches of river cane.

As we broke for lunch, we sat silent for a time, chewing ham sandwiches my grandmother had prepared. We sat listening to rustlings in the brush, a breeze caressing the tops of the canes and the live oaks farther above, and he said to me, "This is where God lives," and said no more.

Freedom. It is a sweet, if elusive, dream.

The lake continues to remind me of its secrets and its power. A storm converged on south Louisiana one early spring. I had scarcely made it home from work when the heavens split asunder and the deluge, peppered with spheres of white hail, converged.

Trees whipped in the front yard like weeds, the tips of many of their limbs severed by the force of the winds and tumbling across the lawn. Already there were standing pools in the grass, and a steady flow along the shallow ravine which drains to Bayou Teche.

Knowing that I should retreat to the sanctuary within the house, but feeling the need to see, I started the truck back up and left again for the lake.

Wind pushed at the truck angrily, trying to shove it from the road while the tires splashed through water along the curb waiting to spiral down into the catch basins. Overhead, pecans and oaks slashed and writhed violently, and sodden leaves flattened against the roadbed. I crossed Bayou Teche, windshield wipers pitching to and fro, and made my way to the levee. Hail pelted the truck, but I could see it was not large enough to do damage.

Where we go when we need inspiration, or simply recharging, is individual to each of us. Some find solace in church, with family, near each other. I find it in solitude. I find it in the storm.

Driving carefully down the levee, watching the trees bend and bow and sway, I understood again how my birthright has shaped me. I was literally born in the eye of a hurricane, have always had an affinity for the storms, mild or powerful. Their ferocious intensity fascinate and frighten me at once, and an uneasy truce between the storm and I has formed over the years. They tolerate me, I believe, like kin.

The lake was a catapult, a hundred, a thousand catapults. I pulled into a sideroad, left the truck running so that the wipers would continue to swipe. Across the expanse, the wind conjured white-capped waves, which the rain sought to beat back down. The waves slapped against the bowing, bending trees, reaching high up their trunks like desperate, starving children. Fishing net buoys made eddies as they fought the mighty sweep of the lake northward.

Along the north shore of the lake, I spied a dim moving shape: A boat, struggling against the wind and rain, making for the tenuous safety of the cut. It was barely visible, but I could discern its bow pounding heavily on the crests, a hunched and haggard figure at the engine tiller. Watching with fascinated dread, the boat made a steady if slow headway, and I determined it was an aluminum skiff, probably about 18-feet long. Laboriously, it continued toward the cut.

I don't know how long I watched it, but it seemed like an eternity. At times, it seemed like he was making no progress at all, then he would suddenly appear to have leaped from one point far away to another closer to me. The wind pushed the lake so hard it made conglomerate waves of the smaller ones, valleys carved out as a gust swept through and pushed the water aside like Moses at the sea. The boat continued its painful trek to the cut, and it was closer. A particularly virulent thunderhead moved closer as well, and the sky darkened even more, so all I could see of the boat was a slight difference in the murk.

Suddenly, that difference veered drastically and aimed itself at me. I realized that, as the sky darkened, the headlights on the truck were probably the only thing the boater could see clearly. I turned on the high beams as he pitched and yawed his way, angled nearly broadside to the wind now.

There is a row of large pilings near what we call "the seawall" at Lake Fausse Pointe, and he was veering close to them, shoved by the wind and rain, but at the last moment, the boater swung the high-swept bow of the skiff around and pitched straight into the wind again. The cut was only a hundred yards away now, but it seemed to take him an eternity to cross the distance.

Then, at once, he was out of the fray, into the channel, and making his way out of the lake. Not easily, to be sure, but essentially out of danger. I flashed my high beams at him, and I think he waved back, but I am not sure.

Pain in my fingers revealed that I had been clenching the steering wheel so tightly my knuckles were white. I retreated back up the levee and rushed as much as I could rush to the landing at Grand Avoille Cove, but the boater was not there. I could not see far left or right, so I spun back out and went to the launch in Charenton and waited. He never showed up. Perhaps he resided in one of the camps along the levee, or had taken a right at the bridge over the cut in Charenton and gone on his way from there. I would liked to have met him, congratulated him on his boatsmanship, perhaps chastised him for letting the weather take him into harm's way, above all, express my relief that he had made it okay.

The storm raged and convulsed as I made slow headway home. This storm, unlike a hurricane, had no eye. It was, on the radar, a band of thunderheads streaming across the southeast like Poseidon's belt. Within homes I passed, people were safe and warm and dry, and the hail had already largely melted away in the lawns.

The storm had no eye but my own, and my eye had witnessed a small victory that day under the ravaging skies and under the torrential rain. The yard was littered with broken tree limbs and leaves. As I turned the key and let the engine sleep, then threw myself into the deluge to run under the awning at the front door, and as I slid my key into the lock, I realized it was probably better that the boater and I hadn't actually met. Walking on the street, in the grocery store, perhaps we'll cross each other's paths one day without recognition. My memory will only be of a dim difference in the deluge, his the flash of pickup truck headlights in the storm. What we'll both remember best is the storm, the raging lake, and the tendril of connection that briefly joined the three of us.

But there are the quiet, reflective moments, as well.

That same week, I fished along the south side of the cove, the pilings stretched out behind me, clear across the shallow cove to Sawmill Bayou. Surely to anyone else they were just a row of old cypress pilings, remarkably intact for being over 70 years old, but just a row of pilings nonetheless. For me they conjured memories and ghosts. Dad limping home with a busted Mercury outboard. The countless warnings, about them, and about the log which crosses the channel right at the mouth of Sawmill Bayou; the sandbars on Lake Fausse Pointe and the huge stumps at the mouth of Peach Coulee. The things I could see, though they were invisible, in my mind's eye. In my imagination, I could envision thousands of cypress and tupelo timbers tied off to those pilings, awaiting the start of their journey down the lake, long before there was a levee; around Big Pass and Little Pass, crossing the finger of land which would one day become Taylor's Point, on to the sawmills which were abundant from Charenton to Morgan City and beyond. Magnificent old growth cypress trunks, a hundred feet long and big around as a dump truck. Right where the row of pilings ended on the south back, a wild persimmon tree grew in my youth, hanging out over the water. One spring the persimmons ripened and as they fell off the tree into the lake the catfish tore them up with mighty explosions of boiling water. Dad took out the fly rod with a large popping bug on the end of the leader and mopped up on 'em that day. Now the rotted stump of that persimmon tree has even vanished.

I coasted up next to one of the pilings and touched it, touched a century of history. A hundred years of ghosts. Could I feel the tearing of a passe partout through the trunk of thousand-year-old timber? Probably not, but I'd like to think so.

The sweat from humid brows, the blood from battered fingers has long been washed from the grain of the pilings by the murky water of the cove, by seasons of forgetfulness and tides of disbelief. The next day when I returned, the water had risen and they were invisible again, submerged to where the things which lie beneath persist, whether we are aware of them or not.

It's here that I learn stories, new stories or those revived from the dim creep of foggy memory. It's here where these words are birthed, and I am but their conduit to any ears that wish to hear.

Fishing and Musing Through Eden

o o o o o o o o o o o o o o o o o o o o o o o o o o o o o o o o o o o

Some go to church and think about fishing, others go fishing and think about God.

—Tony Blake

Counting Coup

Lightning, jagged and spectacular, crashes from cloud to cloud. Magnificent and dazzling against the broiling black thunderheads, they leap like celestial panthers from fold to billow.

Though I know I should retreat, seeking shelter in the truck which is parked a couple hundred yards away on the seldom-used road, there are fish rising, undaunted by the conflagration overhead. A patch of willow off-center of the pond is motionless: This storm, while raging in the skies above me, has brought no wind as yet.

Because I have seen no bolts strike the ground or any of the taller structures nearby, I persist, just a little while longer. Fish are rising; there are ringlets and circles on the surface of the pond everywhere I look. The air is charged, I can feel the hair on my arms standing on end from the electrostatic energy.

Only a damn fool would do this, I thought to myself, then immediately replied, *Well, it's not the first time you've been called a fool and probably not the last. Takes one to know one, pal.*

To the south, distant and unheard, traffic is a column of multi-colored, speeding ants racing to work, rushing home to cook supper, change clothes for that late evening meeting, collapse from a long, exhausting day. I tuck the butt of the rod under my left elbow and drop the leader into my outstretched right hand to inspect the tip for abrasion. I would like to pity those rushing insects along the highway just barely in range of my vision, but I am not so lofty. Were they closer, they would probably gawk at the fool fishing on the pond as lightning flashes warnings overhead and thunder growls threats so fearsome the ground trembles.

Perhaps, as I pity them, they'll pity me. I would like to believe that, rather than rushing down a cattle shoot coerced by deadlines, paychecks and obligations, they are instead off to meet a lover, join friends for a supper, spend an evening watching the storm from a screened-in porch. They'll perhaps pity me in obverse, thinking me without family, without friend, without love, relegated to this lonely pond out of sheer boredom and neglect. As if those things are shackles which would prevent me from being here. I suppose we'll never understand each other. I'll never understand the need to struggle so mightily up that imaginary ladder, and they'll never understand the family, friends and love that stand beside me on the banks of a little pond where the fish are rising in swarming glee.

Gotta live a little, I reminded myself. *Gotta live a lot. Youth is not necessarily wasted on the young.* Though the grass and weeds have grown tall over the summer months, if I keep the rod tip high as the line loops out behind me, snapping it forward just as I feel the barely perceptible tug when it reaches full measure, I can avoid the backcast snags. I lay 40 feet of line out, not perfectly, not even prettily, but adequately for a novice. At the end of the leader, a small chartreuse fly with rubber legs has just settled onto the surface near the edge of the willows.

Before I can even gather the line in my left hand to mend the slack, simultaneously the water churns and thunder smacks deafeningly, both startling me. I wince from the thunder and snatch back on the rod, the tip of which bends over nicely with the weight of a respectable fish on the fly.

Feels wrong, I think, and in a second of decision, I lower the rod just a tad then snap it back again, setting the hook a bit more firmly. The fish makes a startled run for the willows. I know that if he wraps my leader around a stem in there he's gone for certain, so I tug back, and lightning leaps from cloud to cloud as if in response, illuminating the pocket of shade cast by the willows overhanging the pond, where the fish is seeking escape.

Across the acres, the cars and mini-vans and tractor-trailers speed on, oblivious, all heat and stench of exhaust and rubber tires. A father looks at his watch and wonders if he'll make his client's dreaded party in time; a single mom dials the radio stations, searching for a better song, hoping she'll make it to the next pay day before any checks bounce; a toddler screams in the back seat, exhausted and tired from tagging along on a long day of grocery shopping, paying bills and looking for a job, startled by the thunder.

I coax the fish away from the willows, and he resists again by rushing out toward open water, and I let him run, drag applied only with my forefinger pressing line against the rod. He races in the same direction as the distant traffic, and I half expect him to shoot out onto the bank and continue, taking my line to the backing, then popping it off the arbor like a clap of thunder. Instead, rebellious, he leaps out of the water, shaking vigorously, attempting to dislodge the fly, but my second hookset holds fast. He dances on his tail for a moment, then falls back into the pond and races—a little more slowly, he is tiring—toward me.

I reel line in as quickly as I can, trying to avoid slack which will allow him freedom to perhaps head back toward the willows, or into a bed of submerged weeds, where he'll wrap my leader around the unseen growth and pull free. When I have the slack line back onto the spool, it snaps back taunt and I guide him away from the weeds, but he has caught his second wind now, and is heading for open water again.

As my small, personal battle unfolds under the storm front which is still holding its rain, I know I am blessed. There's not much else one can think about while fighting a decent fish on a fly rod in a small pond full of willows and weed beds, but somewhere in the back of my consciousness flashed confirmations. That, after all I've sought and all I've found, it was pulling down the ladder and throwing it into the ditch that made me happy. That, when all is said and done, the only regrets I have are the miles wasted on that concrete, crooked spine. And that, in the end, I can truthfully say I am happier today, this minute, with this job, this home and in this place with these people I know and sometimes love, than I have ever known myself to be.

At last, the bass is spinning tight circles near my feet, and I wait for him to settle down, then place my thumb gently, respectfully, under his lower jaw and lift him out of the water. Three pounds, I guess. Not bad for a light fly rod. I thank him for the battle. We were, after all, only counting coup, and I immersed him into the water again, let go his jaw. He didn't rocket off like the lightning flashing overhead—rather, he meandered along the bottom, heading out toward deeper water, unrushed, unburdened, unencumbered. Free. Defeated this day, perhaps humbled, but whole to fight again another. This is the way of dignity. It is not necessary to kill him. It is only necessary to best him, as I have been similarly bested by other rising fish on other ponds many times before.

I stood and my back ached, my shoulder snapped a little, or perhaps it was a minor clap of thunder. I glanced at the highway, and could have sworn it was a few miles farther away than the last time I looked.

Boat Dogs

Some dogs are dry land dogs, some are water dogs, some are boat dogs, some are all of the above. It has become increasingly obvious to me that Mocha is no boat dog.

Shadow, my dearly-departed first English springer spaniel, was a water dog and a boat dog by instinct. Shadow loved the boat. He'd stand with his back legs on the bottom planking and his front legs on the deck as we'd make our way to the lake, ears flapping like brown flags in the wind, wagging his nub of a tail in delight. Shadow, perhaps the most intelligent dog I've ever known, would sit on the back seat of the boat while I was fishing, watching everything, curious about any little speck of debris that floated by, and absolutely had to sniff any fish that I happened to luck out on bringing into the boat. If I threw a fish back without letting Shadow sniff it, he would pout until I caught another and let him sniff it.

Mocha is an adorable, loving, beautiful English springer. She's kind, energetic, friendly, eager to please and is definitely not a boat dog. I've only taken Mocha in the boat once before, a trip she didn't particularly enjoy much. I decided recently to try her again, since she was fairly young the first time.

I let her sit in the front seat of the truck, where she whined and woofed in delight on the way to the landing. When I prompted her to jump in the boat with me from her perch on the dock, she obeyed without hesitation, eagerly sniffing everything in the bilge. When I started the engine and throttled up, she suddenly remembered that she didn't like boats at all.

She curled up around my feet and put her head between my calves the whole ten minutes it took to get to the lake. I patted her head, and she whined. I thought, well, maybe she just doesn't like to be underway, she'll be better when we get to the lake.

Alas, no. Mocha is not a boat dog. While I fished, she wandered around aft aimlessly, whining and complaining. She'd try to settle down and take a nap, but her whining kept her awake. When another boat would pass, Mocha would prop herself up on the gunwale and whine to it, as if saying, "Please take me back to my nice fenced-in back yard!"

I caught very few fish because of the recent bout of high winds we've been having, but those few little ones I did, I let Mocha sniff. The first one she was fairly interested in sniffing, but the next three might as well have been rubber chickens for all she cared. She did not sniff. She just looked at me and whined, "Okay, you got one, can we go home now? I think I'm seasick."

As I fished along a wide canal, the boat passed near a clump of water lilies. Mocha, having little experience with boats or water lilies, apparently thought this was dry land and an escape. I wasn't watching her, but I suddenly heard this loud *Kerplunch*! I spun around, thinking I had disturbed a gator, and there was Mocha, trying her dangdest to swim out of the water lilies—a patch of which had glued itself to her head, looking like a funny cap—and back into the boat. I grabbed her by the scruff of the neck and hauled her back aboard, where she promptly shook the water off herself and onto me. The water lily cap did not budge, however, and I had to peel it off of her, at which point she lay down and proceeded to pout. If there had been a gator in that clump, I imagine she would have made an English lunch.

But the next clump of lilies we passed by, *kerplunch* again. I hauled her back out, she shook the water off herself and onto me, I held her head in my hand and said softly, "Shadow would *never* have been that stupid."

She licked me in the face, begging to go home. I took her home. The fish weren't biting anyway.

At the landing, I commanded her to stay in the boat until I got it into the trailer, so she wouldn't run around and get hit by a car or something. She didn't like this idea at all. There was dry land, just a few feet away, I was on it, why couldn't she be? She kept trying to disobey, but I gave her stern warnings not to. Finally, I hauled boat and dog out of the water and said, "Come on, Mocha."

She sat there on the back seat, looking at me.

"Mocha, come on, you can get out now," I said.

She arched her ears up at me, and cocked her head. She yawned, then she lay down on the seat and stared at me.

"Come on, it's time to go home."

Her eyelids blinked sleepily. I wasn't about to ride her home in the boat, so I went and prodded her out. As soon as her feet hit the ground, she made a beeline to the truck door I had left open.

"Mocha, *no*!" I screamed, but she didn't listen. She flew into the truck and plopped her still wet, smelly self into the passenger seat. I was going to ride her in the bed of the truck. But I got in, holding my breath—the smell of wet Spaniel is not refreshing—and we went home, where I released her at last, noting the big soaked spot on the cloth seat. She ran great spiraling circles around the yard for about five minutes, then on her own rushed through the gate to the back yard. I swear, if she had the sense, she'd have closed it an locked it behind her.

She's not a boat dog. I have to get used to that idea. While Mocha enjoys walking by the bayou behind the house, taking an occasional brief swim, boats are not her thing. Nor does she appreciate the sniffing of fish.

I miss having a boat dog, but I have to get used to the lack of one. I briefly entertained the notion of a boat cat, but realized at once that Patches would not only never fit the bill, she'd probably be so irritated by the adventure there would be bloodshed. I can pretty much guess, though, that she'd never jump out into a patch of water lilies.

But if she did, I'm sure if there were a gator in those lilies it'd be history.

On the Fly

Mostly I fish flies now. I won't lie, there are times when, rather than go home empty-handed, I'll resort to a spinning rod and tackle or earthworms. I'm not proud. But given the opportunity, however slight, I'll fish flies.

Quite the eccentric, it's always amusing the looks and comments I receive while fly fishing.

See, around these here parts, many fishermen use a fly rod. But in large majority, they simply use it as a long jigging pole for reaching into brush, trees, etc. to snatch out fish, mostly *sac-au-lait* and bream. Fly fishing as it originated usually brings up images of guys in waders standing in crystal-clear streams catching rainbow trout, a species of fish most Louisiana anglers seriously doubt actually exists. If they actually got ahold of one, it would be an *etoufee* in a heartbeat.

Out at a rather public pond a few months ago, surrounded by other fishermen who were throwing more usual baits without success, I was plucking little bass out regularly.

Finally one of the guys strolled over to me and asked, "You ain't from around here, are you?"

"Sure am," I said, unhooking a largemouth from an olive wooly bugger. A wooly bugger is a fishing fly, you understand, not something from a Wes Craven movie. "Born and raised in Charenton."

"Well, where'd you learn how to do that?" the gentleman asked.

"What, catch fish?"

"No," he said, "catch fish with *that.*" He pointed to my rod.

"Oh, my dad was a fly fisherman."

"Ahhh," the man said knowingly. "So *he* wasn't from around here." He strolled off them, shaking his head and muttering, "Darndest thing I ever saw."

Actually, dad was born in Ft. Worth Texas, but he didn't start fly fishing until he moved here in 1946. But armed with a fiberglass fly rod and a Martin reel, the man was a deadly weapon on the water. I learned a lot from him about fly fishing, though we fished conventional tackle much of the time.

"Bought one of those once about 40 years ago," one gentleman said to me on a pond. "Never used it."

"You can't catch bass around here with that," another asserted with a no-doubt-about-it tone. I immediately proved him wrong by taking a 16-inch large-mouth right in front of his eyes.

"You ought to go to Montana or something, where you can really use that," a kind lady said to me one day. I said it's in the plans.

"You're so eccentric," a buddy said of my fly fishing habit.

Eccentric? Me? I guess so. I guess because I like fly fishing, like my boats wooden and my house cypress, I am somewhat eccentric. Here, anyway. There are, in fact, fly fishing clubs in New Orleans, Baton Rouge and two in north Louisiana.

"You look like the guy from that movie," someone said. "You know, what's the name of it? Something about a running river."

He was speaking of course of *A River Runs Through It,* based on the autobiographical novel by Norman Maclean. I thought about asking if I reminded him of Brad Pitt or Craig Sheffer, but I decided I didn't want to know.

It was Mr. Maclean, in fact, who penned that, "If our father had had his say, nobody who did not know how to catch a fish would be allowed to disgrace a fish by catching him."

My friends are learning, however, certain rules about fly fishing. The most important of these is never to walk or stand behind and to the right of me, because when casting, I've got 60-70 feet of line with a very sharp hook at the end slinging around like a cobra. Also, they have learned that, given the option, I prefer to be reminded of Tom Skerritt.

That's not to say I don't still fish conventional tackle. If the wind's too bad, for example, and I can't get a good casting stroke, I'll pull out the spinning gear rather than have to go home. But given the opportunity, I'd rather fish flies than anything else.

But it got me to thinking about why. Why fly fishing? It's kind of a pain, in a way, managing all that line at my feet, finding a spot with enough room for my back cast, dealing with leaders and tippets and tiny knots with lousy vision. I guess I am eccentric, but I appreciate the purity of it. That's not a hoity-toity statement. I'm not getting noble or anything. But the art of fly fishing is an ancient one, and based on the concept of "matching the hatch" or giving the fish whatever they're feeding on, at least an imitation thereof.

The cast is tiresome to learn, but once mastered (which I have not completely) it is as graceful and beautiful a thing as any art. A perfect 60-foot cast that lays a small black gnat precisely where a fish is rising on the pond delights me. A less-than-perfect cast which piles 60-feet of line in a messy nest at my feet just makes me concentrate on my timing a little better.

Once the basic cast is mastered, it's time to move on to the roll cast and the double-haul. I have done pretty good with the roll cast so far, but the double-haul is still a feat of perfect timing and synchronicity which eludes me.

But I have also learned that, in many situations, fish will take a fly when they'll take nothing else. There may be many reasons for this, but I suspect it is because the fly imitates natural food more than any other, and that they aren't accustomed to seeing flies like they are plastic worms, spinner baits and the like. However, when someone asks, "Is it hard to learn?" I say, "Oh, terribly. Takes years and years of practice. Drives you nuts. I almost had to start prescription medications because of it." That usually makes them go back to their spinner baits and leave the art of fly fishing to me.

But in fact, one of the pioneers of moving fly fishing from the trout streams of the north to other species and waters was Tom Nixon of Lake Charles. Tom, who passed away last month of cancer, introduced the fly rod as a deadly instrument for fishing bass and bream. Rev. Harry Boyd, of Winnsboro, is one of the most renowned modern bamboo rodmakers in the nation.

But I guess what it's really all about is that when standing at the edge of a quiet, green pond when the fish are rising, curling line at the end of that graceful wand, I feel like I've learned something important. To me, anyway. I know you're not all anglers out there, and sometimes these diatribes about it evoke numerous yawns. Still, when I consider that of all the things I could learn in this mixed up world fly fishing is the one I chose, I have no regret. It's taught me patience, concentration and some form of grace I never knew I possessed. In some way I can't really describe with words, laying a line out over the water with a fly rod somehow connects me to it more than other ways of fishing.

Someone provided me an Internet link to something the other day that showed me I am far from as obsessed as I could be.

What they showed me was a bait vending machine.

I kid you not, kind folks. It looked like a soft drink machine, except it's blue and it has pictures of fish on the front, which I assume lights up in the dark, so the night fisherman will have access to bait without stumbling around and stubbing his toe on the curb. It weights 765 pounds, stands six feet high, and takes $1 and $5 bills. It's refrigerated, of course, and can carry up to six items. It also works off regular 110 power, so you can put one in your restaurant or beauty shop if you think it would generate some income.

It seems strange, somehow, that you can go to a vending machine, put in a five, and get worms or crickets or four other items, though I don't know what those could be. I assume shiners are not included, since there doesn't appear to be an aquarium inside to contain them, and besides, how would the machine dip them out?

There's something inherently wrong with the idea of a fishing bait vending machine. I don't know what it is. When I go to buy worms (since I don't have a worm farm in my own yard and Dad's is long since gone) I always check to make sure they're wiggling in the box. You always have to make sure your fishing worms are wiggling, or you might spend $2.50 for a box of stinky, decayed slime. How do you check to make sure your worms are wiggling in a vending machine? Who do you ask for a refund? If you get a box of dead worms, do you put in another five and hope you get a live one? Sounds suspiciously like gambling to me.

I would be ashamed to buy bait from a vending machine. I would have to go incognito, disguised in a trench coat and floppy hat, with a fake mustache glued to my lip, and park my truck two blocks away so nobody would connect me with the vending machine. And what if little kids have some money in their pockets and mistake the machine for a snack vendor? Maybe they'll think the button that says "WORMS" are those candy gummy worm things. The rest is just too gruesome to imagine.

This is fishing technology run amok if I ever saw it. I griped a few weeks ago about sparkly bass boats which cost more than I make in a year, and electronic fish finders, all that stuff. But a bait vending machine takes the cake. Sure, there have been times when I wanted to go fishing but couldn't find bait, but to buy it out of a vending machine? I'd rather stay home and watch Bill Dance. I may have very little sense, but I do have my dignity.

The only upside to this is that if there were a bait vending machine at every boat ramp in the area, you could just kinda hang around it for an hour or so in the morning. You could pretend you're checking your fishing line, or the grease in your trailer bearings, but you'd actually be watching the people using the vending machines to see what bait they're buying. That way you'd know what the fish are biting on. This is assuming, of course, that a true, self-respecting angler would stoop to buying bait that way. Still, it sounds like a plan.

Now, what would be good would be a vending machine for line, corks, hooks, flies or mosquito repellant. Actually, I don't use off-the-shelf mosquito repellant anymore, after having learned that the best all-around insect repellant is Amber Romance, which you can get from Victoria's Secret. Again, I kid you not. I hijacked a lady friend to buy it for me, and when she asked for it, the clerk at Victoria's Secret said, "Oh, the stuff the fishermen and hunters use?" I didn't hear this all myself, because I was trying to figure out how .02 ounces of silk can make underwear. It really works, though, and you don't smell like DEET, and if you don't catch any fish to make you smell fishy, you can go eat out at Mr. Lester's afterward and order fish.

Doesn't matter. I'll still fish out of a little wooden boat with a homemade paddle (which is only backup in case the trolling motor gets stuck on a log.) I'll still buy my bait from Jay's in Baldwin when I need it, though I mostly fly fish now. A fishing fly vending machine would make quite a good profit off me, for certain.

Either way, I'll smell really nice while I'm on the lake.

There is a small pond in a subdivision development area perhaps two miles from where I live.

It was, in years past, a crawfish pond, but when the main road for the subdivision was constructed, they borrowed quite a bit of dirt from the edges around it, and it is about two acres today. There are some deeper holes, but on average it's about four feet.

Nobody else fishes it, probably suspecting that since it's so new and recently disturbed there's not much chance of more than a few small bluegill. I stumbled on it about two months ago, and found I could regularly pick out small bass, about ten inches, and a few bluegill with no trouble. Sometimes people come and work their hunting dogs in it, but I have never seen a length of monofilament, a battered bobber or any other sign that it's being fished other than by me.

I talked with the developer of the subdivision, and he told me that plans for a future phase of construction call for enlarging the pond to a forty-acre lake. Estate-style homes will be built around it and sold for a good penny. It's a few years away yet, but after that I won't be able to fish there anymore. So I spend a good bit of time working it.

Having been raised in a small wooden boat fishing lakes from the moment I could sit up straight and hold a fishing rod in my hands, ponds are new experiences to me, and difficult ones. I am slowly learning that while they share many characteristics, ponds are not mini-lakes. This particular water has a patch of willows in the center of it, but there are no trees whatsoever around its bank. There is brush along the water's edge, and the little bass and bluegill love to hide in there and assault a Spook anytime it gets within four feet of their lair. Knowing the age of the pond, the fact that once crawfish were harvested out of it, I suspected there might be bigger fish in it, but even running a wooly bugger or Clouser deep produced on a few feeble nibbles.

But I go there regularly, because it's far enough from any highways that I can only dimly hear the cars passing; it's easy casting with no trees around, though the line at my feet does tend to snag on stubble a lot. The developer keeps the area mowed fairly often. It's one of those places I've dedicated myself to becoming intimate with, this one more than any other, because I know it's demise is sure. When it's dug out, there will be a large mortality factor in the fish population, but the developer said it would be stocked again. I haven't kept fish out of it, releasing all the little bass, even the occasional one that makes the fourteen-inch minimum.

There's something of a sadness though, when I work that pond. It's a pretty place, and I think I'd like to have a house of my own near it, but with no neighbors crowding me and throwing their own lines into my secret little spot. The bass are so underfished, they hit nearly anything I throw at them. Sometimes, when the wind is up and my five-weight is giving me too much trouble casting, I return to spinning tackle and pull the little bass out with spinnerbaits. Each eight- or ten-inch one will probably not grow much more, after the pond is redug and enlarged to a lake for estate homes and well-to-do residents, but they'll be replaced by Florida-strain largemouth. I don't dislike the Florida bass, they're pretty and they get big. But native bass hold much more appeal for me. Perhaps my eight thousand years of ancestry on this land is why I like the indigenous bass more than the Florida variety. They seem to belong more to that little pond tucked away in a partially developed segment of a subdivision's sudden sprawling growth. They remind me, in a way, of myself.

Casting tiny sinking fly, I let it run down where I suspected there was a deeper hole in the north end of the pond. The wind was threatening to kick up again, that plague that fishermen will remember the early part of 2003 for. I let it sink, made a jerking retrieve, sink again, and repeated the process.

A dull thud transmitted through the line to my hand and I snapped back the rod tip. The thud immediately transformed into a dead weight, and I was sure I had hooked bottom. It was so firm, in fact, that I actually had time to walk about thirty feet down the bank, counter to the direction my line was angled, to attempt a de-snagging tug, when the snag suddenly shot out toward the middle of the pond.

It took nearly fifteen minutes before I caught a glimpse of what was swirling around down there, stripping off line, then letting me nudge it slowly toward the bank, only to catapult away again and leave my spool spinning out even more line than before. But at last, when I coaxed it close enough to the shallows near the edge of the pond, a flash of green-white both reassured and terrified me: Not a catfish, not a choupique, this was a largemouth bass.

He made two or three more half-hearted runs, but he was tired. The bank of the pond drops about a foot and a half to the water edge, and when I managed to coast him up to the lapping surface, I had to step out and into the mud to wrap my thumb under the jaw of a four-pound largemouth. I was caked in wet mud to my right knee, but stood there amazed and delighted. I never would have believed there were fish that size in that little, young pond.

The way I grew up, in a slightly-better-than-poor Indian household, with a father who could catch fish in a pothole on the street, fishing was meant for escape, for sport, for relaxation, for father-son bonding, and fish were meant for the table. In my later years, appalled by the fishing pressure in the basin and the lakes of my parish, I have begun practicing catch and release almost exclusively. I only keep bluegill for the table now. But I thought about the certain demise of the pond when the roaring diesel excavators move in, and the likely death of this native largemouth, as beautiful a creature as I've ever seen come from home waters. When the hydraulics pull the buckets down into the mud to begin creating a pristine lake for homeowners who'll have finely manicured lawns leading out to its banks and who'll either fish it or ignore it in favor of the golf course to be built in another part of subdivision, the habitat this fish will be destroyed and surely him along with it.

It's a quandary I have never faced before. It's said the people of Easter Island once lived in a dense woodland. Little by little, they used up an extremely finite resource, until at some point, some inhabitant of the island, fully knowing what he was doing, cut down the very last tree standing. I wonder what went through his mind when the axe made its first blow to the last tree in his entire world.

Or maybe he'll somehow escape the chaos of enlarging the pond into a small lake, compete for food with Florida largemouth, perhaps having a few of the stocked fingerlings for a snack along the way. Maybe he'll escape the hydraulic buckets, survive the muddying of the water until the sediment settled, and forage for insects and baitfish, managing to survive until the ecosystem restored itself.

What would you do? Take advantage of the resource which, more likely than not, will end in tragedy and waste? Or play the unlikely odds that the fish might survive, to be caught another day by some other lucky angler.

I won't tell you what I did, released it or took it to the table. It's a question maybe we all should think about, and that's the point of this story. A little pond out somewhere, unnoticed except by one angler, who can have a dramatic impact on it in his own way, but not so harsh as the fate which looms on the horizon. Perhaps you've never kept fish for cooking, or perhaps you're a convert to catch and release like me. If your favorite lake or stream were facing almost certain loss of its population of game fish in the near future, would that justify the taking of fish? Or would you stick to your principles?

No, I won't tell you what I did with that fish, because somebody on one side of the fence or another is going to be upset. But I believe the question is worth thinking about on a windy or rainy day when the fishing is impossible. Maybe it'll give the one who ponders it a greater understanding, one way or the other, of this sport, the resource and the thing it is within us that makes us so enamored by it.

Or why, in the last moments of an orange-swept sky at dusk when all eternity seems to fall in on itself around that little pond and the man standing on its bank, it seems to matter so much.

June

June, and the dog days of summer have come to laze around like old hounds under pecan trees, slits of eyelids twitching at gnats in the heat. Summer people, gray-eyed and thin, lounge on straight-backed kitchen chairs under the porch overhang, propped back against droplap cypress siding which has never seen the likes of paint.

The memory of winter firmly put to rest, June accepts summer with open arms. There was little spring this year, the transition to the heat of summer was almost unnoticed. Outside in the yards I pass, tomato plants tied to every manner of support climb and reach for that yellow face shining in the sky, setting blossoms and bearing fruit, while cucumbers, peppers and okra follow suit. Weeds stick their noses between the tomatoes' ankles—dandelions with yellow faces of their own, crabgrass and portulaca circling their roots.

The rivers are falling; June bugs gather on the window screen under my outside lights, all hard and brown and shiny. Sometimes they strike so hard I hear the Whack! of their exoskeletons against the frames. Now and then, tiny green frogs visit to show me their bellies, clutching the screen with long toes and puffing their throats pinkly at me.

The blue wort and oxalis and wild onions are gone, but the lantana is thriving in the oppressive heat. My fig tree is setting many shoots, though it's only three or four feet tall. I pinch off the tiny fruit it sets so that it may dedicate more energy to developing roots and above ground growth. Farther behind the house, Bayou Teche runs brown and muddy and swift. I walked along these very same banks as a child, searching through the underbrush for signs of rabbits. Armed with first a Daisy BB gun and later a Benjamin pellet gun which had been my grandfather's and was probably the straightest shooting, most accurate gun I have ever known, I never killed anything except dry cypress seed balls and the occasional tin can.

Behind my parents' house, at the bayou, there was an old dilapidated camp which in better days was home to my uncle, Fred Stouff. Uncle Fred had it fixed up nice, from photos I've seen, but he died when I was too young to remember him, and in the later Junes of my youth honey bees occupied an entire wall of its weakening structure. A hurricane years before had damaged it severely, and it was never repaired. Now and then I'd go poke around beneath its sagging rafters and carefully make my way over its rotting floors. There was an old cedar wardrobe in there that I hauled out with the intent of refinishing and putting in my room, but I never got around to it. Eventually it ended up in the hands of my best friend, who also never got around to doing anything with it, and later still, it was finally refinished into a beautiful gun cabinet by his father Jim Presley.

I found a stash of five or six buffalo nickels in the old camp one June and pocketed them to look for more, but the honey bees objected to my disturbance and ran me home, where I sat in my room and thumbed the nickels over and over between my fingers. Most were dateless, as buffalo nickels tend to become, but one was marked 1923. That was the year before my father was born.

My Uncle Ray gave me my first pocket knife. I lost it somewhere in the pasture behind my parents' house digging in a crawfish hole. Don't ask me why I was digging in a crawfish hole with a pocket knife because I have no idea, but I lost it in the mud bug's den. After Hurricane Andrew, when they came with excavating equipment to bury much of the debris that the storm had left, I watched to see if they would dig up my pocket knife, but I never saw it fall out of the bucket. It was tradition in our family that the uncle gave the nephew his first pocket knife. I have no brothers or sisters, so I have no nephew to give a pocket knife to. Sometimes that saddens me in a way I don't quite understand.

June in those days was barricaded by barbed wire on the land owned between us and my grandparents, which also served to keep the horses in. We had four of them: Two quarter horses, a Tennessee walker and my first, a Shetland pony named Nancy. Even though I had outgrown Nancy, we kept her because we were so attached to her. When we'd barbecue in the back yard and all the family would come over, Nancy would rattle the fence with her hoof and snort for as long as it took, until finally Dad would open a pony Jax or Falstaff and pour it down her throat, which she gulped up lavishly, then wandered off, content at last.

Between my grandparents' house, where I live now, and my parents' house there was nothing but horse pasture except one big pecan tree way up front. One stormy day in June, my mom was walking over to my grandparents' when lightning hit the pecan tree just as she was beneath it. The tree split in half with a deafening crack and the halves fell away from each other. Mom, who has always had nerves of steel, just kinda looked at it and kept on walking.

Meanwhile my grandmother was on the front porch watching all this and screaming for Mom to run for her life, but Mom just padded on over.

"Lee," Ma Faye asked, a nervous wreck by then, "why didn't you run?"

"Well," Mom explained calmly, "it was already over by then, and you know, lightning doesn't strike twice in the same place."

Ma Faye and I would grind coffee beans by hand in an old coffee grinder she had, and the dark roasted scent of them drifted lazily through hot June days. Ma Faye would always add a shard of egg shell to her coffee when she brewed it, saying it took out the bitterness. We'd pick June tomatoes in the garden that my grandfather plowed every year with a Montgomery Wards front-tine tiller. He always gave me a whole row to plant whatever I wanted. In July, the figs would finally come, and those we saved from the birds and squirrels became fig preserves which sat on the counter in Ma Faye's kitchen until the mood struck her to spread some on toast with a little real butter.

June was the first full month of vacation, and the summer stretched out before me always seemed endless and never empty. There was a whole bayouside to explore, honey bees in the old camp to brave in search of more buffalo nickels, rabbits to stalk with my Benjamin, always knowing I'd never hit one with the pellet gun, always knowing I wouldn't even try to. There were weekends when Dad would wake me early, and we'd get in the old boat and go to the lake all day, coming home with plenty of bull bluegill and perhaps a few bass. Mom would heat the cooking oil in ancient black iron skillets and call the family to come over while Dad and I cleaned the fish. I did the scaling, he gutted them and cut off the heads, under the pretense that I might cut myself badly with the sharp knife, but I knew he was sparing me from the grisly duty.

At some point in the young summer, we'd pile the Charenton Stouffs into the car and make the long trip to visit the Ft. Worth Stouffs, or vice versa. Wherever the annual visits would occur, the evenings would usually culminate into a small concert, with Dad, my Uncle Ray, cousins Jim and Lynn, and Ma Faye all playing instruments and singing old bluegrass or country-western tunes.

Thunderstorms visit the landscape of June, dropping torrents, blazing lightning and rumbling thunder. While today I pop open an umbrella and seek to avoid the deep water rushing along the curb, in Junes of my youth I'd rush out in a raincoat and hood to watch the big drainage ditch near the house swell and churn. I'd throw sticks into it and race with them toward Bayou Teche. Along the path leading to the bayou, small rivers of water also formed, carrying leaves and twigs and bugs to an eventual dispersal into the stream ahead. There, the ditch would widen and send swirling maelstroms out into the Teche, to vanish somewhere downstream. Later, when the rain subsided, I'd hook a worm under a bobber and throw it right into the bayou where the ditch emptied, and catch little bluegill and catfish who were congregated there feeding on the prey the rushing water delivered to them.

Ama'tpan na'mu

Awakening to thunder from a late afternoon nap, flashes of brilliant lightning lanced through the windows, burning my eyes with white magic.

There were massive black storm clouds outside the window when I peeked through the curtains. Though there was no place I needed to go, I put on my shoes, grabbed my keys and went to the truck, feeling the need to chase the storm.

Across the miles along the road of my life, I have always chased storms. I feel an affinity with them, some kinship which trembles and sparks in air charged with by the lightning. So not really knowing where I would go, I chased the storm broiling to the north, and the road led me to the Atchafalaya Basin Protection Levee, which I crossed and found myself on the southern shore of Grande Lake.

Ama'tpan na'mu. Beneath my feet, the broken white clamshell was like bleached bone. It stretched out for a mile to the east and west, a fingernail of raised mound deposited here a basketful at a time by my ancestors. This was

Ama'tpan na'mu, a very large village which looked out over part of *Sheti*, that great series of interconnected lakes from which we took our name in kinship.

I parked the truck away from the attendant's shack, for today this is a boat landing, bulldozed at some point in the early part of the century so that fisherman could launch into Grande Lake here. I can still walk along the edge and find bits of broken pottery, some plain, some ornate. When I was a child, I would stand here with my father and we couldn't see the other side of Grande Lake, but decades of man's tampering with nature have taken their toll, and the northern bank is now easily visible. Grande Lake is but a shadow of its former self. Much like the people who share its ancestral name.

Over that now-near treeline of cypress and willows, a blackness as absolute as midnight churned and spit silver fire at the earth. The bolts found some ground below, discharged into the swampy watersways beyond. It was here, on *Ama'tpan na'mu*, that an entire village stared in amazement as a Spanish ship sailed up Grande Lake, having entered the Atchafalaya River from the Gulf of Mexico and made their way north. These were no mere Spanish colonists, no priests and missionaries: These were Consquistadors, set upon their mission by God, they supposed.

We call it the Beach now. It rather looks, from a distance, like a white sandy beach, until closer examination reveals the crushed and compacted clamshell. The clam species *rangia* was abundant when these lakes were sometimes brackish, and Chitimacha would feast on them, using the discarded shells as a sort of building material, pre-historic concrete as it were. It kept their feet out of the mud in Louisiana's frequent rains, provided a stable base for erecting palmetto huts, and the stark whiteness of it was a pristine backdrop to easily see a big, black water moccasin snake slithering up on the children.

Overhead, silver warriors throw spears from inside the black clouds, spears that turn into jagged, spectacular lightning bolts. The crash of them is created by a thunderbird, lurking somewhere in those same billows, beating its wings like a gargantuan raptor. There is no rain. I watch the lightning, not a second goes by without a magnificent blast of power, pitched down by silver-faced dead.

When the galleons arrived on Grande Lake and approached *Ama'tpan na'mu*, the *na'ta* of the village refused them. He forbade them to come ashore. If I look beyond the scattered wreckage of old oil drums lashed together as buoys, derelict boat trailers and assorted metal and wooden junk, I can nearly see small children, their faces stricken with amazement, looking out at these huge wooden vessels with their great sails, the strange, iron-clad men upon them, their faces so pale and bearded. I can see the *na'ta*, standing firm in his protection of a single village among dozens in the nation. What might have gone through his mind? Surely he could not have imagined that he was the first to witness the end, those who would, with the passing of time, reduce his thriving nation from tens of thousands to a handful of survivors numbering less than fifty.

If I follow the village shell bank by boat, as I did last spring, to the east away from the ramp, there are shallows in which huge redears gather for a short few days each year. I chased them with the rod, they were fat and bold, but I tried to disturb them as little as possible. They have come from the few remaining depths of Grande Lake to make their spawning nests in the hard shell shallows of *Ama'tpan na'mu*, where nearly five hundred years ago, the village *na'ta* refused the Spanish, and steel was brandished, cold and glistening white, like the lightning bolts crashing and crackling with God-given power out across the lake.

It saddens me, sometimes, that we do not know his name, that *na'ta*, the chief of the village of *Ama'tpan na'mu* who stood, surely afraid and uncertain of his actions, against their blades. But the Spanish were beaten back, forced to leave, and they made their way down the lake and river, accosted by Chitimacha warriors all along the way as the alarm was sounded from village to village. Eventually they reached the safety of the Gulf of Mexico, and that first tragic encounter ended.

Traveling northwest by boat, I can enter the terribly shallow waters of *Cok'tangi*, "pond lily worship place," which the Spanish called Grande Avoille Cove. The levee intersects it now, and its other half to the south is a favorite spot for fishing bream and bass in the spring, though in the summer it's shallow waters are too hot to support much of a fish population. If I travel southeast, around Taylor's Point and into the river proper, I can traverse the entire Atchafalaya basin with its winding oilfield canals, natural bayous, hidden ponds and pools.

But lighting is flashing everywhere, and thunder is resonating, trembling the clamshell mound. The storm is moving just north of me, to the southwest, and skirting the edge of the lake. I can see gray rain coming. Soon it will fall and *Ama'tpan na'mu* will glisten under it. A chief, when the word *na'ta* was no longer used, is buried somewhere on this mound, forbidden interment in Christian cemeteries during the mid-1800s, for after the Spanish retreated that fateful day, they made alliances with another tribe far to the east, and returned in force. The first chapter in the demise of the people of the lake was written in the war that followed.

Ama'tpan na'mu was long dead, it's people scattered and decimated, when the Union army landed here to assault rebel troops stationed in Franklin in what would become known as the Battle of Irish Bend, just a skirmish by true reckoning, but a part of local history and folklore. Irish Bend is *Oku'nkiskin*, "old man's shoulder," a steep twist of Bayou Teche to the southeast.

The storm is passing, carrying its spears of lightning and silver warriors with it. Clearing skies behind, peeking sunshine and scattered rain. I am reminded that I have not fished this side of the levee since last fall. Perhaps I'll bring the boat in some weekend soon, put it over into Grande Lake from the shell beach of *Ama'tpan na'mu*. I have probably missed the big redears, what we here call chinquapin, but there are still bream and bass moving along the canals and through the cypress.

I start the truck and head for home, leaving the old village behind, white and still. I make my way home, to *T'kasi'tunshki*, which the French named Charenton. As I am climbing the road which crosses the levee, in the rearview mirror I can almost see, in the gray misting of rain augmented by a few shining sunbeams far behind, massive, parchment-colored sails, mahogany bows, glistening swords, and one steadfast man standing at the water's edge on *Ama'tpan na'mu*. His name is forgotten, but his courage will live on in the hearts of some long after the storms have passed.

Noise

It's the noise that gets overwhelming sometimes.

The noise, the constant pandemonium. Western culture, in all its facets of expansion and growth, has carried with it the sheer din of noise. A friend once asked, *How can they hear the Voice of the Great Mystery when they never stop making noise?* I have no answer for him.

The noise came from Europe, it's clanking machinery, booming guns, rattling sail rigging and clattering armor. Industrialization came, the ear-splitting whine, the clanking assembly lines, the shrieking sirens.

In all the earth there is no place dedicated to solitude, said Chief Seatl, once the teeming multitudes with their clamoring noise came upon him. It permeates us today, makes our bones resonate brutally, assaults our brains, causes our hearts to misbeat. Though we tune it out, relegate it to that phenomenon known as "white noise", the effect on us is resolute: The constant chaos of noise batters us down, wears us thin, but when the silences come they make us uneasy, restless, as if we are trying to hear something. We think it's the ringing phones, the passing traffic, honking horns, roaring machines. But what we are missing in the rare silences, that which makes us so anxious, is the voice of the world.

Europe, with all its rapid expansion and leaps in technology, shielded its people, and ours, from the voice. From the noise grew squalid slums, coal-blinded and choking families, sewerage running along cobblestone streets, murder and despair. French workers, those who could still hear above the noise, threw their wooden shoes, *sabots,* into the powered looms threatening their families, their existence, to break them down. Thus the word *sabotage* was born of the need to hear.

I sit here writing this, and the air conditioner is growling, the police scanner chattering, the traffic outside on Wilson Street churning like doomed sojourners. I sit at lunch and the cell phones ring, the dishes clatter, people try to speak louder than their companions to be heard, just to be heard above the fray. People talk all at once, ignoring each other, trying to be heard.

What is they want to say? Who do they want to hear them?

Noise. It's like concrete. It insulates us from our ancestors, from the earth beneath us. Noise drowns out the sound of running water, the voices of our kin long dead. Perhaps that why I spend so much time on quiet water casting flies for fish—the silence. The echo of the past whispering on the wind, through ancient cypress, along shell-lined banks and shores.

I walk on concrete and it hurts my feet; I touch the cold brass knob of my door and it burns my skin. The air-conditioner shields me from the outside world, the television churns out music and conversation and gunshots and news broadcasts to remind me that reality is, in fact, measured in the diagonal.

I need the silences sometimes. The escape into quietude, searching, waiting for the single moment, that flash of an instant, when it is revealed to me that there is a purpose to all things under heaven. Such revelations do not come to human beings when they are inundated by noise, insulated by concrete.

How can they hear? my friend asked. I do not know. Perhaps most of us don't want to hear. We are too concerned, too frantic, too desperate with making money, finding solace from material things, working our way up ladders that end at the precipice into a bottomless abyss. To hear would mean those things would become less important. Generations ago, my father's people would give away all they owned to others, to demonstrate that what we have is not nearly so important as what we are, what we treasure is not corporeal or solid.

I stood on the bank of a pond this week, catching small bream and bass. A sudden movement just under the surface of the water not far away alerted me to the presence of a large fish. A very large fish. Stealthily, like a spectre, it moved just inches below the surface but sent out a huge v-shaped wake as it moved through a liquid world of muted silence. I could see the swirling from the swish of its tail. I poised, ready to lift my fly line from the water and cast to it, but stopped. What if I hooked it? There would be a mighty splash with the strike, a whizzing of line through the reel, a struggle, a frantic rush for escape, and the final moments of a brilliant, dragon-laid sunset would shatter. Worse, the silence of that watery depth which the big fish moved through would burst, disrupted with the ensuing fray. I didn't make the cast. Sometimes it just enough to listen, and to see. There will be other fish, other days. Time must be taken, now and then, for silence. I packed up my rod and sat on my tackle bag as the final moments of the day continued to unfold, watching the risings over the surface of the pond. Crickets chirped, bullfrogs bellowed. Now and then, a distant bird would call, but not very loudly.

Five years ago, I was blind as well as deaf. I walked concrete and complained about the mud or dust on my shoes. I covered myself with noise, to shield me from the things for which I might be ridiculed, elicit words of concern for my well-being. With the death of my father, the passing of a brand from him to me that I never even knew existed, the noise subsided. Just a little. Just a half a decibel. But I heard. Just enough. Whispers can be loud enough.

So don't be too concerned if the words here darken and grow cloudy; don't worry if the air seems to thicken around this page and grow heavy, hard to breathe. It's just the noise, and the whispers. They are at constant odds. Sorting them out requires catharsis, of a sort. Sometimes, you must chase thunderbirds, ride with silver warriors, to make sense of it all.

Memorial Day being a half-day at work for us newspaper people, I didn't get to head out for a little line-throwing until evening.

After putting out the day's paper, my gal and I decided to head for New Iberia, La., for lunch and a movie. The lunch was a buffet, and I succeeded in causing myself severe distress with repeated trips to the bar. The movie was a comedy and that helped me feel a little better.

After a much-needed nap, it was a couple hours before dark so I loaded a couple rods into my tackle backpack and drove over to the pond I frequented all last year alone. Since this spring, as reported earlier, I have been dismayed to find that the maroons have taken it over. I still go there though, stubbornly refusing to let the Philistines completely kick me out of what was my private sanctuary.

There was no one around this particular evening, as I had hoped. The maroons, I believed, were recovering from barbecue and beer. I had brought an eight-foot four-weight I just picked up used, a great little rod. Since the sun was still bright and a little wind kicking, I chose to start things off with a Jitterbee under a VOSI.

I don't know the geographical extent of the VOSI in the fly fishing world, but it is quite common in Louisiana. VOSI stands for "Vertically Oriented Strike Indicator" and, simply put, is a very small oblong perch cork cut in half. As one of the premiere fly anglers in our area, Catch Cormier, noted, no self-respecting fly fisherman would be caught dead using a perch float, thus "VOSI." It works very well.

All last year when I fished this pond, I caught not a single bream. From April to December when winter finally caught up with me, I caught oodles of small bass, a lot of medium bass, and a handful of lunkers. Since being overrun by the maroons, I have been catching quite a few bream, very large ones now and then, and lots of small ones. I am sure that this means the maroons have reduced the population of large predatory fish in the pond.

The Jitterbee/VOSI resulted in a few nice bream and a decent bass. There were dark thunderclouds rolling in, but no rain, and when the sky turned overcast, I switched to a popper, my trusty Accardo Spook.

When a car pulled upon the nearby road, I knew the tranquility was over. I recognized the car. It had been here several times before.

Out hopped a younger man and his wife or girl, carrying baitcasting rods. Also out of the car emerged Sugar.

I don't know what breed Sugar is, but she's a medium-sized tan dog with the energy of a tornado and the hearing of a rock. While I was working a stand of willows off-center of the pond, the couple started working their baitcasters along the north bank, fanning out and shouting at each other from fifty yards apart.

And Sugar began to play.

Sugar leaped over their lines if they dropped their rod tips too low. Sugar raced through the tall grass like a maniacal Greyhound with faltering directional skills for now and then she'd barrel into their legs.

"Sugar!" the young man would yell, teetering for balance. "Calm your butt down!"

Sugar does not understand these things. When told to calm down, Sugar leaps into the pond. At some point in her life, Sugar learned to associate the words "calm down" with jumping into the pond, and shows her only true obedience in life by doing so at once, usually right in front of the young lady, who get soaked and commences to fussing.

The couple tends to work the bank like they are running a marathon. Casting and walking, casting and walking, displaying the time-honored wisdom that if there isn't a bite on one cast within a twenty-foot stretch of bank, there ain't no fish there. I try to keep the patch of willows positioned between us, so they can't see the fish I'm taking, but at that pace it's fruitless.

At last they near the corner of the pond, and Sugar takes notice of me. It is as I feared. Shooting off, belly low, Sugar gallops for me, tongue flapping, while her master is yelling, "Sugar! Come back here! Sugar!" and I am praying he does not say the words "calm down."

They work their way completely around the pond three times this way, casting once every twenty feet, yelling at Sugar, yelling at each other, catching the occasional small bass, and hollering at me from one hundred and fifty yards, "Sure ain't biting today, huh?"

By and by, a buddy of theirs pulls up on a four-wheeler and, being a pal and all, tries to distract Sugar by racing around the pasture near the pond so that Sugar will chase him. He soon tires of this, of course, and goes back to chat with his friends.

Now, every time they make one cast and move twenty feet, with Sugar bounding into the pond with a colossal splash if she even hears the man tell the girl "Keep you rod tip down," because she thought she heard "calm down," there is also the sound of the four-wheeler cranking up and moving twenty feet, then shutting off, and discussions about football, work, family, friends and the fact that the fishing sure sucks here.

Tiring of my spot behind the willows and feeling cocky, I move behind the other anglers a respectable distance to fish the south side of the pond. Sugar bounds around me, tangling in my legs, nipping at the butt of my rod. The young man is yelling, "Sugar, Sugar, *SUGAR-SUGAR-SUGAR!*" and Sugar hears naught. So to be helpful, I shout, "Sugar, calm down!" and Sugar immediately leaps into the pond, drenching the young woman, who then yells, "SUGAR!" At which point Sugar rockets toward me again, and begins a tango with my legs, causing me to accidentally step on her toe. She yelps and runs off, pouting.

After their fifth circumference of the pond, they load up and leave, yelling at Sugar all the way to the car. I have caught about eighteen fish, they have caught two. I hear, "We'll try tomorrow, maybe they'll be biting then." And off they go, Sugar's head out the back window, yelping at me in farewell.

It's nearly dark, and I pull a few more fish out of the pond, avoiding the murky, muddy areas where Sugar calmed down. Just as it is getting too dark to see the Spook or a strike, the silence is absolute, the sky tranquil. For just a split second, in the complete stillness, I find myself missing Sugar.

Then I get my flask out of my tackle back and take a good stiff belt to regain my senses.

You don't get to be a zealot without stepping on a few toes along the way.

Fishermen, particularly fly fishermen, are zealots. Don't try to deny it, you know it's true. We are not emphatic about our hobby, we are not enamored of it, we are infatuated, we are obsessed. We are zealots. Fanatics.

But what gets me is people who, in the interest of small talk, leave themselves wide open when asking something like, "So, did you get to go fishing this weekend?" while having lunch.

I'm sure they intend it as innocent small talk. Then, when you launch into a tirade about where you went, what fly, what rod, what leader, the weather, the feeding patterns, and so forth, their eyes glaze over and they are suddenly very fascinated with their pasta.

People don't understand us. People who don't fish, that is. And the inevitable extension of that is, people who fish but don't fly fish don't understand us.

Admittedly, I don't understand us sometimes either. This whole fishing thing. What's the point? Oh, don't give me that speech about communing with nature, touching our heritage, appreciating the battle of wits and skill. I'm the one who writes all that dribble remember? Much as I believe it's true, there are moments when I sit back and look at myself and wonder to what possible end does becoming such a fanatic serve?

I am lucky in the respect that I no longer have a wife who tells me I should not or cannot buy that new rod. On the other hand, such safety features would probably keep me from getting the electricity cut off. My girl does her best to keep me in check, I have to give her due credit. Yet there's no control mechanism for my fanaticism. I am mostly untethered, unencumbered, without oversight. I can get up and go fishing practically anytime I want when I'm not at work. I can gleefully leave the house behind with a sink full of dishes, a laundry basket full of dirty clothes, the lawn up to my knees and the truck having changed colors due to the grime on it.

My father was not quite the zealot I am, but I do come by it honest. My mother recently observed to my girlfriend that, "I think he likes fishing even more than his daddy." This is quite a statement, for in my mind, my father was the most dedicated fisherman I ever knew. However, he had the priorities of a wife, family, demanding work at the plant, and two or three part-time at-home jobs for extra money. Still, there were many weekends I recall dad getting bit so severely by the bug we didn't see him from Friday afternoon until Sunday evening during the daylight hours.

Last year, I fished almost every single day. After work, before work, each day of the weekend, unless something absolutely unavoidable caused me to miss out. If my job as a journalist required me to cover a city council meeting or the like, I had my rod and tackle bag in the truck, sitting in City Hall anxiously watching the clock and trying my best not to suddenly scream, "Oh, get on with it, will you?" during some tiring discussion among council members regarding employee health insurance while dusk was fast approaching. That's not obsession? Sure it is. And when someone asks me, "Did you get to go fishing this weekend," over lunch on Monday, you can bet your bottom dollar they're going to get the whole play-by-play with emphatic zealotry.

Those like me go through great pains to go fishing. We juggle schedules, people and responsibilities. Say it's Wednesday after work. You know you have a dinner date with your girlfriend or wife, and you need to stop and get groceries because the refrigerator is about as barren as a tundra. On top of that, you are wearing your last clean pair of jeans. What you do is, invite the girlfriend to go fishing with you until dark, which she'll either decline or accept, either way, you've gained her approval because it's going to take her until dusk to get ready to go out anyway. So you throw an ice chest into the back of the truck or car, race through the supermarket for your groceries, throw it all in the ice chest with a bag of ice, then haul butt down to the pond to fish for two hours. When the sun goes down, you high tail it back to the house, put up your groceries, shower while your jeans are running through the dryer with a wet towel and four scented fabric softener sheets, dash out, get dressed and finish tying your last shoe just in time to answer the door when your girl knocks. Of course, if you have a wife or live-in girlfriend, slight alterations to this plan are in order.

Football fanatics have it made: They only have to make such arrangements when the game is on. The best we can hope for is rain to achieve some semblance of a normal, responsible lifestyle, but then, we all have a slicker suit, don't we?

So we slap at the alarm clock at 6 a.m. Monday through Friday, groggily complaining that we have to get up to go to work, fall back asleep, the alarm goes off again, this process repeats itself until we haul ourselves out of bed, cussing about the injustice of it all, still so half-asleep we make coffee with flour, all the while complaining about having to get up so early. But on Saturday morning we leap out of bed an hour before sunrise and stand there at the boat launch or on the water's edge, patiently, eagerly awaiting for just enough light to shine so we can cast, or drive the boat without running into a barge.

This is our lot in life, as fishermen. What I find especially odd is that while I was a dedicated tackle and bait fisherman, fly fishing has made me all the more obsessive. I guess that's to be expected, since I enjoy the fly rod so much more.

All of which does nothing to explain why we brave stinging and biting insects, snakes, bears, falling to our deaths, drowning and all other manner of risk to chase fish. Our non-fishing wives, girlfriends, friends and co-workers look at us as if we're some sort of head case, mildly amusing but to be pitied.

Pity me all you like. Just don't ask if I had a chance to go fishing. Your pasta's not nearly so interesting as my fish stories!

The Cast Not Taken

There were oodles of small bass, some no longer than four inches, most less than twelve, hitting at nearly any fly I chose to offer them.

The bream were hungry, too, after a spate of bad weather and repeated storm fronts finally settled out. Just playing out a few feet of line, ten feet from my boots, strikes would startle me into a bad hookset.

At its south end, this pond makes a v-shaped transition into a gentle, shallow slope. Even though the undergrowth along the bank here is slight, I usually stand in the water in my knee-high mudboots because it's easier. I can cast to each side of the pond where it makes this apex.

While unhooking a spunky little largemouth, movement just on the peripheral caught my attention. I looked up, and something huge was moving through the water, just under the surface, making an arrow-shaped wake as it went. The angle of the light was such that I could not see it, but the creature must have been huge. I knew—or at least strongly suspected—there were no alligators here. As the wake moved near shore, it diverted back toward deeper water, then continued a meandering, leisurely traverse of the shallow bank to the east.

Of course, I knew it was a bass, or did I just want it to be? No alligators here, no beavers, no nutria. Nothing else in this pond could have left such a swelling in its passing. The rod in my hand was a four-weight, with decent moderate-fast action and a healthy backbone, but even the two or three pound fish put an uncomfortable bend to it, urging me to coaxe them gently. Whatever was moving along that shallow bank, startling small bream so much they leaped nearly ashore in terror, might be more than this little rod could handle.

I put the small bass I had just unhooked into the water carefully, silently. Should I cast? The popper on my tippet was one of my favorites, which the fish in this pond seldom turn down. I was confident in my reel's drag system, believed the rod might just suffice if I played my cards tenderly.

Just then, the fish made a wide, sweeping turn and its wake now spread behind as it moved toward me again. I was still as stone. A dozen yards away, it veered west, and just ahead of its arrowpoint, a significant maelstrom suddenly swirled as the fish casually, without much fanfare, slurped down some prey. It continued a slow trek along the west side of the pond.

Finally I made a decision: The rod's under warranty. I played out some line, and with what was probably the best cast a passable caster at best ever made, sent the popper just ahead of the moving wake, about to lay down.

Right then, a car pulled up on the road which passes near the pond. In a frantic lurch, I snapped the line back. It fell into a muddled pile right behind the wake. The fish kept moving, undisturbed.

The anglers who come here, hardware casters, catch a fair number of bass out of this pond, but I've never seen them catch anything very large. In fact, there are few large fish here, I believe. I have caught only three impressive largemouth in it over nearly two years. It is, however, one of the few places where I regularly outfish the spinnerbaits and plastic worms.

Two persons leaped from the car and rushed to the far edge of the pond, casting at once. I was far enough away, at the other end, that they could see me but not the massive wake moving now back east, circling, little bluegill jumping away like raindrops splattering on glass. The fish, perhaps sensing this new presence, kept to my end of the pond.

I cursed fate quietly. Here I am, in the presence of the grandpappy of what is surely a largemouth bass, and I don't want to cast to it because I might hook it and reveal that, in fact, this pond is home to at least one huge fish. Of course, if I land him, I'll release him after taking a few photos, and the baitcasters will see this, return later to bombard the water endlessly in search of a prize to bring to the taxidermist and adorn their living room wall.

What to do? I was nearly trembling with anxious indecision, and I must have looked quite the fool standing there, rod hanging low, looking out over the pond, apparently right at the two new arrivals. I retrieved my line and cast far from the wake, which was continuing to move here and there inside the point of the pond. Occasional slurps revealed the fish was in fact actively feeding.

I could imagine it down there, just beyond my vision, a behemoth of epic proportions, just meandering along, king of all it knows. No other occupant of the pond dared cross it. That was perhaps why it moved so slowly, so carefully, so silently as to sneak up on prey without spooking it. Across the pond, the two anglers were catching small bass and putting them back at once, which relieved me. But the monster wake in front of me had turned now, and was heading north.

"Come back," I whispered, not even really aware that I was doing so. "Come back, you don't want to go over there, come on, come back..."

When the big wake turned and sucked down a Junebug, I realized I had not been breathing. It veered then, off course, back along the west bank. I praised it quietly.

During the last twenty minutes of light, the bass never ceased moving along my end of the pond, feeding quietly. At last, when the two visitors finally packed up and left, I was left with too little light to see very well. There was no sense in casting, I couldn't be sure where the wake was, though I thought I caught the brief outline of it to the right. I broke down my rod and packed it away, made the long walk back along the pond's bank to the waiting truck on the road.

Just as I was passing the northern corner of the pond, before entering the overgrown meadow between it and the road, a splash behind me nearly made me jump out of my skin.

Turning, a huge ring of ripples was expanding outward, just a few feet from dry land. Immediately, the shadow of a huge, finned back arched again, and in the dimness of the fading day I thought I saw a magnificent tail briefly surface then vanish again. The ripples slowly faded, and the darkening pond settled into smoothness again, save for a lone, v-shaped wake moving off south, slowly, no need to hurry, no need to fear anything.

"Good night, old man," I said to it softly. The big fish always knew I was there, I realized, and it always knew the other two fishermen were there. Fish don't get to be that big without knowing such things.

Back in the truck, I turned around on the road and eased away, glimpsing just the barest sparkle of starlight that marked the pond's existence, out beyond the concrete. As I drove away, I was glad I had never made that cast.

Something Broken

It was eight years ago that I idled down that long narrow driveway for the first time in too long.

We were both at our worst, that old house and I. As much as myself, the old place was facing its own trauma, its particular grief. My grandmother's old Caprice was still in the garage, and the old house leered at me with a face I didn't recognize, though I shouldn't have been surprised. We had grown estranged, distant.

I remember sitting in the truck for awhile, locking my gaze with it. I stared into its window glass eyes, wondering if there were anything left here for me, the wayward son, the one who had turned his back on it and all those within. Behind it, overgrown brush and thicket threatened to advance further, devouring the house, causing it to vanish as the world took over in the absence of loyalty.

I don't want it, I had said to her. *I won't be around here. Let someone else have it.* Even that day in the drive, I still saw it as only a temporary haven, a stopover on my way to something else, as yet unknown. It glowered down at me, all bone-white and steep of roof, small porch like a snout. It reproached me for my absence.

The key complained about the lock, the lock resisted the key, but at last the bolt turned and I let swing open the front door. The smell was dark, musky, faint hints of dog and stale air. I had expected that: My father had finally let the dog and cat go to new homes when he reluctantly conceded she'd not be coming back to rejoin them.

I didn't enter. I studied the siding, dirty and in disrepair. The stop chain had broken, and the screen door hung open. Everywhere there was the blight of emptiness. Behind me, in the back of the truck, was everything important enough to me to take here. Inside the house was everything important to my grandmother over seven decades of her residency here. I stood there, more beaten down than I had ever been. I had fled just that morning, my life in shambles from broken dreams and hanging promises without stop chains.

Of course, I knew this place. I had always been here. Part of me still was. I knew the linoleum covering the floors, but had forgotten the perfect white oak hidden beneath it. I knew the marble coffee table just there near the sofa, the big white-framed mirror on the wall, the torn and ragged sofa witness to the dog's months of loneliness. I knew the alcove behind the living room, had slept there many a time, safe and secure. But I had been gone for years, struggling through forging a life, building its foundations, nailing up its framing, raising its roof, but my craftsmanship was tawdry. It collapsed around me, splintering and cracking loudly, until all that remained was a jumbled debris field.

Unloading the things from the truck, I glanced at the old brown easy chair in the corner, and winced against the pain of the statement, *I don't want it.* I imagined the pain it must have caused her, me, her only heir, her only grandchild. Though I had not intended it that way, it was like saying, *I don't want you.*

She had looked up at me, there in that old brown chair, a half-finished beaded necklace on a loom in her lap, and her eyes were black, moistening pits of hurt. *Burn it, then,* she said, voice trembling like falling roof trusses. *Promise me you'll burn it to the ground.*

But I resisted the guilt, the vow, reminding myself I'd just be here for a little while. Just long enough to put myself back together, find those pieces that had fallen away, see where they fit, snap them back into place. There was much to be done to make this old place liveable again. I walked-through it, checklisting the work ahead of me, and marveled at how two years of emptiness can diminish a house. It's doors must be opened and closed, its floors walked on, its ceilings soaked with voices and laughter, and yes, even crying.

Over the months that followed, I worked at getting it comfortable again. I painted its walls, not even bothering to fix the cracks in the sheetrock. I wouldn't be there long enough. I had landed a job again, and spent my evenings working on the old house. I stripped up all the decrepit linoleum and, in the living room and kitchen, released the old wooden floors my grandfather had installed. Nights I slept under its protection again, but I reminded it that I would be gone again soon. Yet there were reminders of her, and of me, everywhere. When I pulled off a piece of baseboard, hidden there was an old mathematics flash card she used to teach me when I was a kid. When I emptied out a dresser, hidden within, was a manuscript I wrote then I was 14 called *Memories of a Grandfather*, a disjointed, rambling work penned more to make sense of his passing the year before than any literary purpose.

It took six months to refinish the floors alone. But I scraped away decades of old varnish and the glue used to hold down the cheap linoleum and dropped the debris into an aluminum pan. When the pan was full, I'd throw it into the waste basket, and when the waste basket was full, I'd carry it outside and dump it into the big garbage container, and when that was full, it would go to the road and be emptied by the big trucks that came twice a week. Little by little, I relieved the house of arthritis and rheumatism, but with every pass of the scraper, I relieved myself of something, too. A wall of wainscoat in the kitchen had buckled and popped loose, cracking in the process. I replaced it, painted it to match the rest, throwing out something broken and bringing in something whole. It's been said there's only one way to hurt a man who's lost everything: Give him back something broken. I was given back something broken, this old house, and over time, without even realizing it, the notion of temporary became permanence, and the thought of leaving it forgotten.

The last time I saw her was an afternoon on, I think, Mother's Day. I had cut the lawn that morning, using her old Snapper mower, and that afternoon, my parents and I had gone to visit. I knew that there were moments of clarity, but they were mostly outnumbered by the fog of her aged focus. She hugged me, there in those white, crisp sheets, surrounded by metal bed rails and featureless furniture.

"I saw you outside the window," she said, and I nearly wept. Here, frail and withered, was the strongest, most elegant and beautiful woman I had ever known in my life, now shrunken, so thin I feared she'd get lost in those sheets one day and never be found. "I saw you outside, the window this morning," she said.

"Did you, granny?" I smiled, swallowing down any hint of dismay lest she hear it in my voice.

She nodded. "You were cutting the grass. You did a good job, baby. Do you have a cigarette?"

She was 92 years old. She was 22 when she had first walked into that old house back on the reservation. Seventy years later, surrounded by sterile walls and white-garbed nurses, I would have forsaken everything I had to give her a cigarette. Everything.

It wasn't much later that the phone awakened me in the dead of night. I stumbled out of bed, picked it up and heard my father's voice crackle, barely in control of his grief.

"Old woman went home," he said.

Home. I mouthed the word soundlessly. I promised him I'd be there at daybreak to help with the arrangements. I sat in the near-dark, moonlight streaming through windows relieved of grime and dirt, casting hazy shadows over the living room. I sat in that old brown chair. Home. Around me, fresh paint reflected the moonlight, and the oak floor twinkled in some spots with satin luster. There was, I thought, so much left to be done. Years of work ahead.

Home. When I was old enough, she would ride me on the lawn mower with her, let me steer. When I was a little older, she let me drive it by myself, and eventually, I was charged with cutting the lawn regularly. Then, for six years, I cut not a single blade, seldom opened a door, rarely lifted laughter into the ceiling. Not until the day I pulled up in the driveway, a truck full of broken dreams and unfulfilled promises in tow, and slid the key into a reluctant lock to gaze in at my own life, wrapped all up with hers.

The pieces of us are rejoining. Oh, the foundation still needs to be leveled, and the northern rooms and upstairs still need to be renovated. There are unpainted trim pieces around the windows, some of which need new glass. But the locks accept my key easily now, and the ceilings are saturated with voices, the floors firm with trust. I still have that old brown chair, and sit there, in the exact same spot, she did for 70 years. Sometimes I wake for no reason, thinking I heard the phone ring. Most times I go right back to sleep, but sometimes I go and sit in the dark in that old brown chair, and she moves through shadows, vanishing in moonbeams, surveying my work, considering my progress. *You did a good job, baby.*

If I live to be 92 years old, I will have been here for 60 years. What then? I've given orders to those that matter that I won't wither away surrounded by strangers and metal bed rails. I don't know where I'll go after this life, but I'll depart it from here. We're still rebuilding, this old house and I, one fragment at a time. Will we be finished by the time I go home? I don't know. Sometimes I doubt it. Sometimes I think rebuilding a life worth living is like rebuilding a house worth living in. Maybe you never really finish. Maybe you never really should.

Things tend to get tangled up in life sometimes, and much as I am loathe to admit it, the runabout has not been wet in too long. Last weekend, I decided to spend Sunday getting her running. Old outboards do not like to sit up for so long. I put in a battery and filled up the fuel tank. When I turned the key, guess what happened?

It started right up.

I shut it down immediately, since I was sitting on dry land at the time, and didn't want to burn her up with no water to pump through the cooling system. So I hooked her up to the truck and we went to the landing. I backed her down, and, still on the trailer, started it again. The water was pumping through, and that 46-year-old Mercury sat there on the transom purring contentedly.

I had to cut the grass. I needed to clean the shop and put up laundry, too. In fact, there were about a dozen things I needed to get done. But there it was, a gleaming mahogany runabout of my own making, a Mercury purring like a kitten on the back, what's a guy to do?

The bayou was abuzz with boats and waterskis Sunday, but I cruised along in my mahogany runabout happy as a bug in a rug. The old Merc performed flawlessly, and I marveled again at how well the boat took rough water, cornered with just a slight acceleration of the throttle, got "out of the hole" as they say, on takeoff. We rode, this boat and I, to Lake Fausse Pointe, skirting the shore from the channel to Bird Island Chute and back around to Eagle Point, passing Cotton Canal and taking a leisurely cruise back through the canal to Grande Avoille

Cove. Of course, I got *those* looks. I was never sure if they were appreciative or demeaning.

As mentioned in the past, my father was a boat builder. Folks used to come from all over Louisiana and adjacent states for his wooden boats, back when such things were considered worth having, when quality craftsmanship mattered. I never built a boat with my father, though we talked about it many times. It is one of my few regrets. I built, after his passing, a replica of his old 12-foot wooden bateau, which came out badly and was discarded. With the runabout, despite it's minor flaws, I felt like I had at least carried on some trifling fragment of his talent.

In 1982, I think it was, I rented the movie *On Golden Pond* and we watched it. I was still living at home, in high school. There was, in the movie, a Chris Craft runabout, and I fell in love with it. I vowed then and there that one day that I'd have one of those. Dad told me about some he had seen in his day, some tidbits and trivia he recalled about them. My father was a bateau and pirogue man. It was in these Louisiana boats which he sought our divinity in the lakes and bayous of the basin. But he was also a craftsman, perhaps the finest I have ever know, and the gleaming lines of a fine Chris Craft mahogany runabout pleased him in the same way it appealed to me.

There were times, make no mistake, when I was building that boat under the garage at home when some problem of construction confounded and frustrated me. In true boat building tradition, I kept a small stool nearby. This is known as "the moaning chair." It is present to sit on and spend a little time being miserable about some tragic bad cut, some broken sheer, some problem for which the solution is elusive. I spent many hours in my moaning chair over those ten months, but often I got my answers from kind folks on the Internet discussion forum for *WoodenBoat* magazine.

Other times, though, sitting and thinking, staring at this concoction of wood and screws and glue, I could feel his presence surround me, and the answer would make itself known, out of the clear blue, out of, seemingly, nowhere. Of course it wasn't out of nowhere. I know precisely from where my answers arose.

Cruising along Lake Fausse Pointe, along its familiar shores and well-known coves and points, I understood that my bright mahogany runabout was not a bateau, not a pirogue. I am not my father. Our paths diverged somewhere along the way, as they must have. I carry with me much of him, his love of his wonderful, magical lake and the thousands of ghosts drifting along its currents and tides; his joy in working wood, in fashioning boats; most of all, his great respect for all things finely crafted, the notion that if it's not good enough to put your name on it, it must not see the light of day. No, I am not my father. He didn't understand the need to write, my chosen occupation, until near the end of his days. He never could quite comprehend some of the decisions I made, and many in retrospect were as foolhardy as he warned.

I made the turn at Eagle Point, remembering that there is a big, sunken stump just around the corner to avoid; along the finger of Cotton Point, I swerved out far from the trees, remembering that there are numerous sunken timbers there, snapped off by hurricanes over the centuries. In Grand Avoille Cove, I made sure to avoid the row of pilings lurking from Sawmill Bayou to the south side of the cove. All these things my father taught me, and whether in a bateau or a runabout, the basic understanding between that lake and I remains the same.

I am not my father, but I am my father's son, and it remembers me as well as I remember it. *That lake will never hurt us,* he said to me. Respect it! Learn its moods and its dangers, but in the end, he said, that lake will never harm a Chitimacha. We may harm ourselves on it, through negligence or foolhardiness, but the thousands-year-old bond between us is strong.

There are flat-topped pond lilies in Grande Avoille Cove again. Small and few as they are, it is good to see them again. Pollution killed them off before I was a teenager. This was, after all, the place we called "pond lily worship place" and to the Spanish it was the cove of the "grande avoille" as they named those lilies. When I was a child, when the cove was full of huge lilies like those, we'd fish near them and lure bass out from their secluded cover. A sunken wooden barge lies on the south shore. As I cruise near it in the runabout, I can just barely make out the shadow of its shape under the murky water, but the spikes which once held its sides together are poking, rusty and crumbling, above the surface. My father took many of those beams which the barge was made up of to construct his house, our house, back after the war. What remains of them, below the dark water of Grande Avoille Cove, is merely another memory.

As I left the cove, to take the channel back home, I realized Sunday was Father's Day. The old Mercury rumbled behind me, throwing a wake of memories, a tail of understanding. The wind was up, and the ripples across the water were like the backs of buffalo, a great herd, undulating over the land in numbers so great they could not be counted, but they could all be killed.

At the landing, I winched the runabout onto the trailer, took her home and wiped her down. She sat there, a boat of no practical purpose, merely a cruising show pony, but when I realize that she came together, came to life, under my hands, hands that are only partially my own, I know that this Father's Day was a day well spent.

Complaining about the weather, a Louisiana pastime, is entirely flexible depending on the current conditions.

Sure, just a few weeks ago I was complaining about the constant rain. Now the rain isn't so constant, and I'm complaining about this miserable heat. I'm a Louisianian, it's tradition.

Of course, the moment I sit down to write this column, regarding the heat and all, a cool front comes through and makes things downright tolerable. However, since I don't have another topic handy in the ol' noggin', let's go with the flow.

But let me tell you, friends and neighbors, in case you haven't noticed it had been downright hot in the afternoons around these parts. Because of this, I have had a bad case of the "don't feel like doing pecan" syndrome from about 11 a.m. to roughly 6 p.m. It's too painfully hot out there.

Just over the last few summers it couldn't have been this hot, and I couldn't have been much younger. I mean, it was just two summers ago I built a mahogany runabout. I worked on the house. Now, just because I am two months or so shy of my 40th birthday, I can't take the heat anymore? Bah.

But if I go outside about 2 p.m. on the weekend to, oh, say pick up the garbage container from the road, well, before I'm halfway back to the house the sweat is pouring in to my eyes, my hair is matted to my scalp and I'm seeing mirages of palm trees, water ponds and Jeanie-clad Arabian girls. A trip to the road to pick up the garbage container is like a journey across the Sahara. I keep wanting to drop to my knees and dig a hole in the sand with a stick in search of water.

I don't know about global warming and all that, but it's hotter than it was. I don't remember it being this hot when I was a kid, when I could explore the bayou all day, ride horses, shoot my BB gun, swing on the swing set in the back yard, whatever. Now it's all I can do to get the key in the door and get in the house before I collapse into a desiccated pile of leathery skin and brittle bones.

The air conditioner runs almost all the time. I don't remember the air conditioner running that much in previous summers. I know my electric bill is a better indicator of global warming than any ice sheet in Antarctica. Talk about sea level change? I could change the level of the basin just by sweating into Bayou Teche.

And when there's that ever-present threat of rain in the forecast, whether it comes or not, it drives the humidity up, which only serves to make it hotter. I look at the weather forecast and see it's going to be 95 degrees, but with the humidity, you get a heat index of 103! Who thought up the idea of heat indexes, anyway? I mean, isn't it bad enough to say, "It's hot as the dickens today," without some smarty-pants know-it-all adding, "Yeah, and the heat index is 105!" It's the summer version of wind chill in the winter. Did I really need to know about wind chill? Does it make me feel any better to know that the wind is making me feel colder, just like the humidity is making me feel hotter? How does this advance the culture of humankind? More importantly, isn't there enough suffering in the world without making up heat indexes on top of everything else?

"Man proposes and the Good Lord disposes," my dad always said, and though I still haven't a clue what in the world that meant, I suspect it had something to do with heat indexes. Next the know-it-alls will concoct some geometric, algebraic, trigonometry-based calculation to determine that the angle of the sun through the earth's atmosphere, compiled with the amount of vegetative growth within 40 feet of an individual, and coupled with the severity of solar flares, has actually risen the simple temperature of 95 degrees on the thermometer to 146 degrees. At 146 degrees, brain fluids begin to boil.

It sure is hot, though, that's the bottom line. I went out to wash the truck this weekend, and vultures were circling overhead by the time I got to the windshield. This morning on the way to work I think I passed the bleached-white skeleton of a door-to-door salvation salesman, an irony in and of itself. Me, I'm just heading to the bajoon for a cold one. A "bajoon" is a decidedly Cajun term for a barroom, usually of a less than outstanding caliber.

I have a half dozen quarts of chili in the freezer. Who wants chili when its 95 degrees in the shade (never mind the stupid heat index, I don't want to know about it.) I have the fixins' for a big seafood gumbo in the freezer, but who wants a hot, steaming bowl of seafood gumbo when it's so hot the crawfish are burrowing to Anchorage, the shrimp are somewhere in the Marinas trench and the blue crabs are just begging to be put in an ice chest.

They say that Neanderthal man could not biologically cope with the change in climate at the end of the ice age, and went extinct either due to heat stroke or interbreeding with modern Homo sapiens. This may mark the event horizon of another extinction wave: My kind, nearly-40ish fat boys who spend eight or more hours a day in air-conditioned offices or meeting rooms, is heading down the road to extinction via climate change. We'll be fossilized, or perhaps mummified, and thousands of years from now they'll dig up our bones and study them in labs, trying to figure out why we expired. If we are in fact mummified, perhaps there will be enough of our internal organs left for tissue samples which will reveal that our sweat glands went China Syndrome and our livers have suffered that inevitable by-product of climate change, too many trips to the bajoon for a cold one.

There's this annoying space in the alcove above the stair that I never finished, and it looks terrible. One day in July I actually got the energy to do something about it.

First I went to the woodshed to find an appropriate piece of lumber to begin the job. However, upon arrival in said woodshed, I remembered that a few weeks earlier I had spent an entire afternoon cleaning it out. In the process, the lumber itself got pretty disorganized. There is, for a woodworker, nothing worse than having your oak mixed with your cypress and having a couple of boards of fir stacked in with your pine. You get the idea.

So I spent two hours organizing by species, width and length. When finally done with this, I selected the board I wanted and brought it to the shop. I started by trimming the edge with the table saw, but the cut was so bad I realized it had been too long since I had aligned the tool. I took time out to adjust fence, miter and blade, but it occurred to me that last Christmas I had bought myself a new blade and never installed it, so I did that too.

When done, I figured I'd be needing my miter saw for the job, and spent some time getting it aligned properly. Then I realized the jointer probably needed tweaking, and went on to that project.

During all this, I realized the shop was a horrid mess, so I moved all the tools around, emptied shelves, vacuumed everything, and put it all back.

Of course, while cleaning up, I glanced in my chisel box and saw a bit of rust staining my shiny Blue Marples, so I cleaned them up and put an edge on all four. This got me to wondering about my hand planes, and sure enough, they all needed a good, sharp edge applied.

Finally everything was in order. I picked up the lumber I had retrieved from the woodshed, looked at it, put it back down and went inside for a much-needed nap.

Getting started is the hardest part. Once rolling, I'm good for the duration. It's just getting started that is difficult. That annoying spot above the stair is still unattended to.

I've been working on this old house for seven years, and I'm not even halfway done. Seven years, though, in the life of a 160-year-old house, is nothing, but it's a significant chunk of mine, considering the men in my family generally head for the Happy Hunting Ground by their mid-70s. Thus, I am nearly 40, I've spent about a tenth of my overall life working on the house, and I'm less than half done with the house and more than half done with myself. A dismal circumstance, to be sure.

Folks shake their heads at me in wonder. "Doesn't it drive you crazy?" they ask me. No, I tell them, I am quite used to living in a construction zone by now. I mean, Patches doesn't give a jolly rip about that annoying spot above the stairs. I have no wife to pester me about the one cabinet door in the kitchen that doesn't match the others, nagging me to build a new one to get everything uniform. With careful deliberation, I have effectively removed that spot above the bar where the sheet rock needs patching from my consciousness. It does not exist unless I want it to. And the various pieces of trim molding which are keeping the living room and "piddling room" from otherwise being completed? The devil is in the details, as they say.

"Is it a Victorian look you're after?" they ask me.

"No," I reply. "I'm actually striving toward middle- to late-Sanford and Son."

But this weekend, with any luck, I'm going to get something done, even it's just cut a piece of wood. It's difficult. There's a new wooden boat eating up my brain right now, and that's a hard temptation to resist. The rain has finally subsided for the most part, and the river's dropping, and they say the goggle-eye are tearing up anything you throw at them in the basin. What's a little hole in the stair alcove? In the whole grand scheme of the universe, completely unimportant.

Renovating a house built by poor Indians is both easier and more difficult than a similar house built by folks who might have had a dollar or two. It's easier because I don't have to worry about a lot of elaborate molding and details. It's harder because they couldn't afford a square, level or plumb bob. At some point, it seems, they couldn't even afford a saw, because many of the wall studs in the kitchen look like they were hewn with axes, dull ones.

Then there's the outside. That's where the big money comes in. It needs to be blocked and leveled soon, professionally. I fight it constantly, and it's not like it's sagging so much it resembles a melting bowl of ice cream, but it's a never-ending battle to keep it relatively horizontal. Much to the puzzlement of everyone I know, and probably you kind folks as well, I absolutely despise the metal roof. Dastardly! I want a shingle roof again, but we're talking blood money now.

"What?" people exclaim, bewildered. "You want to remove a 50-year metal roof that's in perfectly good shape to put on shingles that might last 20 years?"

"Yes," I say. "It looks like a battleship."

"Dumb!" they say. "Foolish! Irresponsible! Slovenly!"

I also want the dormers it had on the front replaced. I don't know when they were removed, probably when that stinking ugly metal roof was put on, but I remember them well, and have photos of them for rebuilding guides.

"Dormers!" folks shout. "Hurricane-attracting disasters, that's what dormers are! You have to climb up there and put plywood over them when a storm comes! You'll fall from the ladder and break your neck! They'll blow out and flood the whole house! Leave 'em alone! Don't put them back! Idiot! Moron! Nut-case!"

So it goes.

One day, too, I'll build a big shop in the back of the house. This is another cause for dismay among folks. They say I should pour a slab and erect one of those convenient, easy-to-assemble metal buildings which will last several lifetimes.

I explain that I want a slab, yes, but a wood-frame shop with siding and roof to match the house.

"Shingle roof on a wood frame workshop!" they scream in horror and flee, surely off to alert the villagers that the creature has escaped, light torches and march on my property like a mob of peasants, shouting, "Give us Frankenstein!"

Well, maybe I'll get some work done this weekend. If so, it'll be done in a traditional, historically accurate manner, that particular style of home construction known only to an enlightened few as "Po' Indian."

You look around at folks on the streets these days, it's like a scene from George Romero's *Dawn of the Dead*: Folks walking around, slack-jawed, sluggish and slow, mumbling incoherently when you speak to them. Summertime zombies, that's what we are. We're walking the streets like zombies looking for Gatorade.

I can fish in spring and fall, or very early in the morning. But after about 10 a.m., it's just too miserably hot to stay out there. Sunday I took off in the boat for the basin. Within an hour I had taken two bass, decent sized, and a couple of small perch.

But then the midmorning heat came in, and the fish shut their mouths and refused to say boo to me. The sweat started rolling into my eyes, making casting accurately a difficult task at best. By 11 a.m., the automatic bilge pump on the boat kicked on, and I was terrified she had sprung a leak. But no, she was just relieving herself of the gallons of accumulated sweat in the bilge.

So I went in. The ride back to the boat launch was so refreshing, I circled a couple times just to enjoy it, then finally coasted in to the ramp and the oppressive, breezeless heat. By the time I got the boat loaded, my shirt was soaked, and by the time I got home, unhooked and cleaned up the boat, all I could do was go inside, shower and change clothes, and collapse on the sofa.

I barely left the house the rest of the day, sucking in air-conditioning like it was the nectar of the gods. I watched a couple of bad movies and one good one, played on the computer, wrote a little, and cussed a lot.

So either I need an air-conditioned lake, or I need a summer hobby that can be enjoyed indoors. This is not an easy proposition. I hate being stuck inside. I am an outdoorsy kinda guy. While I had been considering a new boat building project, Sunday's fishing trip forced me to realize that the last thing I want to be doing is working outside on a boat.

Fishing and boat-riding are the only water sports I enjoy. I don't ski, tube, hydroslide or swim. Not to say that I can't swim, but I grew up with repetitive inner ear problems, and my early years were pretty much swimless, so it's not a pastime I grew fond of. I can swim well enough to save my life (I think) should the boat overturn or something, but recreationally, not my cup of tea.

Perhaps I could take up painting. Gary Drinkwater sent me a lovely work he recently created, for which I am most grateful, and it got me to thinking maybe I want to try painting. But then I realized, as talented as Gary is, maybe we had better strike a deal: I won't paint, if he doesn't take up writing. I might get outgunned!

One of the local area's most talented artists is Francis Todd, whose work with film is magnificent and many times hauntingly beautiful. But Francis specializes in outside photography, so there we go again. Much as I love photography, the idea of photographing fruit baskets on my kitchen table just doesn't float my boat.

"Maybe you could work on the house, cheesehead," you say. This is true, except that in order to do so, I have to go out to the shop. It's miserable in the shop, and going in and out is surely a guarantee of pneumonia.

I started trying to tie fishing flies. It's difficult, considering my vision is so poor, but it's an inside job. I started by tying some simple flies called the Jitterbee, a Louisiana-created little jewel for bluegill which looks like a bee. The Jitterbee is tied with chenille, which is pretty coarse stuff, and I can just about see it well enough that I tied a half dozen of the worst looking Jitterbees ever. They look like there was a bad gene pool in the hive, and I doubt any self-respecting perch will have anything to do with it.

Then I wanted to experiment with more traditional flies using feathers and fur. I was creating some monstrosity which vaguely resembled a One Eyed One Armed Flying Purple People Eater when I decided that it needed a little hairy fluff on the tail to finish it off nicely. I also decided it needed to be black and tan. I had no black and tan deer hair in my fly tying box.

Then I spied Patches, napping on the sofa.

She opened one eye to watch me suspiciously as I approached with the scissors.

"Just a little nip," I said. "You'll never miss it."

She yawned, and flexed her claws. I got the idea, and finished off the fly with some red and yellow I already had. Really doesn't matter. The fly resembles a nuclear waste-mutated Junebug suffering from lycanthropy. It's also so big I would probably need a tarpon rod to cast it.

So that's out as a summer hobby. I figured then that, since I couldn't actually build a real boat, I might build model boats and ships. I started looking at models of boats I like on the Internet: Chris-Craft runabouts, the U.S.S. *Constitution*, stuff like that. Model kits cost an arm and a leg and a firstborn son thrown in. I could almost build a real boat for what the models cost. Since most of my monthly pay is going to the electric bill from running the air-conditioner and copious amounts of consumable liquids, there's no money left over for model boats.

Crochet? Ha. Whittling? I'd slice my thumb off, and the mess is terrible, all those shavings mixed with blood. Cooking? I've gained too much weight from laying around on the sofa all summer already. Body building? I've built enough body from laying around on the sofa all summer already, thank you very much.

Now and then I go outside when it gets near dark just to survey the ranch. I am fearful that the vinyl siding will melt off the house, but so far so good. I check to make sure Mocha has plenty of water and isn't roasted. Now and then I think about cutting the grass, but usually decide it's still too hot. Besides, if I let it grow enough, perhaps it'll create a canopy over my whole lot, like in those haunted house movies, and provide perpetual shade. At that point, the undergrowth will die off from lack of light, and I can sell the lawnmowers and weed eater for some cash.

If you're thinking this entire column sounds suspiciously like it originated from the mind of a heat stroke victim, you're probably right. It's too stinking hot.

July

July brings with it the desire to wander.

It was in July, overwhelmed by toils and debacles, that I took to the road to visit a friend in Lawton, Oklahoma. I packed my Mustang with enough clothes to last for a week and, not really knowing the way, took to the road and let the wheels spin away misery.

The trip was uneventful until just north of Wichita Falls, when a storm settled over the plains. I passed car wreck after car wreck, and the rain came in heavy sheets. When one particularly brilliant lightning bolt flashed, I saw far in the distance a tornado so huge it seemed to be miles wide. This was more than I could stand, and though I was only an hour from Lawton, I found the nearest motel and hid for the night.

While in Lawton, I visited Fort Sill, and the cell in which Geronimo was held for the last of his days. Voices in a language I could not understand still whispered within those dank mud-brick walls, and the heavy iron door was rusted by tears. Later in the day, I visited the great warrior's grave, said a few words of thanks and respect over it. Standing there at his last resting place, I could imagine Geronimo riding free and unfettered over his home lands, but imprisoned here, far from home, buried away from his ancestors. It matters not to the Western-descended where they are laid to rest, mostly. But to men like Geronimo, little was more important. Still is, to me.

It put me in mind of a July many years earlier, when I stood at the top of a mesa in Arizona, in a village called Oraibi, which was the oldest Hopi settlement in their lands. That night, the Kachinas had danced, coming out of the darkness under a sky with an impossible number of stars. Though the part of me that is Western-descended knew these were the village men dressed in the garb of ages-old spirits, a part of my soul also knew what those Hopi men knew: For a time, while they danced, they became the individual Kachina they represented.

They danced great circles around the fire, sang songs so ancient the words conjured forth ghosts from the rock and sand, ghosts which had roamed here before contact, chased buffalo when the herds were so large they covered hundreds of square miles. I sat in reverence and awe.

That long-ago July, I climbed the face of rock into a cliff dwelling high above the desert sands. I wandered through the remains of Anasazi shelters, explored a kiva and heard a raptor screech somewhere much higher above. The Anasazi, a Navajo word for "ancient strangers" or "ancient enemy," vanished without a trace from these remarkable structures around 1300 AD Inside one of their small homes, I touched adobe walls and saw the finger and thumb prints of their builders, forever captured by the then-wet adobe. From the edge of the settlement, far, far in the distance, I could see more mesas, more desert and the greater blue of a sky than I had ever known.

There was a long-dead riverbed near where I was staying with friends, and I walked it under a sweltering July sun. I noticed material, like slate, imbedded in the dry sides of the vanished river, and pulled one out. It was pottery, a piece as large as my hand. There were layers and layers of this, and I pulled out many more, finding some plain and ocher, some with exquisite paintings still perfectly preserved: a wolf, a warrior, a woman, a great bird. Suddenly regretful that I disturbed them, I placed them back into the sandy riverbed and left them in peace.

As the Kachinas danced that night, the drums beating and resounding across the mesa, a part of me was stirred which I never was aware of before. Back home in Louisiana, I realized, was a marvelous legacy of culture equally as rich and vibrant as this, but lying dormant, half-asleep. In its fitful dozing, the ways and spirits of my own people were seeking rebirth. I thought of the four columns of the Hopi, and the four sacred trees of my people. I thought of dry riverbeds holding broken pottery, and the shell reefs of our ancestral worship place dredged into oblivion for the value of its material, as skeletons rolled out and were discarded into the lake.

A Hopi woman had prepared a feast for us after the Kachina dance: beef stew with barely enough meat in it to make you or I a decent steak. Fry bread in abundance, and corn, squash and beans. Singing, laughter and kind-hearted teasing lifted out across the desert like thunderbirds taking flight. The entire village contributed to a basket of fruits and vegetables which a Kachina presented me during the dance, an honor not to be mistaken.

In Flagstaff, Arizona, on my way back to the airport to take the great silver bird home, we passed a convenience store with a hand-lettered sign in the window reading exactly: "No Dogz Or Indians Alowed."

July flashes hot, scorching concrete streets and burning tender flesh. A land of desert, and a land of water, I had moved from one to the other and back again. I noticed my grandmother's hands, fingers and palm full of bandages from minor lacerations while splitting river cane to make baskets; I noticed my grandfather's lithe, nimble fingers fashioning silver and turquoise; I noticed my father deftly cutting wood away from a block to slowly, painfully reveal the warrior and his dog trapped within, set free.

I long to wander again in July. I hunger for frybread cooked at high altitude, the only way to make good frybread. I ache to stand at the head of the Serpent Mound, to scurry among the ruins at Cahokia. I want to climb cliffs and explore kivas, search for *wendigo* with cousins in the fir-carpeted hills, make an offering of tobacco at Grand Village in Natchez. My kin are still alive all over this great land, and while we were once 500 nations strong, we persist in July despite signs hung on convenience store windows and annihilation by absorption.

In July, it is good to belong to such a large and far-reaching family.

Why is it the Apaches wait to die—that they carry their lives on their fingernails? They roam over the hills and the plains and want the heavens to fall on them. The Apaches were once a great nation; they are now but few, because of this they want to die and so carry their lives on their fingernails.—Cochise

With a storm on its front porch, July opens its doors to the clamor of summer. It is here that summer has become an adolescent—temperamental, moody and resentful. It rebels against law, rallies against commonality and oppresses all within the scope of its influence. Summer is an overlord. Summer is a terrifying but beautiful angel descending from the clouds with purpose of either glory or dismay.

This July has been earmarked by two or three visits with my mom per day in the rehabilitation center at Franklin Health Care, where we believe she will be released this week to return at last to a home which is growing faded and thin from missing her. Each time I go to that house, to retrieve some item she needs or drop off her mail and newspapers, I notice that the colors of the paint are subdued, the varnished wood turning dull, the light from bulbs lethargic. It misses her presence there, the sound of the grandchildren knocking on the front door, the aunts and uncles dropping by to visit, the running of water in the bath and the clink of pots and pans on the stove. Left that way, I am sure it will one day fade away entirely, its existence spent.

Visiting her daily, in the first days of her long trek back toward mobility, I was at first afraid of what I would find there. While I am not one of those people who fear old age—in fact, in many ways I look forward to it—the often associated partners of aging are what make me fearful. And though I encountered people who were so faded I could see through them, see the backs of their wheelchairs through their chests, see the hallway in front of them through their backs, I learned soon enough that there were enough brightly lit eyes there to spread a little joy. At first I'd speak to them, "Good morning," as I passed and received a surprised look that I had actually done so. Later, I could not get the words out of my mouth before some elder shouted, "Good morning!" before I could say it.

There was a July long ago when we would go visit my grandfather in the hospital along the outgoing tide of his life. My mom would pass by and tickle his feet first thing when she entered the room, and he'd shout, "Diddy!" That was her nickname among some of the family, though I don't know exactly why. They called my dad late one night because Emile had an accident and he rushed off to the hospital alone, but returned to say everything was okay, he had just fallen and bumped his head. The next night when we went to visit, I noticed a skull-sized hole in the sheet rock wall.

Emile Anatole Stouff was bigger than anyone in the family, though one July in his youth he had contracted polio and one of his legs never grew in girth, though it was the proper length. Throughout his life, he had to buy two pairs of shoes when he needed new ones, and throw half of them away, a situation which irritated him greatly. But he was well over six feet tall, had a chest like a 55-gallon drum and a booming voice to match. He was so dark there was no mistaking he was Native, and he had a smile which would raise the sun from behind a thunderhead whether Nature wanted it to or not.

One morning, as I was walking across the parking lot to visit my mom, there was a lady and two children, little girls, getting into a car. An elderly gentleman in a wheelchair shouted something to them I couldn't hear, and the girls immediately ran over and gave him big affectionate hugs, singing, "Bye, pop!" with broad, happy smiles. It is for moments like this that there is a July. It is for such sights that July always comes back around.

If my life were a calendar, I would be in July. Slightly more than midway. I flip the pages and look through the August, September, October and November of my days, and wonder where I'll sit and who'll give me smiles and hugs in December. There are no greater joys than hugs and smiles in the December of a life.

But in Julys long gone by, I was surrounded by as closely knit a family as you could find. Parents and grandparents were my entire world, and when, one by one, they followed the thunderbirds to that place where all my relations are singing songs, it came down to me and my mom. In Julys past, we traveled in a pack when one of us was feeling poorly, supporting them and each other. Today I have friends, loved ones, treasured companions, but within I am somehow alone.

Lydia Marie Gaudet Stouff, it was said back in 1947, would never fit into the Stouff family. "She's too meek and timid," my grandmother told my dad. "She's too quiet and shy." It was true, in a family that tended to all talk at once for half an hour at a time then all suddenly go quiet and simultaneously say, "What?" before beginning the loud chatter again. But she surprised all of them by continuing to be quiet and shy, but popping off the occasional zinger remark that left everyone momentarily speechless then prompting gales of laughter.

That humor still stands tall under the hot sun of this July. Upon her arrival, she was aided to her bed with a little help from the staff, and they praised her for her progress. As she lay back down, she popped an index finger in the air and said, "I'm a cranky 76-year-old woman, so you just better watch out." Visitors in her room at the rehabilitation center are often reduced to tears by her dry, casual wit. Behind her, though I am sure only I am aware of it, my father and grandparents are standing there, laughing in a soundless chorus.

We thankfully have far to go before her December, and like all of us should do, I shall cherish each and every date of the calendar of her life.

There was a sweltering, humid July once when we barbecued outside my grandparents' house under a huge pecan tree that Hurricane Andrew took down decades later. I had my first camera, a Kodak Brownie, and took fuzzy, grainy pictures of all of them. In one, my unsuspecting grandfather is about to be doused with bug spray from behind by my mom. In the hazy background of the photograph, an old outhouse still stands, long disused, and farther back still, Bayou Teche is a quiet observer to the lifetimes being played out on its banks.

Within a sweltering July night, just after bedtime, the phone rang and my father rushed to answer it.

"Nick!" my grandfather yelled over the phone line. My grandfather never used the phone at any time before or after that in my recollection because he was hard of hearing. "Get over here, the old woman fell in the yard!"

We rushed over and learned that Ma Faye had fallen off the front porch of the house and broken her hip. She lay there for who knows how long, shouting for the old man to come help her, but his hearing aid was turned down and he never heard her. Finally, in excruciating pain, she managed to get one of her shoes off and throw it at the window near where he sat in the house, and he went outside to see what all the commotion was about.

Now and then we'd take the camp boat Dad built out to Grand Avoille Cove and spend a July day fishing and eating sandwiches Mom and Ma Faye had made that morning, while the men folk drank a few Jax or Falstaffs. Sometimes Dad would tow the bateau behind and he and I would go fish some of the better areas of Lake Fausse Point and cook them up in a skillet of grease on a propane crawfish boiler. Mom would catch catfish and goggle-eye perch. The goggle-eye were indisputably hers once they made it to the table, all golden brown and crispy. My mom would get in a fight with a circular saw for a fried goggle-eye, as they were her very favorite fish for eating.

Mom had surgery of some kind one July when I was very young and was out of the house for a week, so Dad and I had to fend for ourselves. It was quite an adventure, as Dad was no cook. He one night took out a batch of fish frozen from earlier in the year and fried them on the stove, creating such a spewing of smoke that we had to throw the skillet out the back door and open all the windows before retreating to the hamburger joint for supper. After that, we survived on ham sandwiches and oatmeal cream pies until Mom got home and set the house in proper working order again.

The ditch in front of our house was dry and full of naked sugar cane stalks fallen from tractors late in the year, but in July it was often overgrown with weeds which Dad would cut with a ditchbank sweeper. The road tended to crumble into the ditch with every passing car, and now and then I'd sit on the old oak tree roots near the driveway and watch as state road crews made half-hearted repairs to it, patches which lasted perhaps a few weeks then would start their slow, steady crumble into the ditches again. I find it amusing today that when you drive onto the reservation from Baldwin there is a state road sign right before the tribal boundary which says "End Maintenance," then you are on the reservation and the road suddenly improves dramatically.

Sometimes my mom and I talk about those Julys gone past. We are its only survivors, and we remember them with smiles or sad shakes of the head. This July my mom is going home, and the paint in the house will grow vibrant again, the wood bright and the light refreshed. This July will be painfully sparsely populated, but within the two of us, there's more than enough love and joy to make up for it.

The Two of Us

It puts one in mind of our own frailty.

This body, this shell of mostly water within a cocoon of flesh and tissue and supported by a frame of bone is a tender, fragile thing. When we are young those of us who are fortunate treat this container for our souls, this urn for our spirit, as if it is indestructible. It is in fact far more delicate than old window glass.

How little we think of the simple things which we do each and every day of our lives. When those simple tasks and pleasures become elusive to us, shackled by chains of pain, what greater treasure could there be? Money, fame, material possessions, all fade to the peripheral when even the most mundane functions are outside our reach.

Tending to someone beloved whose body has grown frail with the passing of decades is not only an awakening but a lesson in humility. What we are, what we perceive as our strengths and fortunes slip quickly into negligible importance as both the injured and the tender struggle through each day, each hour, each minute. We sit, when she is feeling well enough to stay awake, and chat in the bedroom, talk about old days, talk about days to come, and I struggle to find encouragement, to keep spirits up. There is, I promise, nearly perfect odds that recovery is near, but near means little when even just six days are reduced to each passing minute. Neither of us have ever been gamblers, preferring the birds in the hand to those in the bush.

When I lightly trot up the steps to my house, or without a second thought lug groceries to the fridge, and as I move a chair out of the way of hesitant, painful feet or throw a heavy iron skillet on the stove to fix supper, I am aware of the non-thought I have given such things until now. Along the road, as miles drift behind me and fewer still stretch out ahead, I see in her eyes a prophecy. What day will it be, what milepost down the road or bend in the river, when this body will be unable to do what it has done before: Cast a fly, unhook a largemouth bass, run a plank of cypress through the saw, hammer a nail.

I'm sorry, she says to me sometimes, and I laugh and say something witty to make her feel better, though I doubt it works. What can I say? She carried me in her body when it was strong and complete, she held me close to protect me when I could not protect myself, fed and clothed me, bandaged my cuts and scrapes. She taught me to walk, to talk, to dress, to read, to write, to laugh. She is now teaching me humility. She is teaching me strength I never knew existed across the entire universe.

Family and friends come and go, telephone, send letters and cards. They are treasured and revered. But in the quietest of the passing seconds and minutes, when the house is still except for the spirit of the old man who still walks there, watching unseen, I know it is her and I and no one else exists in this entire lonely world. If I could stretch my memory back along the road to where I first stepped foot on it, I might remember when everything I knew was her and my need, my dependence on her. At this end of the road, our roles are reversed and there is, after all, a circle to which we all return.

Everything the Power of the World does is done in a circle. The sky is round, and I have heard that the earth is round like a ball, and so are all the stars. The wind, in its greatest power, whirls. Birds make their nests in circles, for theirs is the same religion as ours. The sun comes forth and goes down again in a circle. The moon does the same, and both are round. Even the seasons form a great circle in their changing, and always come back again to where the were. The life of a man is a circle from childhood to childhood, and so it is in everything where power moves.—Black Elk.

So it is without regret that I dedicate the miles ahead to this person as she dedicated many miles behind to me. Our pace is slower, our step heavier, but we move along it and watch the signposts, study the crossroads and stop now and then to let our eyes cherish a field of blanket flower or listen to the murmur of our father and husband in the movement of water flowing alongside the way. We have many miles to go, she and I, but the safety and the comfort is in knowing that we'll not traverse them alone.

Counting the minutes, the seconds. There is healing to come, relief on the horizon, but release from pain will not break the circle, nor part the steps on the road. There's nothing in heaven above or earth below which can do that.

With recovery after the slow, painful weeks, we felt there was no more need for "sitters." So one Friday, I moved back to my house after a long absence.

I live only three houses down from Mom, so I'm not far from her call. It's been a rough two months to be sure, but we both survived. She taught me strength and determination which will always be an inspiration to me.

Patches and Mocha were, of course, delighted to have me back home. The house was a mess, and several hours of cleaning were in order before I felt comfortable enough to take a nap, with Patches curled up under my arm, of course.

It didn't take me long to fall back into my normal routine: napping, fishing and not mowing the grass when I should. While my neighbors on either side of me cut their lawns this last weekend, mine still looks like some sort of adolescent facial growth. I fully intended to mow it, you understand, but there was fishing to be done which had fallen by the wayside over the past few weeks, by thunder. A man's gotta have his priorities straight.

My dear darling mom likes to keep the house cool. Really cool. Though at first my teeth chattered at night, I got used to it. When I went home, I kept feeling hot. Now, Mom's house is about 10 years old, whereas mine is 160 years old. In other words, Mom's house can cool to 70 to 72 degrees and not run up too high of an electrical bill. My house would eat up a month's salary assuming I could even get it that cool without giving the air conditioner a nervous breakdown. So I adjusted the thermostat a couple degrees below what I usually keep it, and slowly moved it back up to my normal temperature over the weekend until I got used to it again.

Sunday, in need of a little outing, I took off to Lafayette to do some window shopping. It didn't take long to realize I didn't need any windows—or at least, couldn't afford them right now—and we went to the bookstore instead.

Bookstores are the only thing better than a library. I love libraries because I can go read a book for free, but when I get attached to a book, I have to keep it near me. It's not uncommon for me to be washing dishes, mowing the lawn (which is uncommon) or taking a shower and I'll suddenly have a compelling urge to read Stephen King or *A Brief History of Time*. Or perhaps *Manual of the Vascular Flora of the Carolinas* (one of my all-time favorites!) and rush to the stacks of books scattered all over the house, cuss madly for an hour until I find whatever my sudden inkling was. So I often read books from the library, and if I get attached to them, go to the bookstore and buy it.

I went to Barnes and Noble with the intention of buying *Standing in a River Waving A Stick* by John Gierach, the author of *Death, Taxes and Leaky Waders* which I had just finished. I ended up with that book, but also two others by Gierach, as well as *Walden* by Thoreau and a picture book of wooden boats. I get as odd a look at the checkout in the bookstore as I do fly fishing on the ponds around here, I can tell you.

Also on our trip, we passed by Academy Sports, where I immediately made a bee-line for the fishing section. If there's anything more dangerous for me than a bookstore, it's a fishing store. I managed to get out with only purchasing a few lures and new fly lines but it was tough. The only thing that really saved me is that Academy doesn't stock that much fly fishing stuff.

All last week, I promised Mom a fried fish dinner sometime over the weekend. Confident that I would be able to deliver on that promise, I strolled out Friday evening to one of my favorite fishing holes and proceeded to spend four hours catching doodly-squat. Fly rod, bait casting rod, spinning rod, nothing, notta, zilch, zero, my hero. This is serious pressure, you understand. You have promised your mom fried fish and can't produce. It was so bad, I couldn't have bought fish in the seafood section of the grocery store. In fact, it was so bad, you couldn't have bought me fish in the seafood section of the grocery store.

Saturday morning and afternoon I tried again, and again Saturday evening. My lures were yawning they were so bored. If you've never seen a plastic worm or a Betts fly popper yawn, you ain't seen nothing.

But Sunday morning, though it wasn't easy, I managed to bring home six fish, and we had a great Sunday dinner of fried fish and taters. On the way back from Lafayette, my friend and I stopped for ice cream from the Borden's place. By the time I got home, I couldn't move.

But in the quiet of the late evening, sitting there with just my reading light on and relishing local author Fielding Lewis' book *Tales of a Louisiana Duck Hunter*, with Patches curled up by my side in the easy chair, it was good to be home. I'd do it all again for my dear darling mum in a heartbeat, though we're both praying we don't have to. But in the end, there's no place like home.

Near midnight, my eyes growing heavy and tired, when the "last page I'm going to read" was eight pages ago, I finally put aside the book and sat there for a few moments. Patches yawned and looked up at me but made no sound.

The reading lamp stretched thin, long shadows across the room; some corners remained dark where the bulb couldn't quite reach, and little pockets of midnight lingered here and there, under the bar, behind the television, beside the Douglas fir huntboard. Where the light did hold sway, everything was warm amber. Night had brought cooler temperatures, so the air conditioner wasn't struggling to keep up anymore, and when it switched itself off, I sat with Patches and listened to the house make those subtle, nearly inaudible sounds it makes at that time of the night. We conversed, that old house and I, for a time while the clock turned midnight and the shadows in the corners jealousy held secrets to themselves.

And I knew as surely as my own name that, at the end of this road, when I draw my last breath I want it to be here. Among these walls, where my hands might be the last of generations of hands that fashioned and molded and crafted a home. A singular, determined purpose overwhelmed me, and I vowed I would have it no other way. A person should be free to choose where the road ends after so diligently following it along so many, many miles. When my road ends it will be full-circle, back here in this beloved old house, where it all began.

The Good Porch and Swing

I need to build a porch.

Never mind that I have a dozen or two other projects going on around the house; forget that I haven't completed the kitchen, or the bathroom, or the living room, for that matter. I need to build a porch.

The front of the house has a small porch under a dormer. It's only about 7 feet by 8 feet, though, and if you try to put two chairs on it to sit, there's no way to open the door. It's not really a good porch for sitting on chairs and watching the day go by, because if one of us needs to go inside to get something to drink or go to the bathroom, we both have to get up and move our chairs to open the door.

Everybody needs a good porch. There's nothing like it for relaxing after a long day. I was watching *Extreme Homes* on HGTV the other night, and these nice folks had build a huge house full of glass windows, which was beautiful. But the husband in the family said they did it to "bring the outdoors closer."

That struck me as funny. If you wanna bring the outdoors closer, go outdoors. Ya folla? I like a house with a lot of glass, but not to bring the outdoors closer. If I want to bring the outdoors closer, I'll live in a gazebo.

That's where a good porch comes in handy. I don't like ground-level porches for some reason. A porch should be at least 18 inches off the ground, and made of wood. That way, the cool, moist air from beneath the porch can sift through the slats to you.

A good porch must have room for a porch swing made of cypress, either varnished or painted forest green, a few chairs, and a table. It must be covered, and optionally screened-in. A good porch is a place where you can sit and watch the cars go by, or watch the bayou flow, or watch hummingbirds visiting your hummingbird feeders. A good porch is a place where you can lift an Abita Amber to passersby on the street and say, "How y'all are?" If you'll notice, people passing by tend to be friendlier when you're sitting on the porch than if you're getting the mail, cutting the grass or walking the dog. It's because they realize that only good people sit on porches, and they wish they were sitting on a porch too.

Sitting and relaxing on a good porch is like being the rancher looking over his spread after a long day of mending fences, branding cattle, tracking down stray heifers and fighting Indians. No, never mind that part about the Indians. But after a hard day on the job, a good porch is where you sit to survey your kingdom. Be it a tenth of an acre or the south 40, a kingdom it is nonetheless.

A good porch is perfect for sipping morning coffee and watching the sun burn off the early mist. It's equally good to sit and have a drink while watching the sunset. A good porch must be roomy and comfortable for a handful of people. Any more than a handful of people, say four or five, and it's no longer a porch, it's a deck. That's the difference between a porch and a deck: Decks are meant for crowds, porches are meant for intimate sanctuary with close friends. This is why so many building supply places sell decks now: If you're not hanging out with crowds of peers or acquaintances beneficial to your career, you're not upwardly mobile. Nobody who sits on a porch is upwardly mobile, they want you to believe. You need a deck, made of redwood, to keep up with the Joneses, they suggest.

There should be plants on a good porch, potted in nice containers, well-fed and watered. If you have a dog, it's mandatory to have your dog sit with you on the porch to bark at anybody that comes by. If you have outdoor cats, it's also required that they lay on the porch rail and stalk bluejays.

The other necessity of a good porch is, if it's screened in, a nice screen door. Not just any screen door, mind you, but a nice one with character and charm, warm and inviting. Aluminum does not feel warm and inviting to me, so of course, my porch will have a wood screen door. Imagine an aluminum screen door in your mind next to a wooden one—which feels more homey, more relaxed and wholesome? The wood one, of course. Aluminum screen doors are for brick homes. I have nothing against brick homes, mind you, but I couldn't live in one again. I did for six years, and having been where I am now for another seven years, I can't imagine going back to a brick home with an aluminum screen door.

The front porch will be about 22 feet long and 10 feet deep, incorporating the existing dormer into the overhang to be constructed. But behind the house there'll be another covered porch that will look out over my 550-year-old oak tree and Bayou Teche. This porch will be the better of the two, because it faces northwest, and the sunsets are spectacular sometimes. This is the porch to use when you don't want to see anybody, like when sitting on the front porch, and you want to keep the rumors from starting, like, "Every time I see him, he's got a drink in his hand." Better to retire to the back porch than be known as a porch-sitting lush.

The back porch is where I can sit and watch the squirrels playing in the maple tree and the old oak. A good back porch must be invisible from the front of the house, so you can at least create the illusion of being isolated. A back porch is where you ignore the bell or knocks at the door if you don't want to be bothered. The back porch is where you can nap on a hammock or the porch swing without waking up and finding the electrical meter reader staring at you.

Good porches must be well thought-out and planned. There's nothing more pathetic than a porch that has not been planned well. It must blend into the rest of the house, not jut out from it like a hangnail. A good porch must be like another room of the house, just with only one wall.

That's the porch I'm going to build, when I get around to it. A good porch, then, is a transition point from indoors to out. It's a place of friendliness, warmth and sanctuary, each to its own time and place. A good porch, in the end, is a place where weariness of the day, toils of the world, fall away between the wooden slats and are forgotten. There's nothing like a good porch for regaining some peace of mind.

Except maybe fishing. Now, if you had a porch you could fish from, *that* would be heaven.

A good porch must, of course, have a good porch swing. I've built a number of porch swings. My first, when I was in my very early stages of learning woodworking, was a bizarre concoction of cypress, cedar and hard maple. It fell apart in a few weeks, as a result of my then-inferior wood working abilities. Luckily, no one was seated on it at the time. The second, third and fourth were cypress, and as far as I know, they're holding up quite well, because I don't own a single one of them still, and nobody's come to complain about broken bones or bruises. Besides, I don't have a good porch yet, remember?

For something like $39.95, you can buy a porch swing at Lowe's or some place like that, made of pressure-treated pine or redwood. That's all find and dandy, but to me, putting a pressure-treated pine or redwood swing on a good porch is like putting bumper stickers on a Shelby Cobra.

In fact, when I was building a cypress swing once, someone who came by the shop commented that I could "buy one at Lowe's for 40 bucks." I don't have to tell you the tongue lashing I gave out that day.

Pressure-treated pine is made by treating the wood with creosote, a coal-tar derivative used primarily in railroad ties and pilings; pentachlorophenol, an oil-borne preservative used frequently for utility poles, and chromated copper arsenate under high pressure.

I don't know about you, but those substances don't sound like something I want to be setting my behind upon. Heck, I can't even pronounce "pentachlorophenol" and the word "arsenate" means "arsenic" which, again, I don't think I want to be exposing to my posterior.

Redwood on a good south Louisiana porch is somehow just not appropriate, at least to me. Might as well make the porch swing out of adobe or mesquite.

So down here, at least for me, a good porch swing must be of cypress. Nice aromatic red cedar might be okay. But there's more requirements for a good porch swing than its material.

A good porch swing must have exactly the right angle at the backrest. Too much, and you feel like you're sinking into the crevice between the back and seat, and your knees are higher than your chin. Too little, and you're about to fly out of it on the forward stroke. Hanging a good porch swing is therefore a delicate feat of balance and geometry that is crucial to its enjoyment. It should not, however, require a slide rule.

When a good porch swing is in motion, it must be in a linear path. It must not, in other words, sway from side to side: It should swing to and fro straight as an arrow. Likewise, it should not creak and groan as if it's about to collapse into a pile of toothpicks with you on top of it.

There should be no jerkiness in the motion of a good porch swing. You should be able to place a canned drink or glass on the arm without it falling off while at a slow swing. There's nothing worse than a porch swing which jerks and jangles, causing your drink to fall off the arm while you're waving at the neighbors across the yard. All this does is verify to your neighbors that, "He's a nice enough fellow, but he has bad taste in porch swings."

While a four-foot porch swing has its place on smaller porches, the ideal porch swing is six feet long or more. That way, you can also stretch out on it for a nap with a pillow tucked under your head. A porch swing should never exceed 12 feet, however, because at that length, it is no longer a porch swing, it has become an amusement park ride, and your neighbors will probably file a complaint with the local zoning authority for operating a carnival in a residential area.

The good porch swing should hang level, too. A porch swing that is hanging just a half a degree off level looks like it's had too much gin. There's no excuse for hanging a porch swing unlevel, except that if your porch is itself unlevel, you may have to adjust the swing accordingly to create the illusion that both are on the same plane.

When you command a good porch swing to begin motion, it must do so without complaint. It should not require more effort to start a good porch swing moving than it does to pop the shoe off one foot with the toe of the other. Undue effort in putting a porch swing into motion is wasted effort that could better be used for swatting at mosquitoes or something.

Once in motion, a good porch swing should continue to swing with only an occasional push to keep up the momentum. If you find yourself having to push again far too often to keep the swing swinging, the porch swing is either out of balance or unlevel, or perhaps you need to skip dessert more regularly.

Stopping a good porch swing should require only a slight braking touch of the foot, slowing it quickly to a full stop. If you find yourself skidding along the porch floor trying to stop your swing from swinging, you have unknowingly installed a stubborn porch swing. Stubborn porch swings are those which exhibit their own patterns of behavior which are contrary to what the owner expects of them. There is, I believe, no rehabilitation for stubborn porch swings, and they are generally dismantled and the wood used to construct chicken coops or rabbit cages.

Now, let me clarify right here and now that if you don't have a porch swing as described, don't be dismayed or angry with me. Life is a never-ending quest. Like Hindu belief in reincarnation, sometimes people have to go through a number of pressure-treated pine porch swings, or redwood porch swings, to achieve the level of karma it takes to have a Zen-like cypress, unpainted porch swing with good manners.

Perhaps this explains why, as of this writing, I have neither a good porch nor a good porch swing. Apparently, I have not been good enough in my previous lives to earn one. Which, in the end, means I probably don't know what I'm talking about when it comes to porch swings, being an immature karma Zen-like entity and all.

It's okay. I may just have to pay more dues in life. If you see me sitting outside on a pressure-treated pine porch swing wearing a haz-mat suit, just chock it down to the fact that reincarnation ain't all it's cracked up to be. I was probably a pine tree in my last life.

Hateful Critters

Fishing, as some of you who do it are well aware, is not all philosophical ponderings and musing about the majesty of nature or the quality of solitude.

Sure, we anglers who view fishing as more than a competitive thing—i.e., hook 'em like you're trying to tear their faces off, crank 'em in like a freight train and sling 'em in the boat—prefer to pontificate about communing with nature, the art, the science. But there are times when fishing gets so utterly ridiculous no such thoughts are forthcoming.

Take a recent trip I made to a fishing hole I frequent. It was about an hour before dark, and I knew that was the best time for my fly rod with popping bugs. I walked a good ways to the pond, and was pleased to find that the wind had gone still.

I wore my mud boots, my Cajun Nikes, because some places I like to stand in the water to avoid tangling my retrieved line in the brush along the bank. Here is the advantage the northern fly fishermen have over us down here: They get to stand in the water and the line just floats. In Louisiana, down south anyway, we have to get our line tangled in all kinds of stuff, because most of us are too cocky or macho to wear a stripping basket on our hip, a kind of bushel to collect retrieved line. We think it looks dorky, so we'd prefer to let our line tumble to the ground and instead of going 40 feet with the next cast, we go 10 feet because the line has snagged on a dandelion, and end up looking dorky anyway.

The brush has grown so high over the summer that, on my very first cast, I snagged a tall weed behind me and nearly jerked the rod out of my hand. So I had to wade out and go unsnag the Spook, finally making a cast that found water. My dad always told me when I was a kid, as he was paddling the boat over to retrieve my tackle from a tree, "You catch a lot more fish in the water, boy." My dad had a gift for understated expressionism.

I placed the fly near a patch of willows which I knew generally held a fish or two. The cast was short, but I popped it a little then tried again. I was aiming for a little alcove under the limbs, but the next cast was so perfect, so absolutely artistic, the kind of cast fly fishermen dream of, that it laid out arrow-straight but softly, the line first, the leader curling forward next, to softly lay itself halfway in the water while the tip found the only outstretched willow limb on the whole pond and wrapped itself around it four times.

No amount of tugging or praying would free it, so I had to break the leader, and lost my Spook. Then I had to walk back to the truck to get a new Spook, tie it on, and walk all the way back to my spot. Ten minutes wasted.

I tried another cast, and waded out again to unsnag from the same tall weed behind me. In the process of doing this, I leaned over too far, tilted my legs too much, and water rushed into my left Cajun Nike. Finally, I laid the fly just where I wanted it: Floating exactly below the limb where my first Spook was now forever lost.

Aggravated, I decided it was time for a smoke, so I tucked the rod under my left arm and stuck a cig in my mouth. While I was lighting it, of course, there was a tremendous splash which startled me so badly I dropped the lighter into the water and the cigarette out of my mouth.

I snatched back the rod while it was still under my arm, and of course, completely missed the fish, though the new Spook sailed through the air right at me.

Here's an amazing thing: It is a feat of skill, timing, balance, holding your mouth right, eating the right kinds of foods, good karma, Zen and meditation in Tibetan monasteries to cast just to the right spot, but a sailing Spook after a lousy hookset will inevitably find the 1/8-inch tip of your rod and smack it, resulting in a hopelessly tangled mess.

While attempting to sort out this disaster, I suddenly said, *"YOWWWW-SUH!!!"* and leaped completely out of the pond—a bit sideways, because my left boot is still full of water—onto the bank, jumping and hollering, until I finally retrieved and threw away the lit cigarette that had fallen into my shirt pocket, burning my fingers too, in the process. But that's okay. It reminded me to retrieve my lighter from the pond.

Any sane individual would have packed up, gone home, and watched Scare Tactics on television at this point, but not me. After the rod was untangled, I waded back out a bit, forgetting again to empty my left boot, and cast back to the exact same spot. I stood at ready, cork rod grip in right hand, line in left, ready to strike, a predator, an angler whose every muscle was poised to drive the Spook's hook into the jaw of that unsuspecting bass lingering beneath the willows.

Of course, the fish never struck. In fact, not a single fish struck for the next 45 minutes.

It was, actually, just before dark, when the light had faded so that I could not see well, that the little rascals started biting.

Because of this, I know fish are smarter than we give them credit for. I just know that a whole pond full of them got together and said, "Okay, right when the sun goes down, let's mess with the blind boy."

Fish are cruel, hateful critters.

All I could see was a kind of flash of dull light when they struck. The last two I could not see at all, and was fishing by ear. Fishing by ear is not an easy thing to do, because the splash you hope is a bass taking the fly might be a bass several yards away eating a minnow or a skeeter. Often you set the hook on nothing, and your fly sails to kiss your rod tip, like the one old aunt we all have that always smells like Listerine.

I did manage to land four fish in the last five minutes which I think were bass, but then, I was judging by feel. When I finally wasn't sure where the pond was anymore, and waded the wrong direction thinking I was headed to the bank and got water in my right boot, too, I figured it was time to go home. During the entire walk to the truck, I could hear the hateful critters splashing and frolicking behind me, saying, "Get some new specs, four eyes!" The notion of dynamite briefly entered my mind.

Back at the house, I squished along unloading my tackle into the house, and went back outside to take off my boots and pour out the water and my socks. I took a quick shower and settled in for the rest of the evening in my chair, already thinking about the next trip.

Vengeance, like sushi, is a dish best served cold.

I've never been much on looking ahead. You know, planning for the future, making a nest egg, all that stuff.

Other than a good whole life insurance policy, which I maintained just so mom and dad wouldn't have to foot the bill to bury me if something happened, especially after all those outboard motors he bought me, I've never thought much of putting aside for retirement. In fact, the notion of retirement seemed pretty impossible anyway.

But last year I had the opportunity to join the newspaper retirement program wherein we put aside a percentage of our checks into something called a Simple IRA which we can't get ahold of until we're 59½ years old without paying some serious penalties. The age 59½ is a rather depressing number, really. I figure, at the age the men in my family seem to pass on to the Happy Hunting Ground, or the Happy Fishing Spot as the case may be, that would leave me 10-15 years of time to enjoy the fruits of putting aside funds for 21 years. There's something irritating about that.

A bunch of folks and I were sitting around talking about retirement accounts at the waterin' hole one night, and I heard mention of things like, "Yes, with my retirement plan, I should be able to live off the interest and leave the rest to my kids."

Now, I don't want to sound like a pedigreed reprobate or anything, but I certainly don't plan to live off the interest, and my kids can set up their own retirement accounts. No way. Soon as it's legal, that whole chunk of change is going in my pocket. In fact, I may just carry it all around in cash, so I'll always be able to buy flies or bait at a moment's notice. I plan to do a lot of fishing, as you can see.

In fact, I've come to think of it not as "my retirement plan" but "my fishing money." Doesn't surprise you a bit, does it?

The advice given to me when investing is, "Don't look at it. Just check it every few years. Otherwise, you get discouraged."

Boy, ain't that the truth. I was never good at waiting for Christmas, either. I'd sneak under the tree and try to fold back the edges of the wrapping paper to see if I could just get a peek at what was inside. So after a month of having my paycheck drafted for my "fishing money" account, I peeked at the results.

Disappointing, to say the least. I had expected a threefold increase in the contribution, for certain. I was tempted to call the company and complain that, at this rate, I'd be fishing out of my hospital bed hooked up to life support, but was told that I had peeked too soon. Grudgingly, I quit peeking.

I asked our company representative, now eight months into the process, if I was ready to retire yet. He said I might be ready, but my fishing fund wasn't. I'm beginning to believe this entire idea is for the birds. It's only redeeming feature, as opposed to burying some money in mason jars in the back yard, is that I can't go dig it up when I decide I need a new fly rod.

To begin with, I'm distrustful of and find financial dealings and institutions highly annoying. For instance, when we get paid around here, our staff accountant is kind enough to take our checks to the bank for us after we sign them and fill out the deposit slips. I was recently informed by the bank that if we want cash back off our checks, they'll no longer allow the accountant to do that on her visit, we have to do it ourselves. Or, we have to write a check out to "cash" and let the accountant cash it.

That irritates the dogmeat out of me. Listen up, it's my money. I am allowing the bank to hold it for me, and if I want to send Charlie Manson to get me some cash when I want it, and all the paperwork's filled out, then by thunder, I expect the bank to give Chuck my dough. What's the deal here? It perturbs the living daylights out of me when they tell me what they're going to do with, how they're going to dispense, when they're going to handle, my money. I'm doing them a favor, I could do some other bank a favor. By the way, I have the same charming relationship with physicians. It's my body, I bow to their expertise and education, but in the end, I'll decide.

But back to my fishing fund. The plan was that at age 59½ at the very latest, I'd drop back to being a correspondent and send in regular columns every week, and spend most of my time fishing. I'm not eligible for Social Security until I'm like 65 or something, and if anybody around here thinks I'm going to be getting out of bed at 6 a.m. until I'm 65 for any other reason than to go fishing, they've got another think coming, I promise.

My fishing fund will work this way and in this exact order:

1) Pay for tackle/bait.
2) Pay for fuel and oil if I'm using the boat.
3) Pay for snacks/soft drinks to bring with me.
4) Pay for photographs of lunker bass.
5) Pay the bills, if there's anything left over.

By this time, I hope, the house will be done so there won't be any of those expenses. I'll have paid for my truck in something like 10 years from now, and I should be able to live off fish, so groceries will be minimal. Patches (yes, I have told her that she will still be here in 21 years, like it or not) will have to develop a taste for bluegill. I never plan to cut grass again after I retire. As Chuck Clark once said, "Three-fourths of the earth's surface is water, and one-fourth is land. It is quite clear that the good Lord intended us to spend triple the amount of time fishing as taking care of the lawn."

So I'm not watching my Simple IRA, but I am confident that while I'm not watching, it's leaping and bounding forward to create the fishing fund to end all fishing funds. At 59½, I'll have only five-and-a-half years until Social Security kicks in, too, and then I'll be able to start travelling and fishing with all that extra money. I just gotta make it the first five-and-a-half years. I am learning frugality even now.

You can picture me already, can't you? I shall be the epitome of "the gentleman angler." I'll wear a narrow-brim fedora that's full of dirty fingerprints, holes from hooking it on my back cast and snatching it off my head and into the water, and a few well-chewed flies on the band. I'll wear khakis and suspenders all the time, and the young whippersnapper fishermen will follow me all around because I know where all the best fishing spots are. I'll get invited to weddings or funerals and become "the official old grit who sits around at weddings and funerals telling stories about fishing." You know the one. Every wedding, funeral or any other family get-together has an Official Old Grit who sits in the corner and tells stories. My dad was the last in a long line of Official Old Grits, and I am proud to one day take up the honorable task.

"Yup," I'll say at the wedding reception of one of my great-great grandchildren. "When I was your age, boy, I caught a six-pound pass on two-pound leader on my fly rod. Had to fight him for six hours. You listening to me, boy?"

"Yes, sir," says the young angler, all rapt attention with my decades of fishing expertise.

"Well, go get me another beer and I'll tell you about the time I caught four goggle-eye on one hook all at the same time," I say, and the lad rushed off to the keg, all quivering with anticipation of this tale, while I'm making it up in my mind before he gets back.

My fishing fund is perhaps the wisest investment I've ever made, especially when you consider that previous investments I've ventured into included marriage, beer-making kits, wooden nickels and lawn mowers.

For instance, the infamous Rez car. This might be considered a "fishing car" by some folks, but on the reservation, the Rez car is a permanent fixture of all households.

Not long ago, someone who was riding along with me in the truck interrupted my usual flow of deep, philosophical observations spiced with the occasional witty interlude to ask, "Why do you drive with both feet?"

Well, first I was a bit nonplused to realize that my passenger was not appreciative that I was sharing the wisdom I had gleaned over decades of life and careful study of all manner of subjects, from the human condition to metaphysics to puppy potty training. But rather than launch into an irritated tirade, I replied, "When you've owned as many junk Rez cars that wouldn't idle as I have, you learn to drive with both feet."

It got me to thinking about Rez cars. I can't say I invented the term, and I'm not sure who did, but the first reference to it I ran into was from Ojibwe writer Jim Northrup: "It's 24 years old. It's been used a lot more than most. It's louder than a 747. It's multicolored and none of the tires are brothers. I'm the 7th or 8th owner. I know I'll be the last. What's wrong with it? Well, the other day the steering wheel fell off. The radio doesn't work but the heater does. I turn the key, it starts. I push the brake, it stops. What else is a car supposed to do?"

My first Rez car was a 1975 Mustang II. It looked like a Pinto with a Mad Dog 20/20 hangover. My dad bought it when I wrecked my mom's car coming back from the *Banner* one afternoon. He didn't fuss, much to my surprise, but he disappeared one Saturday morning and returned with two cars, a Malibu for

Mom and the Mustang for me, neither less than 10 years old. He threw me the keys and said, "Here, you gotta wreck something, go wreck that." And I proceeded to do so with wild abandon for the next several years.

What distinguishes a Rez car from the basic old jalopy that many of us po' folks have driven? They may look similar, but there are important differences. A Rez car, first and foremost, resides on the reservation. It usually has for company a former Rez car which is now sitting up on blocks in the yard under the promise of, "I'm going to fix that up one day." In the southwest, a Rez car usually smells like sage and sweetgrass. In our part of the world, it usually has a duck feather stuffed into the visor or hanging from the rearview mirror—assuming that both visor and rearview mirror are in fact still installed.

A Rez car does not idle at a stop sign, so you must keep one foot on the brake and another on the gas to keep it running. Thus I have learned to drive with two feet. That's also why I have never owned a standard shift. I don't have enough feet to go around.

Any Rez car underwent important and required upfront maintenance at purchase. You cannot simply buy a used car of unknown pedigree without putting it through a thorough upgrade, and this involved installing a stereo cassette deck and speakers of at least 100 watts per channel. After this installation, you took care of the minor things, like changing the oil, belts and filters, but the stereo had to come first. Cruising around the Sonic on Saturday night without a stereo blaring AC/DC was unthinkable, whether the oil in the car was the consistency of bearing grease or not.

My father's most famous Rez car was a Plymouth Duster. It was green, and about the ugliest thing ever to come out of Detroit. He changed the engine with a little help from my uncle in the garage after 275,000 miles on the little straight six, and it kept on going. Dad's Rez car always smelled like carbon black from so many years at the Columbian Chemicals plant. When he retired, the carbon black smell refused to go away.

My second Rez car was a 1971 Torino GT. It was bright yellow with black racing stripes and fast as all get-out. The previous owner had the unfortunate experience of being behind the wheel at the time the drive shaft decided to drop out into the street. It seemed like the perfect Rez car to me, so I bought it for $250 when it came up for sale. The trunk lid and hood were more rust than metal at that point, and the quarter panels always rattled with mysterious sounds. One morning I went out to leave for work and found that the driver's side front quarter panel had finally rusted through and a half-inch drive ratchet with a nine-sixteenths socket had fallen out of it. That explained the rattle.

Later, I purchased my grandmother's 1976 Caprice Classic. This car was the size of a Bradley fighting vehicle, but in far too good a shape to be a genuine Rez car. A few years of ownership by me corrected that. The Caprice was about six feet wide, but the dashboard instrument panel was eight feet wide and would clip mailboxes as I passed down the street. I kept a picture of my senior year girlfriend on the dashboard, right next to the speedometer, which incidentally, pegged out at 140 mph. Incidentally, my senior year girlfriend was a real babe, so I was always speeding, and after enough tickets, I took her picture down and put it in my wallet.

I returned to true Rez car ownership with a 1978 Cougar. In Rez tradition, all this time the Mustang II was sitting on blocks under the promise of, "One day I'm going to fix that up," while possums made nests in the trunk and cats delivered litters behind the carburetor. None of these cars, with the exception of the Caprice, would idle without using both feet. The Cougar's left sideview window kept falling off, dangling by the remote control cable which didn't work, because the screw holes were stripped. I'd keep using larger screws, which would strip again, and the mirror would usually fall off while on a date with a new girl. This was not the least bit embarrassing to me, but usually, my dates never understood the philosophy and symbolism of a Rez car. Go figure.

The Cougar's interior driver's side door panel was attached by only two clips, and the armrest by one screw. If you slammed the door too hard, the entire door panel would end up in the passenger seat. The cruise control still worked, but the horn and headlights had their bad days and good days. Not that it mattered. As long as the cruise control worked, all was okay.

The final Rez car I remember owning was a Ford Ranger pickup that my dad gave me. It had replaced the Duster years before, and finally he decided he and Mom didn't need two vehicles, so he gave me the Ranger. The Ranger was four different colors, none of them intentional. The dominant color was gray primer, but it only occupied large spots of the surface, giving the truck a decidedly leprous look. But the little six cylinder in that truck was a pulling son of a gun, despite the fact that it used two quarts of oil a week and smoked like a mosquito truck. When I first moved into my house, I was clearing the land in the back, and using the truck to pull out old fencing through which numerous small one- or two-inch trees had grown. The truck would rip the fence right out, posts, trees with it. The only time it ever failed me at this was when the bumper came off.

You understand that all Rez cars owned by me served double duty as fishing cars, too. All were equipped with trailer hitches, even the Mustang. To own a vehicle without a trailer hitch was like not having tires, it was useless. At any give time, if you opened the trunk of any of my Rez cars (assuming you knew how to untangle the clothes hanger where the lock used to be) you'd find tackle boxes, nets, fishing rods and packs of bait that had been petrified by the heat. There was rarely a spare tire or jack, but there was always a set of jumper cables.

Of course, today I drive a pickup I bought new, so it is really not a Rez car, but I still drive with two feet. I figure, if I own it long enough, it will become a Rez car. I'm a strong believer in tradition, you know. Sometimes it just takes me a little while to get there.

Still, all that talk of retiring put me in mind of how distrustful I am of corporate financial conglomerations.

See, I still subscribe to the theory of burying it all in Mason jars. My grandfather used to tell me that when he was a little boy and they grew short on funds around the house, his great aunt would lock all the kids inside the house and leave. They'd watch her through the windows as she walked down to the bayou, disappeared in the trees for a long while, then returned with a few coins. And yes, I've worked the area over with a metal detector and found no coins to speak of, but learned that the family menfolk apparently didn't mind Jax or Falstaff in a can when they couldn't get bottles.

That's the way I was raised. I still have a *thing* about checking accounts and credit cards, though they are dang convenient. My dad never had a credit card his entire life, and if I had been smart, neither would I have had one my entire life. But that's another, dismal, story.

I take it back: They used to send dad credit cards regularly. You know, "special offer" things. He cut them up to make guitar picks. I kid you not. They make an excellent, medium-stiff pick. Come in lots of pretty colors, too.

So allowing someone to take X-percent out of my check each week, send it to the New York Stock Exchange where a bunch of strange people yell, scream, talk on cell phones and make gestures at each other which, in more genteel company, could be considered rude, is a leap of faith the caliber of which the Knights Templar would envy.

When I first considered getting into this whole bizarre thing, I told a representative that I wanted to invest in mutual funds.

"That's a good choice," I was told.

"I know," I said. "Besides, Jim needs the support."

"Jim?"

"Yeah, Jim. I just feel so sorry for the guy. Marlin just stands there in an air-conditioned studio while Jim has to go wrestle the crocodiles and chase down gazelles on foot."

"Marlin?" he asked, puzzled.

I was starting to feel like I had made a terrible mistake. "Marlin Perkins and Jim Fowler?"

"Eh?"

"We're not talking *Mutual of Omaha's Wild Kingdom* when we're talking mutual funds, are we?"

"Er, no."

"Oh. Well, how's cod liver oil futures?"

That was the end of my first timid steps into the world of putting aside for a fishing fund, until I joined the retirement plan here. I guess I was kinda gun shy after that. Like a bass who's bit too many popping bugs, I shied away from anything that even remotely smelled like it might make me some money. Perpetual poverty seemed far preferable. Who was I to dare think I could put aside a little nest egg to fish with in the future, when poor Jim is out there risking getting his leg bitten off by a rhino? I don't think I could live with myself if anything happened to poor Jim on my account.

I am also a little insulted that I was invited to join a retirement plan known as a "Simple IRA." What's up with that? Are they trying to say I'm too stupid to invest in anything else? Or that I'm too cheap for a Complex IRA? Lemme tell you something, friends and neighbors, there ain't nothing stupid or cheap about me, by thunder. Simple IRA, my eye.

But one way or the other, I'm gonna be outta this bizarre habit of getting up every weekday morning, going to work, coming home, starting all over again. It makes no sense. When the Indians ran things around here, there were no taxes, no debts, plenty of buffalo, medical care was free, women were pretty much in charge though men liked to pretend it was them (that much may not have changed) and we fished, hunted and made boats all the time. The colonists actually thought they could improve on our system by bringing in the New York Stock Exchange. Go figure.

See, it all started with gold, this idea of a retirement account. Really. The early explorers in the Americas were mostly after gold. In some cases, they told the Indians that they suffered from a horrible, painful illness which only gold dust could relieve them of. Now, the Indians soon figured out this was a load of buffalo hockey, and started letting each other know about it before the Europeans got there, so that when the explorers arrived and started asking about gold, the

Indians would just smile, point west, and say, "Little farther." At which time the explorers would go about their merry way, blissfully seeking gold until they hit the Pacific Ocean, and then went, "Hey, wait a minute! Do you think those Injuns back in Tennessee were kidding us?"

Though I understand that horrible, painful illness, of which mine can only be relieved by a bamboo fly rod, it was this lust for gold which led to the idea of retirement plans and mutual funds that had nothing to do with Jim Fowler and Marlin Perkins but eventually led to Martha Stewart's downfall, so it can't be all bad.

The California Gold Rush was a Simple IRA of the time. Folks who were wondering how the heck they'd be able to quit their jobs one day rushed to California to set up a retirement account in the form of bags of gold which they would then invest unwisely in whiskey, brothels and gambling. Kinda like a 19th century Enron, if you think about it. During all this, the Indians were looking down from a tall hill and thinking, "Geez, that must *really* hurt!" then promptly went off and built a canoe to go fishing.

All of which leads to now, in which a little half-breed Indian from Charenton joins a Simple IRA to create a fishing fund for when he retires, probably too old and arthritic to hold a fly rod anymore, which doesn't matter, because his vision will also be so bad he couldn't see a pond if he fell in it. Whereas, in the old days, he'd have been fishing all his life, without any need for funds, and a Simple IRA was a bunch of grizzled Irish prospectors shooting each other over their claims in California. There is an unsubstantiated rumor that the California tribes actually started the gold rush, in the hopes that the prospectors would shoot enough of each other and they'd all go home and leave the Indians alone. Instead, they got Disney and Universal Studios, and Hollywood to make movies about how noble and brave they were. All they really wanted to do was go fishing.

Pardon me. I have to go call my financial planner. I'm wondering about those cod liver oil futures again.

August

August. Waves of heat pass across the concrete spines which bind a nation together, shimmering like wraiths. America, which Kuralt realized is really a land of rivers, is but a mirage somewhere past the event horizon.

In August, the air thickens and is hard to breathe, the heat pounds upon our brows like iron hammers, drawing salty sweat instead of blood. There are mosquitoes humming in the ears, and flies tapping at the window glass. At night,

August is slightly relieved by the absence of the sun. But the darkness is heavy with radiant heat. It sinks low and puddles in fence corners, along fanning tree roots and between the edges of perception.

By this time of year, the garden my grandfather planted was but a struggling, barely surviving chaos of spindly, nearly leafless tomato plants and dry corn stalks. The cucumbers had long given up the ghost, and the peppers had surpassed thriving in the summer to fall victim to the heat as well. Weeds choked everything, unmolested, until the tines of the tiller returned in the fall to ready the soil for cabbage and squash and radish.

We found a nest of yellow jackets in the ground in the front yard by a patch of hackberry trees one August. They had stung my grandfather as he passed by. I watched with dreadful fascination as he carefully laid the end of a garden hose at the entrance of their nest in the ground. Then, inserting a funnel into the other end of the hose, he poured a gallon of gasoline into the hose and down into the nest. The hackberries, true to their indestructible nature, were the only things that survived. When I was told it was safe to be near it again, I studied the dried-up hole marking the entrance of the nest, but there was no movement. I could imagine their poisoned husks down there below the ground. Years later, as an adult, I would prescribe a similar remedy to a nest of yellow jackets that burrowed near the palms in the front yard, attacking me several times when I mowed. I used water and dishwashing detergent, though, a slightly more environmentally friendly solution.

A mother cat wandered into Dad's workshop one August and had a litter of kittens, which I preened over despite her warnings to keep my distance. I eventually garnered her trust with canned tunafish, and the scrambling, mewling kittens were allowed to my hand under her watchful eye. She was big and black, with bright yellow eyes and a shiny coat. The kittens were multi-colored, like fall leaves to come in just a few months. I would sit cross-legged with them, and they would scurry across my lap, topple from my legs with infant imbalance, mewling and fussing for attention with shiny, intelligent eyes. Eventually, the mother left the kittens when they were old enough, and we farmed them out to neighbors and family.

August slows the spin of the planet, as if drawing the strength from the earth as surely as its inhabitants. Nothing moves very quickly in August, save the speeding ski boats and roaring highway denizens. It is almost as if time winds down, and in Augusts past, the nearness of the end of summer vacation loomed like a threatening storm. Children in August are red-faced and moist, huffing to a stop just long enough for a cool drink then leaping into August again. Old dogs stare at them from under wooden porches, reluctant to answer their invitations to play fetch. Even the wings of hummingbirds become more visible, pushing the heat-laden air of August beneath them, burdened by summer.

Sometimes in August I would find old maps in my father's workshop. Maps of the basin, maps of the state, maps of the world. Some children are fascinated by maps, and in August I would sit beneath a broad shade tree and with my forefingers trace the routes of highways, roads, trails and most lovingly of all, rivers. I could conjure speculative visions of what each bend in the river or road would reveal, towns with names I could not pronounce, cities which took up large globs of ink on the printed sheets, lakes which seemed to be etched by glacial geology. With an old set of the World Book of Knowledge added, I could follow the roads and rivers and put my thumb on the Alamo while reading about the valiant battle fought there; I could guide my forefinger to Yellowstone or Yosemite, view photos of Half Dome and El Capitan. Maps led me across oceans in August, to Stonehenge and Venice, to the frozen north and the Marquesas. I traced the voyage of the *Nautilus* according to Jules Verne, and found the birthplace of Tolkien.

My mother's hydrangea were resplendent with blue composite flowers, lining the front of the old house and hiding the pillars. If there were rain, each little flower in the blossom would hold a drop of rainwater, like a small reality slowly dissipating under the returning sun. The yellow irises would be full of sparking droplets inside and out, bowing their heads under the weight of the moisture, slowly raising them to the sky again as they dried. Along the bayou behind the house, August brought low water and briars which tore at pants leg and tender skin. Poison oak leaped from the parched ground to wind snakelike up the trees, but I had learned early on to readily identify and avoid it. Here and there patches of bloodweed grew tall and lush, thriving in the heat, and I was always reminded by my grandmother that crushed bloodweed applied to a rattlesnake bite will keep you alive long enough to get medical attention.

If we were brave enough to stand the heat in August, my father and I would take the boat down Cotton Canal, where the water moccasin snakes hung from the trees like horrid Medusas. He was careful to avoid and not irritate them, but now and then one would come after the fish we had in the boat. He usually dispatched them with a paddle or a .22 pistol. There are cottonwood trees, or at least there were, in Cotton Canal, and I was never sure if it was named for the cottonmouth snakes or the trees.

If the entire year were like August, a day would be a week, a week a month, months stretch into years with the heat-slowed plod of time. Sometimes, in

August, it seems that time is a whirling top losing its inertia, spinning down to a wobble, but still maintaining a delicate balance on its tip to lurch forward into autumn.

The Way of Things

There is a way of things in the world.

I am not at all sure if it is universal. "If the doors of perception were cleansed everything would appear to man as it is: Infinite," William Blake wrote.

The doors of perception. Do they open and close with the accumulation of years, experiences, biases, practicalities? These are the questions to which answers can only be found within the same doors. It's a paradox. A puzzle inside of a quandary.

The world through which my road snakes and my waters course is bifold. It is existence creased and folded into halves. There is that part of me that passes through a reality as solid and cold as a table top, and another which expands into hypercubes, reaching.

As a youngster, when I would motor the boat into that area of Lake Fausse Pointe known as Peach Coulee, my perception was that of an oppressive...something. My best friend, the brother of my soul if not my blood, and I both noted that while trees swayed slightly there was no breeze; tides moved in that canal when they were still elsewhere on the lake, and silence was so absolute it was tangible, nearly solid. Now and then we would hear a mysterious sound: A whistling, far in the woods, accompanied by a sort of *Whup! Whup! Whup!* As if someone were bashing a hollow limb against the trunk of a tree. Then, as abruptly as it began, it lapsed into silence.

Peach Coulee, even on the brightest of days, always seemed dark. As if shrouded in perpetual near-twilight. Viewed through a thin veil. My grandfather hunted Lafitte's treasure there, never found it, though he claimed to have come close several times. Metal detectors refused to function along the canal bank, the east side of which is an Indian mound. A close friend of mine's father claimed to have been chased out of Peach Coulee by...something. Something hazy, unfocused and indistinct, nearly a dozen feet tall, crashing through the brush, snapping trees, and making a whistling, hollow-thumping sound. My friends and I regularly witnessed lights, four or five of them, dancing over the coulee at night. They are, my father's people said, the spirits of a family who ate a white deer, and where transformed for the transgression.

On one fishing expedition down the coulee, the brother of the soul and I were suddenly surrounded by a flock of tiny yellow finches with black feathered masks. They swirled around us like a whirlwind of dandelion petals, a perfect circle in flight, as if lifting away another fragment of a world no longer believed in. Then as one, they darted off above the trees, heading west. I have never seen another yellow finch on the lake since that day. It as if they took their leave of it, and of me. I miss them sorely.

I returned there this spring after many years, and found that the door had swung on its hinges somehow, nearly shut, perhaps firmly closed. Peach Coulee was bright and cheery with singing birds. Wind touched at the willow and cypress and they swayed. I offered tobacco anyway, sprinkling it on the raised east bank. Did a door swing shut? Or did the accumulation of practicalities, responsibilities, living in ponderous linear time change my perception?

If everyone stops believing in something, does it cease to exist?

Just a few weeks later, I was fishing along a different shallow, narrow canal on the lake. It was an overcast, gray day, but the fish were biting and I followed them down that black-water slew. While unhooking one pretty little chinquapin, I nearly dropped him into the bottom of the boat when it began: A whistling, *whup whup whup* sound, very nearby. I heard crashing and snapping, and no, I never saw what was in that woods making the sound. I was too terrified to retreat, too fascinated to flee. But then it abruptly stopped, and I denied myself the use of the electric trolling motor, and with my father's handmade cypress paddle I coerced his old wooden boat out of the canal as quietly as I could.

Doors. They open and they close. I know what it is I heard that day. What they used to hear on Peach Coulee. What chased my friend's father away. *Neka sama.* It reached out from fire and snatched children into the flames if they ventured too close. It crashed through the swamp, whistling and pounding resonance. I do not speak its name while on that ancestral lake, for to do so would invoke it, and I am not sure of the measure of its desperate struggle to survive against disbelief.

Doors of perception. They open and shut, they creak and slide. Their locks have keys, but they are tucked above the frame, lodged in the crack between the walls of practicality.

Linear time can hold no doors, save those which open one way. My father's people lived in circular time, and therefore all things came back about to where they were. Imagine time, then, as a circle, no beginning, no end. Europeans lived in the necessity of linear time, a straight line beginning with the Creation, segmented by the Crucifixion, and ending at the Apocalypse. In linear time, doors only open one way, and there is no returning through them. It *must* be linear to have a beginning, a middle, and an end. In Indian perspective, there was no beginning, middle or end. Crawfish created the world, and is still doing so today. All things perpetual. All things ever-renewing. Perceptions shape need, and need shapes reality.

Neka sama cannot survive in linear time, I think. Peach Coulee cannot persist in linear time. It only moves forward, and in that perpetual velocity, when something is forgotten, it ceases to exist.

Born of two worlds, with polar perceptions, I sway precariously sometimes between linear and circular existence. When I am moving straight as an arrow through the cosmos, Peach Coulee is a singing, wind-swept place of light. When I am swirling the circle of aeons, *Neka sama* crashes through the swamp like a juggernaut dream, like a hulking, gargantuan prophecy.

This is the way of things. This is the perception the divisions of my blood have conjured. These are the doors which open and close without my consent.

It is not just dubious entities in the swamp or mysterious places. The doors of my perceptions also open on *kich*, that little mottled-brown bird which visits sometimes and speaks to me, though I do not understand its words. It is also a small patch of woman's potato I found on the lakeshore in a shallow, sandy bottom. It is searching for medicines in the fields, though I never see them.

What I dread is that something is passing, and I have no power to stop it. I am *so* proud of the success, the stature, my people have secured for themselves over the last decade. I am honored and humbled by our perseverence, our survival, our giant footsteps forward.

Yet, I fear that something is passing, something is lifted by the wind and spirited away each fall. Here at my desk, surrounded by buzzing computers, ringing telephones and the flourescent bulbs which make my head ache, perception becomes cloudy, sluggish and half-sleeping, like a rusty lock on a door stuck in its frame. It's easy, if I allow it, to disbelieve. In the chaotic fray of this unbidden linear existence, black-masked yellow finches carry away another tiny splinter of a peripheral world.

Much as I want to cling to them, perhaps it is better for let them be whisked away. The belief of one man cannot be enough. It cannot sustain them. I cannot sustain them, because I must travel through too much of this demanding, confining linear time to earn those brief forays into the circle. I am made captive by absorption.

Yet I can hope that the obverse of belief may be true: It may not matter if you believe in something or not, so long as something believes in you.

I don't apologize for my perceptions. They are the way of things, at least for me.

Now, I don't even remember what I was looking for that day in the old boat shed where, for 41 years, my father kept the 12-foot wooden bateau he built for us to go fishing in.

But as I was rummaging around the assorted, to be truthful, junk in there, my eye caught a glimpse of dark maroon and chrome. I pulled it out from under a decade of dust and there, the two sections carefully tied with nylon string, was dad's old fly rod.

Standing in the semi-darkness of the boat shed, holding that old rod brought a wave of memories and emotions.

This is what it all means to me, I thought to myself. This is why. The "why" of all things that are me.

I took the rod home and put it away for a few months. I researched. The cork grip was badly deteriorated the eyes rusty and the varnish barely clung to the fiberglass. I researched, and when I felt ready, I ordered a new grip and guides.

One weekend, I dedicated myself to spending my spare time exclusively with that rod. Exclusively with my father.

—

The little boat, a year older than me, never misbehaved. It drifted bow forward, or it remained at calm balance, whatever he required of it. With a paddle in one hand, he could with little effort move the little boat where he wanted while continuing to cast the fly rod or spinning tackle. The little boat was as careful and graceful a craft as I have ever known.

I watched in awe as he laid out 40 feet of line and, at the end of the monofilament leader, a yellow and black popping bug softly touched the water. No sooner had it found the water than it erupted and the line went taut, the rod bent, and dad negotiated a palm-sized chinquapin into the boat.

Did I know I was watching an artist? No, not at five or six years old. My own casting was awkward and only by accident did I hook many fish. He was patient. He was, honestly, more patient in that boat than any other time in his life, and one would think the opposite would be true. But in the boat, bringing in the bluegill, he was at his happiest, and perhaps that invokes patience.

—

With a razor knife, I carefully cut the varnished thread that held on the guides, including one he had re-wrapped himself. After they were removed, I cut off the old grip with the knife and, using a rag soaked with lacquer thinner, stripped the rod of its old varnish easily.

Using an idea someone had suggested to me, I set up my variable speed drill in a jig and chucked the end of the butt section of the rod into it. I used a piece of wood with felt on it to support the other end, and by setting the drill to slowly rotate the rod, I sanded it smooth with 220 grit paper.

The grip came with a quarter-inch bore, so I used rattail files to ream it. As I worked my way close to the proper size, I began test-fitting it, continued to ream, until the new grip fit properly with just a little persuading. Then it was time to install the guide eyes.

—

The rod had no name. I would imagine he bought it at Scelfo's Sporting Goods, but I can't be sure. He had a Martin Automatic reel on it, the kind you wind up and when you pull the lever the reel would automatically retrieve the line.

Perhaps I was about 10. It was spring, and we were on Lake Fausse Pointe, of that I'm certain. The musky, watermelon-like smell of bedding bream was heavy. Dad flipped a worm and hook in a sort of circle made by a growth of cypress knees, and the bull bluegill snatched it away like a maniac.

We took a few out this way, then dad suggested we try the fly rods. He had just given me my first one that year, a new graphite model. While he made perfect casts which caught fish on nearly every occasion, my casts were sloppy and haphazard, reaching the little circle of cypress knees where the bream were nesting only once out of every three attempts. But now and then, we'd both have fish on at the same time, our automatic reels screaming, rods bent over like willow branches, and we'd pull slab perch out of the lake, laughing together. There was no better time to be alive, no better place to be. We worked that little spot with out fly rods for nearly an hour, and in the end, I had boated eight huge bream and dad had taken about 20. Life was good.

—

Wrapping the feet of the guides with thread was an effort in concentration, delicacy and meticulous, neck-aching, back-throbbing misery which took me several tries to get close to right. I found out the right way to do it, eventually, and had the butt section of the rod finished, with new chrome guides and gold thread. It looked, with the new grip and hook keeper, fantastic.

The tip section came next, and I was much better and wrapping by then. Only the smaller guide where the tip tapered so thin gave me much trouble. Finally, I set the tip onto the rod with epoxy.

The rod sections then went back to the drill jig I had made, and with an artist's brush I coated the thread wraps with epoxy one at a time. I let the jig rotate half an hour while the epoxy hardened, so that the constant turning and centrifugal force would keep the epoxy smooth and uniform. I sat nearby, watching, and in the spinning of the rod on the jig, the memory of a flywheel spinning came to mind.

—

The hood of the Mercury was off and lying in the bottom of the boat. The crank rope had broken. Dad took a piece of bow line and wrapped it around the flywheel of the engine and with a mighty tug, spun the flywheel fast enough that the points fired and the engine roared to life.

We were fishing Peach Coulee, and it was only midday when the crank rope broke as dad was about to drive us deeper into the canal in search of more respectable fish. We had caught a few choupique, fun fish to fight, disgusting to look at. Dad would hit them over the head with the butt of his paddle to stun them while he unhooked the fly. To paraphrase John Gierach, if you want a fish to play teach you how to waltz, ask a bass. If you want a fish to dig a ditch, ask a choupique.

Confident that with his improvised starter rope we would be safe getting home, we idled down Peach Coulee to where it splits off into the swamp. Way back there, farther than we ever went, he told me there was an old farm. The foundations were still there when he saw it in the 1940s, and he could discern the rise and fall of field rows in the ground, though large trees were growing among them. Whatever possessed a farmer to find a spot of high, dry ground out there in the swamp to eke out a living escapes me even to this day.

—

I thinned Helmsman spar varnish 50 percent with mineral spirits. Using a one-inch foam brush, I varnished the rod four times while it was slowly spinning on the jig, letting it dry four to six hours in between coats. A light sanding and another coat.

By Sunday night, the rod was done, propped up against a window, drying. It looks fantastic, but not so different as to not still be dad's rod. I was careful to get the same style grip, and the same style guides as original. The tip has a decided curve downward: A battle scar of who knows how many fish it has fought, won against, or lost. All shiny with new varnish, chrome guides and cork, it could have just come off the shelves at Scelfo's that day my father bought it.

In a week or so, when I'm sure the varnish has dried and hardened, I'll finish it out with a buffing wheel on my drill press and a little polishing compound. Then

I'll put a fly reel on it, about a six-weight I should think, and that old rod and I will take a trip to the lake, or to a pond. It doesn't matter which. Though the grip is new, when I hold it the rod resonates memories through my hand. When I dry-cast it in the yard, the whip of the tip flourishes with reminders.

Then, both of us renewed, that old fiberglass, no-name rod and I will chase bass or bluegill and if, as dad always said, I'm "holding my mouth right" I might even catch one or two. I won't fish it a lot, but a good rod deserves to be fished now and then. There is a way of things in the world.

Convergences

Legacies can become a part of our own pallet even if they are not necessarily our own.

Bear with me while I give you some background. Several months ago, I was corresponding by e-mail with a pal I had made on the Internet discussion forum for *WoodenBoat* magazine. We were chatting about bamboo fly rods, and Doug mentioned to me that he had a few old cane rods that had belonged to his grandfather. I expressed interest, and Doug kindly sent me down two of them to choose from after I cast them and inspected their condition. I would, we agreed, return the other and pay the postage.

When the package from Connecticut arrived, it was an aluminum cylinder, a capped tube designed for storing fly rods. I removed the cap and took out two antique rods in cloth bags.

One rod was unmarked, and though of fine craftsmanship, it had suffered some "sets" in the linear cane, resulting in a rod that was no longer straight but dipped and jutted at odd angles. The other rod immediately caught my attention by the etching on the reel seat identifying it as manufactured by the Goodwin Granger Co. of Denver, and by the signature on the bamboo just forward of the cork grip which read "Granger Victory."

I knew that Grangers were highly-sought rods, and the Victory was a legendary model of the Granger line. So I e-mailed Doug and explained to him that, even in the rod's current condition of terrible varnish meltdown, it was worth a little something which was a little more than I could afford. Doug replied by asking me if I intended to buy, sell and trade these rods or if I intended to fish them. Of course, I have no interest in collecting for the sake of collecting when it comes to bamboo fly rods, and I said as much.

"The rods are yours," he said, noting that he'd rather see his grandfather's rods used and enjoyed rather than grow dusty in some display. I gratefully agreed, and promised to send him some boiled crawfish up to Connecticut this fall.

Tons of research, reading and practicing on wooden dowels later, I felt brave enough to work on the rods. I took the unnamed rod first (which, according to some other kind folks I consulted on the 'Net, was probably a higher-grade Montague or Horrocks-Ibbotsson model, both of which were mid-grade companies) and scuffed up the varnish with 0000 steel wool. I straightened the cane under a heat gun and left it clamped in place to straighten. It came out of the clamps as close to straight as I could hope to get it. One line guide needed to be rewrapped, which I did, and then I applied three coats of spar varnish to the entire rod using a variable-speed drill on a jig I concocted.

Satisfied that the first rod came out pretty good, I got to work on the Victory. Luckily, it required no repairs per se, but I stripped the varnish from it with lacquer thinner, preserving the signature line on the cane, and applied five coats of spar varnish on my jig. A little polishing of the nickel silver metal parts, and both rods came out looking like a million bucks.

The second rod casts an eight-weight fly line decently, but it is clearly a notch or two down from the Victory, which casts a five- or six-weight fly line so dreamily it brings tears to the eye. I e-mailed photos of the finished rods to Doug and asked to know a little more about his grandfather, that I might think of him when I take his rods out to fish here in south Louisiana, far from the trout streams and lakes they knew in the north.

John Louis Blake was born in 1902 in Richmond, Va. He was raised by an aunt and uncle due to the tragic death of his mother and some unknown problem regarding his father. The aunt and uncle either ran or owned a sawmill on the James River. Doug said because John Louis Blake was "an orphan" he was expected to work as the hired help was expected to work, but he wasn't paid for it, like the family. He spent any spare time he had in a little camp that he and his brothers and some pals built on the James River.

Later in his life, he came across an ad in the University of Virginia newspaper for a typesetter, reporter and editor. Though he wasn't a student at the university, he applied for and got the job.

After a rather risqué issue of the student paper got the attention of the faculty, John was threatened with expulsion from the university, the one he wasn't even attending. To avoid further embarrassment and confusion the school found him a job at a local newspaper with an arrangement to "keep quiet" about the college paper incident.

John Louis Blake worked for dozens of newspapers and companies for many years. He was friends with E.W. Scripps and William Randolph Hearst, telling Doug great stories about both of those legendary media giants. He eventually became a major officer in the Scripps-Howard corporation, and then president of the Great Northern Paper Co., with an office on top of the Pan Am building in New York.

He retired in about 1968. His grandson recalls him having a fierce, cranky temper typical of a dyed-in-the-wool old newsman, but also a great and dry sense of humor. When in the mood, he could be downright goofy and silly, Doug fondly recalled. His wife was the powerhouse in the family, though, and tended to keep John straight when he got too grumpy with the grandkids.

Mr. Blake was also a talented painter, astronomer, machinist, sailor, fisherman, bird hunter and bonsai gardener. He designed and printed his own Christmas cards every year until the last few of his life, on his own small printing press in his basement. Doug said everyone knew what the Christmas cards would look like by Thanksgiving because of the inky impressions on Granddad's hands and clothes.

John Louis Blake died in 1988.

Some people stroll through flea markets and antique stores and bring home items which knew the touch of other hands, the whisk of other fingers against them, the spirit and souls which still resonate somewhere deep inside. Sometimes, when we are alone and the movement of the thin places allow those special convergences to occur, we may sense them, those voices, those whispers, those touches.

I will think of John Louis Blake each time I fit the ferrules of one of his rods together and sight down the guides to check the alignment. I will, I hope, honor him somehow when I attach a Pflueger reel to the seat, thread the leader and fly line through the guides and tie on a good bass fly.

Perhaps John Louis Blake landed a great many trout or steelhead or salmon on those rods, as well as some smallmouth bass and bluegill. Within the cork grip, perhaps I'll sense that old Granger resonate again with the flick of a weight-forward line shooting through the guides, or the tremble of a respectable fish taking a bow into the tip many years ago. Here is the fly rod of a man I would liked to have known, a man his grandson chose as a role model, a man who rose from orphaned poverty to become a major corporate figure, but still knew the wonder of a good bamboo fly rod and a feisty fish on the end of a leader. That he was a writer and newspaper man makes the legacy of those fly rods even more special to me. This is the way of things, at least for me.

So you see, it isn't about the fishing. It isn't even really so much about the fish. It's about the reaching, the thin places where the convergences happen. It's the narrow taper of a bamboo fly rod again glowing amber in the sun and conjuring line like a sorcerer's wand, rather than sitting dusty in a closet collection.

And though I may or may not be half the fisherman John Louis Blake was, may or may not catch half as many fish as he did, my hope is that some part of him will fish with me and his old bamboo fly rod. And I would hope as well that these words would give an old newspaper man some satisfaction.

> *All things on earth point home in old October: sailors to sea, travelers to walls and fences, hunters to field and hollow and the long voice of the hounds, the lover to the love he has forsaken.*—Thomas Wolfe

October

Across the splinter of land outside my window, leaves scatter like frightened covey of quail, startled by October winds. There are pecan leaves, oak leaves, a few straggling magnolia leaves thick and dry and brittle like leathery flesh. Spider lilies have poked their red, showering heads out of the back lawn, resplendent but gaudy.

The carnival used to come in October. The rides and the duck shoots and the cotton candy, all would arrive in boxed, hinged wagons, which sprang up mysteriously overnight and filled the evenings with tinny calliope music and the scent of buttered popcorn. The ding-ding-ding of games of skill, the call of attendants for the Ferris wheel echoed across autumn. In the morning they would be gone, pulled up and off to the next town, leaving me to wonder if they perhaps never existed at all. I would kick along through the discarded tickets and soda cups and crumbling tent stake holes, wondering if carnivals were real or imagined.

There is, when the summer begins to fade and autumn peeks its brown head around the corner, the instinct to move. The call of October demands we move on, stock and store, make warmth, find sanctuary. Summer is the middle-aged wariness of still reckless youthful spirit; autumn is the hastening ache of passing years, the golden moments until winter, the ending of the circle.

Into October I was carried by the storm, to be born and spend all the Octobers to follow kicking my way through autumn. October birthdays are like the fall: relieved by the cooling days, rested by the lengthening nights, secure in the success of the harvest. Birthdays in October are reflective and considerate; birthdays in May, by comparison, are unworried and reckless.

Overhead, the winged migration has begun. I count songbirds and teal and geese as they arc silently above me. Along the bayouside one evening before dark, a giant owl swooped low and perched in a cypress not far away. He sat there, back to me but head twisted around over his wings to stare at me.

The dog and I survey October from the parcel of land we call home, once again ignoring the call to move on. She sniffs at the season, her fur bristles at the urge to travel, but she remains here with me, confined, rooted to this place. We walk the bayouside in search of summer with all its careless days and nights. There are small, red flowers peeking from the weeds, like bleeding hearts, a bouquet for the funeral of what we seek.

Is it the inability to move, the captivity of summer, which makes me think of endings? October is the time for thinking of it, for the circle is coming about to where it began, and in these final months of the calendar some things must die so that others may be born.

It is in fall that I best understand the doors which open and close around me. With the accumulation of years, experiences, biases and practicalities, I nearly missed them. But ancient wings guide me in autumn, and the world through which my road snakes and my waters course is bifold. It is existence folded into halves, one linear the other circular, and they are at polar extremes of each other.

I watch the dog as she canters around the bayou bank, and I wonder, where would she go in October if she were not shackled to me? Would she follow the birds overhead to some southern latitude where winter holds little sway, or would she move upland, to build herself a little den among the pines, surrounded by needles and brown grass for warmth, chasing mice and beetles for winter's substance? She sniffs warily at the base of a tree, looks up at me, bewildered, but knowing that I won't follow, she shuffles off toward a browning patch of elephant ears, condemned.

The bayou is thick and muddy, but catfish strike at shad near the surface, making ringlets in the wake of their rises. In October the final months of a fisherman's time are fading, and before long it may be time to put the rods and tackle up for the winter months to come, snuggled into the house with its artificial heat, awaiting spring like a prisoner.

Noticing the rising fish, the dog pounces to the weathered wharf, rushes to the water's edge to see. Debris, fragments of summer, float by and she cocks her head at them curiously. The bayou flows south, and we should be following it, she knows. I know it, too, but am helpless to comfort her. Disenchanted, the dog leaves the wharf and searches the ground for the scent of freedom.

Things clutter my mind as the dog and I walk through autumn, things which blind me to the full measure of October: Obligations and responsibilities, things financial and material, grand illusions which permeate an existence yearning for simplicity. I long for Octobers with carnivals and last-minute fishing trips in old wooden boats, of moving, of stocking and storing, of harmonizing with the season again.

I call the dog and we head back toward the house, but I don't put her into the fenced yard. I let her walk with me to the shop, and I find my keys. We get into the truck, the dog and I, and she spins excited circles on the passenger seat at this unexpected excursion.

There are no storms to chase this October, the sky is brisk and clear. Were there a thunderhead on the horizon, the dog and I might break the speed limit to catch it, hoping to glimpse my birthplace in the thunderhead. When the sky is black and thunderheads loom, I search the billows for Ustupu. Through a tragic series of vengeful deeds, Ustupu's six hunting dogs were turned into balls of flame and along with the boy catapulted into the skies. To this day, he calls the dogs back to him: *Apuck*! Come! He calls them by their names: *Kins-put! Tep-kani! Kuc! Kapainch! Neka! Kutep!* A Chitimacha can call Ustupu down from his eternal chase, but once earthbound again, Ustupu will not desist until he has killed every Indian alive on the earth, and he can only be sent back by a command in the Chitimacha language. No one knows the words which will send him back now. No one believes. When there are thunderheads in October, I watch the clouds for Ustupu and his dogs, but I dare not utter his name.

We ride for an hour or two, windows rolled down, and the dog is craning her neck out of the cab, sniffing at fall, ears flapping in chill wind. I investigate off roads and side lanes, peeking through treelines, across cane fields being skinned by combines. Summer is still there, in the groves of cypress, within the black water ponds and along the ditchbanks, but October is reaching outward with brittle fingers.

Finally we return home, and though we have actually gone nowhere but full-circle, the slight detour has somehow satisfied the calling of October. Mocha goes back to the fenced yard, nibbles at her food bowl a moment and sips at cool water, then curls up beneath the awning of the woodshed to sleep.

Inside the house, I kick off my shoes and lie down on the sofa, noting the silence brought by the dormancy of the air-conditioner. Patches prowls up to lie at my side and I scratch her ear. She rubs the side of her head against my arm adoringly. As cats sometimes do, she moves close to me, puts her face close to mine and studies me intently, as if she is trying to understand me, seeking some flicker of October in my eyes. Then, either satisfied with what she found or having found nothing at all, she curls up at my side and lowers her head on her front paws, blinking drowsily.

I sleep, and dream of brown-white panthers bristling with the first new locks of winter's coat, and owls, twisting their necks around to stare at me from tall trees in October, while storms churn and rains fall on distant horizons where the carnivals have gone, and the boy chases his six great dogs past the edge of the world.

October is the season for listening in the dark.

One night, when the cool air was sufficient to keep the mosquitoes at bay, I sat down on the front steps to watch the night and listen to autumn while awaiting a visitor for the evening.

The dog whines behind the fence, so I release her, and bounding in great, fall-frenzied circles, she cuts through the darkness of the front yard like a phantom hound. I let her run through October, careful that she doesn't venture too close to the road and its rushing, reeking automobiles, their headlights like daggers ripping gashes into the curtain of October. Sometimes, I think, we're too much like Dorothy and Toto. Sometimes, it's better not to see the wizard.

I sit there on the front step, and the old house looms up like a sentinel behind me, but I can feel the pecans turning drowsy, though the cedars and the magnolia nearby will remain awake through the coming winter. This is my month. In October, as Robert Blake wrote, the doors of perception are cleansed, and everything appears to me as it truly is: Infinite.

There is a way of things in the world. In October I am most cognizant of it. Mocha stops, sometimes, stares with ears perked at nothing, takes a tentative step forward toward empty air, then shakes whatever it is she saw or sensed off her spine and frolics near the hackberry. In the dim light of the half-moon, she seems half-complete: The white patches of her coat glow, but the liver colored portions blend into the night. It is as if she is half-real.

I walk down away from the porch and turn to look at the house. The windows glow amber from the incandescent light within, but above the peak of the gable, stars wink down at me. The house looms, large and solid, a constant in an ever-expanding universe. Even the stars alter their positions as the seasons unfold, but the old house remains steadfast, an anchor in a sea of change.

Nearby, there are two sago palms, planted by my great-grandmother, Delphine, to commemorate the death of her only daughter, Constance, nearly a century ago. Constance died of a fever before she was barely a teen. Even Delphine, a medicine woman, could not save her from European disease. The palms were once a dozen feet tall, but an October hurricane cut them back, and now they rise just above my head. At Easter, Delphine would cut fronds from them, and the family would make pilgrimage to Bayou Portage, to picnic upon the old mound there, blending the roots of their indigenous ancestry with the infusion of their Catholic beliefs. They remained true to both in a startling feat of duality.

Mocha sits at my feet, whining for an ear-rub, which I grant her. As soon as my hand is away, she bolts again, sniffing along the driveway in search of some stray that passed there weeks ago. Were it not for the streetlights, and the glow from the windows, and the illumination from the other homes nearby, the darkness would be absolute. The air is pleasant and cool, bringing the scents of dry leaves tumbling through October. I breathe it in, relishing the memory of leaping into piles of leaves as a child, hearing them crackle and snap under my weight, my father fussing me for disturbing his work. Leaping into piles of leaves in October is a joy no one should miss.

I sit back on the steps, and the dog canters to me, lays her head on my knee and beseeches me with her odd eyes: The right one is brown, but her left eye is brown at the top and blue at the bottom, segmented horizontally like the ocean from the land. I wonder which half of it she sees the peripheral of October best with. My own eyes are half-alive: The right requiring minor corrective lenses, the left nearly useless, capable of distinguishing only vague shapes and colors without detail. If my sight were "perfect" would I see October as I do now? The Creator, it is said, balances all things, giving more to what has been lessened.

But I comply with her wishes, and together we walk out behind the house, toward Bayou Teche, where the darkness is more complete. The dog tracks near me, unlike in the day, as if she is feeling protective, somehow aware that my vision is not as keen in the darkness as her own. One parcel of the yard we cross, I know, bears the remains of a many, many dogs who once walked with someone along the way to the water. They were all buried there over the generations, followed by pups which scampered carelessly through October to grow into their feet, live out their lives, and rest finally in that corner of the old property with its kin. My beloved Shadow lies there, and so does Chance, in the good company of the many faithful that preceded them. I listen in the October dark, and perhaps I hear them, but who can say? Sometimes people dart their eyes away from me when I speak of October and the things glimpsed within it. I am never sure if I have made them uncomfortable with what they have unwillingly seen themselves, or if they are fearful of the non-conformity that's been spoken. Seeing in October has no place in a world of imagined ladders, perpetual plodding and mythical deadlines.

We reach the ridge of the bayou, heightened when the Teche was dredged long, long ago. Mocha stands looking down, but I can only see a dim discoloration which I know is the water. Usually she would run there, to investigate the water's edge for things of interest, but tonight she lingers in the envelope of darkness with me. Crickets whistle loudly, chiming and calling each other across autumn. In the bright sky, studded with diamond stars and a half-moon, shadows whisk by, indistinct and quick. There are ancient wings alight in October.

Reluctantly, the dog and I trudge back to the house, and headlights turn into the drive. Mocha waits for my command, bristling with excitement, until I tell her, "Go on," and she rushes to my visitor, giving welcome in spiraling leaps of October joy. Visitors in October are like fruit preserves and pumpkin pie, treats to be relished and cherished.

Morning comes too soon. I make the routine happen again, for I am well practiced on the stage of this half-life. I plod through he mythical deadlines and leave the dog whining behind the fence as I motor down the drive. For the next eight hours, I am surrounded by concrete and sheetrock and steel. October is far away. Seeing is blinded by disbelief surrounding me like locusts. I sit behind this computer screen, a thief robbing me of my eyes, shake off the numbness in my right arm, try to keep the ringing phones, chattering and chaos of duality from driving me mad as I count the artificial minutes until I can flee again to October and wooden porch steps. Outside, not far from where I sit within the fray, Bayou Teche flows quietly, persistently, carrying with it comfort and sanctuary. I think of sago palms and dirt mounds, and mourn little girls dead of fever before they became young women.

Blindness is temporary. When the hands of the gold clock on the wall with its maddening, swinging pendulum release me, the dog and I will walk through October again, to see what we can see.

The Haul-Out

There are three lights in the carport; beyond the cascade of illumination at the open front, the darkness is only pinpricked by a few porch lamps and street lights. Cars pass by now and then, and off somewhere on the edge of the reservation a dog is wailing at the moon.

I stand and look out at the night for a moment, and the sky is clear and cool. Across the majesty of the cosmos expands incredible beauty and awe-inspiring complexity, making me feel insignificant and humble. A speck of celestial dust, this rare and wonderful old earth and those of us who live upon it too seldom look up to consider the great mystery of Creation.

But I turn away and start with fresh sandpaper on the transom of the old wooden bateau sitting on its trailer under the carport. Bow facing the night, it seems ready to lurch into the darkness, using some street lamp or bright star as a marker, a signpost. For weeks we have labored, this old boat and I. Her bottom was scarred and battered from too many drifting, wayward logs on the lake, too many encounters with the boundaries which lurk beneath the surface of *Sheti.* Upon turning her over and placing her on sawhorses, the boat's underside was a sturdy, unbreached barrier between its passengers and the water, but it had paid a cost for its vigilance. Together, under night skies and sunny days, we were both resurrected.

Now, with the boat's bottomside planking smooth and whole again, painted and clean, she sits right side up facing the night. Her sides are resplendent with fresh, new oil-based paint, hunter green with a black waterline, and the nicks and scrapes soothed along her gunwales. The transom has been stripped of paint and a soft spot discovered, the first I know of in the boat's long life. With careful and sparing application of epoxy, that minor bit of decay will vanish.

As the sandpaper scrapes along the old fir plywood, clearing away the last specks of paint, it occurs to me that these hands are two years younger than the boat beneath them. They are also at least partially the hands of its builder.

I have, at times, considered carefully wrapping the old boat in canvas tarps, sealed against the elements, protected from rodents and bugs. Something so important, so treasured, at times I am reluctant to use it for its intended purpose. I'll build one just like it, I tell myself, and keep this one from harm. It was in every way my cradle, the safe and happy den from which I was reared.

But as I see it now—gunwales flaring outward to the sweep of the upturned bow before curving slightly back inward to the head block—and touch the memory of it falling at my feet in specks of sawdust, I know it cannot be packaged and stored away. If there is a pivot and a crux to my existence, a fulcrum to lift all the hardships and joys of my life, it is this old wooden boat. A spot of rot, no larger than a half-dollar, is no less a mirror of my soul than the solid steadfastness, the sweeping grace and the cargo of memory than my own regrets and successes. As long as a spark of life and a wisp of breath persist within me, this old boat and I are bound to each other. I could no more put it aside than I could cut off my own hands.

What defines us is unique to the individual, I think. I am defined by this old bateau. Everything that I am, good and bad, is to be found in its lap-joint oak frames, laminated transom and wide sprayrail. Within a few moments in a small wooden boat my character and my soul were forged.

Next day, as October brings a crisp nip to the air, I rub down her varnish with a scuffing pad and carefully apply two new coats of spar. The brush flowing over the deck leaves tiny furrows of varnish, like the wake of the old boat across the lake, which settle and flow out to become glassy-smooth again. Within an hour, it has dried to a satin luster, the rich fir plywood glowing amber beneath. Inside, there are more nicks and scars to be tended to, but by the weekend, she should be back afloat, in her element, returning me to *Sheti* and ancestral promises. Each passing year when this old boat returns, with me in its folds, mark another season in two lives. For as long as there are home waters and old wooden boats, there are promises kept. We are home again.

Leaves spiral down around me, blown off tree limbs by October, scurry across the ground like dancing wraiths. I set free the dog and she lies with her head on her paws watching me replace the cap piece of the transom with a new piece of mahogany. A few pecan leaves flutter and come to rest inside the hull, trembling under the slight breeze sweeping over the gunwale. The varnish flows from the brush, around the gentle curve of the head block, though I am careful to avoid the stainless steel rubrail along the sides. There may be specks of dust in the finish, but this is October, and the boat and I will carry it with us until the next haul out, until the next remembering.

Many times has this old boat drifted into these words, many times has the thought of it swept into these ramblings. This old boat has carried me from the cradle, it will carry me to the grave, as faithfully as it always has. And when at last I look back on my life in the last fleeting moments of breath, it shall be condensed into a few moments in a small wooden boat, a microcosm, a digest of existence well-spent.

It is family member and friend; it is mentor and guide. Within its hull, out there on the waters of my ancestors, I am complete. What will happen to it when I am gone, I cannot guess and perhaps should not ponder. It is enough to know that it has carried me well, and that I have tended to its needs as best I could. There are many things in a life which mark the measure of a man. Few would consider the devotion to an old wooden bateau a significant yardstick. There are moments in this life when such disregard leaves me speechless and mournful.

The things which matter in my life are not disposable; the things that require the most care, the most fretting anxiousness, are the most treasured. She has carried me through thunderstorms and squalls, across a lake which stood up on its hind legs and threatened to devour me and the old father at the tiller; she is by no means frail or delicate, for she has been pitched airborne by impacts with logs and stumps at full throttle, but she requires care.

And as I stand now, slightly more than amidships in this life, I believe I understand that caring is the greatest gift of all those given me by a few moments in a small wooden boat.

When the door swings closed behind me, there is freedom in the air.

Though my head aches, my eyes throb and my right arm is numb, all from too many hours in front of a computer, I rush home, collect the dog and the boat, and escape into October.

My father's people lived in circular time, and therefore all things came back about to where they were. Imagine time, then, as a circle, no beginning, no end. Europeans lived in the necessity of linear time, a straight line beginning with the Creation and ending at the Apocalypse. In linear time, doors only open one way, and there is no returning through them. It *must* be linear to have a beginning, a middle, and an end. In Indian perspective, there was no beginning, middle or end. Crawfish created the world, and is still doing so today. All things perpetual. All things ever-renewing. Perceptions shape need, and need shapes reality.

The world through which my road snakes and my waters course is bifold. It is existence folded into halves, one linear the other circular, and they are at polar extremes of each other.

Springer spaniels are dogs of the fall. Bred in northern latitudes, they are not accustomed to summer's heat, but in the fall the dog is bounding with autumn energy. She twists circles in the boat as we make our way to the lake, and though she usually is at my feet during the ride, emboldened by the fall.

Riding the gentle, crystalline surface of *Sheti,* the waters of my blood, I recall when my best friend—the brother of my soul if not my blood—and I now and then would hear a mysterious, distant sound along the lakeshore: A whistling, far in the woods, accompanied by a sort of *Whup! Whup! Whup!* As if someone were bashing a limb against the trunk of a hollow tree. Then, as abruptly as it began, it lapsed into silence.

It was two decades ago. But the dog and I returned this October to that same canal along the lake, searching for an October gone by.

The water is copper; water-sodden cypress stumps, jagged and dangerous, poke their amputated trunks from the surface. I navigate the boat far clear, and the dog woofs at them, but then, she may only be speaking to October in the same way I am.

The canal is there, perpetual. As I throttle down and turn toward it, I remember: On one fishing expedition down the coulee, the brother of the soul and I were suddenly surrounded by a flock of tiny yellow finches with black feathered masks. They swirled around us like a whirlwind of dandelion petals, a perfect circle in flight, as if lifting away another fragment of a world no longer believed in. Then as one, they darted off above the trees, heading west. I have never seen another yellow finch on the lake since that day. It as if they took their leave of it, and of me. I miss them sorely.

The cypress needles have begun to brown and dry; down the canal, with the dog perched on the deck sniffing with flaring nostrils, I idle the old boat with something like reverence. This is where October is concentrated. Everywhere else is dilution, watered-down and thinned with the solvent of disbelief. But here, in this ancient canal, is the nucleus of October.

Stories swirl and permeate this old canal, like October finches. A close friend of mine's father claimed to have been chased out of here by something hazy, unfocused and indistinct, a dozen feet tall, crashing through the brush, snapping trees, and making a whistling, hollow-thumping sound. My high school chums and I regularly witnessed lights, four or five of them, dancing over the coulee at night. They are, my father's people said, the spirits of a family who killed and ate a white deer, and where transformed for the transgression. Fifteen years ago, on an overcast, gray day, the fish were biting and I pursued them down that blackwater slew. While unhooking one pretty little chinquapin, I nearly dropped him into the bottom of the boat when it began: A whistling, *whup whup whup* sound, very nearby. I heard crashing and snapping, and no, I never saw what was in that wood making the sound. I was too fixed by fascinated dread to flee. But then it abruptly stopped, and I denied myself the use of the electric trolling motor, and with my father's handmade cypress paddle I coerced his old wooden boat out of the canal as quietly as I could.

I know what it is I heard that day. What chased my friend's father away. *Neka sama*. It reached out from fire and snatched children into the flames if they ventured too close to the hearth. It crashed through the swamp, whistling and pounding resonance. I do not speak its name while on that ancestral lake, for to do so might invoke it, and I am not sure of the extent of its desperate struggle to survive against disbelief.

But when I kill the motor, after it coughs once and goes silent, there is nothing here but October, the essence of it, unviolated. We drift with the current down the canal, looking at the shell bank on the right, where *Sheti imasha* walked for millennia. October has cut down some of the underbrush, revealing trash, bottles, cans, burned out stumps and logs, old ice chests and fishing net floats, the refuse of July left unrotten for winter. October plays no favorites, pulls no punches: October shows us the faces we don't wish to admit are in the mirrors of our souls.

The dog whines discontent, jumps the front bench seat to sit near me, looking out at the canal. She hears the resonance. She feels the thickness and purity of October. I admire her. Her existence is neither circular nor linear. It merely is. For me, it is not just dubious entities in the swamp or mysterious places I sometimes glimpse. The doors of my perceptions also open on *kich*, that little mottled-brown bird which visits in the spring and speaks to me, though I do not understand its words. It is also a small patch of woman's potato I found on the lakeshore this summer growing from a shallow, sandy bottom. It is searching for medicines in the fields, though I never find them.

But in the drifting ease of the canal's flow, I fear that something is passing, something is lifted by the wind and spirited away each fall. It's easy, if I allow it, to disbelieve. Outside the chaotic fray of my unbidden linear existence, black-masked yellow finches carry away another tiny splinter of a peripheral world. Much as I want to cling to them, perhaps it is better to let them be whisked away. The belief of one man cannot be enough. I cannot sustain them, because I must travel through too much of that demanding, crippling linear time to earn these brief forays into the circle. I am made captive by absorption.

There are no sounds, no movement. The dog perks her ears at squirrels and an egret, but no flashes of yellow finches spark the air. October may be at its most intense here, but even at the heart of the world fires sometimes smolder. *Neka sama* is not here. Only the pastel memories of fading watercolors linger, smeared and mingled to obscurity by forgetfulness. Even October, I realize, can be made sterile from poison.

We leave with the engine humming destiny, that old wooden hull slicing effortlessly through vanishing legacy. The dog and I follow the canal backward, scanning the trees for old promises, searching in vain for secret gates in a forgotten garden.

November

November is fickle and undecided.

Brief breaths of cold flow southward, exhalations of Old Man Winter's distant presence, but largely November is comfortable and mild. A carpet of fallen leaves is turning the now slowly growing lawn brown, and skeletal trees stand sentinel watch across the yard.

There are Novembers past which come to mind when cool winds tug at my clothes and hair, urging me to follow them toward the equator. Last November it was already much colder, and in Novembers long ago, I bundled up in far more clothes than was necessary to march off to the tribal school while my ever-vigilant mom watched me cross the street, before Charenton Road became Chitimacha Trail, and in days when anybody who came up the road was known to us, and if they weren't, it probably meant trouble. Now and then, I'd be spending a November evening before dusk investigating bugs or playing with a cap gun, and The Walking Man would pass by on the road, heading west, gazing silently at me, but never slowing. I'd stop and watch him pass, all thin and ramshackle and towing an invisible burden, and it seemed like the trees and the house and the yard shrank away from him. His face, I would write decades later, reminded me of Little Big Horn, all full of bullet holes and horseshoe tracks. I remember those Novembers and the person I thought of as The Walking Man, but I never knew who he was, and one November he didn't pass, nor the next. I have not seen him in a dog's life of Novembers, but I believe I know his name now.

Here, in November, the year is an old man, robbed of its youth, fading from the circle, lost in some spiraling convergence of memories. November lives vicariously in June, July and August, drowsily recalling summer's youth. In a few weeks we will sit at the table and give thanks for a year of prosperity, toils, joys, sadness—we give thanks for resting quietly in November as the trees slumber and dream deep, slow dreams of long tendril roots shooting down into the aeons.

The storms of summer, and the threat of them, are behind now. So are the rains, and the ground cracks and heaves, brittle, summer-weary. In Novembers long slipped by, I huddled in the fore of the old boat as my father guided us to the fall lake water, where we'd recall spring and the fitful, splashing of cool weather emboldened bass and bream.

The days are shorter now, as if November is a time of night. For Thanksgiving dinner the five of us would converge on the dining table and give thanks, feast, lie around and make quiet conversation between naps. For supper we'd reunite once more, eating more carefully, still full from the noontime excess. Darkness would have come by then, and if there were time, we'd visit some of the kinfolks in town, and I remember sitting in the backseat of the old car, watching the headlights slice through November, narrow beams reaching out for a future which was just out of their range and unseeable. I'd crane my neck to see over the side of the car door, out the window, to look for November in the darkness. I'd watch the speeding edge of the headlights, hoping they'd catch up with some November hence that might show me where I would be, what I would be, and whether I would be happy there. Now and then, white flying things would flurry by, and I thought they were insects, moths, but I think now they were clairvoyances whose details were overwhelmed by the headlights of the car.

As we'd turn back into the drive at home, between the two big oaks, I remember how the headlights became twin scythes, cutting through the harvest of darkness, arcing around as the car made the turn, and the old green house that my father largely built burst into view under the glare. I'd be tired and cranky, too full of baked ham and lemon icebox pie, to do more than collapse into sleep. If it was still warm, I'd sleep with no covers under the ceiling fan; if the cold had come, I'd wake in the middle of the night to go warm myself by the big gas space heater in the living room, the house's only source of warmth. The heater and the ceiling fan and the house are gone now, ravaged by an August storm, but this November I ride through the nights, my gaze much higher than the door frame of the truck now, still looking toward the edge of the headlights and the undiscovered country they pursue. But now I am no longer seeking a promise. Now I am seeking only a covenant of continuation. A warrant that the peace I've found is perpetual.

The headlights flare and swipe, and there is the house of my grandparents, and great-grandparents, and many more kin, and November is around it like their ghosts. There is a skeletal frame of a wooden skiff on sawhorses under the garage, bow facing me, and the headlights of the truck leap through it, under, around and over it. I put the truck in park and watch the light dance around the house, around the skiff, across the browning grass and fallen leaves. At last I am seeing what I looked for riding home Thanksgiving nights in November so many, many years ago. The flurrying shapes of white precognition have come round at last. My future is November. My place is here.

The dog woofs at me from behind the fence, and I go pat her head and rub her ear, but I don't let her free. Instead, I retreat to the house, sit down in the comfort of my well-worn chair, listening to November make the house move and creak as the temperature changes. Some 160 Novembers have passed through, around, under and over this house and its former occupants, and I miss the ones I knew and those who died before I was born. November is a time for loneliness that is without regret. Loneliness can be relished, the ache of it somehow comforting, in November. The fly rods stand in their cases in the back room, tackle bags at their bases. They may be used again this fall, but the sweep of line through November is different: It is crisp and certain, it is lonely and solitary. Fishing in November is at no other time perfect with solitude.

My eyes are tired; the hour is late. I clean up, change, and lower myself into bed. The cat comes and sniffs my hands, my arms, smelling November all over me, before settling down to sleep. For a moment, just before I am completely asleep, the ceiling fan over my head is different, the room is littered with comic books and plastic model cars, the old space heater is glowing orange through the doorway, and the sentinel presence of the two people in the room down the hall is strong and clear. Half their absence tugs at my fading consciousness, and the other gives me counterbalanced peace.

And I drift off to sleep, to dream boyhood dreams of November, drives through the dark, walking men, and leaves falling and circling, toward the year's final hours.

Fall is a hard time to start new projects, or even continue old ones.

Last weekend, I decided it was high time I finished the kitchen. There's very little to be done: A cabinet door needs to be replaced, which I'll build myself, a lot of trim molding and a few other odds and ends.

So Saturday, I set about getting the shop in order. The shop is supposed to be a wood working shop, but for the past year or so it has done very little of that. It has been used as a bamboo fly rod refinishing shop, a working on the lawn mower shop, a refinishing the bateau shop and a give Mocha a haircut shop. Very little wood has been cut.

I began by setting the jointer back true, because the last time I tried to use it the tables had apparently gone out of adjustment and when I tried to edge-joint a board, I started making wedges. After that, I rubbed down the cast iron table of the table saw with steel wool to remove the slight rust that had built up on it, waxed it, and reset the fence, splitter and miter gauge. Then I did the same to the miter saw. A good cleaning of the entire shop left me ready to start finishing up that kitchen.

And for the next two hours, I thought about what to do first. I popped open a Diet Coke and smoked a cig while considering. Should I work on that corner molding? I didn't feel like going to search for a long enough piece of fir in the woodshed. So I'll rebuild that cabinet door. But then I'd have to glue up some panels, and wait for them to dry. Oh, I could finish the last couple of feet of beadboard under the kitchen cabinet, but that would require going in and out of the house, creating a mess of sawdust inside that I didn't feel like cleaning up afterwards. So I popped open another Diet Coke and lit another cig, checked my hand tools for sharpness. I found my chisels were rusty, so I cleaned and oiled them. I also found my hand planes were dull, and spent an hour sharpening those.

During all this, I wondered if I had any sand paper left after refinishing the boat, and I did, but not much, so I ran to Wal-Mart to get more. When I got back, I realized the band saw hadn't been tuned in months, so I set about doing that. When complete, I opened another Diet Coke, smoked a cig, and wandered over to chew the rag with my neighbor for awhile, telling him all the projects I was about to embark upon.

When done rag-chewing, I wandered back over to the shop and cleaned the windows, which were dismal with sawdust accumulated a year ago. While doing so, I noticed that I was running low on latex gloves, so I got out my notepad and started making a list of everything I needed to restock on: glue, gloves, box cutter blades, WD40, and so forth. It occurred to me then that I was out of varnish, lacquer, thinner and good finishing brushes, so I put those on the list too. Oh, and I remembered that I had broken three of the brad point bits in my drill set, which I needed to replace because they were most often used, and put that on the list.

By the time I finished the list, I realized I didn't have enough money to buy half of what I needed, so I turned off the shop light and went inside to take a nap. Preparing to work is exhausting, you understand.

Sunday, feeling remorseful, I got up in the morning and after my coffee went to visit a pal who is building an entertainment center, a big one, in maple. As always, I was inspired by the project, which is taking shape very nicely, and I rushed home to my own shop, popped open a Diet Coke, lit a cigarette, and stood around for the next two hours wondering where all the bright-eyed, bushy-tailedness had gone off too. So I gathered up the dog and we went fishing in the bayou, where we did not get a nibble.

After that, I put Mocha back in the yard, grabbed a tape measure, and went inside to my piddling room. Or what will be my piddling room, when it's done. I figured, if the kitchen didn't want to cooperate philosophically, the piddling room surely would. I took some measurements for the desk I'm going to build out of cypress to put in there, but noticed that my fly rod case had fallen over. It was the case that holds my bamboo Granger, and it's not a good thing for it to be lying over, so I picked it up and set it back straight.

Or at least, that's what I did in my *mind*, but in reality, it must not have worked that way at all, because the next thing I knew I was standing on the bank of a pond, and the Granger was in my hand, and an Accardo "Spook" popping bug was at the end of 60 feet of line, where it had just lodged its sharp barb into the jaw of a bass.

I told you. I get distracted.

A co-worker was complaining the other day that it took her husband a week or two to replace a small piece of siding on the house. I laughed and commented that it was a good thing I didn't have a wife, the way I handle my renovations. Maintenance is one thing, and I keep on top of it fairly well, but I have been living in something that looks like a construction zone for nearly six years now, and it's like a time-lapsed nature documentary. If you just watch it, you won't see anything happening, but if you use time-lapsed photography, like they use to show a flower opening over a span of hours or days, you will notice that things *are* getting done, on some geologically slow scale akin to the movement of the continental plates. I am like Orson Welles in those old wine commercials: "I will renovate no house, before its time."

But I'll order the few things I need soon, and get down to it. Winter is a good time to work in the house, because the shop is actually the old patio/breezeway of the house, so I can run the heaters in both without going in and out opening and closing doors, jacking up the utility bills. All the noise tends to make Patches hide until it's over for the day, though, and she sneezes a lot with all the sawdust. She refuses to use the Kleenex I put out for her.

However, you *do* realize that I get distracted. I may, in fact, get distracted again, and rather than order some things for the house, accidentally and completely innocently, order the plans for that 16-foot skiff I've been wanting to build.

Have pity on me. I am priority-challenged.

Of course you know, I hate cold weather.

Not that it's been all that cold. But you'd be surprised what I consider cold. The nights lately have been cold.

In fact, while I was standing outside Franklin City Hall Tuesday evening, smoking a cigarette with chattering teeth—if you don't think this is a difficult arrangement, please reconsider—I finally came to the realization that I need to move to the Keys.

Having realized this, I set about digging out my winter clothes from the closet. I went through six shirts Tuesday before coming to the dismal conclusion that none of them fit around my belly anymore. This was enough to put me in a pretty foul mood. If there's anything I absolutely despise more than cold weather, hanging crown molding and sitting through city council meetings, it's buying clothes. This is why you'll usually see me wearing faded, threadbare clothing for months then all of a sudden pop up with a new wardrobe. It's because I put it off until I simply can't stand to look at myself anymore, or else my pants rip when I stoop over.

Shopping for clothes—particularly when you've gone up a size—is murder. I hate it with a passion. If I new that all brands were sized the same, I'd easily run through the clothing section and throw in 10 shirts and some long johns and be done with the whole sordid business. But no, this brand of shirt in a medium may fit perfectly, while the next might fit like a tent or a leotard. One makes me look like Homer Simpson. This is why I have to try on every single shirt of a different brand because if there's anything I hate worse than cold weather, hanging crown molding, sitting through city council meetings and shopping for clothes, it's returning something to the store where you got it. It's so Orwellian.

A few months ago I was given, well in advance of winter, a pair of fleece socks, which I am looking forward to trying out, as soon as I remember where I put them.

The interesting thing about winter is living in my old house. Just Wednesday night, the front door suddenly refused to close properly. With the change in temperature, it wouldn't shut tightly enough for the latch to engage the strike plate, and I ended up having to perform major reconstructive surgery on it at midnight, with the door open and the cold air coming in, while the heater is roaring away, trying to compensate. I was cussing up a storm, I can tell you, and probably disturbed the neighbors when I decided the best way to get the door to fit properly again was with a sledge hammer.

Add to that, the house doesn't heat evenly. It's like, the living room and kitchen are fairly comfortable, the back rooms and bathroom are a little nippy, but my bedroom is like a sauna. I am, all winter long, constantly fiddling with the vents, trying to find some equilibrium and doing lots of cussing and searching for my sledgehammer. What puzzles me is that the bedroom faces north, and due to the layout of the house, absolutely never sees direct sunlight. However, it's hot as the dickens in winter and exceptionally cool in the summer, which I don't object to at all. I think it's one of those places the parapsychologists find where the physical laws of the universe are somehow warped.

I am also one of those people who hates wearing long sleeves. Long sleeves make me feel claustrophobic and suffocating. Now, I don't mind wearing short sleeves with a jacket or coat, but a long sleeved shirt feels to me like a straight jacket, and I am always looking around in search of the padded truck. So often you'll see me wearing short sleeves under my jacket in 30-degree weather, otherwise I might suddenly start babbling about the voices in my head and gasping for air.

Patches believes that in wintertime I transform into her personal heating system. I cannot sit, lie down or otherwise become immobile without her instantly snuggling up beside me. I used to think, "Aww, *cher*, my little kitty loves me so much!" until I began to realize that I am little more to her than an electric blanket. Not to suggest that she isn't affectionate toward me, but in the end, I'm just a big overstuffed quilt in her mind.

It gets annoying. I sit down to have my supper in my living room chair, and Patches is there. I don't allow my pets to beg for food or otherwise get too close when I or my guests are eating, but in wintertime I have to run her off. Usually she knows quite well that, when I am eating, she must give me plenty of space. In winter, the rules in her mind seem to go south. So I run her off, and she sits in the middle of the floor staring at me. Not begging for food, mind you. Patches has never, ever begged for food. She is standing watch for the moment I put my plate away so she can jump up and turn up the thermostat on her personal heating device: Me.

However, the forecast for the next week or so isn't too bad, save for one little strange thing. The weatherman is calling for a 51-degree low Sunday night, then 36 degrees Monday night, and back to 59 degrees Tuesday night.

Wishy-washy weather is a winter-hater's worst nightmare. I hope Patches doesn't snore.

This is how my morning routine plays out.

The clock goes off at 6 a.m., and still asleep, I hit the snooze button. It is tuned to a rock and roll radio station, because country and western makes me convulse.

The clock goes off again every eight minutes. Meanwhile, the first alarm is a signal to Patches that it is time for me to get up, so she comes and chews on my hair or licks my nose. This draws me closer to consciousness, a step at a time, until the alarm goes off again and I look at it, thinking I am dreaming, then realize I'm not, and leap out of bed because it's 6:24 a.m.

Straight to the coffeepot, I brew up four cups and run to the closet to get clothes. I pick pants and a shirt and in the half-asleep daze manage to known down all the spare clothes hangers from the bar. In the process of picking them up and putting them back, several pairs of pants fall off their hangers, and I just leave them on the floor of the closet and slam the door shut. They will stay there until sometime next month.

It's off to brush my teeth and shower then. I throw my clothes on the cabinet, squeeze a little toothpaste onto the brush and, because the lights are so bright to my still-dilated eyes, I nearly shove the brush up my nose, but manage to escape with only a bruised upper lip and a slight abrasion inside where I pushed it against an incisor. The tooth-brushing with minty paste helps wake me up a little more.

It takes at least three minutes to get the shower temperature right in the old house. I learned this the hard way when I first moved there. The plumbing is so old and reworked so many times, there are pockets of cold or hot water in the system which only emerge after a minute or two, so if you set the temperature and get in, you're likely to be hit by a sudden freezing gallon or two, or a scalding gallon or two.

But once I'm sure I'm not going to be deep-fried or put into suspended animation, the shower wakes me up fairly well. After brushing my hair and getting dressed, I make it to the coffee pot and with trembling, caffeine-desperate hands manage to get one of the four cups into my mug and only one all over the kitchen counter, leaving me two cups remaining.

Feed the cat, check my email, and try to find socks that match, an effort in futility the likes of which the world has never known. There are always two with slightly different weaves or just a shade off color from each other, though I only buy black socks in an attempt to make my life a little simpler. Once I get a pair that I believe will look the same from 150 feet up in a helicopter, it's time to locate shoes which were kicked off wherever I happened to be after I came in the night before: Perhaps under the bar, maybe behind the sofa, once I found them in the laundry basket.

During all this, properly breakfasted, Patches follows me around the house, close on my heels, as if enjoying the show. I think she is mystified by all this preparatory stuff. Cats, after all, wear their clothes all the time and bathe with their tongues, and they do not drink coffee. I sit down to put on my shoes and socks, and Patches wants to sit in my lap, so I must move her out of the way, put on a sock, lean back to take a sip of coffee, and she jumps right up again. We repeat this process four times, one time for each sock and each shoe.

It is now 6:50 a.m. and I make a mad dash to the truck, start it up, put it in reverse to back out the drive, and realize I left my smokes in the house. Back in, retrieve them, realize I left the coffee pot on, turn it off, then rush back to the truck, realize I didn't lock the front door of the house, go do that, back in the truck, back up, turn the truck around in the circle drive, get to the street, head back to the house cursing like a railroad man, go back inside to get my wallet.

Patches is curling around my feet and mewling with each re-entry, delighted that I'm finally home again.

Obeying all traffic laws, I make my way to the office, and every slow moving vehicle in the State of Louisiana is on La. 182 between me and Franklin, including cane tractors, sight-seers from Tokyo with digital cameras, school buses, scooters, garbage trucks, horse-drawn wagons full of Amish children and oxen with ploughs. I also catch every signal light on red and if I decide to cross the bayou at Charenton and take La. 87 to Katy, the bridge will be letting a tug through pushing six miles of barges at .5 miles per hour. To turn off Katy Bridge road onto La. 182 requires waiting for 18 vehicles to pass coming from Baldwin, and when the last one is gone by, there are 18 coming from Franklin. This process repeats itself several times until finally there is a safe opening. Meanwhile, people lined up behind me are blowing their horns and telling me to, "Take a picture next time, ya bum!"

There are inevitably people ahead of me turning on ever street between the city limits and Wilson Street, and I must slow down for each of them to do so. Doesn't matter, left or right, somebody's going to turn down every street ahead of me. I often think I see the same car pull out in front of me a block or two down then turn off all over again, but perhaps that's paranoia.

Finally at the office, I rush across the street to the courthouse to get a Diet Coke, fumble with my keys in the front door of the office, drop them four times, and manage to get inside the building just in time to drop my Diet Coke can and see it roll clear across the lobby, so I have to go get another one from the courthouse to avoid the explosion.

I sit, check my email, reply to those that require it, delete those that don't, and reach atop my desk to get my camera so I can download the pictures I took the day before for that day's paper, and realize I left it on the kitchen bar at home.

The Indians had it made, you know that? No clocks, no deadlines, no specific time to be anywhere except when you get there. Wake up in the morning, stretch really good, piddle around until you feel like going to throw out a fishing net or line, maybe shoot a deer, tan a few hides, make some beadwork or sharpen your arrow points. Chat with the old folks for awhile and learn about your ancestors back 62 generations, start feeling a little hungry, go check the fishing gear and get breakfast, take a nap, spend the afternoon chasing the cute Indian girls around the shell mound. Take another nap. Go play stickball, maybe count a little coup with the neighboring tribe, then have a nice supper and go to bed.

And for this we were considered uncivilized.

This is the way my evenings routinely go, if there's no meetings I have to attend.

I get home and park the truck, tired and ready for a nap. I fumble through the keys on my ring, again wondering what half of them go to, but afraid to throw them out because I might need them. Finally I find the right one and get in the front door.

Inside the house, Patches is whining happily. I tell her, "Hello, sweetie," and kick off my shoes, empty my pockets and head straight for the sofa. There are four pillows on the sofa and loveseat: Two of them are well-flattened from years of napping, and two are still new and firm. I must make sure I have one of the flattened ones, otherwise I will get a neck ache.

Laying my head on a well-flattened pillow, Patches jumps up and chews my hair for a moment then turns circles four or five times until she is content to lie down right under my chin. I'm dozing off already, so I don't mind. We nap this way for an hour or so.

I wake up with the yuck mouth. You know, that, "Who stuffed cottonballs soaked in lacquer thinner down my throat while I was sleeping?" feeling after a good, hard nap. I head for the fridge and a Diet Coke, disturbing Patches from her nap. She naps much longer than I do. The first few gulps of Diet Coke alleviate the yuck mouth, and I feel better, sit down in my chair to wake up a little more.

While sitting there, I try to decide what I'll do for the rest of the evening. If there's nothing good on the tube I wanted to see, I'll consider whether it's cold out or not. If it's not, I may go fishing or work in the shop, unless it's dark already, then it's just the shop option. If too cold, I'll read and play on the Internet.

At some point my stomach will start grumbling and I search for something for supper, which is always a daunting task. I hate shopping for groceries. It invariably puts me in a bad mood. The prices first and foremost put me in a bad mood. I can't believe what they sell a gallon of milk for nowadays, and coffee! Jeesh! Then when I have my basket up at the aisle, I have to argue with the cashier at one store about whether or not I have one of their savings cards. I do have one, but that's only because when the store first started this promotion two big stock boys wrestled me to the ground and forced me to fill out the paperwork under threat of having Raid shot up my nose.

"You can save three cents on frozen television dinners!" they exclaim.

"I don't eat television dinners!" I protest.

"Fine! You can save 14 cents on a pot roast!"

"I don't cook!" I say.

"Great! You can save a buck on diet pills!"

I got a card, but I don't take it out when I get to the register. They always have to ask me if I have it, at which point I usually give my speech regarding why they put items on sale to only cardholders, when they could make a lot more money if everybody could buy it, and also how much I despise the fact that they are probably actually using these so called "savings cards" to track my buying habits, which must really give their computers a fit, because generally my purchases consist of ham, Oreos, Treet, toilet paper, Abita Amber and a jar of Hellman's mayonaise. If I have a little extra money, I may also get some peaches and a can of condensed milk.

"You saved four dollars and thirty-eight cents!" they proclaim after checking me out.

"But I spent eighty-five," I say. "How the heck much does a peach cost these days, anyway?"

So I fill out my check, and they have to call for someone to come approve it, then I have to show them my driver's license and tell them my place of employment, and then they tell me to "have a nice day."

Too late. I stalk off through the parking lot mumbling to myself about how much I wish Ike Godsey was around. At least he'd advertise in the newspaper.

Anyway, I was talking about my evenings, and supper. So I decide to have half a peach with a slice of Treet on it, doused with mayo. No, just kidding. Whatever it is, I sit down and enjoy it, then either read, watch the tube or play on the 'Net. Sometimes, if I'm in the mood, I'll write a little about this or that, some fiction perhaps, maybe a bit of my memoirs.

Long about 10 p.m. I started getting sleepy, so I change clothes and lay on the sofa again, just getting a practice run for the bed. Patches knows this routine, she comes and lays down with me, but won't fall asleep, because she knows I will just wake her up when I move to the other room. When finally I can't keep my eyes open, I get up, make sure all the doors are locked and the porch light is on, then snuggle in.

At this point, Patches goes through her routine: She jumps in the bed, circles me exactly three times. No more, no less. She walks around my feet, up my side, over my pillow—pausing only to sniff or possibly chew on my pony tail—and then back around. Finally she'll try to lie across my legs. I hate this, and she knows it. But she'll very softly put one foot on my calf and freeze, waiting like a statue. If I don't react, she'll put another foot, and wait for a few minutes again. Believing that I am fast asleep, she'll spread herself out across the backs of my knees to sleep, at which point I'll say sternly, "Patches, get off!" and she complies immediately. She will then, grumpily, find another spot by my side to settle in for the night.

So as I doze off, I am already thinking of all the things I must do the next day, and sure I am forgetting half of them, probably the most important half, and will end up in some sort of trouble over it.

December

The things removed from me, and those cast away, become like dreams just awakened from, rapidly fading into diminutive mist.

In December, my father left us. December is a time of passings. Here, in the final days of a deceasing year, the pages of the world flutter like ancient wings.

How can I not think of him when December comes 'round the bend in the road? We sat down to Thanksgiving dinner last week, and while the table was full with loved ones, missing was an empty seat and the old man at the head of the gathering. Last Thanksgiving of his life he struggled through a dinner, short of breath, pained in giving thanks, but determined not to fail at this final act of celebration of a life. He would not live to see Christmas.

Sometimes, when the air thins with December chill, and spectre warriors on horseback ride circles around the old oak tree in the back yard at night, I think about the decade that we were estranged. Out of touch, rendered unable to communicate by perceived Decembers of difference. I lost a decade of wisdom from him, a decade of thoughts and learning and laughter.

December, and the wooden casket of its final resting is propped open, awaiting, an eagle feather within, comforted by silken billows. A wooden skiff is slowly taking shape under my garage, and I sometimes stand and study its lines as its skeletal form takes shape, conversing with him, imagining his replies to my queries on its beam, rake and sheer.

The choices I have made in my life, particularly since my father went to join his grandfathers, have been tumultuous and far-reaching. I have hurt others with some of these choices, but in the interest of self-preservation I cannot have regrets.

If I could see the doors which are hidden from me by the blinders of perception, I would slip through one and go to visit people who could teach me songs unsung for centuries, sitting in a tight circle under the Raintree; if I could guide my father's old bateau through some invisible gate between two cypress trees and emerge into a distant past on the other side, I would cut dugout canoes with copper adzes, split cane with my teeth, burn tobacco and cedar on a white-bleached shell mound along *Cok'tangi.*

If this road—this winding, perilous path through which I day to day move—would take a bend or a shortcut into the thin places, I would rest there for awhile before having to return to that ever-moving spline which carries me through to an open casket waiting in a December of my own. There, I would whittle leaping panthers from cypress knees with an old Case pocketknife.

In December, as the year comes around to where it began, a mind's-eye painting of tinsel and brightly-colored glass twinkles in the reflection on an old Catalina television set, and I am snug and warm under a blanket on the sofa of that old house I was reared in. For years now I have had no tree, no lights, no decorations in December. Holidays have not the meaning to me they once had, and I miss those joyful anticipations. But the empty chair at the table expands, reaching outward, until it finds the empty place in my heart and together, those two emptinesses overwhelm.

December. A wake and a funeral for another year falling rapidly into ancestry. Is there no joy in December? I am surrounded by it, relish and embrace it, but every smile pangs deep inside where a small boy whose entire world reached no farther than those four old people of whom only one survives. Every cheerful holiday word echoes back and forth into silence broken only by recollections of a Shetland pony and a reddish-brown quarter horse named Kate who shared my birthdate. Each twinkling string of lights is a hypnotist's charm, entrancing me back to shiny silver roll-cap guns smelling like burnt gunpowder, tattered welded-wire fences and round wooden posts confining a Weimaraner named Prissy, and old wooden boats tucked away for the winter, holding the promise of spring between its gunwales.

But yes, there is joy in December. A Thanksgiving feast prepared by my mom in November was, while melancholy, lifted up by laughing voices and clattering silverware; lemon ice-box pie and chocolate cheesecake afterwards led to blissful misery, and outside, rain fell in sporadic bursts, cleansing. I enter December under a cold night, but I know that I will be warmed by the love which surrounds me and grows stronger with each passing season.

December, and there should be a tree, bedecked with ribbons and glass and tinsel and green garland. Perhaps there will be, this year. Perhaps there will be lights framing the front door of the old house, outlining the eaves, demarcating the gables. Perhaps, this December, there should be passings.

In less than a month, a new year will come, and with it another journey through the circle. Some things can be depended up, some things are perpetual.

When the air warms and the pecan tree in my front yard buds, I'll carry John Louis Blake's bamboo fly rod into my father's old wooden boat and head for *Cok'tangi* once more, while the final touches are being put on my new skiff, preparing it for passage to Buffalo Cove or Round Island, and new journeys to come. It is as it should be. December should always be carried into January. There is no such thing as a new year. It is only a numerical value. Each year carries with in every year that has gone before, and only within those cumulative epochs can we understand what it means to exist in December.

When December comes 'round at last, carrying with it the shortest day of the year and the longest night, there are legacies and promises to keep. Some December hence will be my last, and if I can look back upon every December gone by and know that I have lived them honorably and most importantly, remained true to all those who came before me, then I have truly lived a life worth living. A handful of words, a few wooden boats and rivers coursing through my veins are enough to rest in peace upon.

It is nothing to die; it is horrible not to live.[1]

Here, amidships, December. I picked up a rod and went to a pond, sure there would be nothing there but time to think, a moment or two to consider December and the brisk finality of it.

I park the truck and grab my rod out of its case, assemble the three sections and string it up. I tie on an Accardo popper fly and set the hook in the keeper. Tackle bag on my shoulder, I jump a ditch of ankle-deep water, make the long trek through underbrush turning brown like muddy fields toward the pond. A rabbit darts away from me, scurrying through the brush but not far away, yet its brown coat is a perfect camouflage in the undergrowth.

At the side of the pond, I pause for a moment and reach down to touch the water: It is cold, colder even than I expected, and I know that any fish will be slow and sluggish, reluctant to rise to anything but an enticing prey put right under their noses. I look out west of the fields surrounding me: The sun is ripping the sky into a flame-filled horizon consuming the day like a holocaust. Scant few clouds drift across that glowing backdrop, rendered to silhouette.

December, and there are few places I'd rather be. I think of Robert Traver, aka Judge John Voelker, and I find that in December I understand the Judge more than any other time. The air so thin and still it seems to want to leap away from the earth, the water cool and silent, undisturbed by even a rising fish across the

---

1. "Les Miserables" Signet Books, Victor Hugo.

surface. There are willow trees in a patch out there, most of their leaves gone now, and their spindly trunks and branches growing so tightly packed look like mazes of impossible passage.

Still I do not put out my line, for the silence and the burning sky are hypnotic. I would like to think that the Judge, in some December of his own, stood on some other pond or stream or lake and knew his truth: To love the environment where fish are found, simply because they are without exception beautiful, and to despise those where crowds of people are found, which are without exception desperate and ugly. How I understand that in December. How I would escape the ugly crowds forever, if I could.

I free the fly from the hook keeper and toss out the leader and a few feet of line, but just let it rest there in the water, noting how the luminescent glow of the dusk makes it seem ethereal, somehow, not quite real, not quite tangible. The fly floats there, imitating some insect prey, but even the ripples made when it again met that watery world have faded, leaving it looking like it rests upon a looking glass of flames.

It is the solitude in December that I cherish, for the rest of the fishermen have gone to the deer stands or given up with the season, and I am at last comforted by the uninterrupted silence. While this pond is a manmade construction, it sits upon land my feet have touched for eight thousand years. Just a few millennia ago, I might have stood here and heard the Mississippi River raging not far away, before she changed her path far to the east. Yet I revere the silence, the pond, the dusk. Because like the Judge, I know that I come here not for some sense of sport but rather, in a world where people spend their existences doing something they despise, this walk through the underbrush to this quiet pond is like a small act of rebellion. Here, as the Judge pointed out, I do not have to seek to impress people, or bribe, or be cheated, or demonstrate some futile and imagined power. Here, in that pond, the company I keep responds only to silence, and humility and, above all, endless patience and tolerance.

"I suspect that men are going along this way for the last time, and I for one do not want to waste the trip," the Judge wrote in 1964, the year I was born, the year I made the first mile into the journey. In December there is peace along the way, finality or not.

I strip out line and the reel whirs and clicks, and I remember the whir and click of an old Martin automatic reel on a Heddon fiberglass rod, and the deft accuracy and lithe grace with which my father conjured the line to a precise target far from the boat, settling his fly there so delicately the water scarcely moved.

December is like that, to me. Graceful and delicate. Precise and magical. December is angular, sharp-edged and glints with winter light.

The sun has touched the edge of the earth, and seems to explode there, sending out fanning rays of glorious spectacle, like choirs singing chords of light, like if you plucked a string of a harp and instead of resonating a note, it released starfire. The moon, a half-disk of cold white, is already arching across the darkening sky, half-eye watching me in December.

Line at my feet, I make a few false casts and lay the fly far away from me, let it rest there for a few moments. The air is cooling more. The cork grip of the rod is still warm from my clutching hand, but the bamboo is chill. I reach into my tackle bag and find the silver flask inside the pouch, uncap it and feel the warmth of good scotch chase away the creeping fingers of winter. Judge Voelker had it right: It tastes better out here, though there's no sensible reason for it. Just as there's no sensible reason for standing on a pond in the middle of nowhere in December, with little chance of enticing lethargic fish to bite a surface popper. The best things in life make little sense at all.

I twitch the fly with a sharp pull of the line through the rod guides, let it rest again. Here, in December, the loneliness which sometimes permeates my life when I am surrounded by the crowd is less painful when I am standing alone on a pond in search of reluctant fish. Again, not sensible. One would think the loneliness would be augmented here, in this quiet sunset, but I am soothed by the dipping sun's fading, by the glow of the pond, by the whispers I can hear far better here than anywhere else.

My life, the sum total of which encompasses all of those who have come before me, is most comforting to me here. All my relations gather around this pond, and in the twilight of the world and of December, stand hand-in-hand and lift their eyes toward dusk, watching, vigilant.

In the end, I am here, like the Judge, not because I consider fishing so almighty important; I am here because I am sure that the supposedly legitimate concerns of people are far less important; I am here, after all, because it makes no sense to be here, and in that very senselessness do I find comfort.

No fish rise to my fly, but it doesn't matter. Dark is nearly upon me. I stay just a few minutes longer, hoping for erudition. Convergence. Opening gates and creaking bolts.

In the last moments of a fading day amidships December, the wait is over.

Grown men don't say such things to each other. But they should.

When the knock came on my door that Sunday evening, the Sunday before Christmas, I expected it to be one of the boys. But it wasn't. It was the brother of my soul, Scott Matthew, who has for over a decade now lived out of state. His current residence is Virginia, and when we speak by phone, he tells me of fishing bronze-backed smallmouth bass in rivers and farm ponds.

We see each other about annually. That's not enough for brothers. But as soon as his face appeared at my door, I was instantly calculating the weather forecast for the next couple weeks, figuring my time off for the holidays though the newspaper job is still demanding, and planning when we could get out to the water.

Throughout my days, whenever something made itself known to me out there on *Sheti*, I have almost always been alone. The only exceptions have been when in the company of this brother of mine. Indians believe in things having meanings. I know no one else who is as attached to the waters and the earth here. I know no one else who feels as deeply, as if his own roots were somehow as far-reaching as mine. He was not born here, but has lived most of his life here.

Grown men don't say as much to each other. They don't toy with niceties. We trade insults jokingly and tease each other's accomplishments condescendingly. Scott and I went to a pond the following Friday and caught nothing. I was disappointed, to say the least. It is one of my most reliable, productive fishing spots, and when he would tell me over the telephone about fishing the Rapidan for smallies, I'd tell him about the largemouth I took from the pond. But it failed me.

The next Sunday, the Sunday after Christmas, we returned. The wind was up, howling, and my fly rod was uncooperative, but we caught a dozen or so small bass out of the pond. Redemption. We returned again that Tuesday, the Tuesday before New Year's day, a new circle. We'd fish near each other for a time, opposite sides of the pond at others. The Tuesday trip resulted in several nice catches, all released. We'd stop now and then and talk, about river smallies and pond bass, about *Sheti* instances and *Co'ktangi* moments, wooden boats filled to the rail with memories.

Grown men don't say what's in their hearts, but they should. The words may come from a reddened face, nearly a whisper of embarrassment, in a world turned upside down, on its head with the backwardness of a culture gone amok. I didn't say so, but I think the brother of my soul knows it. We sat and shared scotch from a silver flask I keep in my tackle bag, watching sunset. A few more bass emerged, cold but feisty, taken on Clousers or spinnerbaits, respectfully returned to the frigid waters from which they were coaxed.

When I was 15 years old, the brother of my soul appeared on my doorstep, unannounced, much the way he did the Sunday before Christmas. He threw me a pack of chewing tobacco and said, "Let's go fishing." He's been appearing on my door, announced or unannounced, and we've been fishing, ever since, though rarely together anymore. He is godfather of my son. He immerses himself in running, cold water chasing smallmouth, and I float along my ancestral native waters or stand aside ponds eight hundred miles apart.

Sundown has much meaning to me. It's beauty notwithstanding, it's a circle closing inside the larger circle of the season, of the year, of a life, of the uncertain tenure of the future. As he and I stood, miniscule and unimportant, under a reddening sky flashing dragonfire across the pond at our feet, I wished to tell him that in all my life, he has been my truest, most constant, most cherished friend. My tongue seemed to turn to sand as I tried, but when I passed him the silver flask and the half-disc of the sun passing under the distant edge of the earth flashed Indian summer beams from the flask into my eyes, I knew there was no need.

Grown men don't say such things, but perhaps they don't need to. Perhaps, such things are simply known. Perceived and understood. Each arrival on my doorstep confirms the bond we share, running like cold rivers and deep as still lakes. While other friendships have faltered and faded, grown distant and dim, those which need not be vocalized have remained fast and true. There are only a handful, the brother of my soul chief among them, but there are others who I know are there at the dialing of a phone, arrival on a doorstep unannounced, always within reach. These are the most treasured gifts of a life.

Yet of all, water only flows between Scott Matthew and I. We shook hands and I told him to be careful on those long, sometimes treacherous highways which will take him back to river smallmouth and mountains. As his truck rolled down my driveway, I picked up the fishing tackle we had used and put it back in its place in the house. Glancing out the window, the truck was gone from view.

Water covers nine-tenths of this wonderful planet. Rivers flow across this continent in a web of connections. Standing in a Virginia river casting to smallmouth or in a wooden boat along Lake Fausse Pointe fly-fishing for bream, the brother of my soul and I are always tethered by water.

Grown men don't say as much. But eight hundred miles away, I believe my brother knows this. It's spoken in the sound of water racing over rock, lapping against deadfalls, winds whistling through trees and illuminated by fiery sunsets, closing circles, until the next unannounced knock at the door.

Aft, December

Now, at last, the year fails and flounders, gasping. There is an open window through which the Reaper will enter and brush December away at last, heralding in the imagined revival of the new year.

If December were the final chapter of the book in which this life is written, its remaining unread pages would be few. If this December were the last for me, would there be no afterword? No epilogue to offer respite?

A year in the life. A season turns and the circle comes around again to where it began. I have found, in the months of this year, great wisdom, boundless love and eternal convergence. It has been a year of blessings, a year of quandary, a season of renewal.

By now, in Decembers swept away by the bristles of time, the Christmas tree would be coming down and soon the scent of baking ham would fill the house, saturating its corners and crevices to linger there for days. The new year would unfold soon, infant, bearing tidings of hope.

So the dog and I take to the road to watch December perish. We have discovered all there is to discover, for this season at least, at home. December is everywhere, and we go to bid it farewell.

Mocha twirls and pants and whines in the passenger seat of the truck, pausing now and then to gaze out of the closed window at the brown world beyond. We take the levee road, passing over the locks and down toward Grand Avoille Cove, where muddy water flows from Lake Fausse Pointe to fill its margins. There are mud flats showing here and there, and birds perch on them, whipping their wings at winter.

If I were to write an epilogue for December, for the year, it would have to be penned here, surrounded by these ancestral waters on these hallowed grounds. What would I write for December? A eulogy, an epithet. Perhaps a sermon. A congregation surrounds me and the dog as we make our way to the lake proper, exit the truck and go to stand, trembling both, near the water. I hear hymns lifted in praise of Creation; I hear words of grace and divinity from behind the pulpit of that wondrous, timeless expanse of water before us. I am in the cathedral of my ancestors. I am in the holiest of holy places.

Mocha canters along the granite blocks that protect the levee from the occasional barrage of the lake against its foundations. She startles a bird, which she chases down the shore, leaping, ears flapping, celebratory in the temple. I follow her slowly, hands in pockets against the cold, but my gaze cannot tear away from the lake.

From January through June, from July to November, and now finally here at rest in December, I have poured out the words which fail miserably to express the way this old lake flows through my veins like earthblood. As I lower myself to sit on a dry log to watch the water, and the dog rushes to my side to share the vigil, it is a wonder to me that I have even tried. Some things cannot be voiced or penned.

Day to day, the people I meet seem to either understand this, or it is as alien to them as an off-world landscape. Those who comprehend, I see water, rushing or still, warm or cold, behind their pupils, hear it whispering back of their voices, lingering and filling the vacancies of their movements. I am always thinking of water: Devouring lunch in the noxious noise of the diner crowd, sitting behind the press table at city hall, resting my head to the pillow after the ugliness of the day has left me exhausted, there is water behind my thoughts.

December. Heartland for the soul. The dog looks up at me, whining, and I rub her ear. In her half-blue, half-brown left eye, I see the margin of water and earth. Long ago, the Creator sundered the water by creating the land, knowing that water is perfection, and man is not perfect. The scientists tell us it was four and a half billion years ago. The fundamentalists say it was six thousand. My father's people do not say. We have no need of it. The circle will come back there again.

An epilogue for December. Another year falls by the wayside, left to shrivel and wither into the dry husk of memory. Everywhere I look on the lake before us, I see myself, under every cypress, motoring across every flow of water, drifting along every inch of shoreline. There are nearly four decades of Decembers out there, incalculable instances of me existing out there, and it is no wonder that if I am cut physically or in the psyche, I bleed lake water.

But darkness is near, and the air is growing unbearably cold. I take the dog back to the truck and we climb the shallow hill back up to the lower levee road, make our way toward home. By and by, we turn back to concrete, and the water is out of sight, but not beyond my awareness. We cross Bayou Teche, still and silent, and shadows lengthen over it, augmented by golden brilliance of sunset. Then we are home, and the water is behind this old house, but as the light fades it becomes half-real, like Mocha's eyes, like my existence.

Aft, December. In not too many more months, spring will return, as it always does. An old wooden boat will be uncovered and, loaded with legacies, carry me back to create more instances of myself out there on *Sheti.* I'll chase fish with a fly rod, and the world will be as it should. Nicholas Leonard Stouff Jr. is there, as are Emile Anatole and Josephine Faye and Lydia Marie and Ray Lanier and Aunt

Mary's wolf and *Neka sama* and songs and laughter and behind them all, the never ceasing, eternal rise and fall of water.

0-595-34316-3

Printed in the United Kingdom
by Lightning Source UK Ltd.
108116UKS00002B/81